北京大学中国语言学研究中心

早期北京话珍稀文献集成

主编 刘云

西人北京话教科书汇编

分卷主编 翟赟 郭利霞 陈颖

华语入门

[俄罗斯] 吴索福 著

中文版

北京大学出版社
PEKING UNIVERSITY PRESS

图书在版编目(CIP)数据

华语入门：中文版、英文版 / (俄罗斯)吴索福著. —影印本. —北京：北京大学出版社，2017.9
（早期北京话珍本典籍校释与研究）
ISBN 978-7-301-28762-0

Ⅰ.①华… Ⅱ.①吴… Ⅲ.①汉语—对外汉语教学—教材 Ⅳ.①H195.4

中国版本图书馆CIP数据核字（2017）第224301号

书　　名	华语入门（中文版、英文版）（影印本） HUAYU RUMEN（ZHONGWEN BAN、YINGWEN BAN）（YINGYIN BEN）
著作责任者	［俄罗斯］吴索福　著
责任编辑	孙　娴　路冬月
标准书号	ISBN 978-7-301-28762-0
出版发行	北京大学出版社
地　　址	北京市海淀区成府路205号　100871
网　　址	http://www.pup.cn　　新浪微博：@北京大学出版社
电子信箱	zpup@pup.cn
电　　话	邮购部 62752015　发行部 62750672　编辑部 62753027
印刷者	北京虎彩文化传播有限公司
经销者	新华书店
	720毫米×1020毫米　16开本　41.25印张　270千字
	2017年9月第1版　2018年10月第2次印刷
定　　价	165.00元（全二册）

未经许可，不得以任何方式复制或抄袭本书之部分或全部内容。
版权所有，侵权必究
举报电话：010-62752024　电子信箱：fd@pup.pku.edu.cn
图书如有印装质量问题，请与出版部联系，电话：010-62756370

19世纪来华传教士记录的官话方言及其历时演变研究
（16AYY002，2016年国家社科基金重点项目）

总　序

语言是文化的重要组成部分，也是文化的载体。语言中有历史。

多元一体的中华文化，体现在我国丰富的民族文化和地域文化及其语言和方言之中。

北京是辽金元明清五代国都（辽时为陪都），千余年来，逐渐成为中华民族所公认的政治中心。北方多个少数民族文化与汉文化在这里碰撞、融合，产生出以汉文化为主体的、带有民族文化风味的特色文化。

现今的北京话是我国汉语方言和地域文化中极具特色的一支，它与辽金元明四代的北京话是否有直接继承关系还不是十分清楚。但可以肯定的是，它与清代以来旗人语言文化与汉人语言文化的彼此交融有直接关系。再往前追溯，旗人与汉人语言文化的接触与交融在入关前已经十分深刻。本丛书收集整理的这些语料直接反映了清代以来北京话、京味文化的发展变化。

早期北京话有独特的历史传承和文化底蕴，于中华文化、历史有特别的意义。

一者，这一时期的北京历经满汉双语共存、双语互协而新生出的汉语方言——北京话，她最终成为我国民族共同语（普通话）的基础方言。这一过程是中华多元一体文化自然形成的诸过程之一，对于了解形成中华文化多元一体关系的具体进程有重要的价值。

二者，清代以来，北京曾历经数次重要的社会变动：清王朝的逐渐羸弱、八国联军的入侵、帝制覆灭和民国建立及其伴随的满汉关系变化、各路军阀的来来往往、日本侵略者的占领，等等。在这些不同的社会环境下，北京人的构成有无重要变化？北京话和京味文化是否有变化？进一步地，地域方言和文化与自身的传承性或发展性有着什么样的关系？与社会变迁有着什么样的关系？清代以至民国时期早期北京话的语料为研究语言文化自身传承性与社会的关系提供了很好的素材。

　　了解历史才能更好地把握未来。新中国成立后，北京不仅是全国的政治中心，而且是全国的文化和科研中心，新的北京话和京味文化或正在形成。什么是老北京京味文化的精华？如何传承这些精华？为把握新的地域文化形成的规律，为传承地域文化的精华，必须对过去的地域文化的特色及其形成过程进行细致的研究和理性的分析。而近几十年来，各种新的传媒形式不断涌现，外来西方文化和国内其他地域文化的冲击越来越强烈，北京地区人口流动日趋频繁，老北京人逐渐分散，老北京话已几近消失。清代以来各个重要历史时期早期北京话语料的保护整理和研究迫在眉睫。

　　"早期北京话珍本典籍校释与研究（暨早期北京话文献数字化工程）"是北京大学中国语言学研究中心研究成果，由"早期北京话珍稀文献集成""早期北京话数据库"和"早期北京话研究书系"三部分组成。"集成"收录从清中叶到民国末年反映早期北京话面貌的珍稀文献并对内容加以整理，"数据库"为研究者分析语料提供便利，"研究书系"是在上述文献和数据库基础上对早期北京话的集中研究，反映了当前相关研究的最新进展。

　　本丛书可以为语言学、历史学、社会学、民俗学、文化学等多方面的研究提供素材。

　　愿本丛书的出版为中华优秀文化的传承做出贡献！

王洪君、郭锐、刘云
2016年10月

"早期北京话珍稀文献集成"序

清民两代是北京话走向成熟的关键阶段。从汉语史的角度看，这是一个承前启后的重要时期，而成熟后的北京话又开始为当代汉民族共同语——普通话源源不断地提供着养分。蒋绍愚先生对此有着深刻的认识："特别是清初到19世纪末这一段的汉语，虽然按分期来说是属于现代汉语而不属于近代汉语，但这一段的语言（语法，尤其是词汇）和'五四'以后的语言（通常所说的'现代汉语'就是指'五四'以后的语言）还有若干不同，研究这一段语言对于研究近代汉语是如何发展到'五四'以后的语言是很有价值的。"（《近代汉语研究概要》，北京大学出版社，2005年）然而国内的早期北京话研究并不尽如人意，在重视程度和材料发掘力度上都要落后于日本同行。自1876年至1945年间，日本汉语教学的目的语转向当时的北京话，因此留下了大批的北京话教材，这为其早期北京话研究提供了材料支撑。作为日本北京话研究的奠基者，太田辰夫先生非常重视新语料的发掘，很早就利用了《小额》《北京》等京味儿小说材料。这种治学理念得到了很好的传承，之后，日本陆续影印出版了《中国语学资料丛刊》《中国语教本类集成》《清民语料》等资料汇编，给研究带来了便利。

新材料的发掘是学术研究的源头活水。陈寅恪《〈敦煌劫余录〉序》有云："一时代之学术，必有其新材料与新问题。取用此材料，以研求问题，则为此时代学术之新潮流。"我们的研究要想取得突破，必须打破材料桎梏。在具体思路上，一方面要拓展视野，关注"异族之故书"，深度利用好朝鲜、日本、泰西诸国作者所主导编纂的早期北京话教本；另一方面，更要利用本土优势，在"吾国之旧籍"中深入挖掘，官话正音教本、满汉合璧教本、京味儿小说、曲艺剧本等新类型语料大有文章可做。在明确了思路之后，我们从2004年开始了前期的准备工作，在北京大学中国语言学研究中心的大力支持下，早期北京话的挖掘整理工作于2007年正式启动。本次推出的"早期北京话珍稀文献集成"是阶段性成果之一，总体设计上"取异族之故书与吾国之旧籍互相补正"，共分"日本北京话教科书汇编""朝鲜日据时期汉语会话书汇编""西人北京话教科书汇编""清代满汉合璧文献萃编""清代官话正音文献""十全福""清末民初京味儿小说书系""清末民初京味儿时评书系"八个系列，胪列如下：

"日本北京话教科书汇编"于日本早期北京话会话书、综合教科书、改编读物和风俗纪闻读物中精选出《燕京妇语》《四声联珠》《华语跬步》《官话指南》《改订官话指南》《亚细亚言语集》《京华事略》《北京纪闻》《北京风土编》《北京风俗问答》《北京事情》《伊苏普喻言》《搜奇新编》《今古奇观》等二十余部作品。这些教材是日本早期北京话教学活动的缩影，也是研究早期北京方言、民俗、史地问题的宝贵资料。本系列的编纂得到了日本学界的大力帮助。冰野善宽、内田庆市、太田斋、鳟泽彰夫诸先生在书影拍摄方面给予了诸多帮助。书中日语例言、日语小引的翻译得到了竹越孝先生的悉心指导，在此深表谢忱。

"朝鲜日据时期汉语会话书汇编"由韩国著名汉学家朴在渊教授和金雅瑛博士校注，收入《改正增补汉语独学》《修正独习汉语指南》《高等官话华语精选》《官话华语教范》《速修汉语自通》《速修汉语大成》《无先生速修中国语自通》《官话标准：短期速修中国语自通》《中语大全》《"内鲜满"最速成中国语自通》等十余部日据时期（1910年至1945年）朝鲜教材。这批教材既是对《老乞大》《朴通事》的传承，又深受日本早期北京话教学活动的影响。在中韩语言史、文化史研究中，日据时期是近现代过渡的重要时期，这些资料具有多方面的研究价值。

"西人北京话教科书汇编"收录了《语言自迩集》《官话类编》等十余部西人主编教材。这些西方作者多受过语言学训练，他们用印欧语的眼光考量汉语，解释汉语语法现象，设计记音符号系统，对早期北京话语音、词汇、语法面貌的描写要比本土文献更为精准。感谢郭锐老师提供了《官话类编》《北京话语音读本》和《汉语口语初级读本》的底本，《寻津录》、《语言自迩集》（第一版、第二版）、《汉英北京官话词汇》、《华语入门》等底本由北京大学图书馆特藏部提供，谨致谢忱。《华英文义津逮》《言语声片》为笔者从海外购回，其中最为珍贵的是老舍先生在伦敦东方学院执教期间，与英国学者共同编写的教材——《言语声片》。教材共分两卷：第一卷为英文卷，用英语讲授汉语，用音标标注课文的读音；第二卷为汉字卷。《言语声片》采用先用英语导入，再学习汉字的教学方法讲授汉语口语，是世界上第一部有声汉语教材。书中汉字均由老舍先生亲笔书写，全书由老舍先生录音，共十六张唱片，京韵十足，殊为珍贵。

上述三类"异族之故书"经江蓝生、张卫东、汪维辉、张美兰、李无未、王顺洪、张西平、鲁健骥、王澧华诸先生介绍，已经进入学界视野，对北京话研究和对外汉语教学史研究产生了很大的推动作用。我们希望将更多的域外经典北京话教本引入进来，考虑到日本卷和朝鲜卷中很多抄本字迹潦草，难以辨认，而刻本、印本中也存在着大量的异体字和俗字，重排点校注释的出版形式更利于研究者利用，这也是前文"深度利用"的含义所在。

对"吾国之旧籍"挖掘整理的成果，则体现在下面五个系列中：

"清代满汉合璧文献萃编"收入《清文启蒙》《清话问答四十条》《清文指要》《续编兼汉清文指要》《庸言知旨》《满汉成语对待》《清文接字》《重刻清文虚字指南编》等十余部经典满汉合璧文献。入关以后，在汉语这一强势语言的影响下，熟习满语的满人越来越少，故雍正以降，出现了一批用当时的北京话注释翻译的满语会话书和语法书。这批教科书的目的本是教授旗人学习满语，却无意中成为了早期北京话的珍贵记录。"清代满汉合璧文献萃编"首次对这批文献进行了大规模整理，不仅对北京话溯源和满汉语言接触研究具有重要意义，也将为满语研究和满语教学创造极大便利。由于底本多为善本古籍，研究者不易见到，在北京大学图书馆古籍部和日本神户外国语大学竹越孝教授的大力协助下，"萃编"将以重排点校加影印的形式出版。

"清代官话正音文献"收入《正音撮要》(高静亭著)和《正音咀华》(莎彝尊著)两种代表著作。雍正六年(1728)，雍正谕令福建、广东两省推行官话，福建为此还专门设立了正音书馆。这一"正音"运动的直接影响就是以《正音撮要》和《正音咀华》为代表的一批官话正音教材的问世。这些书的作者或为旗人，或寓居京城多年，书中保留着大量北京话词汇和口语材料，具有极高的研究价值。沈国威先生和侯兴泉先生对底本搜集助力良多，特此致谢。

《十全福》是北京大学图书馆藏《程砚秋玉霜簃戏曲珍本》之一种，为同治元年陈金雀抄本。陈晓博士发现该传奇虽为昆腔戏，念白却多为京话，较为罕见。

以上三个系列均为古籍，且不乏善本，研究者不容易接触到，因此我们提供了影印全文。

总体来说，由于言文不一，清代的本土北京话语料数量较少。而到了清末民初，风气渐开，情况有了很大变化。彭翼仲、文实权、蔡友梅等一批北京爱国知识分子通过开办白话报来"开启民智""改良社会"。著名爱国报人彭翼仲在《京话日报》的发刊词中这样写道："本报为输进文明、改良风俗，以开通社会多数人之智识为宗旨。故通幅概用京话，以浅显之笔，达朴实之理，纪紧要之事，务令雅俗共赏，妇稚咸宜。"在当时北京白话报刊的诸多栏目中，最受市民欢迎的当属京味儿小说连载和《益世余谭》之类的评论栏目，语言极为地道。

"清末民初京味儿小说书系"首次对以蔡友梅、冷佛、徐剑胆、儒丐、勋锐为代表的晚清民国京味儿作家群及作品进行系统挖掘和整理，从千余部京味儿小说中萃取代表作家的代表作品，并加以点校注释。该作家群活跃于清末民初，以报纸为阵地，以小说为工具，开展了一场轰轰烈烈的底层启蒙运动，为新文化运动的兴起打下了一定的群众基础，他们的作品对老舍等京味儿小说大家的创作产生了积极影响。本系列的问世亦将为文学史和思想史研究提供议题。于润琦、方梅、陈清茹、雷晓彤诸先生为本系列提供了部分底本或馆藏线索，首都图书馆历史文献阅览室、天津图书馆、国家图书馆提供了极大便利，谨致谢意！

"清末民初京味儿时评书系"则收入《益世余谭》和《益世余墨》，均系著名京味儿小说家蔡友梅在民初报章上发表的专栏时评，由日本岐阜圣德学园大学刘一之教授、矢野贺子教授校注。

这一时期存世的报载北京话语料口语化程度高，且总量庞大，但发掘和整理却殊为不易，称得上"珍稀"二字。一方面，由于报载小说等栏目的流行，外地作者也加入了京味儿小说创作行列，五花八门的笔名背后还需考证作者是否为京籍，以蔡友梅为例，其真名为蔡松龄，查明的笔名还有损、损公、退化、亦我、梅蒐、老梅、今睿等。另一方面，这些作者的作品多为急就章，文字错讹很多，并且鲜有单行本存世，老报纸残损老化的情况日益严重，整理的难度可想而知。

上述八个系列在某种程度上填补了相关领域的空白。由于各个系列在内容、体例、出版年代和出版形式上都存在较大的差异，我们在整理时借鉴《朝鲜时代汉语教科书丛刊续编》《〈清文指要〉汇校与语言研究》等语言类古籍的整理体例，结合各个系列自身特点和读者需求，灵活制定体例。"清末民初京味儿小说书系"和"清末民初京味儿时评书系"年代较近，读者群体更为广泛，经过多方调研和反复讨论，我们决定在整理时使用简体横排的形式，尽可能同时满足专业研究者和普通读者的需求。"清代满汉合璧文献萃编""清代官话正音文献"等系列整理时则采用繁体。"早期北京话珍稀文献集成"总计六十余册，总字数近千万字，称得上是工程浩大，由于我们能力有限，体例和校注中难免会有疏漏，加之受客观条件所限，一些拟定的重要书目本次无法收入，还望读者多多谅解。

"早期北京话珍稀文献集成"可以说是中日韩三国学者通力合作的结晶，得到了方方面面的帮助，我们还要感谢陆俭明、马真、蒋绍愚、江蓝生、崔希亮、方梅、张美兰、陈前瑞、赵日新、陈跃红、徐大军、张世方、李明、邓如冰、王强、陈保新诸先生的大力支持，感谢北京大学图书馆的协助以及萧群书记的热心协调。"集成"的编纂队伍以青年学者为主，经验不足，两位丛书总主编倾注了大量心血。王洪君老师不仅在经费和资料上提供保障，还积极扶掖新进，"我们搭台，你们年轻人唱戏"的话语令人倍感温暖和鼓舞。郭锐老师在经费和人员上也予以了大力支持，不仅对体例制定、底本选定等具体工作进行了细致指导，还无私地将自己发现的新材料和新课题与大家分享，令人钦佩。"集成"能够顺利出版还要特别感谢国家出版基金规划管理办公室的支持以及北京大学出版社王明舟社长、张凤珠副总编的精心策划，感谢汉语编辑室杜若明、邓晓霞、张弘泓、宋立文等老师所付出的辛劳。需要感谢的师友还有很多，在此一并致以诚挚的谢意。

"上穷碧落下黄泉，动手动脚找东西"，我们不奢望引领"时代学术之新潮流",惟愿能给研究者带来一些便利,免去一些奔波之苦,这也是我们向所有关心帮助过"早期北京话珍稀文献集成"的人士致以的最诚挚的谢意。

刘　云

2015年6月23日

于对外经贸大学求索楼

2016年4月19日

改定于润泽公馆

导　读

郭利霞

《华语入门》藏于北京大学图书馆和首都图书馆，也藏于俄国国家图书馆，作者吴索福（Усов, Сергей Николаевич, 1891—1966）[①]，汉学家，1891年9月21日（俄历1891年9月9日）出生在俄罗斯梁赞省米哈伊洛夫村。1906年开始在满洲生活，1917年毕业于哈尔滨商业学校、伊尔库茨克军事学校，1921年开始在中俄工业学院（今哈尔滨工业大学）教授俄语，兼华、俄语教授，担任预科生教务主任十余年。后曾任中东铁路东方语课程负责人。1945年到铁路局翻译室任职，后在北京重工业部做翻译，1949年起在华北大学工学院（今北京理工大学）任俄文专修科主任（郑焱 2009：280），1954年回到苏联，居住在梁赞。1966年去世，葬于斯科尔谢公墓。妻子玛尔加莉塔·彼得洛夫娜（Маргарита Петровна, 1904—1987），儿子列昂尼德（Леонид, 1934—1985）。

吴索福编写的俄语教材有《俄文津梁》《我对于教学俄文的一点经验》等，编写的汉语教材有《汉语口语》（俄文文本）(1926)、《汉语口语教材（1—3）》（与郑艾堂[②]合作，1926—1927）、《汉字教法问题》(1927)、《俄汉词典》（与叶宗仁合作，1929）、《汉语口语复合教材》（与

[①] 刘云博士提供了吴索福的俄文生平资料，石汝杰老师和王红厂老师帮助翻译核对了著作目录和生平简历，谨致谢忱。

[②] 合著的作者名郑艾堂、叶宗仁、郑泽冰均是音译。另外，《汉语口语》也可翻译成《汉语会话课本》。

郑泽冰合作，1930）、《第二阶：汉语口语研究》（1931）、《俄日汉词典》（与阿夫多诺莫夫、松野合作，1938）、《中国语入门》（1954），均在哈尔滨出版。①

《华语入门》1937年由北京法文图书馆发行出版，根据作者的计划，这是四卷本的汉语教材，笔者手头只有卷一的中文版和英文版，至于另三卷是作者未完成还是散佚了，不得而知。从英文版的前言中可以得知，计划中的第四卷包括经济、政治和法律等内容。英文版扉页和"作者的话"中注明《华语入门》改编自俄文版《汉语口语》（Kitaiskii Razgavornii Yazik）第六版。本书英文版的翻译、校订和大部分出版事宜由迪瑞德（C. Tyrwhitt）负责，中文版的翻译、校订工作由迪瑞德、何化黔完成。笔者目前还没有搜集到《汉语口语》教材或其他相关资料，因此我们仅对现有的中英文两本配套初级教材加以介绍和分析。

《华语入门》中文版是中文课本，内容全部是中文，供师生课上使用；英文版是注音、英文翻译和讲解，依照中文版内容的顺序，全部标注拼音和英文解释，供学生课前自学使用。本文所依据的是北京大学图书馆的影印本。

一、《华语入门》中文版

（一）体例、内容等

中文版全书共250页，体例为："教学说明"、二十五课课文、"温故知新"（用于复习）、"生字名词表"（即生词总表，分课列出）、插图（分课列出）。其中"教学说明"单独编页。

"教学说明"指出学生（原文为"外国学员"）在老师（原文为"中国

---

① 吴索福的著作信息可参考 http://www.russiangrave.ru/person?prs_id=30。

教员"）讲解新课前预习的方法：学生先要预习生词的拼音和意义，然后看拼音通读句子并做到可以将其翻译成英文，最后再把英文翻译成中文，翻译用拼音就可以，但要注意语法是否正确，如果有错，要知道错在哪里。预习充分了，到老师讲的时候多少总有一些印象，就容易理解了。

老师讲课的方法是：先要仔细地讲解新内容，学生理解后再让学生跟着说，注意有错必纠；然后用图片引导学生自己说，一看发音，二看学生的记忆效果。学习课文的时候，老师先来读一遍课文，让学生认真听，然后让学生跟着读，最后让学生自己读，老师要注意读得是否正确。学生熟悉了课文以后，老师可以提问，引导学生用所学的内容回答，目的是练习会话。

为了练习语音，英文版书后（354—355页）列有一个《练习四声表》，每次上课老师可用五分钟让学生练习。方法如下：首先学生模仿发音，然后学生跟着老师读，最后学生自己读。老师要特别注意发音是否正确。

每次上课都要复习以前学过的内容，以免遗忘。

二十五课课文的编排以词语为纲，兼顾各种语法结构，如第一课共有七组词（详见下表）。第Ⅰ、Ⅱ组每组有3个生词，打乱词语的顺序，列出了六种不同的排列组合形式，如："1.书，纸，本子""2.纸，本子，书""3.本子，书，纸"，目的是让学生反复学习以熟练掌握。第Ⅲ组"有"与前两组词语穷尽性地组句，共列出9句话，如："我有书""他有本子"。第Ⅳ组"没有"与前三组词语共生成9个句子，其中有6个复句，如："他没有书，他有纸""您有书，没有本子"。第Ⅴ组"有……没有"是本课句型，共有7组一问一答的句子，如："您有本子没有？——我没有本子，我有纸"。第Ⅵ组词"铅笔、钢笔"，同样是跟前面的"有、没有、有……没有"组成句子。第Ⅶ组出现的疑问语气词"么"，与前六组出现的动词、名词组合，构成了7个疑问句，既有单句，也有复句，如："您有书么？——我有书""您没有书，您有纸么?——我没有书,我有纸"。

表一 1—5课生词表

	第一课	第二课	第三课	第四课	第五课
第Ⅰ组	书 纸 本子	一 两 三 四 五	这 那 是 不 (这是)(这不是) (那是)(那不是)	毛笔(枝)	先生的 学生的
第Ⅱ组	我 您(你) 他	个(本子)	是 不是	甚么	这/那本书 这/那张纸/桌子 这/那个人/东西/本子 这/那把椅子 这/那枝钢/毛/铅笔 这/那位学生/先生 这/那几(本/张/个/枝/位)
第Ⅲ组	有	张(纸)	这是……不是 那是……不是	人(个) 东西(个)	是……是
第Ⅳ组	没有	本(书)	这是几? 那是几?	先生 学生 位	大 小
第Ⅴ组	有……没有	枝(钢笔)(铅笔)	也	谁	长 短
第Ⅵ组	铅笔 钢笔	几	桌子 椅子	的 我的 您的 你的 他的	知道
第Ⅶ组	么		六 七 八 九 十 把(张桌子)(把椅子)	谁的	茶(个)水(个) 饭(个)
第Ⅷ组					碗(个) 茶碗 饭碗 玻璃杯(个)

其余各课对生词的处理方法大同小异,均是"新词语+旧句型"或"旧词语+新句型",学习新的词语和句型时不断复现之前的内容,这其实是直接法常用的替换练习。一般生词中出现名词时,句子中会给出相应的量

词,如第六课第Ⅱ组"那位先生有几个姑娘?——他有两个姑娘"。同组内的词语必有内在联系,如 第七课第Ⅰ组"多、少"、第十四课第Ⅰ组"贵、贱"、第二十课第Ⅲ组"新、旧"均是反义词;第十一课第Ⅶ组"您好啊、谢谢、请、请坐、再见"均是日常寒暄用语;第十六课第Ⅰ组"红、黄、绿、白、黑、蓝、颜色"均为颜色词,第Ⅳ组"墨水儿、粉笔、黑板"均为教学用品;第二十三课第Ⅴ组和第Ⅵ组生词分别是邮政局和电报局常用词,前者是"邮政局、邮票(一分票)(三分票)(半分票)、来信、去信、回信、票",后者是"电报局、电报(份)、打电报、来电报、去电报、上海";第二十五课第Ⅴ组"病、得病、大夫、治、医院"均是医院场景用的词语。

"温故知新"以问答形式为主,分十六个话题,是对前面二十五课的综合复习。

插图共12页。主要是两类,一类是辅助教学的,如量词的使用(235页)、器物的形状(236、237页)、数字的表述(237页)、地图(243页)等;另一类是反映当时的社会实况,如课堂(241页)、邮局(244页)、车站(244页)、饭馆(245页)、影院(245页)、医院(246页)等。

值得一提的是,全书词、短语、句子需要重读的音节前都标了调号。如:第二十二课第Ⅶ组"1.他从²那里²拿来的²牛奶?——他从⁴那儿拿来的"。

(二)语言特点

《华语入门》作为一部汉语教材,客观上记录了当时北京话的一些语言特点。词汇特点,如"女儿"叫"姑娘"(第六课);"学堂、学校"并用(第二十三课),不过北京口语中"学校"用得更多[1];"教室"说成"讲堂";有儿化词,如"演电影儿"(第二十四课第Ⅲ组);用"个"来形容茶、水、饭(第五课第Ⅶ组)。

---

[1] 依据《华语入门》(英文版)第256页注释95。

语法特点以选择问句和反复问句为例分析。

全书选择问句有使用连接词的,如"(是)……是……""(是)……还是……(呢)"等,也有不用连接词的,即无标记选择问句,前者如:"那所红房子是中学校是小学校?——是中学校"(第二十三课第Ⅱ组)、"是那位大学生写的字好,还是这位小学生写的字好呢?——还是那位大学生写的好"(第十课第Ⅷ组)。后者如:"他们卖中国书,外国书?——他们中国书,外国书,都卖"(第二十一课第V组)。

选择问句中还有由一对反义形容词构成的,如:"那个本子大小?——那个本子小"(第五课第Ⅳ组)、"这枝钢笔长短?——这枝钢笔不长"(第五课第Ⅴ组)、"他的牛多少?——他的牛多"(第七课第Ⅰ组)、"这个大本子贵贱?——这个大本子很贵"(第十四课第Ⅰ组)。

同样是北京话教材,比《华语入门》早的《汉英北京官话词汇》(1911)和《华英文义津逮》(1913,第三版)均未见这种由反义形容词构成的选择问句,仅《官话指南》(1903)中有1例:"你雇的这个车干净不干净,车厢儿大小,骡子好不好?"(131页)。张丹星(2013)考察的八部清末民初北京话语料中,仅《语言自迩集》有用例,可见,《华语入门》对这一格式的记录比同时期的文献更充分。

全书反复问句格式有VO-neg-VO、V(O)-neg-V(O)和VO-neg,如:"您的儿子写字不写?"(第九课)、"您吃饭不吃饭?"(第九课)、"那本书您念不念?"(第九课)、"先生来了没有?"(第十一课)。综观清末民初的八部语料,"VO-neg-VO"格式在早期语料中的比例总体来说高于后期语料,随着时间的推移,"VO-neg-VO"格式的地位被"VO-neg-V"取代(张丹星 2013)。《华语入门》正好能反映从"VO-neg-VO"到"VO-neg-V"的历时过程。书中无一例"V-neg-VO"格式,在其他语料中出现频率也很低。总的来看,反复问句的表现符合清末民初北京话后期特点。

二、《华语入门》英文版

（一）体例和内容

英文版（*A Course of Colloquial Chinese*）共365页，全书包括：目录、前言、作者的话、学生使用注意事项、威妥玛式拼音表、正文25课、课后复习、注释索引、拼音索引、英文索引、练习四声表。正文前的部分单独编页，声调表未加页码。本书有详细的注音和讲解，可供学生自学之用。

"前言"说明这是《华语入门》四卷本中的第一本，专为俄国学生学汉语而编。本书适用于汉语初学者，理论依据是"直接法"：

（1）中文老师必不可少，且只能说汉语。由于均有威妥玛式注音和英文翻译，每课后面还有语法注释，老师做到这一点应该不难；

（2）课文采用会话形式，目的是让学生早早地掌握简单的口语结构；

（3）每课后面都有语法注释，目的是向学生循序渐进地介绍汉语的语法特点；

（4）全部课程旨在帮助学生从初级基础会话知识学到第四册经济、政治、法律等相关内容；

（5）即使学生零起点，也可使用本书。

"作者的话"说明了本书内容的出处，向中英文两个版本的合作者致谢，并说明这是暂定本。

"学生使用注意事项"详细说明学生应如何使用本书，教师应如何安排教学，如下课前几分钟练习声调、每次上课前要安排复习等等。作者认为中文版无需设计声调，英文版有一个《练习四声表》，学生再跟着老师勤加练习，声调很容易掌握。书中需要重读的音节拼音标为黑体，以区别于其他音节。作者特别指出汉语的特点是一字多义，为了不让学生困扰，第一次出现时并不给出所有翻译和解释。随着学习的推进，学生慢慢会了解其他意思，这样学习词汇才能事半功倍。

《威妥玛式拼音表》给出了威式拼音及其对应的英文音节和词语，不过作者也说明，有些音只在中文里有，因此不可能找到准确的英文对应，有的连大概的对应都不太可能找到，如ng、ü在英文中就没有对应的音。

正文中25课课文的体例是：(1)生词、威妥玛式拼音（右上）和英文翻译（右下）；(2)例句的注音和英文翻译，译文如果内容少，就和注音在同一行呈现，如果内容多，先拼音再翻译，两部分独立呈现。

"课后复习"生词带拼音，没有英文翻译，文本部分的安排与正文一致。

"注释索引"按注释的音序排列，包括：注音、汉字、注释序号；"拼音索引"按生字拼音的音序排列，包括：拼音、汉字、英文释义、所在课文、所在段落；"英文索引"按生字英文释义的音序排列，包括：英文释义、汉字、拼音、所在课文、所在段落。作者设计不同索引的目的是方便学习者根据自己的需要查阅相关内容，如需要了解某个语言点就去"注释索引"中查找，想了解某个中文词语的中文解释就去"拼音索引"中查找，需要了解英文词语用中文怎么说，则去"英文索引"中查找。

《练习四声表》从中文版二十五课课文中挑出五个汉字，是用来练习声调的。

（二）词语翻译和语法注释

词语翻译一般只给出英文中对应的词语，不过有些细节值得注意，名词的英文翻译给出了单复数两种形式，如第1课第Ⅰ组"书—book(s)"。有些则给出了不限于课文的多个意思或多种用法，如 "张"是纸、桌子、纸币、文件、皮、票的量词（第2课第Ⅲ组）；"枝"用于笔、花及其他长条形的东西（第2课第Ⅴ组）；"位"表示礼貌（第4课第Ⅳ组）；"饭"指食物或米饭（第5课第Ⅶ组）；"哪"是句末语气词，有时也作疑问代词（第10课第

Ⅳ组）；"旧"可形容时间、人、地方、事物（第20课第Ⅲ组）等。

  语法注释在每课的最后部分，全书接排，共有103条注释。这些注释大都抓住了汉语的特点，如重视语序和虚词、量词是汉语特有的等等。前三个注释首先说明了陈述句、否定句、疑问句的语序和格式。注释4①指出汉语动词没有屈折形式，所有人称和数量形式都相同，如果需要说明人称和数量，动词前面会加代词或名词。8指出汉语没有相当于英语冠词the、a的词语，"书"可能翻译成：book, a book, the book, books。10指出量词是汉语独有的，量词用于数词和名词之间，回答问题时常常省略名词，如："您有几个本子？——我有两个。"74指出"把"用来强调句子的宾语，英文翻译时通常省略。

  有些注释涉及语用，如25对"您"和"你"的区分；46说明英汉顺序相反，汉语说"张先生"，英语则说Mr. Chang。类似的，81指出，街道名称，名称在"街"前，如"买卖街"；66"您姓甚么？"语法上是正确的，但是很少使用。

  有些注释可以互参，如77"那"后标明可参看17；78（a）"儿"的更常见用法可参见59。

  作者对语言的变化也很敏感，如5指出he, him, she, her, it都用"他"，但最近也出现了"她"和"牠"。

  这些词语翻译和语法注释大部分都是学习者不易掌握的或容易混淆的，作者的分析多能切中要害。当然也有错讹，我们将在第三部分加以分析。

三　《华语入门》的得失

  （一）《华语入门》反映了较先进教学理念

  《华语入门》（英文版）"前言"说明本书运用的教学法是"直接法"。

---

① 下文如无特别注明，均省略"注释"二字，只保留注释的序号。

本书成书阶段，直接法还是比较先进的方法，和翻译法相比，最明显的优势是更有利于培养口语能力。

编排设计上，无论是一课之内从生词到对话，还是全书从二十五课课文到"温故知新"，都是从机械练习过渡到交际练习。

在教学内容方面表现为以下几点。(1)重视口语表达，如88"开"口语中常用动词重叠形式，89"关"口语中后面通常要加"上"。重视语音，特别是声调，每课都安排了声调练习，有些词还标了变调，如314页"旅馆"的"旅"标的是2(3)，表示本调是上声，变调为阳平。中文版中需要重读的音节前标了调号，英文版需要重读的音节用了黑体。(2)重视句型学习，每课都有需要掌握的句型，而且用替换法不断重复练习。(3)话题选择上，"温故知新"均是与学生日常生活密切相关的内容，包括：家庭、购物、服装、饭店、住宿、学校、邮政局、电报局、电影院、医院、宾馆、商人等。可以此了解当时学生学习生活的情况以及当时社会经济的情况，如邮票有半分票、三分票等。

在英文注释方面，对重点和难点的把握比较到位，复杂的词语分阶段解释。如"的"出现了两次(19、30)，"就"也出现了两次(62、103)，多处指出跟英语不同的语序(46、81、100)等。

《华语入门》重视复习和交际，教学法上比较成熟，实用性很强，虽然作者说这只是暂定本，但编排很合理，也比较严密，已经具备了现代口语教材的雏形。

(二)《华语入门》的不足

《华语入门》英文版扉页就有"Provisional Issue"字样，"作者的话"更是明确说明这只是暂定版本，印数有限，欢迎批评和建议。可见作者认为教材不够成熟，需要进一步修订。在笔者看来，本书的不足除了个别明显错误外，也有同时期西人编写汉语教材的普遍局限的地方。

《华语入门》中有些描写分析明显是套用印欧语系语法范畴,因而有削足适履之嫌。

作者把汉语的时态分为将来时、现在时、过去时。很多解释涉及时态,如12说"不"否定现在时或将来时。同样,汉语没有格范畴,16则认为"的"是领属格的标志,65认为"给"是与格,72把"拿笔"的"拿"看作工具格。显然是套用了印欧语的语法系统。

作者注意到了汉语中的结果补语,不过仅限于例举,如61"完"做结果补语,102"好"做结果补语,却未加以概括总结。

有些解释不准确,如"这、那"分别解释为this, these和that, those(15页);67把副词"很"当作最高级;20把"是这本书大是那本书大?"当作比较级。

总之,《华语入门》在一定程度上反映了北京话的特点,但其语料具有异质性,不能看作一时一地之语的记录,这是我们在研究时需要特别注意的。

参考文献

陈士廉(1987),哈尔滨工业大学忆往,《教育学研究——〈台湾及海外中文报刊资料专辑〉》第4辑,书目文献出版社,北京。

韩永进、王建朗主编,民国时期文献保护中心、中国社会科学院近代史研究所编(2015)《民国文献类编(教育卷846)》,国家图书馆出版社,北京。

吴启泰、郑永邦(1903)《官话指南》,上海别发洋行,上海。

易永谊(2016)魏池、魏智对北平汉学的贡献,《国际汉学》第1期。

张丹星(2013)《清末民初北京话的选择问句和反复问句研究》,北京大学硕士学位论文。

郑　焱(2009)《沐浴夕阳》,北京理工大学出版社,北京。

華語入門
壹 叁

華語入門

卷壹

著作者　哈爾濱法政大學校教授 吳索福

繙譯者　迪瑞德　何化黔

出板者　魏　智

排印者　北京西什庫印刷所

發行者　北京法文圖書館

教學說明

(一) 中國教員與外國學員第一天見面語言當然不通現在預備了一個途徑若能照着行去兩方面的語言慢慢的就可以通了

(二) 教員沒講新字以前學員必須把所應講的功課先要預備一回但是怎樣預備呢

(甲) 應來回細看拼音及意義

(乙) 將拼音及意義都看過以後用拼音要念成句子到了能繙譯出英文來為適可這樣就便於閱看文法了

(丙) 再用英文譯出漢文來就用拼音不必用漢字須注

意文法有無錯誤及其錯誤在甚麼地方這是為學員預備的方法等到教員講的時候多少總有一些印象並且容易明白了

(三) 凡教員對於教學法當然都是很明白的不妨也寫在下面一點

(甲) 教員應先將沒講過的新意思不厭煩瑣的講幾次叫學員聽過以後再用比方叫學員跟着說如說錯了必須改正聲音如有不對再告以發音地位務要叫學員說對為止其次指着圖畫叫學員重說也要注意發音並且還要看他記憶力怎麼樣

(乙) 將一課本文念與學員聽聽了以後就叫學員跟着念再叫他自己念要注意念的句子有無錯處聲音是否正確

(丙) 學員課文熟習以後可以提出句子來問學員叫他回答每次更叫學員用課本的句子來問教員這是練習會話的要緊方法

(丁) 更爲練習發音起見在課本後列成一表教員在每一堂時間內用五分鐘叫學員熟聽方法

(一) 模仿發音

(二) 教員發音叫學員跟着發音

(三)叫學員自己發音最要緊的是要注意他發音對不對

(四)

(戊)每次功課別忘了溫習從前所學的免得遺忘

以上所說不是要限制非用此方法不可不過為得是兩方面語言容易通的起見所以指出一個途徑來教者與學者或能免去許多困難作教員的或者還有比這個特別好的方法也未可知

第一課

I 書 紙 本子

1 書，紙，³本子
2 紙，³本子，書
3 ³本子，書，紙
4 紙，書，³本子
5 書，³本子，紙
6 ³本子，紙，書

II 我 您(你) 他

1 我，您，他
2 您，他，我
3 他，我，您
4 我，他，您
5 您，我，他
6 他，您，我

III 有

1. 我有₁書
2. 您有₃紙
3. 他有₃本子
4. 我有₃本子
5. 您有₁書
6. 他有₃紙
7. 我有₃紙
8. 您有₃本子
9. 他有₁書

IV 沒有

1. 他₂沒有本子
2. 我₂沒有書
3. 您₂沒有紙
4. 他₂沒有書,他有紙
5. 您₂沒有本子,我有本子
6. 我₂沒有紙,您有書
7. 您₂有書,他₂沒有書
8. 他有₃紙,₂沒有書
9. 我有₃本子,₂沒有紙

V （有○沒有）

1 我有₃紙沒有？

2 他₂有₃本子沒有？
您₃有紙
他₂沒有本子

3 您₁有書沒有？
我₃有書

4 他有₃紙沒有？
他₂沒有紙，他有本子

5 您有₃本子沒有？

6 他有₁書沒有？
我₂沒有本子，我有紙
他₃有書

7 他有₃書，有₃本子沒有？
他有書₂沒有本子

VI 鉛筆 鋼筆

1 您有₁鉛筆
2 他有₁鋼筆
3 我₂沒有鋼筆,我有鋼筆
4 您有鋼筆,我₂沒有鉛筆
5 他有₁鉛筆沒有?
6 他₃有鉛筆
  我₂沒有鋼筆,我有₁鉛筆
  沒有?
  您₂沒有鋼筆,您₃有鉛筆

VII 麽

1 您有₁書麽?
2 他有₃本子麽?
  我₃有書
3 我有₁鉛筆麽?
  他₂沒有本子
4 他有鋼筆麽?
  您₃有鉛筆
5 您沒有書您有₃紙麽?
  他₂沒有鋼筆,他有鉛筆

我沒有書，我₃有紙

6 他沒有₃本子麼？
  他₂沒有本子

7 您沒有₁書麼？
  我₃有書

第二課

I 一兩三四五

1. 一，兩，三，四，五
2. 四，三，五，兩，一
3. 三，五，一，四，兩
4. 五，三，一，兩，四
5. 兩，四，一，五，三

II 個（本子）

1. 一₄個本子
2. 三₁個₄本子
3. 四₄個本子
4. 他有₃五個本子
5. 我有兩個本子，₂沒有三個本子
6. 您有₄四個本子麼？
7. 我沒有四個本子，我有兩個本子

III 張（紙）

1. 兩張紙
2. 五張紙
3. 您有一張紙
4. 我有三張紙
5. 他沒有四張紙，他有一張紙
6. 您有五張紙麼？
7. 我沒有三張紙麼？

您沒有三張紙，他有三張紙

IV 本(書)

1. ⁴四本書
2. ³五本書
3. ⁴我有¹一本書
4. 他有¹三本書
5. 您有兩本書²沒有五本書
6. 我有₄一本書麼?
7. 他₂沒有三本書麼?

他沒有三本書,他有₄一兩本書

V 枝（鋼筆）（鉛筆）

1. 一枝鋼筆
2. 兩枝鉛筆
3. 我有三枝鋼筆
4. 他有四枝鉛筆
5. 您沒有五枝鉛筆，我有
6. 他有四枝鋼筆麼？他沒有四枝鋼筆，他有三枝鋼筆
7. 您沒有兩三枝鉛筆麼？我有兩三枝鉛筆

IV 幾

1. 幾³個本子？
2. 一²個本子
3. 幾³張紙？
4. 兩³張紙
5. 我³有幾³本書？
6. 他³有四⁴五本書
7. 他³有幾³枝鉛筆？
8. 您³有一¹枝鋼筆，他³有幾³枝鋼筆？
9. 他³有五³枝
10. 他³有一本書，有幾³個本子？
11. 他³有一本書，四⁴個本子
12. 您³有幾³張紙？
13. 我²沒有紙，我有本子
14. 他³有幾³枝鉛筆，幾³枝鋼筆？
15. 他³有五³枝鉛筆，一¹三四枝鋼筆

第三課

I 這 那 是 不

（這是） （這不是）
（那是） （那不是）

1. 這是書
2. 那是紙
3. 這是三個本子
4. 那是五個本子
5. 這²不是鋼筆，⁴那是鋼筆
6. 那²不是四本書，那是³兩本書
7. 這是本子，²不是紙
8. 那是⁴一本書，²不是₁三本書

II 是 不 是

1. 這是¹鉛筆麼?
2. 這是³紙麼?
3. 那是³本子麼?
4. 這不是¹鋼筆麼?
5. 那不是¹書麼?
6. 那不是¹鋼筆麼?

是,這是鉛筆
不是,這是³本子
那是³本子,⁴這是本子
是,這²不是鋼筆
不是,那²不是書,⁴這是書
不是,那是¹鉛筆

III （這是○不是）
（那是○不是）

1 這₄是₃紙不是？
　這是紙
2 那₄是鋼筆不是？
　那₂不是鋼筆，那是₁鉛筆
3 這是₁書不是？
　是，這是書
4 那₄是₃本子不是？
　不是，那是₃紙

IV （這是幾？）
（那是幾？）

1 這是幾枝鋼筆？
2 那是幾枝鋼筆？
3 那是幾個本子？
 這是五個本子
4 這是三本書，那是幾本？
 那是四本
5 這是一枝鉛筆，這是幾枝？

 這是兩枝
 那是幾個本子，幾張紙？
 那是五個本子，四張紙

V 也

1. 這是書，那³也是書
2. 我有本子，他³也有本子
3. 這²不是紙，那³也不是紙
4. 您沒有鋼筆，他³也沒有鋼筆
5. 那是鉛筆，這³也是鉛筆麼?
6. 他有本子，您³也本子麼?
7. 他有本子，我²沒有本子
8. 這是³五張紙，那³也是五張紙麼?
9. 不是，那是⁴四張
10. 我有一枝鋼筆，他³也有一枝麼?
11. 他³也有一枝
12. 那是兩本書，這是幾本?
13. 這³也是兩本

10 他有三個本子，²您³有幾個？
我³也有三個

11 您有本子，您³也有紙麼？
是，我³也有紙

12 他有鉛筆，他²沒有¹鋼筆麼？
他有鉛筆，³也有鋼筆

VI 棹子 椅子

1 我有¹棹子，他有³椅子
2 那是棹子，這³也是棹子
3 您³有椅子沒有？
4 我²沒有椅子，我有¹棹子
4 那是³椅子不是？
5 不是，那是¹棹子
他有棹子，³也有³椅子
他³也有椅子

VII 六七八九十把（張棹子）（把椅子）

1. ⁴六張紙
2. ²七個本子
3. 這是¹八本書，那是³九枝鉛筆
4. 我有²十張紙
5. 他有⁴六張棹子，您有¹七把椅子
6. 那是³幾把椅子？
7. 那是¹八把椅子
   您有²十張棹子麼？
   我沒有十張棹子，我有³九張
8. 這是⁴六把椅子，那³也是六把椅子麼？
   不是，那是¹八把椅子

第四課

I 毛筆(枝)

1 您²有毛筆沒有？
  我³有毛筆
2 您有³幾枝毛筆？
  我有¹七枝毛筆
3 他³也有毛筆麼？
  是，他³也有毛筆
4 那是²毛筆不是？
  不是，那是¹鉛筆，⁴這是
  毛筆
5 這是³幾枝毛筆？
  這是¹八枝

II 甚麼

1 這是₂甚麼？
這是₁桌子

2 那是₂甚麼？
那是₃椅子

3 您有₂甚麼？
我有₂毛筆

4 他有₂甚麼？
他有₁鋼筆

5 ₄這是本子，₄那是甚麼？

6 這是本子，那₃也是本子
我有紙，₁他有甚麼？
他有₁鉛筆

華語入門　第四課

III 人(個) 東西(個)

1. 這是⁴六個人，那³也是六個人
2. 那是³九個，這是²七個
3. 幾個人有³桌子？
4. 十個人有²桌子
5. 幾個人有³椅子？
6. 四個人有椅子
7. 一個人有³兩枝毛筆
8. 五個人有³幾枝？

6. 五個人有²十枝
7. 三個人有¹三個，六個人有³幾個？
8. 六個人有⁴六個
9. 這是¹書
10. 那是²甚麼東西？
11. 那是³本子
12. 您有²甚麼東西？
13. 我有¹桌子

IV 先生　學生　位

1. 我₁是先生
2. 他₁是₂學生
3. 那是₄六位學生
4. 這是₃兩位先生
5. 您有₃幾位先生?
6. 我有₂一位先生
7. 他有₃幾位學生?
8. 他有₃十位學生
9. 先生有₂甚麼東西?

10. 他有₂甚麼東西?
11. 他₃也有桌子
12. 那是₁鋼筆,₄這是甚麼東西?
13. 那是₁鋼筆,這是₂毛筆
14. 我有鉛筆,₂您有₂甚麼東西?
15. 我有₂毛筆,有₁鋼筆

第四課

8. 先生有₁書有₁鋼筆

9. 學生有₂甚麼東西?

10. 學生有₂毛筆, 有₁鉛筆

11. 他₄是₁先生不是?

    不₁是, 他₁是₂學生

12. 這是₃幾位學生?

    那是₂八位

V 誰

1. 誰₂是₁先生?

   他₁是₁先生

2. 誰₂是₁學生?

   我₃是₁學生

3. 誰₂有₁先生?

   他₁有₁先生

4. 誰₂有₃兩把椅子?

   我₃有₃兩把椅子

5. 誰₂沒有₃紙?

1. 他沒有紙
2. 誰有棹子，沒有椅子
3. 我有棹子沒有椅子?

VI 的 我的 您的 你的 他的

1. 我³的鋼筆
2. 您²的本子
3. 他¹的學生
4. 您是他¹的學生麼
5. 我是他⁴的學生他是您²的先生麼?
6. 不是，他²不是我的先生那是我³的毛筆麼?

7 那₄是您的毛筆
這₂不是您的₁鉛筆麼?
那₂不是我的鉛筆,那是
他的鉛筆

VII 誰的

1 這是誰的椅子?
　那是他₁的椅子
2 那是誰的椅子?
　這是我₃的椅子
3 您是誰的學生?
　我是他₁的學生
4 他是誰的先生?
　他是我₃的先生

第五課 先生的 學生的

1
1. 這¹是²誰的書?
2. 那²是²先生的書
3. 那²是²學生的鉛筆麼?
4. 那⁴是²學生的鉛筆
5. 這²是²您先生的棹子麼?
6. 是,這⁴是²我先生的棹子
7. 那²是²您學生的毛筆麼?
8. 不是,那²不是²我學生的毛筆

II
那/這 本 書
那/這 個 人/東西
那/這 本 本子
那/這 枝 鉛筆/毛筆/鋼筆
那/這 把 椅子
那/這 張 紙/棹子
那/這 位 先生/學生

幾(本/張/個/枝/位)

1. 這本書是³我的,那張紙是¹他的
2. 這把椅子是¹先生的,那張棹子是²學生的
3. 這個本子是²誰的?

3 這個本子是⁴那位學生的
4 這兩枝鉛筆⁴是他的不是?
　不是,是⁴這位先生的
5 這幾枝毛筆是²您的麼?
　是,這幾枝毛筆⁴是我的
6 那幾枝鋼筆³也是您的麼?
　不是,是⁴那位學生的
7₂誰是您的先生?
　⁴那位是我的先生
8 這位是²誰?
9 那位先生有³幾位學生?
　那位先生有²十位學生

III 是○是

1. 這是₃紙是₃本子?
   這是₃本子

2. 那位是₁先生是₂學生?
   那位是₂學生

3. 這張桌子,是₂您的是₁他的?
   這張桌子是₁他的

4. 那把椅子是₁先生的是₂學生的?

5. 那把椅子₂不是先生的,是學生的
   那是₁三個是₄四個?
   那不是三個,₃也不是四個,那是₃五個

IV 大⁴小³

1 這張⁴桌子⁴大，那張桌子³小

2 我的書⁴大，您的書³小

3 那個本子⁴大小？

4 這本書⁴大小？

5 這本書⁴不小

6 先生的本子是⁴大的是這本書⁴大是那本書⁴大？

7 ⁴這本書⁴大，那本書小²是您的學生⁴是他的學生大？

8 我的學生²沒有他的學生大這兩張紙是²誰的？⁴大的是¹他的³小的是³我⁴的

9 這把椅子₄大不大?
10 這把椅子₂不大
那張棹子₃小不小?
那張棹子₂不大不小

V 長短

1 這枝鉛筆₂長,那枝毛筆₃短
2 這枝鋼筆₂長短?
3 這枝鋼筆₄不長
您的鉛筆₂長短?
4 我的鉛筆₃短
是₂您的鉛筆長是₁他的鉛筆長?
我的鉛筆₂沒有他的鉛筆長

5. 學生的鉛筆是²長的是³短的？

學生的是²長的

VI 知道

1. 您知道¹他是²誰麼？

我知道，他是¹先生

2. 您知道他有³幾位學生？

他有⁴四位學生

3. 那個人是誰，²您知道⁴不知道？

我¹知道那個人是誰，那個人是²學生

4. 您知道²那張⁴大棹子是

2 誰的不知道？

1 我知道，那張大桌子是先生的

5 您知道他有甚麼東西不知道？
我不知道他有甚麼東西

6 您知道那兩枝鋼筆是誰的？
我知道，長的是先生的，短的是學生的

VII 茶(個) 水(個) 飯(個)

1 這是茶那是水

2 您有茶沒有？

3 我沒有茶，我有水
他沒有茶？

4 這是甚麼？
這是飯

5 那也是飯麼？
那不是飯，那是茶

6 這個飯是₂您的，那個茶是₂誰的？

7 那個茶是₁他的
這是您學生的₂茶麼？
是，這₄是我學生的茶

VIII 碗(個) 茶碗 飯碗
玻璃盃(個)

1 那是₂甚麼東西？
2 那是₃幾個碗
3 那是₂一個碗
先生有₂茶碗，學生有₄飯碗
4 這是₂甚麼碗？
這是₄飯碗

5 那¹是玻璃¹盃麼?
是，那⁴是玻璃盃
6 是茶碗⁴大是飯碗⁴大?
飯碗大，²茶碗小
7 您有茶碗，³也有玻璃盃麼?
是，我³也有玻璃盃
8 這三個飯碗是²您的麼²
²不是我的，那²八個²茶碗是是我的

9 您有幾個玻璃盃?
我有³九個玻璃盃
10 那是²甚麼碗?
那是⁴飯碗

第六課

I 書棹子 飯棹子

1. 這是²甚麼棹子？ 這是¹書棹子
2. 誰⁴有⁴飯棹子？ 那個人有飯棹子
3. 這張⁴大書棹子是²誰的？ 我⁴不知道是誰的
4. 是⁴飯棹子⁴大是¹書棹子⁴大？ 書棹子²沒有飯棹子大
5. 那位先生有³幾張⁴飯棹子，³幾張⁴書棹子，⁴您¹知道⁴不知道？ 我¹知道，他有¹三四張書棹子，³五六張飯棹子
6. 那張書棹子⁴大不大？ 那張書棹子²不大，⁴這張⁴飯

棹子⁴大

II 父親　母親　兒子　姑娘

1 這位是²誰？　這位是³我的⁴父親
2 他是²誰的³母親？　他是⁴那位²學生的³母親
3 你父親有³幾個兒子？　我父親有⁴四個兒子
4 那位先生有³幾個姑娘？　他有³兩個姑娘
5 那位姑娘有²甚麼？　他有¹玻²璃¹盃
6 你³的兒子⁴大小？　我³的兒子²不⁴大
7 這個茶碗是²我¹兒子的，那個飯碗是我¹姑娘的
8 這張書棹子是²誰的？　這張書棹子是²我⁴父親的

III 羊（隻）牛（頭）猪（口）

1 這是²羊不是？ 是，這⁴是²羊
2 這是²羊麼？ 那²不是羊，那是²牛
3 這是牛，那⁴是²甚麼？ 那是¹猪
4 那是³幾口猪？ 那是³五口猪
5 這是³幾隻羊？ 這是¹七隻羊
6 那¹八頭牛是³你²母親的麼？ ⁴是我母親的
7 他的猪⁴大³小？ 他有⁴一口⁴大的，四口³小的

IV 肉 羊肉 牛肉 猪肉 斤

1 這是²羊肉，那是²牛肉
2 這是³幾斤羊肉？ 這是¹三斤羊肉
3 那是³幾斤牛肉？ 那是²十斤牛肉
4 這是²甚麼肉？ 這是¹猪肉

V 魚 條 塊

1 這是³幾條魚？ 這是³兩條魚
2 那是³幾塊猪肉？ 那是³六塊猪肉
3 是⁴這條魚⁴大是⁴那條魚⁴大？ ⁴那條魚⁴大，這條魚³小
4 那塊肉有³幾斤？ 那塊肉有¹八斤

5 這₃條魚有幾₃斤？ 這條魚有₄六斤

VI 麵包 茶葉 咖啡

1 他有₄麵包麼？ 他₂沒有麵包
2 這₂是誰的茶葉？ 這是₁先生的茶葉
3 這₁是咖啡是₂茶葉？ 這是₁咖啡
4 那是₃幾斤麵包？ 那是₄六斤麵包

VII 二

1 十₁一，十₄二，十₁三，十₄四，十₃五，十₄六，十₁七，
十₁八，十₃九
2 二₄十，三₁十，五₃十，八₁十

3 二十一，三十二，五十四，六十五，七十八，
八十九，九十九

4 四十四個人，七十二斤茶葉，八十五條魚，二十
三隻羊，三十五斤羊肉

5 四十六頭牛，五十二塊牛肉，六十七斤牛肉，

6 七十四口豬，八十一塊麵包，九十二斤茶葉，
十八斤咖啡，十四斤豬肉，四十五塊豬肉，五十
五斤魚，

第七課

I 多 少

1 羊肉¹多，豬肉³少
2 茶葉¹多，咖啡³少
3 您的牛¹多，我的牛³少
4 他的牛¹多³少？他的牛¹多
5 是²茶碗多，是⁴飯碗多？茶碗¹多，飯碗³少
6 是¹先生的書多，是²學生的書多？
7 您是¹先生麼？是，我⁴是先生書多，誰的書少，我不知道²誰的

II 多少

1. 這是多少隻羊？ 這是四十二隻羊
2. 那是幾頭牛？ 那是六頭牛
3. 他有多少斤茶葉，多少斤咖啡？ 他有二十五斤茶葉，三十八斤咖啡
4. 您的兒子有幾位先生？ 我的兒子有一位先生
5. 那是多少位學生，這是幾位先生？ 那是四十位學生，這是兩位先生
8. 您是誰的先生？ 我是那位學生的先生

華語入門　第七課

III 十幾　幾十　二十幾　五十幾

1. 那是¹多少斤魚？　那是²十幾斤魚
2. 這是¹多少張書桌子？　這是²十幾張書桌子
3. 這位先生有¹多少位學生？　他有¹幾十位
4. 您有³幾十個玻璃盃？　我有⁴幾十
5. 那⁴二十幾張飯桌子是²誰的？　我⁴不知道是誰的
6. 這是³七十幾枝²毛筆？　這是七十²二枝

IV 字

1. 這是³幾個字？　這是³三個字
2. 那是¹多少個字？　那是¹八十¹三個字

V 們 我們 你們 他們

3 這是⁴「飯」字不是？這²不是⁴「飯」字,這是¹「鉛」字
4 是⁴這個字是¹「書」字,是⁴那個字是¹「書」字？這個字是¹「本」字,那字是¹書字

1 你們有甚麼？我們有²毛筆
2 誰有書桌子？他們有書桌子
3 誰沒有飯桌子？我們沒有飯桌子
4 先生們有多少枝鉛筆？先生們有²十³幾枝鉛筆
5 這³幾十張書桌子是²學生們的不是？⁴是學生們的

VI 我們的 你們的 他們的

1 那條魚是₁他們的麼？ 是，那條魚是他們的
2 這口猪是₂您的麼？ 不是我的，是₃我們的
3 那五十九斤咖啡是₂誰的？ 那五十九斤咖啡是₃我們的
4 這四十二張書棹子，是₃你們的是₁他們的？ 這四十二張書棹子是₁他們的，那三十六張₄飯棹子是₃我們的

VII 百 零

1 ₄一百，₄二百，₄六百，₃九百

1. 一百零₁一，三百零₄四，七百零₁八
2. 八百₁一十，九百₄四十，二百₃五十
3. 一百一十₃九，二百三十₄六，五百四十₁一，
4. 九百八十₄二
5. 四₄百個₂茶碗
6. 九百二十₁一斤₁咖啡
7. 八百九十₃五個₂人
8. 七百零₁七斤₂茶葉
9. 五百₁一十五個₁玻璃盃
10. 六百七十₁塊₄麵包
11. 七百八十₃把₃椅子
12. 九百₃九十個₄字
13. 二百零₃五隻₂羊
14. 一百₁八十口₁猪
15. 四百₁七十頭₂牛

華語入門　第七課

VIII 千

1. 一千⁴，二千⁴，八千¹
2. 一千⁹百³三十⁴六，兩千¹八百二十³五，八千⁴百⁷十¹一
3. 三千²零²三，八千⁴百²零七，六千²零五十四，九千²零五百
4. 三千⁴百²個²茶碗
5. 四千⁶百⁹十¹三頭²牛
6. 七千³百⁶十³九口¹猪
7. 八千⁴百²五十¹八條²魚

8 四千零₂一個₃本子，五千三百二十₄四個₄飯碗

9 九千九百九十₃九枝₂毛筆

10 六千三百七十₁八隻₂羊，五千四百三十₄二斤₄麵包

第八課

I 都 甚麼的 百多 千多 幾百 幾千

1. 這[1]都是[2]羊肉，那[1]都是猪肉

2. 你們都有[2]甚麼東西？我們有[3]本子，有[1]鉛筆，有[1]書桌子，有[3]椅子，甚麼的

3. 那[1]三百多枝鋼筆，這[4]一千多張紙，[1]都是[4]那個人的麼？是，[1]都是他的

4. 你們有幾[3]百斤茶葉？我們有[1]三百斤

5. 這是多少[3]斤咖啡？這是幾[1]千斤

II 這些 那些

1 這$_1$些個本子$_1$都是$_2$誰的？ 這些個本子都是我$_2$兒子的，$_1$不$_2$都是他們的，$_3$也有我們的

2 那$_1$些羊都是$_1$他們的麼？

3 這些口猪是您的，那些頭牛$_3$也是$_2$您的麼？ 不是，那些頭牛是$_4$那個人的

III 〈問答〉

(一) 這是$_2$甚麼東西？ (二) 這是$_1$棹子

(一) 這是$_2$甚麼棹子？

(二) 這是$_1$書棹子

(一) 這是₃幾張書棹子？

(二) 這是₃兩張書棹子

(一) 這兩張書棹子₁都是₂您的麼？

(二) 不₁都是我的，這張₄大的是我的，那張₃小的₂不是我的

(一) 那張小的是₂誰的？

(二) 那張小的是₂學生的

IV〔問答〕

(一) 那位姑娘₁都有₂甚麼東西？

(二) 那位姑娘有₁書，有₃紙，有₃本子，有₁鉛筆，有₂毛筆，甚麼的

Ⅴ（問答）

(一) 他有多少枝鉛筆多少枝毛筆？
(二) 他有十幾枝鉛筆二十幾枝毛筆
(一) 您的兒子有幾張紙，幾本書，幾個本子？
(二) 我兒子有五張紙，八個本子，九本書
(一) 那個人是甚麼人，您知道不知道？
(二) 我知道，那個人是先生
(一) 他是誰的先生？
(二) 他是我們的先生
(一) 你們是幾位學生？

VI 〔問答〕

(一) 那是₂甚麼？
(二) 那是₃碗

(一) 那是₂甚麼碗？
(二) 那是₄飯碗

(一) 你們有₃幾位先生？
(二) 我們有₃兩位先生

(一) 你們的先生有₄多少位學生？
(二) 一位先生有₁三十多位，一位先生有₄四十幾位

(一) 你們六位有₃幾位先生？
(二) 我們是₄六個學生

(一) 那是₂您的₄飯碗麼？

(二) 那₂不是我的飯碗，那是₁他的飯碗

(一) 您₃也有₄飯碗麼？

(二) 是，我₃也有飯碗

(一) 你們₃有₄飯碗麼？

(二) 是，我們₃也有飯碗

(一) 那₁些茶碗是₃你們的麼？

(二) ₄是我們的

VII〔問答〕

(一) 誰有₃椅子？

(二) 我們有椅子

(一) 你們有多少把椅子？

(二) 我們有二十多把椅子

(一) 他們也有椅子麼？

(二) 他們也有椅子

(一) 是你們的椅子多是他們的椅子多？

(二) 我們的椅子多，他們的椅子少

(一) 他們有多少把椅子？

(二) 他們有十幾把椅子

(一) 你們的椅子大不大？

VIII 〔問答〕

(一) 那個人有²羊沒有？

(二) ³有羊

(一) 是，他³也有牛

(二) 他³也有²牛麼？

(一) 是²羊多是牛¹多？

(二) 他的羊¹多，牛³少

(一) 我們的椅子²不⁴大不小

(二) 是你們的椅子⁴大是他們的椅子⁴大？

(一) 我們的椅子²沒有¹他們的椅子⁴大

IX 〔問答〕

(一) 他有$_1$多少隻羊幾$_3$頭牛？

(二) 他有$_3$幾百隻羊八$_1$頭牛

(一) 那些口豬$_3$也是$_1$他的麼？

(二) 不是，他$_2$沒有豬

(一) 這些塊肉都是$_2$甚麼肉？

(二) 有$_2$羊肉，有$_2$牛肉，$_3$也有$_1$豬肉

(一) 這些塊肉，那些條魚，$_1$都是$_2$誰的？

(二) 都是$_4$那個人的

(一) 這條魚$_4$大不大？

（二）這條魚₄大

X〔問答〕

（一）那位是₂誰？
（二）那位是我₄父親
（一）那位是₃你₃母親麼？
（二）是，那位⁴是我母親

（一）那枝₂長鉛筆是你₄父親的麼？
（二）不是，那枝₃短的是我父親的，那枝₂長的是我₃母親的

（一）那個玻璃盃是₂誰的？

(二)那個玻璃盃是誰的，我不知道
(一)那個咖啡是你母親的麼？
(二)是我母親的
(一)那是幾斤茶葉，幾斤咖啡？
(二)那是三斤茶葉，五斤咖啡

第九課

I 作(做) (棹子) (椅子)

1. 這個人作₁書棹子,那個人作₄飯棹子
2. 你們₄作₃椅子麼?
3. 您作椅子,₃也作₁棹子麼?
4. 那位₂學生作₂甚麼?他₄作₃椅子
5. 那個人作₂甚麼棹子?
   棹子
   是,我們₄作椅子
   我₃也作棹子
   那個人作₁書棹子,₃也作₄飯

II 作書

1. 先生作₁書不作? 先生₄作書

華語入門 第九課

2 是₁先生作書是₂學生作書？
3 你們的先生作₁書不作？他₂不作書

III 做飯

1 您母親作₂甚麼？ 我母親作₄飯
2 您的₁姑娘作₄飯不作？ 他₂不作飯
3 他₂不作飯，他₄作₂甚麼？ 他₂不作甚麼
4 你們的飯是₂誰作？ 我們的飯是₄那個人作

IV 寫

1 誰寫字？ ₃我寫字
2 先生₃寫字麼？ 先生₃也寫字

V 念

1. 那位學生⁴念¹書麼？那位學生⁴念書
2. 您⁴不念書，您⁴作²甚麼？我³寫字
3. 這個字⁴念²甚麼？這個字念「紙」
4. 那本書您⁴念不念？我²不念
5. 那兩位姑娘是²誰念書？是那位⁴大的念書
6. 那位先生的²兒子⁴念書不念？他⁴念書

3. 您的²兒子³寫字⁴不寫？他⁴不寫字
4. 您的²姑娘寫字，他²有²毛筆麼？他²沒有毛筆，他有¹鋼筆

7 你們³有¹書念⁴麼？ 他³有書念，我²沒有書念

VI 會

1 你⁴會作⁴飯麼？ 我⁴會作飯
2 他⁴會作²甚麼？ 他會作¹桌子，也會作³椅子
3 您的²兒子⁴會作書不會？ 他²不會作書
4 那位學生會寫¹多³少個字？ 那位學生會寫³幾²十個字

VII 喝

1 他們¹喝²茶麼？ 他們¹喝茶
2 誰²不喝³茶？ 我³不喝茶
3 您¹喝³水麼？ 我¹喝水

VIII 吃

1. 你₁吃₂甚麼？　我吃₄麵包
2. 你的₂兒子₁吃₂羊肉₄不吃？　他₁吃₂魚
3. 你的₁姑娘₂吃₂魚₄不吃？　我吃₁猪肉
4. 你是吃₁猪肉是吃₂牛肉？　我的兒子₄不吃羊肉
5. 那位先生₁吃₂甚麼？　他吃₄飯
6. 您₁吃₂飯₄不吃飯？　我₄不吃飯

4. 他是喝₁咖啡是喝₂茶？　他₁都不喝
5. 那位姑娘₃有茶喝₂沒有？　他₃有茶喝
6. 我有茶，您₁喝不喝？　我₁喝

華語入門　第九課

7 您吃₂甚麼₄肉？我吃₂羊肉
8 您的₄父親吃₂甚麼₄肉？我的父親吃₁猪肉
9 您的母親也吃₁猪肉麼？不是，他吃₂牛肉
10 那個人₃有₄飯吃沒有？他₃有飯吃
11 那兩個人，誰有飯吃，₂誰沒有飯吃？他們₁都有飯吃

IX 要

1 那位先生₄要作₂甚麼？他要₃寫字
2 那位學生₄要作₂甚麼？他要₄作₃椅子
3 您的₂兒子₁要吃₂甚麼？我的兒子要₂魚
4 您的₄父親是要寫₄大字是要寫₃小字？

我₁的₃父親要₃寫₃小字
5 您₃的₃母親要₃喝₂茶₄是要喝₃水？他要喝₂茶
6 那₃幾個姑娘₄是要念書不是？是，他們₄是要念書
7 您₄要喝₁咖啡麼？我₄不喝咖啡，我要喝₂茶
8 他₄要作₁棹子麼？不₂是，他要作₃椅子
9 你₄要念₄這本書麼？是，我₄要念這本書
10 您₄要吃₂牛肉麼？不₂是，我要吃₁猪肉
11 您₄不吃羊肉，您₄要吃₂甚麼？我要吃₄麵包
12 您₄要吃₄飯麼？是，我要吃飯

第十課

I 今天　昨天　明天　了

1. 今天你們念書不念？
   今天我們念書。

2. 昨天你們念書了麼？
   昨天我們沒念書。

3. 明天你們要念書麼？
   明天我們不念書。

4. 您今天要作甚麼？
   我今天要作飯桌子。

5. 您今天寫字了麼？
   我今天寫字了。寫了多少個字？寫了二百多個字。

6. 那位學生明天作書桌子不作？
   他明天不作。

7. 昨天您作甚麼沒作？
   昨天我沒作甚麼。

II 的

1. 這張₄飯棹子是₂誰作的？這張飯棹是₁他作的
14. 您吃了₄一碗飯麼？是，我吃了₄一碗飯
13. 您喝了₄一碗茶麼？不是，我喝了₃兩碗
12. 那個人吃了幾碗飯？那個人吃了₄一玻璃盂咖啡
11. 他₃也沒喝茶，他喝了₄一碗飯
10. 他₃也沒喝茶麼？
9. 您的兒子吃飯了麼？他₂沒吃飯
8. 他喝了₃幾碗茶？他喝了₃兩碗茶
8. 他的姑娘喝₂茶不喝？他₄不喝，他₁喝了

華語入門　第十課

2 那個飯是您³母親⁴作的麼？⁴是他作的
3 那張書棹子是您的²兒子⁴作的麼？⁴是我兒子作的
4 這些本書是²誰作的？⁴是那位¹先生作的
5 那一玻璃盃²茶是²誰喝的？是我姑娘喝的
6 那些¹塊魚¹都是²誰吃的？都是¹他們吃的
7 那個字是²您³寫的麼？²不是我寫的，是¹先生寫的
8 那本書是²您念的麼？⁴是我念的

III 還

1 那位學生有書，²還有甚麼？他還有³本子
2 那位先生有兒子，²還有¹姑娘麼？他²還有姑娘

六十八

3 這位要念書，還要作甚麼？他還要寫字

4 您今天作飯，您明天還作飯麼？我明天還作飯

IV 哪

1 你們的先生作甚麼哪？他作書哪

2 您母親作甚麼哪？他作飯哪

3 那位學生念書哪麼？是，他念書哪

4 那個姑娘作甚麼哪？他寫字哪

V （還○哪）

1 您的父親喝咖啡了沒有？還沒喝哪

2 你們吃飯了麼？我們還沒吃哪

華語入門　第十課

3 他們₁都₂有茶了麼？他們₂還沒有哪

4 您兒子念書了沒有？他₂還沒念哪

5 您有了鋼筆了麼？

6 您還念書哪麼？是，我₂還念書

7 那位學生還寫字哪麼？他₂還寫字哪

VI 好不好

1 那張桌子作的好

2 這把椅子作的不好

3 那些個本子作的好不好？

4 那位學生寫的那幾個字，好不好？

5 那位學生寫的那幾個字，好不好？有好的，有不好的

⁴大字寫的³好，³小字寫的⁴不好

5 你們⁴四位²誰寫的³字好？

6 這本書⁴作的³好不好？

7 那個飯⁴作的³好不好？

8 那位學生⁴念的³書³好不好？

VII 還是 啊 呢

1 那位是₁先生啊，₂還是₂學生呢？他是學生，₂不是先生

2 那張棹子是₁書棹子啊，₂還是₄飯棹子呢？

3 那是₁書棹子

這些個字是₃你寫的啊，₂還是₁他寫的呢？

⁴我們₁都寫的好

那位學生₄念的₃書₃好不好？他念的₃好

VIII 還是 好吃

1. 是₂牛肉好吃是₂羊肉好吃？ ₂還是₂羊肉好吃
2. 這兩張桌子，是₄這張大是₄那張大？ ₂還是₄這張大
3. 是你₄父親的書₁多是你₃母親的書₁多？
   ₂還是我₄父親的₁多，₃母親的₃少

4. 你是₁今天念書啊，₂還是₂明天念書呢？
   我今天₂不念，₂明天念
5. 這把椅子是你們₃兩個人作的啊，₂還是你₂一個人作的呢？ 是我們₃兩個人作的
1. 都是₁他寫的

4 是¹您¹姑娘的鉛筆²長是您²兒子的鉛筆²長?

5 是²茶碗⁴大是⁴飯碗⁴大，²還是飯碗⁴大，²茶碗³小²還是我¹姑娘的鉛筆²長

6 好³呢?是²那位⁴大學生寫的字³好，²還是這位³小學生寫的字好³還是那位⁴大學生寫的好

第十一課

I 甚麼也 誰也 甚麼都 誰都

1. 那位學生有²甚麼東西？ 他²甚麼²也³沒有
2. 您的先生有²甚麼書？ 他²甚麼書³也³沒有
3. 那個人會寫²甚麼字？ 他²甚麼字³也³不會寫
4. 你¹吃²甚麼？ 我²甚麼²也³不吃
5. 他⁴會²作²甚麼？ 他²甚麼³也³不會作
6. 您有²甚麼³紙？ 我²甚麼³紙³也³沒有
7. 你們²誰²作²飯？ 我們²誰²也³不作飯
8. 他們²誰²喝茶？ 他們²誰³也⁴不喝茶

9. 誰²也³沒²有鉛筆？

10. 誰²也³沒²有書

11. 誰²有¹書？

12. 他²是²誰？　誰²也³不⁴知道¹他²是²誰

13. 你²會¹作²甚麼棹子？　我²甚麼棹子都¹會作

14. 你²們²有²甚麼書？　我²們²甚麼書¹都²有

15. 那²個⁴人⁴會作²甚麼？　他²甚麼¹都²會作

16. 甚²麼人¹都²有

17. 誰²要吃²飯？　誰²¹都²要吃²飯

　誰²要念²書？　誰²¹都²要念²書

II（問答）

- (一) 你們₄作₂甚麼？
- (二) 我們作₁桌子
- (一) 你們₄作₂甚麼桌子？
- (二) 我們作₁書桌子，作₄飯桌子，甚麼的
- (一) 你們₄會作₃椅子麼？
- (二) 我們也會作₃椅子
- (一) 你們₄作₁的桌子椅子₃好不好？
- (二) 我們作₁的桌子椅子₃好

III （問答）

(一) 您₄父₄親₄作₂甚麼哪?

(二) 他₄作₄書₁哪

(一) 您的₃母親₄作₂甚麼哪?

(二) 他₄作₄飯哪

(一) 您的₂兒子₂還₄念書哪麼?

(二) 他₂不念書

(一) 您的₁姑娘₄會寫字₂不會?

(二) 他₂還₃小哪，還₂不會₃寫哪

IV 〔問答〕

(一) 您¹今天⁴念書了沒有？
    我¹今天⁴念書了

(二) 也³寫⁴字了麼？
    沒²寫字

(一) 您¹今天²還要寫字麼？
    我¹今天⁴不寫字了，我²明天寫字

(二) 那些¹個字⁴是您³寫的麼？
    不²是我寫的

(一) 是²誰寫的，您¹知道麼？

(二) 我₁知道，是₁先生寫的

(一) 那本書₄是您₄念的不是？

(二) ₄是我念的

V（問答）

(一) 先生！您要₁喝₂茶麼？

(二) 我₄不喝茶，我₁喝咖啡了

(一) 您要₁吃₄飯麼？

(二) 我₄要吃飯

(一) 您要₁吃₂甚麼？

(二) 您₃有甚麼，我₁吃甚麼

第十一課

(一) 我²有²魚,²牛肉,²羊肉,¹豬肉,您¹吃²甚麼?

(二) 我²要吃²魚

VI 來 去

1. 來了¹三個學生
2. 去了²八個學生
3. 您今天²來不²來?
4. 學生¹都²來了麼?
5. 先生²來了²沒有?
6. 昨天²來的⁴那個人是²誰?
7. 您⁴作²甚麼去?

我今²天²來

學生¹都²來了

先生²還²沒來哪

那²是我³⁴父親

我¹吃⁴飯去

8 他₂昨天作甚麼₄去了？　他₄念書去了
9 那位學生₄去了麼？　他₂還₂沒去哪
10 你們₂十位₃幾個人去，₃幾個人₂不去？
11 來了₃幾位了？　來了₂七位了
12 誰₂還₂沒來哪？　都來了
　₄六個人去，₄四個人₂不去
13 ₁張先生₂來了沒有？　₁張先生₂還₂沒來哪
14 ₁書先生₂來了沒有？　₁書先生₂來了

VII 您好啊 謝謝 請坐 再見

1 張先生，您₃好啊？　好好．₂您哪？　謝謝₃也好

華語入門 第十一課

VIII 請

1. 您³明天³請¹張先生¹吃⁴飯麼？是⁴，我⁴明天³請¹他吃飯
2. 您⁴要請¹包先生¹作⁴甚麼？我⁴要請¹他³寫⁴字
3. 你³請了³幾個人？我³請了²八個人
4. 是²您⁴要請¹他，是¹他⁴要請²您？
5. 是¹他⁴要³請³我，不²是³我⁴要請¹他

2. 張先生，請您¹喝²茶？⁴謝謝，我¹喝一碗了．
   請您¹吃⁴肉．⁴謝謝，我¹不吃，我¹吃了

3. 包先生，您²來了，³請坐，⁴謝謝，²您請坐

4. 包先生您⁴要⁴去麼？⁴是，⁴再⁴見，⁴再⁴見

第十二課

I 問

1. 他₄問₂誰哪? 他問₁張先生哪
2. 先生₄問₄學生₂不問?
3. 您₄問他₂甚麼了? 我問他₃有₁書沒有
4. 你要問₂誰? 我要問₁先生

II 回答

1. 先生問學生，生學回答₂麼? 學生₂回答
2. 先生問₂您，您₂回答₄不回答? 我₂回答
3. 您問₁他，他₂回答了麼? 他₂沒回答

III 說話 跟 句

1. 一個人₄問，一個人₂回答；那是兩個人₁說話
2. 您說₂甚麼哪？ 我說₁他來了
3. 他要跟₂誰說話？ 他要跟₂您的姑娘說話
4. 這句話是他說的麼？ ²不是他說的
5. 您要跟₂誰念書？ 我要跟₁張先生念書
6. 他是跟₂誰來的？ 他是跟₁他母親來的
7. 您的₂兒子是跟₂誰₄去的？ 是跟₁他₄父親去的
8. 你說了₃幾句話？ 我₂一句話₃也沒說
9. 你₃有₄話₁說麼？ 我₂沒有話說

IV 明白 跟

1. 我說的話你₂明₂白麼？　我₂明白
2. 書先生說的話你₂明白₄不明白？
3. 他說的話我₄不明白
4. 學生有₄不明白的，要問₂誰？　要問₁先生
5. 那枝鋼筆跟這枝鋼筆，₁都是₂您的麼？　不₂都是我的，那一枝₂長的是我的，那枝₃短的₂不是我的
6. 這位學生跟那位學生，₁都會寫字麼？　₁都會
7. 您有₂甚麼東西？　我有₁書跟₃本子

10. 這句話₄是誰說的？　是₃我說的

V 對 不對

1 那個字寫的對麼？ 那個字寫的對
2 他回答的對不對？ 他回答的對
3 您要請先生麼？ 對了，我要請先生
4 他說的那句話對不對？ 他說的那句話不對

VI （我說）（您說）（你說）（他說）

1 您說是這個大是那個大？ 我說是這個大
2 他說是今天作好啊，是明天作好呢？ 他說明天作沒有今天作好
3 那位學生說，鉛筆是長的好啊，是短的好呢？

VII 再回

1. 先生，請您₄再寫一個字好，我₄再₃寫一個那個字您₃寫了沒有？我寫了兩回了
2. 您請他₄再來一回麼？我請他₄再來一回
3. 這句話先生說了幾回了？他說了₁三四回了
4. 您說的話我₄不明白，請您₄再說一回。好好，
5. 先生，請您₄再寫一個

4. 您說₁他們兩個人₂誰作的好？先生說是₄這個學生念的書₃好啊，是₄那個學生念的書₃好呢？先生說他們₁都念的不好
5. 他說是₂長的好

VIII〈請問您哪〉好些個 一點兒

1 請問₂您哪，這碗茶是₂誰₁喝的？

2 請問₂您哪，那個人是₂誰？ 那個人是₁張先生

3 那₃好₁些個人₄作₂甚麼哪？ 他們₁說₁話₄哪

4 學生₁都₂來了麼？ 還有好₃些個人₂沒來哪

5 您₁喝咖啡₄不喝？ 我₁喝一點兒

6 我₄再寫一回 那個字我₂還不會寫哪，請您₄再寫一回．好好
我₄再說一回

6 請您₄再₁喝一點兒．謝謝，我₄不喝了．

7 他說的話您₁都₂明白了麼？我₄一₃點兒₃也不明白．

第十三課

I 姓 名子 叫

1 您⁴姓²甚麼？ 我姓¹書¹
2 您⁴叫²甚麼²名子？ 我名子叫⁴道²明
3 張先生的²名子叫²甚麼？ 張先生的名子叫¹知¹生
4 人²有²名子，東西³也²有²名子麼？
5 請問²您哪，那個東西⁴叫²甚麼²名子？
  那個東西⁴叫²毛筆
6 這個碗名子叫²茶碗，那個碗名子叫²甚麼？
  那個碗名子叫⁴飯³碗

II 完 就 叫

1. 這⁴本³書⁴您¹念⁴完²了麼? ⁴念⁴完了
2. 您¹喝完了²茶了麼? 還²沒喝完哪
3. 那⁴幾個⁴大字寫完了,⁴那⁴幾十個³小字兒還²沒寫哪
4. 您吃完飯⁴就¹喝咖啡麼? 是,我吃完飯⁴就喝咖啡
5. 先生問您,您⁴就²回答麼? 是,他問我,我⁴就⁴回答
6. 他叫您⁴作²甚麼? 他叫我念¹書
7. 先生⁴叫學生⁴作²甚麼? 先生叫學生³寫⁴字
8. 我³母親⁴叫我作甚麼,我⁴就作甚麼

III 錢〇塊錢〇毛錢〇分錢

1. 請問²您哪，這是²甚麼東西？那是²錢
2. 您³有²錢麼？我³有²錢
3. 您³有¹多少²錢？我³有²一塊錢
4. 一塊錢是³幾²毛錢？一塊錢是²十毛錢
5. 一毛錢是³幾²分錢？一毛錢是²十分錢
6. 這是¹多少²錢？這是²一塊⁴四毛錢
7. 那是³幾毛錢？那是³五毛³五分錢
9. 他⁴叫我來我⁴就來，他⁴叫我去，我⁴就去
10. 我跟他說完了話，⁴就去

IV 要

1. 您₄要₂甚麼？ 我要₃紙
2. 他₄作₂甚麼來了？ 他要₂錢來了
3. 他要₃本子作₂甚麼？ 他要₃寫字
4. 那₃兩張棹子，您₄是要₄大的是要₃小的？
5. 我₃有棹子，我₁都不要
6. 這張₄飯棹子，他要₁多少錢？ 他要₃五塊₃五毛錢

8. 這兩塊₃五是₂誰的？ 這兩塊₃五是₁他的
9. 這₄四毛₃五是₂您的麼？ 不是我的，是₄那個人的
10. 他有₃幾塊錢？ 他有₃五塊錢

6 他⁴作²甚麼⁴去⁴了？　他⁴要²錢去了

V 給

1 您³給他₁多少錢？　我給他⁴四塊⁴二毛錢
2 先生³給您₁書了麼？　先生還²沒給我書哪
3 您⁴父親³給了您幾枝₁鋼筆？　他給了我⁴一枝
4 這本書是誰給您的？　那本書是²錢先生給我的
5 您⁴要給他³甚麼東西？　他⁴要甚麼，我³給他甚麼
6 他母親³給了他³幾毛錢？　給了他³兩毛錢

VI 給

1 那個⁴字是²誰³給你³寫的？　那個⁴字是²錢先生給我寫的

2 您給²誰⁴作⁴飯？　我給我³母親作飯

3 誰²給學生作⁴書？　先生給學生作書

4 那把椅子是給²誰⁴作¹的？　那把椅子是給¹張先生作的

5 您給²誰⁴念書哪？　我給我的¹姑娘念書哪

VII 買賣

1 我³給他²錢，他給我東西；我是³買東西

2 我³給他東西，他給我²錢；我是⁴賣東西

3 他⁴作²甚麼⁴去了？　他³買²東西去了，他買甚麼⁴去了？

4 他們買茶葉，³也買咖啡麼？　是，他們³也買咖啡

5. 您買了幾斤羊肉，幾斤豬肉？
6. 我買了一斤羊肉，二斤豬肉
7. 你們賣甚麼肉？我們賣牛，羊，豬肉
8. 他們賣甚麼東西？他們賣麵包
9. 這個麵包多少錢？這個麵包一毛錢一斤
10. 這條魚是多少錢買的？是一塊多錢買的
11. 那個茶碗是給誰買的？是給我姑娘買的
12. 那張飯桌子賣多少錢？賣十塊零五毛錢
13. 那隻小羊兒你賣給誰了？賣給 張先生了

第十四課

I 貴 賤 很 不大好

1. 買東西₂錢₁多是₄貴，₂錢₃少是₄賤
2. 這位寫的字₂不大好，那位寫的₂很好
3. 那張桌子₄貴，這把椅子₄賤
4. 這頭牛₄是₃五十塊錢₃買的，您說₄貴不貴？
5. 我說₃很貴
6. 那枝毛筆₄一毛錢，₄賤不賤？
7. 這個₄大本子₄貴賤？這個大本子₃很貴
8. 那個人₄賣的東西₃很賤

8 ⁴貴的₂不貴，⁴賤的₂不賤

II 貴姓 賤姓

1 您⁴要問他⁴姓₂甚麼，您就說⁴貴姓
2 他⁴問您⁴貴姓，您要₂回答⁴賤姓
3 您⁴貴姓？ ——賤姓₂錢
4 那位⁴貴姓？ ——他姓₂張

III 講 功課

1 您₁今天₃有₁功課麼？ ——今天我₂沒有功課，₂明天有功課
2 昨天您₃有₁功課麼？ ——昨天我₃有功課
3 今天₂誰給你們₃講的功課？ ——₂白先生今天給我們₃講

IV 意思

1. 請問₂您哪，不貴是₂甚麼意思？
2. 這個字有₃幾個意思？
3. 您₂明白我的₄意思麼？
4. 他們兩個人有₃兩個意思．這個人的意思是要₄念書

4. 昨天₁包先生講的功課，您₁都明白了麼？
   我₁都明白了
5. 這本書先生給您講₃完了麼？還₂沒講完哪
6. 今天的功課我₄不很明白，請您₄再給我講一回

,₄那個人的意思是要₃寫字

V 告訴

1 請您₄告訴我，今天先生₂來不來？今天先生₄不來
2 您₄問他₄作₂甚麼去，他₄告訴您了麼？他₂沒告訴我
3 他有₂甚麼意思，沒₄告訴您麼？
4 我跟您說的話，請您₂不要告訴他。是，我₂不告訴他
5 這句話是₂"誰₄告訴您的？"是₄那位₁姑娘告訴我的

VI 太

1 這口豬₄賣十五塊錢，您說貴不貴？十五塊錢₄太貴了

2 這枝鉛筆⁴太²長，還有³短一點兒的麼？
3 他說的話⁴太¹多了，叫他³少說幾句
4 他寫的那個字⁴太³小了，叫他寫⁴大一點兒

VII 丈夫 太太

1 這位是²誰？ 是我⁴丈夫
2 您是他⁴太太麼？ 對了，我⁴是他太太
3 他是¹姑娘是⁴太太？
4 那位太太⁴姓²甚麼？ 那位太太姓²錢
5 張太太²昨天⁴作²甚麼去了？
6 您丈夫³買²甚麼東西去了？ 他³買¹東西去了

他給³我們的姑娘¹,兒子們,買¹書去了

VIII 〔問答〕

(一) 先生跟²誰說話哪?

(二) 先生跟²學生話說哪

(一) 先生跟¹他們說²甚麼哪?

(二) 先生問學生哪

(一) 先生問學生,學生²回答了沒有?

(二) 學生²回答了

(一) 回答的⁴對不對?

(二) 回答的³很對

IX〔問答〕

(一) 那位先生⁴貴姓?
(二) 姓²白
(一) 他叫²甚麼²名子?
(二) 我⁴不知道他叫甚麼名子
(一) 白先生³也給³你們講功課?
(二) 對了,³也給我們講功課
(一) 他講的功課³好不好?
(二) 他講的功課⁴太好了,我們²沒有⁴一點兒不明白的

(一) 您³好啊? ³請坐,³請坐

華語入門　第十四課

(二) ³請坐，³請坐
(一) 請您¹喝茶
(二) ⁴謝謝
(一) 您²昨天⁴作甚麼去了？
(二) 我昨天³買¹東西去了
(一) 您買²甚麼去了？
(二) 我買¹書去了？
(一) 您的書是¹多少錢³買的？
(二) 三¹塊四²毛錢買的？
(一) 他們賣¹書，²還賣²甚麼東西？

(二) 他們還賣³本子，鋼筆¹，鉛筆¹，甚麼的
(一) 他們的東西⁴賣的⁴貴⁴賤？
(二) 他們的東西²不貴
(一) 請問²您哪，這本書您是給²誰買的？
(二) 是給我⁴太太買的
(一) 給²誰買的？請您再說一回
(二) 是給我⁴太太買的
(一) 您的太太⁴念書哪麼？
(二) 對了，⁴念書哪

華語入門 第十四課

X （問答）

(一) 貴⁴姓？

(二) 賤姓¹包．您²貴⁴姓？

(一) 賤姓²白．包先生，您⁴作²甚麼來了？

(二) 我要請您給我們³講功課

(一) 你們³幾個人⁴念書？

(二) 我們¹三個人念書

(一) 那兩個人是²誰？

(二) 那兩個人，²一位是¹張太太，²一位是¹張太太的⁴丈夫

(一) 他們²來了麼？

(二) ²沒來，他們²明天來

(一) 好，³請他們明天來

(二) ⁴再見，⁴再見

(一) ⁴再見，⁴再見

第十五課

I 屋子　間

1 這是²甚麼？　這是¹屋子
2 那是³幾間屋子？　那是⁴一間屋子
3 那間屋子⁴大小？　那間屋子⁴不很大
4 這間屋子²是您的麼？⁴是我的

II 裡　在　(在〇裡)

1 那間屋子裡有²甚麼東西？　那間屋子裡有¹桌子，有³椅子
2 您的⁴丈夫在⁴那間屋子裡⁴作²甚麼哪？

他在那間屋子裡跟₂錢先生說話哪.

3 請問₂您哪,₁包太太買的茶葉₄在₄那間屋子裡哪麼?

4 先生寫的₄那個字,在₄這本書裡₃有沒有?

5 在這本書裡₂沒有

6 在₄這個茶碗裡₃有茶麼?

7 在₄那個飯碗裡₃有飯麼?

8 這個玻璃盃裡₃有₁咖啡麼?

那個玻璃盃裡₂沒有咖啡,有₃水

在飯碗裡有₄飯,是₄一碗飯. 在飯碗裡₂沒有飯,是

在這個茶碗裡₃有茶

在那個飯碗裡₂沒有飯

III 窗戶　門

1 你們吃飯的那間屋子有幾個窗戶？有兩個窗戶
2 那四個窗戶大小？那四個窗戶都不小
3 您念書的那間屋子有幾個窗戶，幾個門？

9 在茶碗裡有茶，是一碗茶。在茶碗裡沒有茶，是一個茶碗
10 在這間屋子裡有多少人？有三十多個人
11 在那間屋子裡沒有人麼？是，在那間屋子裡沒有人

2 一個飯碗
2 一個茶碗

IV 房子　所

1 那²是²您的²房子麽？對了，那⁴是我的房子
2 您有³幾所房子？我有⁴一所房子
3 那所房子有¹多少間¹屋子？有十間屋子
4 那所房子³好不好？那所房子²不⁴大好

4 這兩間屋子₁都有³兩個窗戶麽？²不是，⁴一間有
　兩個窗戶，⁴一間有²一個窗戶
5 這個門作的³好不好？這個門作的⁴不好
6 是⁴這個門⁴大是那個門⁴大？⁴那個門⁴大

有³五個窗戶，³兩個門

V 住

1. 您住³幾²間屋子？ 我住⁴六間屋子
2. 誰²在⁴這所房子裡⁴住？ 錢太太在⁴這所房子裡住
3. 這是²您住的²房子麼？ 是，這⁴是我住的房子
4. 那間屋子是²誰住？ 那間屋子是³我跟我⁴丈夫住
5. 他住的⁴那間屋子有³幾個門，幾個窗戶？ 他住的那間屋子有²一個門，兩個窗戶
6. 這所房子是²誰的？ 是¹包太太的

VI 家

1. 您家裡有³幾口兒人？ 我家裡有³五口兒人

2 您家裡₁都₂有甚麼人？ 我有₁父親，₂母親，₃太太，還有一個₂兒子，一個₁姑娘

VII 學堂（個） 地方（塊）

5 您的丈夫₄在家裡哪麼？ 他₄在家裡哪
4 您的先生₄在家哪麼？ 他₂沒在家
3 您太太在家裡₄作₂甚麼？ 他在家裡給₃我們作₄飯
1 這所房子₄是你們₂學堂不是？
2 這個地方₃有學堂沒有？ ₃有學堂
3 學堂是₄作₂甚麼的地方？ 學堂是₄念書的地方

第十五課

4 他們ˊ學堂裡ˇ有ˇ多ˉ少ˇ位ˋ先生？有ˇ十ˊ幾ˇ位ˋ先生

5 您ˊ的ˉ姑娘在ˋ學堂裡ˇ念ˋ書哪ˇ麼？

6 您ˊ的ˉ兒ˊ子在ˋ家ˉ裡ˇ念ˋ書麼？不ˊ是，他ˉ還ˊ小ˇ哪，在ˋ家ˉ裡ˇ念ˋ書

7 是ˋ這ˋ個ˉ學堂ˊ學生ˉ多ˉ，是ˋ那ˋ個ˉ學堂ˊ學生ˉ多ˉ？不ˊ是，他ˉ在ˋ學堂念ˋ書

8 這ˋ一ˊ塊ˋ地ˋ方ˉ是ˇ我ˇ的，那ˋ一ˊ塊ˋ地ˋ方ˉ是ˋ他ˉ的
是ˋ那ˋ個ˉ學堂ˊ學生ˉ多ˉ，這ˋ個ˉ學堂ˊ學生ˉ少ˇ

VIII 舖子

1 賣ˋ東西ˉ的ˉ地ˋ方ˉ叫ˋ甚ˊ麼ˉ名ˊ子？賣ˋ東西ˉ的ˉ地ˋ方ˉ叫ˋ舖子

2 在ˋ這ˋ個ˉ舖子裡ˇ，賣ˋ甚ˊ麼ˉ東西？

3. 在²這個舖子裡賣²茶葉，咖啡，甚麼的
4. 賣¹書的舖子是²甚麼舖子？賣書的舖子是²書舖
5. ²甚麼舖子賣¹棹子，賣³椅子？
   棹椅舖賣¹棹子，賣³椅子
6. 賣²牛，²羊，¹猪肉的，這個舖子叫²甚麼²名子？
   那叫⁴肉舖
7. 在肉舖裡³也賣²魚麼？ ³也賣魚
8. 這個麪包房是²您的麼？ ⁴是我的
9. 這個地方有²甚麼舖子？
   這個地方²甚麼舖子¹都有
10. 書舖裡³也賣³紙，¹鋼筆，¹鉛筆，²毛筆麼？ ³也賣

10 您的太太在₄那個舖子裡₃買₂甚麼？

他在那個舖子裡₃買₁玻璃盃

第十六課

I 紅 黃 綠 白 黑 藍　顏色

1. 那²所²紅房子是²學堂麼？"對了，"是²學堂
2. 這兩個⁴綠窗戶⁴大小？　這兩個綠窗戶⁴大⁴的³很
3. 那³張棹子是²黃的不是？　"是²黃的
4. 您買了³幾斤¹黑麨包？　我買了⁴二斤黑麨包
5. 白麨包⁴貴賤？　白麨包⁴貴一點兒
6. 這³幾張紙⁴是⁴綠的不是？　這幾張紙²不是綠的，是²藍的
7. 這³枝鉛筆是²甚麼²顏色的？　這枝鉛筆是¹黑顏色的

8 茶碗₃有₂紅顏色的沒有？　茶碗₂甚麼顏色₁都有

II 地板　頂棚

1 那間屋子的₄地板是₂甚麼顏色的？　是₂黄顏色的
2 地板是₂甚麼顏色的₁多？　地板是₂黄顏色的多
3 這幾間屋子的頂棚是₂甚麼顏色的？
4 這間屋子的頂棚是₂白的麼？
   這間屋子的頂棚₄是₂白的
   這屋子的頂棚₂不是₂白的是₂藍的

III 牆（面）

1 那間屋子的₂牆是₂甚麼顏色的？　是₄綠顏色的

2. 這間²屋子有³幾⁴面牆？ 這間屋子有⁴四面牆
3. 這面牆¹跟⁴那面牆⁴是²一個²顏色麼？ ⁴是一個顏色
4. 這面牆有²門，那面牆有¹窗戶
5. 這面牆有³幾個門，³幾個窗戶？ 這面牆有²一個門，²一個窗戶

IV 墨水兒 粉筆 黑板

1. 您要買鋼筆，²還要買²甚麼？ 還要買墨水兒
2. 您要²甚麼²顏色的⁴墨水兒？ 我要買²藍顏色的
3. 這個墨水兒是²甚麼²顏色的？ 這個墨水兒是²紅的
4. 這兩枝²粉筆是²誰的？ 那兩枝粉筆是¹先生的

華語入門　第十六課

V　畫兒　畫

5 粉筆有₂白的，也有₂紅的麼？粉筆₃也有紅的
6 這是₂甚麼東西？這是₁黑板
7 這塊黑板₄大小？這塊黑板₂不大
8 在你們那間屋子裡有₃幾塊黑板？有₃兩塊黑板
9 這間屋子裡₃有黑板沒有？這間屋子裡₂沒有
1 那張畫兒是₂誰的？這張畫兒是₂黃先生的
2 這本書裡₃有畫兒沒有？這本書裡₃有畫兒
3 您₄會畫畫兒麼？我₄會畫畫兒
4 您₄會畫甚麼？我甚麼₁都會畫

VI 筆 拿 拿筆

1. 這是甚麼筆？ 這是毛筆
2. 那是甚麼筆？ 那是鉛筆
3. 這枝筆是您的不是？ 這枝筆是我的
4. 您要拿甚麼？ 我要拿鋼筆
5. 您要拿筆麼？ 是，我要拿粉筆
6. 你的兒子要拿甚麼？ 我的兒子要拿茶碗

5. 那兩張畫兒畫的好不好？
6. 那兩張畫兒畫的太好了
   這張畫兒是您畫的麼？是我畫的

7 您₁的₁姑娘₄要拿₂紅鉛筆₄是要拿₄綠鉛筆？

8 我的姑娘要拿₄綠鉛筆

9 我₄要拿₂甚麼東西？ 你要拿₄飯碗

10 您拿₁鉛筆₄作₂甚麼？ 我₄要寫幾₃個字

11 先生拿₂甚麼₃筆寫₃字？ 先生拿₂粉筆寫字

12 先生拿₂粉筆寫字，學生拿₂甚麼₃筆寫₃字？ 學生拿₂鋼筆寫字

13 這幾個字是拿₂甚麼₃筆寫的？ 這幾個字是拿₂毛筆寫的

您₄會拿₂毛筆寫字麼？ 我₄會拿₂毛筆寫字

14 您說是拿₁鋼筆寫的字₃好啊，₂還是拿₁鉛筆寫的字₃好呢？我說₂還是拿₁鋼筆寫的字好

第十七課

I 上 在○上 掛

1. 在⁴這張畫兒上⁴畫的是²甚麼？
2. 在⁴這張畫兒上畫的是²學堂
3. 先生在¹黑板上³寫了³幾個字？
4. 先生在黑板上寫了³兩個字
5. 那張棹子上³有²甚麼東西？
6. 那張棹子上有¹鋼筆，²還有⁴墨水兒
7. 「黃²」字在我們的書上³有沒有？「黃」字在我們的書上³有
8. 在⁴那張畫兒上，⁴畫的那³兩個人，是¹先生是²學生？

²一位是¹先生，²一位是²學生

⁶在⁴這面牆上⁴掛的是³幾張畫兒？

⁷那面牆上⁴掛的是³兩張畫兒

³那面牆上⁴掛的⁴那張畫兒是²誰畫的？

是²|白先生畫的

II 把

1 請您把⁴那張畫兒³給我

2 請³把⁴那枝粉筆給¹他，我³給他了，⁴謝謝

3 誰³把⁴那張畫兒給¹包先生了？

³我把⁴那張畫兒給他了

華語入門　第十七課

4 他²把¹這¹碗咖啡¹都喝了
5 誰²把⁴那¹條魚¹都吃了？
　您的²兒子把那條魚¹都吃了

III 拿來、拿去

1 請您把²那⁴幾個¹玻璃盃²拿去
2 請您把²那⁴幾塊²白麵包給我拿來
3 那張書棹子²拿來沒有？
　　²拿來了
4 誰²把⁴那³張飯棹子²拿去了？
　　²錢先生的兒子²拿去了
5 那把⁴椅子⁴是給²誰²拿來的？
　　是給²您拿來的
6 這¹些個²毛錢兒是誰²拿去的？
　　是²黃先生拿去的
7 您³把⁴那¹三斤茶葉給我拿來，³把那³五斤咖啡給他拿去

IV （拿○ 來去）

1. 他²拿²甚麼來了？ 他拿²粉筆來了
2. 請你³給²我拿一碗茶來
3. 請你³給他拿墨水兒去
4. 他要拿²甚麼來？ 他要拿¹玻璃盃來
5. 您⁴作²甚麼來了？ 我拿¹書來了
6. 黃先生⁴要²拿²甚麼去？ 他要拿¹黑板去
8. 請³你把⁴那一碗茶給我拿來
9. 請³你把⁴那碗咖啡給他²拿去
10. 那張畫兒給誰²拿去的？ 給²您的⁴太太拿去的

V 大學堂 中學堂 小學堂

1 請問²您哪,這個地方³有⁴大學堂沒有?

2 那兩位學生是⁴大學堂的²學生麼?

3 他們⁴是大學堂的學生

4 這個地方³有大學堂

5 那位姑娘在²甚麼學堂⁴念書? 他在₁中學堂念書

6 那個₁中學堂有₁多少學生? 有⁴二百多位學生

7 您⁴要拿⁴墨水兒去了麼? ⁴是,我²拿⁴墨水兒去了

8 您⁴要拿⁴飯碗去麼? ²不是,我²要拿²茶碗來

9 錢先生拿了³幾枝筆來? 他拿了³兩三枝來

5 您₂兒子在₂甚麼學堂₄念書哪？他在₃小學堂念書哪

6 藍先生是中學堂的₁先生麼？不是，他是₄大學堂的先生

VI 吃墨紙

1 這兩張₁吃墨紙你是給₂誰買的？是給我姑娘，₂兒子，₂一個人₄一張

2 那吃墨紙₁都有₂甚麼₂顏色的？紅，黃，藍，綠，白，₁都有

3 拿₂毛筆寫字₄要吃墨紙不要？拿毛筆寫字₂不要吃墨紙

4 拿₁鋼筆寫字₂沒有吃墨紙₃好不好？

沒有吃墨紙₄不好

5 那吃墨紙₄大張的₁多少錢，₃小張的₁多少錢？

大張的₃兩毛₃五，小張的₄一毛₄二

第十八課

I （問答）

(一) 那所房子是₂誰的？

(二) 那所房子是₂白先生的

(一) 您知道是₁多少錢₃買的？

(二) 是₁七千多塊錢買的

(一) 那所房子有₃幾間屋子？

(二) 有₁八九間屋子

(一) 那幾間屋子的₄地板是₂甚麼₂顏色的？

(二) 是₂黃顏色的

II （問答）

(一) ²您²那³所房子₄是²您一家兒₄住麼？

(二) ²不²是我一家兒住，是我們³兩家兒住

(一) ²您住³幾間？

(二) 我住₄四間

(一) ⁴那²幾間²誰住？

(一) ³頂棚³也是²黃的麼，

(二) ²不²是²黃的，是²白的

(一) ²那²牆是²甚麼²顏色的？

(二) 有²紅的，有₄綠的，³也有²藍的

(二) 那幾間₂藍家住

III 〈問答〉

(一) 這₄是₂學堂不是？
(二) 這₄是學堂
(一) 這₄是中學堂麼？
(二) 這₂不是中學堂，這是₃小學堂
(一) 在這個學堂裡有₁多少位₂學生？
(二) 有₁三百多位學生
(一) 有₁多少位₁先生？
(二) 有₄二十多位先生

第十八課

IV （問答）

(一) 那個舖子是甚麼舖子？

(二) 那是桌椅舖

(一) 桌椅舖賣甚麼東西？

(二) 桌椅舖賣桌子，椅子，甚麼的

(一) 他們都賣甚麼桌子？

(二) 他們賣書桌子，也賣飯桌子

(一) 椅子他們也賣麼？

(二) 是，那是大學堂

(一) 那是大學堂麼？

(二) 椅子他們₃也賣

V 〈問答〉

(一) 這張畫兒是₂誰₄畫的？

(二) 這張畫兒是₃我₄畫的

(一) 您₄丈₃夫也₄會₄畫畫兒麼？

(二) 他₂不會畫畫兒

(一) 在牆上₄掛的那張畫兒，₃也是您₂畫₄的麼？

(二) 對了，₃也是我₄畫的

(一) 那張畫兒是拿₂甚麼₃筆₄畫的？

(二) 是拿₂毛筆畫的

華語入門　第十八課

(一) 您拿毛筆畫畫兒拿₂甚麼筆寫字？

(二) 拿₁鋼筆跟₁鉛筆寫字

VI 〔問答〕

(一) 請您₃把₄那枝₁鋼筆給我拿來

(二) 您要鋼筆₄作₂甚麼？

(一) 我要₃寫字

(二) 您拿鋼筆寫字，您₃有₄墨水兒麼？

(一) 我₃有墨水兒

(二) 您有甚麼₂顏色的墨水兒？

(一) 我有₂藍顏色的墨水兒

一百三十六

(二) 請您把那張₂白顏色的₁吃墨紙₃也給我拿來

VII （問答）

(一) 你在₂甚麼學堂₄念書哪？

(二) 我在₄大學堂念書哪

(一) 你們的₁先生給你們講功課，₃也給你們₃寫字麼？

(二) ₃也給我們寫字

(一) 你們的₁先生拿₂甚麼₃筆給你們寫字？

(二) 拿₂粉筆給我們寫字

(一) 拿₂粉筆在₂甚麼₄上寫字？

(二) 在₁黑板上寫字

VIII ³那

1. ³那枝₁鉛筆是³你的？ ⁴那枝₂長的是我的
2. ³那枝₁鋼筆是₁他的？ ⁴這枝₂短的是他的
3. ³那張₁桌子是⁴飯桌子？ ⁴那張₄大的是飯桌子
4. 這兩個本子，³那個本子是³好的？
5. 請問²您哪，³那把₃椅子是²您買的？
6. ³那兩把₃小的是我買的
7. ³那幾間屋子，³那間屋子的₁窗戶是⁴綠的？
8. ³那間₃小的是綠的

IX 這ᴿ那ᴿ在這ᴿ在那ᴿ

1 您⁴在⁴這ᴿ作²甚麼哪？我在這兒畫畫兒哪

2 他的書⁴在這裡哪麼？他的書²沒在這兒

3 誰²在那兒³講功課？|錢²先生在那兒講功課

4 那位¹姑娘在¹包先生那兒⁴念書麼？他⁴在那裡念書

7 那幾個舖子，³那個舖子⁴賣的東西⁴賤？

8 那幾個舖子的東西⁴都不賤

³那¹句話的意思您⁴不白明？

⁴這一句話的意思我不明白，請您⁴再給我³講一回

X 講堂　課堂

1. 這間屋子₄是₃講堂不是？是₄，這間屋子₄是講堂
2. 這個講堂裡有₃幾個₂門，幾個₁窗戶？
3. 這個講堂裡有₁三個窗戶，一個門
4. 講堂是作₂甚麼的地方？講堂是₃講₁功課的地方
5. 這個墨水兒是在₃那兒₃買的？是在₄那個舖子裡買的
6. 請問₂您哪，那位學生在₃那兒₄念書哪？我₂還₄不知道他在那裡念書哪
7. 是₄大學堂的課堂₄大，是₃小學堂的課堂₄大？

大學堂的課堂⁴大，小學堂的課堂³小

5 這個課堂裡的地板是²甚麼²顏色的？
6 這個課堂裡的地板是²黃顏色的
7 這個課堂裡的牆都是²甚麼²顏色的？
8 這個課堂裡的牆都是²藍顏色的
9 這個講堂裡的頂棚是²甚麼²顏色的？
10 這個講堂裡的頂棚是²白顏色的
11 講堂上¹都有¹黑板麼？⁴是，講堂上¹都有黑板
12 這個課堂裡⁴掛的那張⁴畫兒是²誰畫的？是²黃先生畫的

10 在那個課堂裡有₁多少₁張₁書桌子?

那個課堂裡有₄二十多張書桌子

第十九課

I 一塊兒

1 他跟²誰²一⁴塊兒念書？　他跟⁴那位學生一塊兒念書

2 您跟²誰²一⁴塊兒來的？　我跟²｜黃先生一塊兒來的

3 他跟他的姑娘一塊兒去的

　您的⁴太太跟²誰²一⁴塊兒去的？

4 您跟²誰²一⁴塊兒³買東西去了？

　我跟｜書先生一塊兒買東西去了

II 父母

1 您的父母₄在家哪麼₁？

我⁴父親在家哪，我³母親沒在家

2 您跟您的父母⁴在²一⁴塊兒住麼？
"是⁴，我跟我父母⁴在一塊兒住

III 孩子

1 那位先生有³幾個²孩子？ 那位先生有³兩個孩子

2 那個孩子⁴要買甚麼¹東西？ 那個孩子要買³紙

3 那兩個孩子³那個孩子⁴是²您的？ 那個⁴大的是我的

4 他家裡有³幾個²孩子？ 他家裡有⁴四個孩子

IV 街（條）

1 這條街²長³短？ 這條街⁴不短

2 在⁴您⁴住的⁴那條街上，有³幾個學堂？有³兩個學堂

3 包¹先生⁴在²甚麼地方⁴住？⁴在買賣街

4 這²條街⁴叫²甚麼²名子？這條街名子叫²學堂街

V 衣裳（件）穿

1 這²是²誰的²衣裳？這²是²我跟我⁴丈夫的²衣裳

2 那是³幾件²衣裳？那是³兩件²衣裳

3 那件²紅衣裳是²誰的？那是⁴那位⁴太太的

4 您穿的²衣裳是²甚麼²顏色的？我穿的²衣裳是²藍的

5 你說是²穿²長衣裳³好，是²穿³短衣裳³好？我說還是²穿³短的好

6 昨天²黃¹先生穿⁴的是²黑衣裳

VI 帽子（頂）戴

1 這⁴頂⁴帽子是²誰的？　這⁴頂帽子是¹張先生的
2 您⁴戴⁴的那⁴頂⁴帽子是¹多少錢買⁴的？　這⁴頂帽子是¹三塊³五買的
3 您¹今⁴天⁴戴帽子來了麼？　我今²天²沒⁴戴帽子來
4 戴²白帽子的那⁴位姑娘⁴姓²甚麼？　他姓²藍

VII 鞋雙

1 兩隻鞋⁴是⁴一雙鞋麼？　⁴是，兩隻鞋⁴是一雙鞋

2 這₄雙鞋是₂您的麼？ 這雙鞋₂不是我的

3 您₁穿的這雙鞋是₂甚麼顏色的？

4 我穿的這雙鞋是₂黃顏色的

5 這雙鞋₂是₂幾塊錢買的？

6 這雙鞋十塊錢您說₄貴賤？

7 這雙鞋₄大一點兒，請您給我一雙₃小一點兒

8 這雙鞋₂是₃九塊錢買的

9 我說₄貴一點兒

VIII 瓶子酒

1 這是₂甚麼東西？ 這是₂瓶子

2 在這個瓶子裡₃有₂甚麼？ 在這個瓶子裡有₃酒

3 您₄會喝₃酒麼？ 我₄會喝酒

IX 酒盃

1 那個₃酒₁盃₂是₃誰拿來的？　那個酒盃是₃我拿來的

2 您喝了₃幾盃酒？　我喝了₄四盃酒

3 請您₄再喝一盃！　₄謝謝，₄不喝了

4 這是₂甚麼？　這是₁玻₂璃₁盃

5 這瓶子是₄酒，那瓶子₃也是₃酒麼？

6 那個瓶子₄是₃酒瓶子？　₄是酒瓶子

4 這瓶子酒是₃幾塊錢買的？

5 這瓶子是₄酒，那瓶子₃也是₃酒麼？

4 那瓶子₂不是酒，是₃水

5 這瓶子是₄酒，那瓶子₃也是₃酒麼？

4 這瓶子酒是₄四塊錢買的

4 這瓶子酒是₃幾塊錢買的？

X 牛奶 奶油

1. 您是喝茶是喝牛奶？我喝牛奶
2. 牛奶多少錢一瓶子？牛奶一毛五，一瓶子
3. 您喝茶要牛奶不要？要牛奶
4. 您昨天買了幾瓶子牛奶？
5. 我昨天買了兩瓶子牛奶
6. 這是幾斤奶油？這是一斤奶油
7. 您吃麪包，吃奶油不吃？也吃奶油
8. 您明天要買幾斤奶油？我明天要買五斤

5. 是玻璃盃大是酒盃大？玻璃盃大酒盃小

8 奶油¹多少錢⁴一斤？ ¹七毛錢一斤

9 牛奶是²甚麼²顏色？ 是²白顏色

10 奶油³也是²白顏色的麼？

³有白顏色的，³也有²黃顏色的

第二十課　I 斤兩

1. 這所房子一半是我的，一半是他的
2. 一斤是十六兩，半斤是八兩
3. 茶葉多少錢半斤？茶葉一塊錢半斤
4. 您買了幾斤咖啡？我買了一斤半
5. 這半瓶子酒有幾兩？這半瓶子酒有十二兩
6. 您要買幾瓶子牛奶？我要買半瓶子牛奶
7. 他昨天買了一斤牛肉，半斤豬肉，四兩羊肉

8 這一條魚有一斤三兩

9 這一半是我的那一半，那一半是您的

II 倒

1 請您給我倒一碗茶來

2 我給您倒一盃酒來，您喝不喝？謝謝，我不喝

3 那碗咖啡是誰給您倒的？是他給我倒的

4 那玻璃盃牛奶是給誰倒的？是給你倒的

5 請您再給我倒一盃酒來

III 新舊

1 這件衣裳是新的麼？這件衣裳是新的

IV 課本

1 錢²學生³買⁴甚麼去了？　他買⁴課³本去了

2 這個課本是¹新²的是⁴舊的？　這是⁴舊課本

3 那位學生⁴是¹新²來的不是？⁴對了，他⁴是新來的

2 這頂帽子也是¹新的麼？　²不是，這頂帽子是⁴舊的

4 那件衣裳⁴太舊了，請您給我買一件¹新的來

5 您¹新買的⁴那所房子有³幾間屋子？　有¹八間屋子

1 錢²學生³買⁴甚麼去了？　他買⁴課³本去了

2 這個課本是¹新²的是⁴舊的？　這是⁴舊課本

3 我們²昨天跟¹今天⁴念的¹都是⁴舊課本，²明天⁴要念¹新的

4 這個課本裡的⁴畫兒是²¹黃先生⁴畫的

華語入門　第二十課　一百五十四

V　中國　外國　國

1. 這是那一國？　這是中國。
2. 那也是中國麼？　那不是中國，是外國。
3. 我們是在中國麼？　是，我們是在中國住。
4. 這國大不大？　這國很大。
5. 中國的地方大不大？　中國的地方大的很。

VI　中國人　外國人

1. 您是那國人？　我是中國人。
2. 您的先生是外國人麼？　我的先生是外國人。
3. 你們學堂的學生都是中國學生麼？

VII 中國話 外國話

1. 中國人說中國話，外國人說外國話
2. 您會說外國話麼？是，我會說一點兒外國話
3. 他的姑娘會說那國話？他的姑娘會說中國話
4. 對了，是外國人
5. 包先生！那兩位學生是外國人麼？
6. 那個舖子賣中國東西，也賣外國東西麼？
7. 也賣外國東西
8. 中國人穿的衣裳長短？有長的，也有短的
9. 不都是中國學生，也有外國學生

VIII

〔外國書〕 〔中國飯〕
中國字 外國字 〔中國書〕 〔外國飯〕

1. 那本書上₃有外國字沒有？那本書上₃有外國字
2. 您寫的₄那個₄字是₃那一國的字？—那是₁中國字
4. 那個中國人說的₄外國話₃好不好？
5. 我說的外國話您₂明白不明白？
   他說的外國話₃很好了
   您說的外國話我₂明白
6. 這₁三個課本₁都是₃那國課本？這兩個課本是₄外國課本，那₂一個課本是₁中國課本

IX 旗子（面）

1. 這²旗子⁴是³你的麼？這面旗子⁴是我的
2. 是⁴在⁴那個中國書舖買的？
3. 這個中國課本是在³那個舖子³買的？
4. 這幾位¹中國學生⁴念外國書不念？
5. 那個人⁴會作¹中國飯麼？他⁴會作¹中國飯
6. 您吃了³幾回中國飯？我吃了³兩¹三²回了
7. 請問²您哪，今天你⁴是吃⁴外國飯是¹吃¹中國飯？
8. 今天我吃⁴外國飯
9. 中國飯³好吃麼？中國飯²很好吃

2. 那³是那¹一國的²旗子？　那是¹中國旗子

3. 中國旗²子有幾³個²顏色？　中國旗子有三個顏色

4. 這面旗子是¹新的是⁴舊的？

5. 在²牆上⁴掛的旗子是²甚麼²顏色的？

6. 在²牆上掛的旗子是⁴綠顏色的旗子

7. 在³講堂上，¹今²天掛²旗子不⁴掛？

8. 今天不掛，²明天要掛

9. 那是⁴外國²旗子麼？　對了，那⁴是外國旗子

10. 外國旗子¹都有²甚麼²顏色？　外國旗子²甚麼顏色¹都有

第二十一課

I 學

1 您跟²誰學¹中國⁴話哪？　我跟²錢先生學中國話哪

2 您³也學³寫中國⁴字麼？　我³也學寫中國字

3 那個姑娘跟他³母親學²甚麼哪？　跟他母親學作⁴衣裳哪

4 你們學堂裡的學生³也學⁴外國⁴話麼？　他們³也學外國話

II 多喒

1 ²黃先生告訴您¹多喒來？　他告訴我²明天來

2 那張畫兒是₁多嚜₄畫的？　是₂昨天畫的
3 您₁多嚜上他₁家裡去？　我₁今天就要去
4 他這件衣裳是₁多嚜₃買的？　我₄不知道是多嚜買的

III 開　關

1 您₄是要開₁窗戶是要開₂門？
2 那個門是₂誰開開的？　是那位₄太太開開的
3 請您₃把那個窗戶₁開開！　好好，我寫₂完了字₄就開
4 那個門₁開開了麼？　那個門還₂沒開開哪
5 請問₂您哪，這個門₁關不關？　這個門₄不關

6 誰把門關上了？
7 請您把門開開，把窗戶關上！我開開門了，也關上窗戶了

IV 〔問答〕

(一) 您跟誰學中國話哪？
(二) 我跟關先生學哪

(一) 關先生今天來了麼？
(二) 今天沒來

(一) 他多喒來？
(二) 他說他明天來

華語入門 第二十一課

(一) 您₄今天₄要₄作₂甚麼去？
(二) 我要₃買點兒東西去
(一) 您₄要₂買₂甚麼東西？
(二) 我要₃買幾瓶子₃酒，幾瓶子₂牛奶跟₃幾斤₃奶油
(一) 您要買東西去，請您把₁窗戶，₂門，₁都關上
(二) 是₄是·我₁都₁關上了

V (問答)

(一) 您在₃那兒₄住哪？
(二) 我在₁中國大街住哪
(一) 您跟₂誰₂一₄塊兒₂來的？

(二) 我跟我₄父母₃一塊兒來的

(一) 你們₄作₂甚麼來了？

(二) 我們₄要買幾件₁衣裳

(一) 你們₄要買甚麼₂顏色的₁衣裳？

(二) 要買一件₂紅的，兩件₂藍的

(一) 在₄那裡₃有賣鞋的沒有？

(二) 在₄那裡₃有賣鞋的

(一) 您₁穿的這雙鞋是在₃那兒₃買的？

(二) 也是在₄那裡₃買的

(一) 那條街上₃也有₁書舖麼？

第二十一課

³有書舖

(二) 他們⁴賣₁中國書，⁴外國書？
(一) 他們中國書，外國書，₁都賣
(二) 那個書舖是₁中國₁書舖麼？
(一) ²不是，是₄外國書舖
(二) 您³也在他們⁴那裡³買書麼？
(一) ⁴對了，我們的課本₁都是在₄那裡買的
(二) 他們₄會₁說中國話不會？
(一) 他們³有₄會的，³有₂不會說的

一百六十四

VI 看

1. 請你們看在⁴這張畫兒上，⁴畫的是²甚麼東西？
2. 您看，這張畫兒上，畫的是²瓶子跟³酒盃，甚麼的
3. 請您看，這⁴是我的⁴課本不是？
4. 您在那裡⁴看⁴甚麼？我在那兒看⁴畫兒哪
5. 你看，是這張畫兒畫的好，⁴還是⁴這張畫兒畫的好？

這幾個字寫的²不大好
這幾個字寫的³好不好？
是⁴，那⁴是您的課本
是⁴這張畫兒⁴畫的好，是⁴那張畫兒⁴畫的好？

華語入門　第二十一課　一百六十五

VII 報(份) 信(封) 看 (書)(信)(報)

1 這是²您買的⁴報⁴麼？是，這是⁴我買的報
2 這是⁴中國報是⁴外國報呢？這是⁴外國報
3 這⁴一份報¹多少錢？這⁴一份報⁴一毛錢
4 您今天⁴要看¹中國報麼？是，我今天⁴要看中國報
5 您看²甚麼¹書哪？我看⁴外國書哪
6 我⁴念書，他⁴看書
7 這一封信是²誰³寫的？是我³母親寫的
8 你⁴要給誰寫信？我要給我⁴丈夫寫信
9 您⁴看的是誰的信？我看的是¹關先生的信

10　您₄在₄那兒₄看₂甚麼哪？　我₄看₄信哪

11　這份報₄是₂您₄看的麼？　⁴是₂我看的

VIII 聽

1　請你們₁聽，我₄要給你們₃講功課

2　先生講功課，₂甚麼人₁聽？　先生講功課₂學生們聽

3　您₁聽，₂誰在₄那裡說話哪？
　　錢₁太太跟₂黃太太在那兒說話哪

4　他₁聽₂甚麼哪？　他聽₃我們兩個人₁說的是₂甚麼話

IX 看一看 聽一聽

1　請您₄看一看，我寫的這封₄信₄對不對？　寫的₄對了

2 您買的酒盃沒給您父親看一看麼？給我父親看了

3 請您看一看，他在家裡沒有？他在家哪

4 張先生來了沒有？我看一看去

5 先生請您聽一聽我念的信對不對？

6 請您聽一聽，他們說的中國話好不好？

好，我聽一聽

他們說的很好了

第二十二課 １ 上○去

1. 您⁴上²甚麼地方去？ 我上他¹家裡去
2. 那位學生⁴上²學堂去了麼？ 他⁴上學堂去了
3. 您²明天⁴上²誰家去？ 我⁴要上¹張先生家裡去
4. 您上¹張先生家裡去⁴作²甚麼去？ 我要³請他給我們講功課
5. 昨天²上⁴您家裡去的⁴那個人是²誰？ 那是我們的¹先生

II 上那兒 上街

1 請問您哪，您今天要上那兒去？ 我要買棹子去

2 您念完了書，還要上那裡去？ 上那個棹椅舖買去

3 白先生上那裡了？ 我還不知道上那兒了哪

4 我上街去，您上那兒去？ 我也上街去

5 你知道他上那兒去了麼？ 我知道他上那兒去了

III 從○來

1 您從家裡來麼？ 是，我從家裡來

2 他從甚麼地方來？ 他也從家裡來

3 您從書舖買了甚麼來了？ 我買了兩本書來

4 這幾瓶子酒是從家裡拿來的麼？

不是，是從舖子拿來的

5 那位先生是從外國請來的麼？

對了，是從外國請來的

IV 從那兒(裡)

1 您從那兒來？ 我從買賣街來

2 這個麪包是從那裡買來的？

是從我們那條街上，那個麪包房裡，買來的

3 上你們學堂，要從那兒去？ 要從中國大街去

華語入門　第二十二課

V 上那兒
　　裡

1 您²昨¹天上³那⁴兒去了？　我上²｜錢先生那⁴兒去了
2 上²那⁴兒作²甚⁴麼去了？　我跟¹他有⁴話說
3 上²您那裡去的那⁴位，貴姓？　他姓²｜藍
4 您上⁴他那⁴兒去了麼？　還²沒去哪
5 您²還上⁴那裡買鞋⁴去麼？　我²不去了，那兒的鞋⁴太貴

4 他們⁴賣的東西¹都是²從那裡³買來的？　都是⁴從⁴外國買來的
5 您²明天²從那裡⁴上²學堂去？　我明天從¹｜包先生⁴那兒，上學堂去

一百七十二

VI 上⁴這⁴(裡兒)

1 他上⁴這兒⁴作²甚麼²來了？他要跟您¹說³幾句⁴話
2 您¹今天上⁴這裡來，您²明天²還來麼？我明天²還來
3 明天是²您上⁴他那兒⁴去，是¹他⁴上²您這兒⁴來？
4 上⁴這兒²來的¹都是⁴作²甚麼²的？都是²學生
²還是他⁴上²我這兒⁴來
5 您²昨天²沒上⁴這兒²來，您上²那裡⁴去了？
我³買東西去了

VII 從那裡兒

1. 他從那裡拿來的牛奶？ 他從那兒拿來的
2. 您從那兒上那兒去？ 我從那裡上學堂去
3. 從那個書舖那兒買來的書，都是外國書麼？ 不是，也有中國書
4. 這頂帽子是從那兒買來的？ 不是買的，是從錢太太那裡拿來的
5. 請問先生，這本書從那兒念？ 從那兒念

第二十三課

I 從這裡兒

1 您₂從₄這兒⁴上那₁兒³去？ 我從這裡上街₃買₁衣裳去．
您₄要買₂甚麼₂顏色的衣裳？ 我要買₂一件₁黑的，₂一件₂藍的

2 他₂昨天₂從這裡₄上那裡₄去了？

3 我₂還₄不知道他上那兒⁴去了哪

4 這本書₄是₂從這兒⁴講的麼？ ₂不是，是從₄那兒講的

5 您從這兒₄是上學堂麼？ ⁴是，我從這兒⁴上學堂

那幾碗咖啡⁴是₂從₄這兒給他們₂拿去的麼？

華語入門　第二十三課

⁴對了，⁴是從這兒拿去的

II 學校　大學校　中學校　小學校

1. 您的⁴丈夫是⁴大學校的¹先生麼？
⁴是，他是⁴大學校的先生

2. 您的¹姑娘在²甚麼⁴學校念書哪？
他在⁴大學校念書

3. 在這兒³有³小學校沒有？

4. 在這裡³有³很多的小學校
在小學校念³完了書，就要⁴上²甚麼學校⁴念書去？
要上¹中學校念書去

5. 那所²紅房子是¹中學校是³小學校？
是¹中學校

III 事情 事（件）

1 您₁今₃天₃有₄事情沒有？ 我今₃天₃有事情

2 您₁今₃天₃有甚₂麼₄事？ 我₄要₃買₁東西去

3 請問，₂錢先生的₄事情₃好不好？ 他的事情₂不₄大好

4 他₂昨天₂沒有事情，₁今天₃也沒有事情麼₂？

5 張先生₄作₂甚麼₄事情哪？

6 他₂今天₃也沒事情

那₂幾位學生是₂甚麼學校的₂學生？

他們是₄大學校的學生

IV 火車站　車票

1. 您上那兒去了？　我上火車站去了
2. 您上火車站作甚麼去了？　我買車票去了
3. 您給誰買車票去了？　我給白先生買車票去了
4. 今天火車站人多不多？　今天人不少
5. 這張車票是綠的，那張是甚麼顏色的？　那張是黃的
6. 我有一件事情要跟您說．請說
7. 這件事情是我的，那件事情是他的
8. 先生有先生的事情，學生有學生的事情

V 郵政局 郵票（一分票）（三分票）
（半分票）來信 去信 回信 票

1 請問²您哪，⁴這條街上³有²郵政局²沒有？

2 您要⁴上郵政局麼？⁴對了，我⁴要上郵政局

3 您⁴上郵政局⁴作²甚麼去？我⁴要買²郵票去

4 您買郵票⁴作²甚麼？我⁴要給我³母親³寫⁴信

5 您³母親給您²來⁴信了麼？給我²來信了

6 是¹多咯來的信？是²昨天來的信

7。您⁴要給誰⁴去信？我要給²藍先生去信

8. 這兩封信都是給¹關先生去的⁴信麼？²不是，
⁴一封是給我³母親去的，⁴一封是給¹關先生去的
9. 您給他們⁴去信，他們²來回信麼？
10. 這是一分票，那是幾分票？那是半分票
11. 有半分票，一分票，還有幾分票？
12. ⁴這張票是幾分的？這張票是⁴四分的
13. ⁴您要買幾分票？
14. 我要買兩張³五分的，⁴四張一分的
    您有三分的郵⁴票麼？我沒有三分的，我有一分的

15. ⁴這⁴張⁴票²是甚麼票？ 這張是車¹票

VI 電報局 電報（份）打電報 來電報 去電報 上海

1. 您在³那兒⁴作事哪？ 我在⁴電報²局作事哪
2. ⁴這份電報⁴是²誰²來的？ 是²毛先生來的
3. 您⁴上電報局作²甚麼⁴去？ 我³打電報去
4. ⁴打電報，²一個字¹多少錢？ 一個字⁴一毛多錢
5. 您⁴是給毛先生³打電報啊，⁴是給他³寫⁴信呢？ 我²還是給他打電報
6. ⁴這份電報⁴是⁴從那裡²來的？ 是從⁴上海來的

7 您給他去電報作甚麼？
我給他去電報叫他上這兒來

第二十四課

I 飯館子

1. 您₁今天在₃那兒₁吃的飯？我在₄飯₃館子吃的飯
2. 是₄在₁中國飯館子吃的，₄是在₄外國飯館子吃的？
3. 是在₁中國飯館子吃的
4. 那條街上₃也有₄外國飯館子麼？也有₃外國飯館子
5. 昨天你們在₄那個飯₃館子吃飯，₁吃了₁多少錢？吃了₃五塊多錢
6. 你們吃飯的₄那個飯館子₄大₃小？那個飯館子₄不小

II 旅館

1. 您在₃那兒₄住哪？　　我在₂旅館₃住哪
2. 在₃那個旅館住哪？　　在₂那個₄外國旅館住哪
3. 您在那個旅館住幾間₁屋子？　　住₃兩間屋子
4. ₄多少錢₄一間？　　₄四十塊錢一間
5. 那個旅館的₁屋子₄大不大？　　屋子₂不大
6. 您在旅館住，₃也在旅館₁吃₄飯麼？　　₃也在那兒吃飯

III 電影院　片子　演電影兒　看電影兒

1. ₄那是₂甚麼₄地方？　　那是₄電影院
2. 電影院是₄作₂甚麼的₄地方？

電影院是演電影兒的地方

3 ²昨⁴天³上那³兒⁴去了？ 我⁴看電影兒去了

4 ²昨⁴天³的片⁴子²好不好？ ²昨天的片子²很好了

5 ²您⁴看的是中國片⁴子麼？ ⁴是中國片子

6 ²您⁴看外國片⁴子不看？ 我³也看外國片子

IV 戲 戲園子 看戲 聽戲 唱

1 請問²您哪，那是戲²園子不是？ 那⁴是戲園子

2 ¹今³天有⁴戲沒有？ 今³天有⁴戲

3 ²您是要⁴看電影兒⁴是要¹聽戲？ 我要¹聽戲

4 ²昨天那⁴個戲園子⁴看戲的⁴多不多？ 看戲的⁴不少

華語入門　第二十四課

5 看電影兒要買票，聽戲³也⁴要買票麼⁴？
看戲³也⁴要買票

6 今天他們唱的，是¹中國戲⁴是⁴外國戲？
今天他們唱的是¹中國戲

7 您⁴會⁴唱¹中國戲麼？我²不會

V 商人 作買賣 作買賣的

1 ⁴那位是作⁴甚²麼的？那位是¹商人

2 ²甚⁴麼是¹商人？商人是⁴作³買⁴賣的

3 作⁴買⁴賣的⁴在³那兒作⁴買⁴賣？
作⁴買⁴賣的在⁴舖子裡作⁴買⁴賣

一百八十六

4 那⁴個人是⁴作²甚麼買賣的？他是賣¹桌³椅的

5 這³個地方³也⁴有外國商人麼？

VI 書記

1 你們學校有³幾個書記？有³兩個書記

2 書記是⁴作⁴甚麼的？書記是³寫⁴字的

3 那兩個書記會³寫那國⁴字？一個會寫¹中國字，²一個會寫⁴外國字

4 張先生叫那個書記寫²甚⁴麼哪？他叫他寫⁴信哪

5 那個寫字的⁴是書⁴記不是？他²不是書⁴記，他是²學生

VII 裁縫

1. 昨²天⁴來的那⁴個人是⁴作²甚麼的？ 他是⁴作²衣¹裳¹的
2. 作⁴衣¹裳⁴的叫²甚麼？ 作⁴衣¹裳的叫²裁縫
3. 那⁴個裁⁴縫⁴姓²甚麼？ 他姓²毛
4. 裁²縫昨⁴天作²甚²麼來了？
5. 我⁴要叫他⁴給我⁴作一件衣裳
6. 那⁴個裁⁴縫會作中國衣¹裳，³也⁴會作外國衣¹裳¹麼？
   他⁴會作外國衣裳，³也⁴會作中國衣裳

VIII 回來 回去 回國（回家來去）北平 南京

1. 白²先生²回來了沒有？ ²還沒回來哪

2. 您⁴要²回⁴去麼? ⁴是，我⁴要⁴回去

3. 您⁴從²這兒⁴就²回⁴去麼? ⁴是，我⁴從這兒⁴就回去

4. 你³們兩²個人一⁴塊兒²回家⁴去麼?
³我⁴回家去，他⁴不回家去

5. 他²是從²那兒²回⁴來的? 他²是從上海回來的

6. 您²從郵²政局還⁴要上³那兒⁴去麼?
⁴不²上那裡去⁴了，我從這裡⁴就要²回家去了

7. 您⁴是從⁴戲園子²回來的麼?
⁴是，²是從戲園子回來的

8. 您⁴的丈夫⁴上³那兒⁴去了? 他²回²國了

華語入門　第二十四課

9 您⁴的太⁴太上³北平⁴去了，多嚜²回來？
10 他¹多嚜²從南京²回來？他¹今天⁴就回來,明²天回來
11 他們回國⁴去了，還²回來不⁴回來了？
12 我⁴不知道還²回來不⁴回來了
13 你²還回學校去麼？是⁴，我²還回學校去
14 您²上火車站去，還²回來不⁴回來呢？
15 不⁴回來了，我²從火車站²還要⁴上電影院⁴去
16 他⁴從北平²回南京去麼？是⁴，回南京去
17 他²回南京⁴作甚麼⁴去了？看他的父⁴母去了
18 他⁴是回²北平⁴去了麼？是⁴，他²回北平去了

17 書記₂回來了沒有？ 還₂沒回來

18 那個₁商人是₂昨天₂回₂國來了

第二十五課

I 作飯的廚子

1. 您₁家₃裡₃有作飯₄的沒有？

2. 作飯的叫₂甚麼？ ₃有一個作飯的作飯的叫₂廚子

3. 您₄的作飯的會作₁中國飯，₄會作₄外國飯麼？

4. 中國飯，外國飯，₁都會作

5. 那個廚子作的飯₃好₁吃不好吃？ 他作的飯₂很好吃

6. 您₄要告訴廚子₂甚麼₄話？

7. 我₄要告訴他₁今天₁多作一個人的飯

II 木匠

1. 請問您，²甚麼人⁴會作¹棹³椅？
2. 木²匠還會作²甚麼？⁴還會作¹窗戶，門，²甚麼的⁴木匠會作棹椅
3. 那個棹³椅⁴舖裡有³幾個⁴木匠？⁴有⁴不³少木匠哪²個木匠作
4. 您說⁴是這個木匠作的棹椅³好啊，²還是⁴那個木匠⁴作的³好呢？
5. 這張棹子跟那幾把¹椅子都是²誰給您⁴作的？⁴都是⁴那個木匠給我作的

III 作鞋的鞋匠

1. 他是⁴作²甚麼的？他是⁴作²鞋的

2 作₄鞋的₄是鞋匠不是？作鞋的₄是鞋匠

3 那個鞋匠在₃那個₂鞋舖裡作₂鞋？
他在₄那個₂鞋舖裡作鞋

4 那幾個鞋舖裡作鞋
他們₂不會作中國鞋，他們會作₄外國鞋

5 這兩雙鞋是那₃個鞋匠₄作的？
是₄那個₄外國鞋匠作的

IV 買東西的 賣東西的

1 我們上舖子₃買東西，我們是₄作₂甚麼的？
我們是₃買東西的

V 病 得病 大夫 治 醫院

1. 錢²先¹生¹今¹天²來³了²沒¹有¹？他²沒⁴來，他⁴病³了
2. 他²得²甚⁴麼⁴病³了？我²還⁴不¹知¹道¹哪¹
3. 張¹先¹生¹的⁴病³好³了²沒¹有¹？還²沒³好³哪
4. 他³請⁴大⁴夫¹了²麼？請⁴了

1. 作⁴買³賣⁴的¹叫¹商¹人¹，還²叫⁴賣⁴東¹西¹的
2. 那⁴條²街¹上⁴賣⁴東¹西¹的¹多¹不⁴多？
3. 這⁴個⁴人²是⁴賣²甚²麼²的？賣⁴東¹西¹的⁴不³很³多
4. 那⁴個⁴買³東¹西¹的⁴跟²誰²說⁴話⁴哪？我³也³不⁴知¹道⁴是⁴賣²甚²麼²的
5. 他¹跟⁴賣⁴東¹西¹的¹說¹話⁴哪

第二十五課

5. 黃²大夫⁴上³那兒⁴去了？他給人⁴治病⁴去了
6. 治病的地方叫²甚麼？那個醫院裡有多少位⁴大夫？
7. 那個醫院裡有¹多³少位⁴大夫？
8. 那個醫院裡的大夫¹都是³好⁴大夫麼？
9. 給²您治病的那位⁴大夫，³也是⁴那個醫院的⁴大夫麼？
10. 對了，他³也是⁴那個醫院的⁴大夫
    這²條街上⁴就²有¹一個⁴醫院麼？
    不²是，²還有¹一個⁴外國醫院哪

VI 辦公 職員 當 行 不行

1. 包⁴先生在⁴電報²局⁴辦¹公麼？他⁴在電報²局辦公
2. 他們那⁴兒有¹多少位²職²員？有¹三十多位
3. 學校裡有先生，³也有²職²員麼？學校裡³也有職員
4. 學校裡的職員³也³講功⁴課麼？他們⁴不講功課
5. 您的⁴父親在⁴那個學校裡⁴是先生²是職²員？他是²職²員
6. 請問您，郵政局²明天⁴辦公²不辦公？明天⁴辦公
7. 職員說辦⁴公，¹商人³也說⁴辦¹公麼？
8. ²藍先生⁴是¹商人麼？商人⁴要說⁴作買賣

他₂不是商人，他是電報局的₂職₂員
9 他在郵政局當₁書記₄麼？　對了，當書記
10 當書記的₂不₄會₃寫字，₂行麼？　那₄不行
11 看電影兒₄不買票，₂行₄不₂行？　不買票₄不行
12 他得的₄那個₄病₂不₄上醫院治去，₂行₄不₂行？
　 不上醫院去₄不行

溫故知新

I 家問答

(一) 您₄貴姓？

(二) 賤姓₁張

(一) 您在₃那兒₄作事？

(二) 我在₃火車站作事

(一) 您家裡有幾口兒人？

(二) 我家裡有₁七口兒人

(一) 您₁都有₂甚麼人？

(二) 我有₄父親，₃母親，我有₄太太，還有₂一個₂兒子，₃兩

個₁姑娘

(一) 您₄父親是₄作₂甚麼的？

(二) 他是₁商人

(一) 您的₂孩子們在₁家裡念書麼？

(二) 不是，我的₄大姑娘在₄大學校念書，我的₂兒子跟我的₄小姑娘在₃小學校念書

(一) 您的₃母親跟您的₄太太在₁家裡₄作₂甚麼？

(二) 他們在家裡給₃我們₄作飯

賣東西　問答

(一) 你們這兒₄賣₂甚麼東西？

二百

我們這兒賣₂茶葉，咖啡，酒₃，奶油₃，牛奶₂，甚麼的

(一) 這個茶葉₁多少錢一斤？

(二) 這個茶葉₁三塊半錢一斤

(一) 咖啡₃也是三塊半錢一斤麼？

(二) 不是₂，咖啡是₃兩塊₃一斤

(一) 奶油₄六毛錢一斤，牛奶₄一毛₄二一瓶子

(二) 奶油₁多少錢一斤，牛奶₁多少錢一₂瓶子？

(一) 你們這兒還賣₂甚麼東西？

(二) 我們這兒還賣₂碗茶，₄飯碗，₁玻璃盃，₃酒盃，甚麼的

III 人 穿的 戴的 問答

(一) 你們也賣麴包麼?

(二) 我們有白麴包, 沒有黑麴包

(一) 您昨天上那兒去了?

(二) 我買衣裳去了

(一) 都給誰買啊?

(二) 我們家裡的人, 我給他們一個人買一件

(一) 買的都是甚麼衣裳啊?

(二) 給我父親買了一件長的, 給我母親買了一件短的, 給我的兒子, 姑娘們都買的是學生的衣裳, 還

給我太太買了一件₄不很長的
(一)₄那些件衣裳₁都是₂甚麼₂顏色的？
(二)我父母的都是₂藍顏色的，姑娘的是₄綠顏色的，我兒子的是₂紅顏色的，我太太的是₂黃的
(一)您買的那件衣裳₄貴賤哪？
(二)有₃九塊₃五毛錢的，有₂十一塊₄半的，那小孩子的衣裳都是₄六塊₃五一件，您說貴不貴啊？
(一)我說₁都₃很賤，一點兒不貴
(二)您₁穿的這件衣裳₃也是₁新買的麽？
(二)₂不是，這是₄舊的，我昨天₄就買了₄一頂₄帽子，一

雙²鞋，²沒⁴買⁴衣裳

(一) 那頂帽子₁多少錢哪?

(二) 兩塊₃五

(一) 那雙鞋是₃幾塊錢₃買的?

(二) 鞋是₂七塊₁八毛₃五買的

(一) 您說⁴是⁴在衣裳舖裡₃買衣裳好啊，²還是⁴叫裁縫在家裡⁴作³好呢?

(二) 我說那³有²錢的還是叫裁縫在家裡作好，那²沒²錢的買一件穿₃也²行了

IV 人 吃的 喝的 問答

(一) 您³好啊？

(二) 好³好・您³也³好啊！

(一) 謝謝，我³也好

(二) 您²從³那兒來？

(一) 從⁴飯館子來

(二) 上⁴飯館子⁴作²甚麼去了？

(一) ¹吃⁴飯去了

(二) 是您²一個人¹吃的啊，²還是¹跟人²一塊兒吃的呢？

(一) 是跟人²一塊兒吃的

（二）跟²誰一塊兒吃的？

（一）有電報局一位²職員，郵政局的一位₁書記，跟北平醫院的²黃大夫，²還有一位₁商人，我們₄六個人一塊兒吃的。

（二）吃的₁是中國飯是₄外國飯？

（一）吃的₂是中國飯

（二）吃的₁都是²甚麼呢？

（一）吃的是²牛，²羊，₁豬肉跟²魚，甚麼的

（二）你們₁喝³酒了麼？

（一）₁喝²酒了

(二) 喝的酒₁多不多啊？

(一) 我們喝的₄不多，就喝了₃兩瓶子，那幾位₃有喝₁七八盃的₂，有喝₃五六盃的₂，我₄就喝了₃兩盃

(二) 你們六位₁吃了₁多少錢？

(一) 吃了₄六塊₄二毛錢

(二) 是誰₃給的₂錢哪？

(一) 是₂黃大夫₃請的₄

(二) 你們吃完了飯，₄作₂甚麼去了？

(一) 吃完了₃飯，₁喝了₃一點兒₂茶，就上₄電影院₄看電影兒去了，看₂完了電影兒就都₂回家₁了

Ⅴ 人住的問答

（一）您⁴在⁴這⁴所房子⁴住麼?

是，我⁴在這所房子住

（一）您住³幾間屋子?

我住⁴一間屋子

（一）您住的屋子有幾個門，幾個窗戶?

我住的屋子有一個門，兩個窗戶

（一）您住的屋子，門，²窗戶，⁴地板，³頂棚跟²牆，¹都是²甚麼²顏色的?

（二）門，窗戶，頂棚都是²白顏色的，四面牆是²藍顏色

（一）在牆上掛₂甚麼東西？

的，地板是₂黃的

（二）在牆上掛₃兩張₄畫兒

（一）在畫兒上畫的是₂甚麼東西？

（二）在畫兒上畫的是₂一隻₂羊，一口₁猪，兩頭₂牛，那一張畫的是一張畫的

（一）在您的屋子裡都有₂甚麼東西？

（二）在我的屋子裡有一張₁書桌子，一張₄飯桌子，四把₃椅子，甚麼的

VI 我們的學堂　問答

(一) 您在₂甚麼學堂₄念書？

我在₁中學堂念書

(一) 你們學堂有₃幾位先生，₁多少位學生？

我們學堂裏有₂十幾位先生，₁三百多位學生

(一) 中國學生外國學生都有麼？

有中國學生，₂沒有外國學生

(一) 中外國的書₁都念麼？

₁都念

(一) 你們學堂裏有多少個講堂？

我們學堂裡有₂十₁三個講堂
(二) 講堂是₄作₂甚麼的地方？
(一) 講堂是₃講功課的地方
(二) 在講堂上₁都有₂甚麼東西？
(一) 在講堂上₁有₁書桌子，有₃椅子，在₂牆上有₁黑板，₄畫兒，甚麼的
(二) 先生拿₂甚麼₃筆在₁黑板上寫字？
(一) 先生拿₂粉筆在黑板上寫字
(二) 學生拿₂甚麼₃筆寫字，在₂甚麼₄上寫字？
(一) 學生拿₂鋼筆在₃本子上寫字

華語入門

(一) 學生們⁴念的¹都是新課本麼?

(二) 不是,² 有的學生念的是¹新課本,³ 有的學生²還是⁴舊課本

(一) 你們在講堂上⁴作²甚麼?

(二) 我們在講堂上¹聽¹先生講功課. 先生⁴問我們, 我們就²回答

(一) 你們的功課³有⁴不明白的地方,⁴要問²誰?

(二) 我們³請先生給我們講

(一) 功課完了你們就²回家麼?

(二) 是,⁴ 功課完了我們⁴就回家去

VII 學堂 學校

學校是念書的地方．有小學堂，中學堂，還有大學堂．先生在學堂裡講功課，學生在學堂裡念書．先生講功課的地方叫講堂也叫課堂．講堂裡有黑板跟畫兒，甚麼的．在這個地方小學堂很多，中學堂，大學堂也不少．

學堂 問話

1 學堂是作甚麼的地方？
2 在學堂裡講功課的是甚麼人？
3 在學堂念書的是甚麼人？

VIII 家

4 先生³講¹功課的⁴屋子叫²甚麼?

5 先生²拿甚麼³筆在¹黑板上寫字?

6 在牆上掛的那張書兒是¹先生⁴畫的, 是²學生⁴畫的?

7 那個⁴外國學堂是⁴大學堂是¹中學堂?

8 這個⁴地方都有²麼學堂?

那所房子有³兩家住, 一家姓²錢是⁴作³買賣的(商人), 一家姓¹張是⁴大夫. 錢家家裡有⁴四口兒人, 張家家裡有三口兒人. 那個姓²錢的有一個¹書舖, 東西²很好, 賣的³也³很賤, 買賣²很好. 那個姓¹張的是在南京醫院裡當大夫

家問話

1. 您家裡有³幾口兒人？
2. 您家裡¹都有²甚麼人？
3. 您跟您的⁴父母在²一塊兒⁴住麼？
4. 您的⁴丈夫在³那兒作事？
5. 您的⁴太太在⁴家裡哪麼？
6. 您的⁴父親是¹商人麼？
7. 您的³母親在家裡⁴作²甚麼？
8. 您有³幾個孩子？
9. 您的²兒子是在¹家裡⁴念書麼？

10 您的₁姑娘在₂甚麼學校₄念書₁？

11 這條街上₃有姓₂白的麼？

12 張家₄是這兒住麼？

13 您的₄父母在家哪麼？

14 他跟他的太太₄住幾間₁屋子？

IX 舖子

那條街上有₃很多舖子，甚麼₁書舖，₁棹椅舖，₄麴包房，鞋舖，₃筆舖，₁都有．他們賣東西有貴的，有賤的．在那兒₃也有外國舖子，作買賣的₃也₁都是外國人．他們的東西₁都是從₄外國₃買來的

舖子 問話

1. 舖子是賣東西的地方麼？
2. 在這條街上都有甚麼舖子？
3. 桌椅舖子賣甚麼東西？
4. 書舖裡也賣本子麼？
5. 那個鞋舖賣的鞋貴賤？
6. 請問您，那個舖子是麨包房是肉舖？
7. 那個外國舖子賣的都是外國東西麼？
8. 舖子裡作買賣的是甚麼人？
9. 在筆舖裡甚麼筆都賣麼？

10 在那個舖子裡³也賣⁴帽子麼?

X 郵政局

我昨天寫了³兩封信,⁴一封是給我³母親去的,⁴一封是給²毛先生去的.⁴這兩封信要買³幾分²郵票,²甚麼⁴地方賣²郵票,我¹都不知道.我⁴就問¹張先生去了.張先生⁴告訴我,這兩封信要買⁴六分票,賣郵票的地方⁴叫²郵政局

郵政局 問話

1 請問您,³那兒有郵政局?
2. 那個郵政局裡有¹多少位²職員?

3 郵政局裡有⁴會說⁴外國話的²職員麼?

4 您的¹先生給²您來⁴信了麼?

5 他⁴上郵政局³買²甚麼去了?

6 那張郵票是³幾分的?

7 昨天您給²誰去信?

8 這封信⁴是¹今天²來的麼?

XI 電報局

我⁴父親給我²來了⁴一份⁴電報・我今天³也給他⁴去了一份電報・他給我²來的電報有²十幾個字,我給他⁴去的電報有⁴二十多個字・³打電報的地方⁴叫⁴電報局・在我⁴住

的³那個地方，有一個³很⁴大⁴的⁴電報局。那個電報局裡職員³很多，上那兒³打電報的³也不少

電報局　問話

1 這封電報⁴是²誰來的？
2 您給他⁴去⁴電報了麼？
3 錢太太給他⁴丈夫去的電報有¹多少個字？
4 打電報，²一個字¹多少錢？
5 打電報要⁴上²甚麼⁴地方去？

XII 電影院　戲園子

人作²完了事情，²很³好是⁴看⁴電影兒去。不看電影兒，

聽⁴戲³去也³很⁴好．演⁴電影兒的地方⁴叫⁴電影⁴院．唱⁴戲的地方⁴叫⁴戲園子．⁴張先生說今天那個戲園子戲²很⁴好，那個電影兒的⁴片子²不大⁴好

電影院　戲園子　問話

1　您上電影院⁴作²甚麼⁴去了？

2　看電影兒³也³要買⁴票麼？

3　電影院³演的片子¹都是⁴外國片子³麼？

4　今天那個電影院的⁴片子³好不⁴好？

5　這個地方³有⁴戲園子沒有？

6　您說⁴是⁴看電影兒³好⁴是¹聽戲³好？

7. 我們說¹聽戲去²行，我們說⁴看戲去²行不行？
8. 昨天你們³幾位⁴看戲去了麼？

XIII 醫院

在我們這兒有一個³很大的¹醫院。那個醫院裡⁴大夫³很多。在那個地方住的人有了⁴病，¹都是上那兒⁴治去。那個醫院的大夫都是²很³好的大夫。我⁴父親的病跟²黃先生的病，¹都是在⁴那個醫院⁴治³好了的

醫院 問話

1. 這兒³有¹醫院麼？
2. 那個醫院裡有¹多少位⁴大夫？

3 那個醫院是外國醫院不是？

4 黃大夫是那個醫院的大夫？

5 在上海醫院裡治病貴不貴？

6 您的病是那個醫院裡治好了的？

XIV 飯舘子

昨天關先生請我們幾個人在飯舘子裡吃飯．我們吃的有牛肉，羊肉，猪肉，魚，甚麼的．我們還喝了很多的酒．我們吃完了飯，關先生就問我們，誰喝茶誰喝咖啡．我們告訴他，我們都不喝咖啡．他知道我們都不喝咖啡，就給我們一個人倒了一碗茶．

我們₁喝₂完了茶，就₁都₂回家去了

飯舘子 問話

1 那個₄飯舘子是₁中國飯舘子，是₄外國飯舘子？
2 在₄飯舘子₁吃飯₄貴₄賤？
3 昨天他們₄四位在飯舘子₁吃飯，₁吃了₁多少錢？
4 你們在飯舘子裡₁吃的₁都是₂甚麼？
5 您請那二位吃飯，₄是在₄飯舘子吃，₄是在₁家裡吃？

XV 旅舘

旅舘是₄住₂人的地方。旅舘有₄大，有₃小，有₄貴，有₄賤，在火車站那兒有一個₃很₄大的旅舘。那個旅舘₂名子

叫北平旅館,北平旅館裡住的人那國人都有。北平旅館的屋子也很大,窗戶也很多。他們說是上這兒來的人,都是住北平旅館

旅館 問話

1 那個旅館大小?
2 在旅館住貴不貴?
3 您在旅館住幾間屋子?
4 在旅館住一間屋子多少錢?
5 您上上海是在旅館住,還是在張先生家裡住呢?
6 您在旅館住,也在旅館裡吃飯麼?

XVI 廚子　木匠　裁縫　鞋匠

1 廚子

(一) 廚子是作₂甚麼的？

(二) 廚子是₄作₄飯的

(一) 您家裡₃有廚子沒有？

(二) 有廚子．

(一) 您的廚子會作₄外國飯麼？

(二) 他₄會作外國飯

2 木匠

(一) 木匠會作₁棹子，₃椅子，還會作₂甚麼？

他們還會作窗₁戶，門，甚麼的

(二)那個木匠作的那張，₄是書₁棹子₄是飯₄棹子？

(一)他作的是飯₄棹子

(二)那張飯棹子是給₂您₄作的麼？

不₂是，是給₄那位先生作的

3 裁縫

(一)您叫裁縫₄作₂甚麼？

(二)我叫他₃給我₄作₁衣裳

(一)他₄會作₄外國衣裳麼？

(二)外國衣裳他₃也會作

4 鞋匠

(一) 您¹穿的這雙鞋是¹新的是⁴舊的？

(二) 我¹穿的是¹新鞋

(一) 在³那個鞋舖買³的？

(二) 在中國大街⁴那個鞋舖買的

(一) 多少錢⁴一雙？

(二) 三塊¹八¹一雙

(一) 您的衣裳都是¹他³給您⁴作麼？

(二) 對了，¹都是他給我作

生字名詞表

一 書紙 本子 我 您 你 他 有 沒有 鉛筆 鋼筆 麼

二 一兩三四五 個 張 本 枝 幾

三 這那 是 不是 也 棹子 椅子 六七八九十 把

四 毛筆 甚麼 人 東西 先生 學生 位 誰 的 我的 您的 你的 他的 誰的

五 先生的 學生的 這幾○ 那幾○ 大 小 長 短 知道

六 書棹子 飯棹子 父親 母親 兒子 姑娘 羊 隻 牛 頭 豬 口

茶水 飯碗 茶碗 飯碗 玻璃盃

肉 羊肉 牛肉 豬肉 斤 魚 條 塊 麭包 茶葉 咖啡 二

七 多少 多少 十幾 幾十 二十幾 字 們 我們 你們 他們

我們的 你們的 他們的 百 零 千

八 甚麼的 ○百多 ○千多 幾百 幾千 這些 那些

九 作桌椅子（做） 作書 作飯 寫 念 會 喝 吃 要

十 今天 昨天 明天 了 的 還 哪 還(○)哪

不好 還是 啊 呢 好吃 好

十一 甚麼○也不○ 誰也不○ 甚麼○都○ 誰都○ 來 去

您好啊？ 謝謝 請 請坐 再見 請

十二 問 回答 說話 句 明白 跟 對 不對 我說 您說 你說

他說 再 回 請問您哪 好些個 一點兒

十三　姓名子　叫完　就叫錢　〇塊錢
〇分錢　要給給買賣　　　　　〇毛錢

十四　貴賤很　不大好　貴姓　賤姓　講功課　意思

十五　屋子間裡　在在〇裡　窗戶門　房子　所住
告訴太丈夫　太太
家　學堂　地方　舖子

十六　紅黃綠白黑藍　顏色　地板　頂棚　牆面
墨水兒　粉筆　黑板　畫兒　畫筆　拿筆

十七　上在〇上　掛把　拿來　拿去　拿〇來　拿〇去
大學堂　中學堂　小學堂　吃墨紙

華語入門

二百三十一

華語入門

十八 那？ 這兒 那兒？ 這裡 那裡？ 在這兒 在那兒 在這裡 在那裡？ 講堂 課堂

十九 一塊兒 父母 孩子 街條 衣裳 件 穿 帽子

二十 頂戴 鞋雙 瓶子 酒 酒盃 牛奶 奶油

半兩倒新舊 課本 中國 外國 中國人
外國人 中國話 外國話 中國字 外國字 中國書
外國書 中國飯 外國飯 旗子面

二十一 學多偺？ 開關看報份信封 看(書報信)
聽看一看 聽一聽

二十二 上○去 上那裡兒？ 上街 從○來 從那裡兒？ 上那裡兒
上這裡兒 從那裡兒

二百三十二

二十三 從這裡兒 學校 大學校 中學校 小學校 事情 事件 火車站
車票 郵政局 郵票 一分票 三分票 半分票 去信
回信 票 電報局 電報 份 打電報 來電報 去電報 上海

二十四 飯館子 旅館 電影院 片子 演電影兒 看電影兒 戲園子
看聽唱（戲） 商人 作買賣 作買賣的 書記 裁縫 回來 回去
回國 回家 來去 北平 南京

二十五 作飯的 廚子 木匠 作鞋的 鞋匠 買東西的 賣東西的 病
得病 大夫 治 醫院 辦公 職員 當 行 不行

華語入門

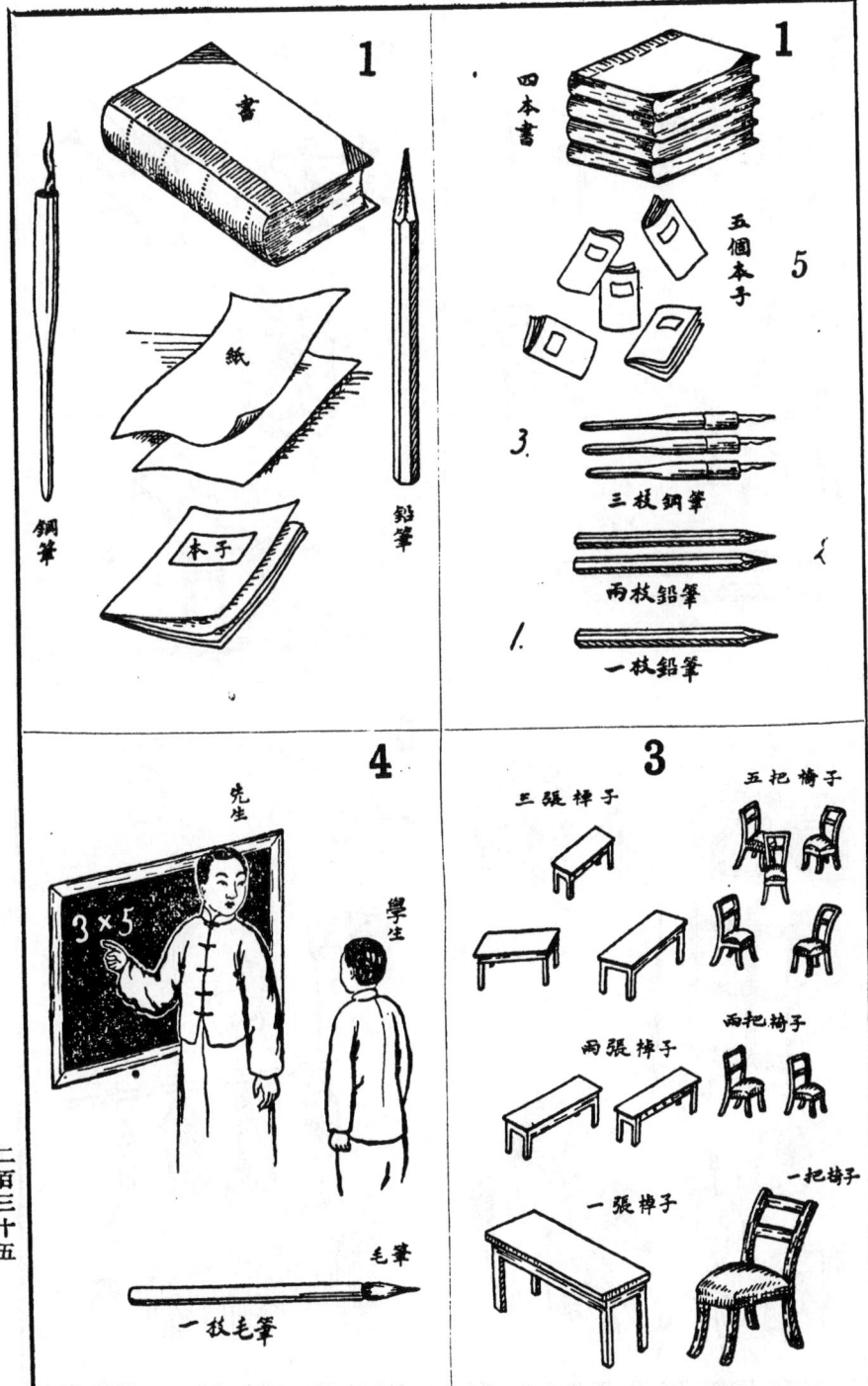

5

大 小

大 小

長
短

5

茶碗　飯碗

茶　玻璃盂

水

6

書桌子　飯桌子

父親　兒子　姑娘　母親

6

竿　一斤是十六兩　斤

羊(隻)　牛(頭)

豬(口)

魚(條)

羊肉　豬肉　牛肉　魚

二百三十六

6

1	2	3	4
10	13	18	12
20	24	27	23
30	35	36	34
40	46	45	49
50	57	54	56
60	68	63	67
70	79	72	78
80	81	84	89
90	92	95	93

6

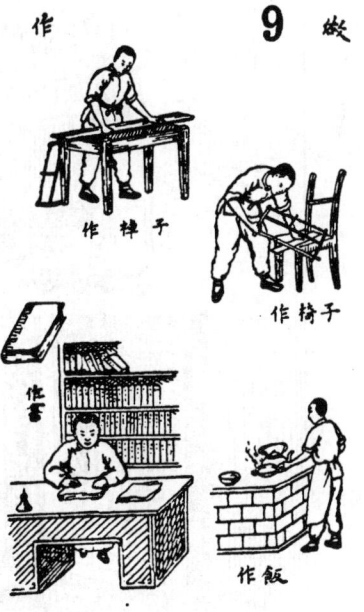

茶葉　茶　麵包　加非　作　做　作桌子　作椅子　作書　作飯

7

100	113	109	167
200	225	276	293
300	301	378	399
400	415	427	455
500	508	549	581
600	628	666	690
700	717	775	788
800	805	833	891
900	932	659	999

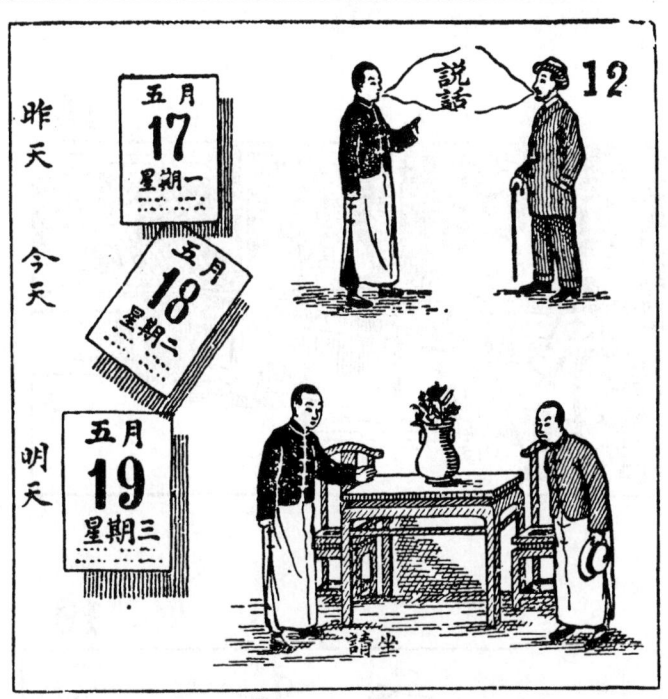

15　鋪子

19　瓶子　倒　酒盃　中國旗子　奶油　牛奶

譚話 20

（圖中文字：中國操手、中華民國、街市、黑板、先生請勿語、書、房門口、圖畫）

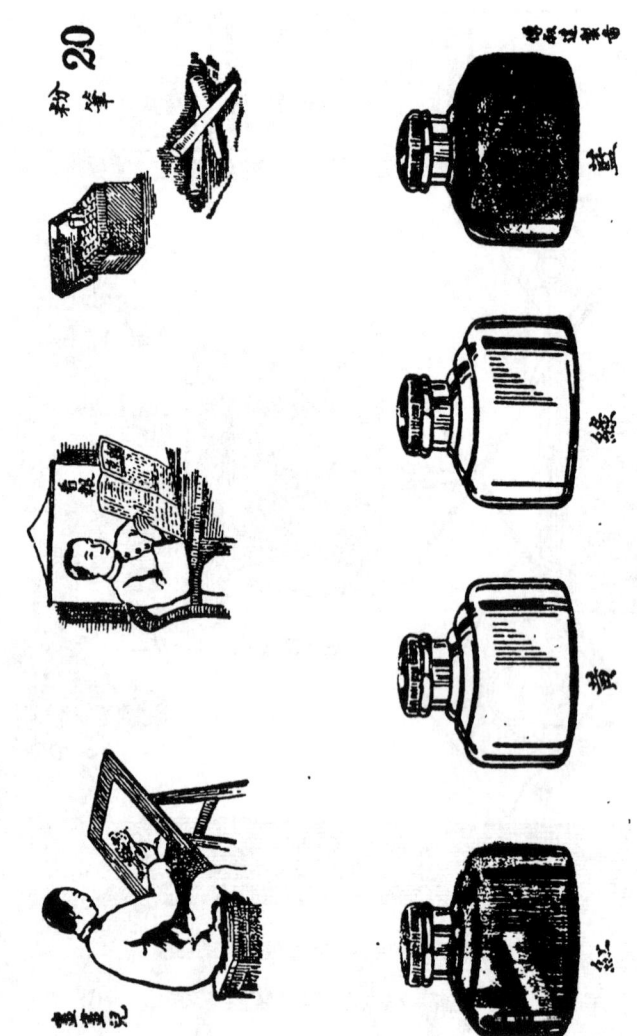

圖球地界世

亞細亞洲

太平洋

澳大利亞洲

印度洋

阿非利加洲

隆巴洲

大西洋

加拿大洲

亞美利加洲

太平洋

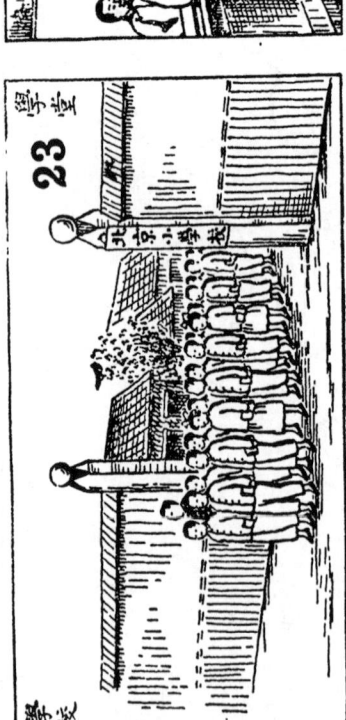

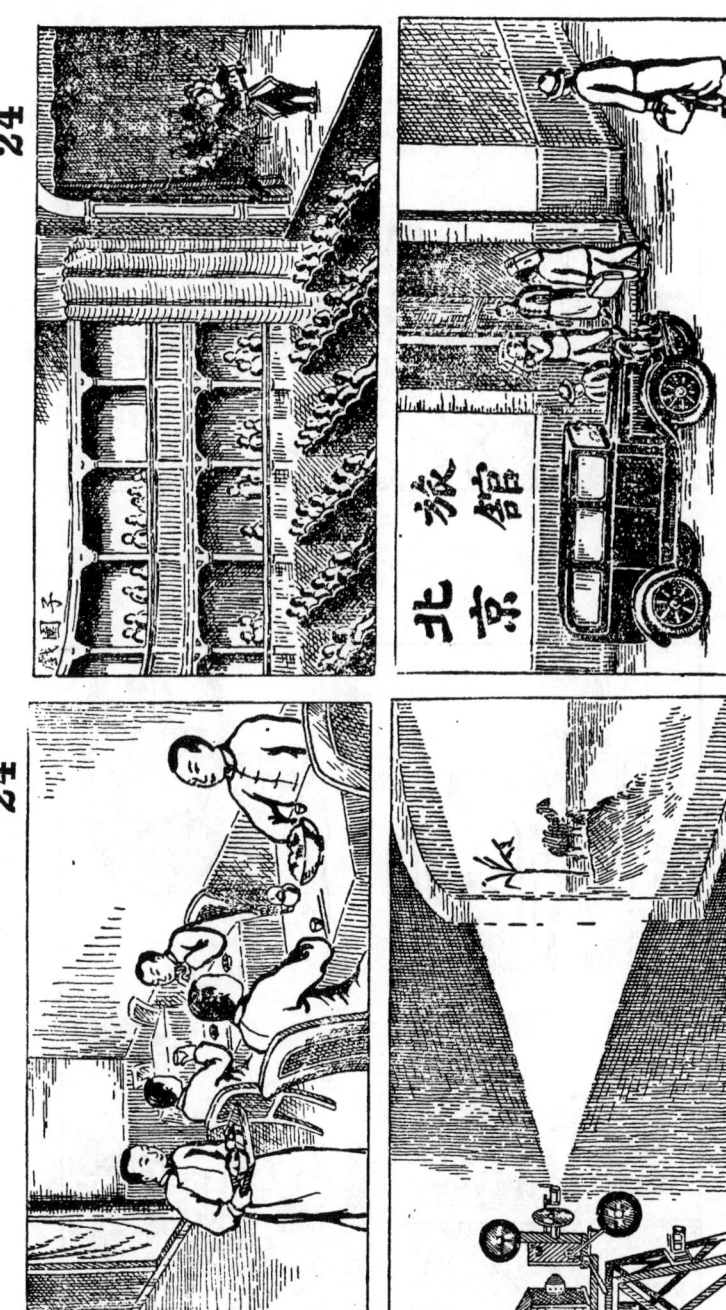

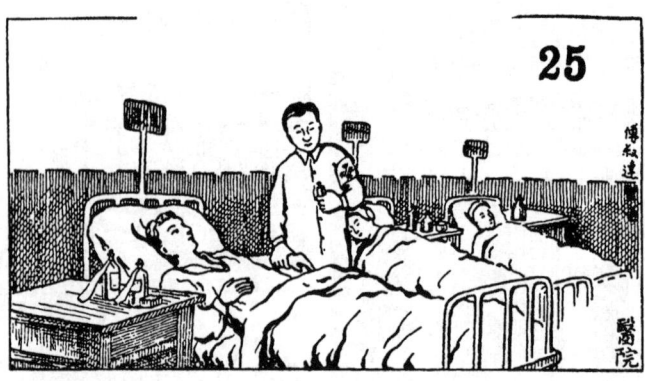
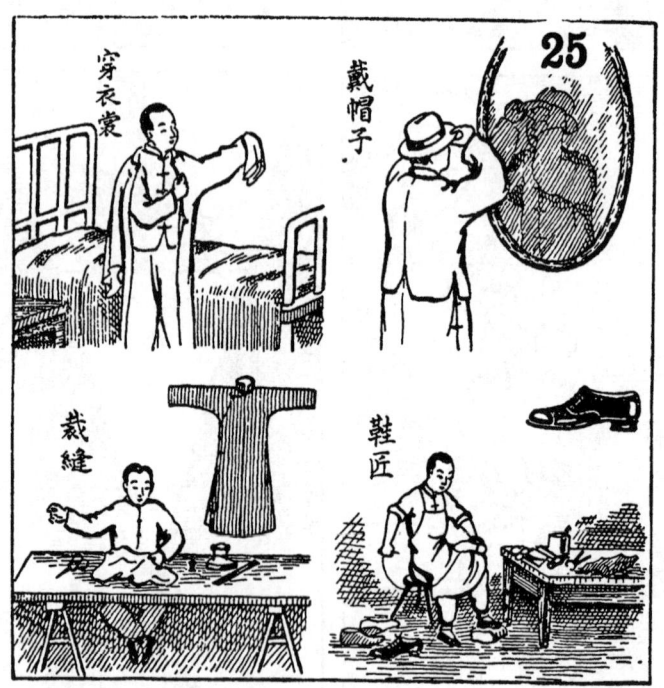

北京大学中国语言学研究中心

早期北京话珍稀文献集成
主编 刘云

西人北京话教科书汇编
分卷主编 翟赟 郭利霞 陈颖

华语入门

［俄罗斯］吴索福 著

英文版

北京大学出版社
PEKING UNIVERSITY PRESS

19世纪来华传教士记录的官话方言及其历时演变研究
（16AYY002，2016年国家社科基金重点项目）

总　序

语言是文化的重要组成部分,也是文化的载体。语言中有历史。

多元一体的中华文化,体现在我国丰富的民族文化和地域文化及其语言和方言之中。

北京是辽金元明清五代国都(辽时为陪都),千余年来,逐渐成为中华民族所公认的政治中心。北方多个少数民族文化与汉文化在这里碰撞、融合,产生出以汉文化为主体的、带有民族文化风味的特色文化。

现今的北京话是我国汉语方言和地域文化中极具特色的一支,它与辽金元明四代的北京话是否有直接继承关系还不是十分清楚。但可以肯定的是,它与清代以来旗人语言文化与汉人语言文化的彼此交融有直接关系。再往前追溯,旗人与汉人语言文化的接触与交融在入关前已经十分深刻。本丛书收集整理的这些语料直接反映了清代以来北京话、京味文化的发展变化。

早期北京话有独特的历史传承和文化底蕴,于中华文化、历史有特别的意义。

一者,这一时期的北京历经满汉双语共存、双语互协而新生出的汉语方言——北京话,她最终成为我国民族共同语(普通话)的基础方言。这一过程是中华多元一体文化自然形成的诸过程之一,对于了解形成中华文化多元一体关系的具体进程有重要的价值。

二者,清代以来,北京曾历经数次重要的社会变动:清王朝的逐渐孱弱、八国联军的入侵、帝制覆灭和民国建立及其伴随的满汉关系变化、各路军阀的来来往往、日本侵略者的占领,等等。在这些不同的社会环境下,北京人的构成有无重要变化? 北京话和京味文化是否有变化? 进一步地,地域方言和文化与自身的传承性或发展性有着什么样的关系? 与社会变迁有着什么样的关系? 清代以至民国时期早期北京话的语料为研究语言文化自身传承性与社会的关系提供了很好的素材。

　　了解历史才能更好地把握未来。新中国成立后，北京不仅是全国的政治中心，而且是全国的文化和科研中心，新的北京话和京味文化或正在形成。什么是老北京京味文化的精华？如何传承这些精华？为把握新的地域文化形成的规律，为传承地域文化的精华，必须对过去的地域文化的特色及其形成过程进行细致的研究和理性的分析。而近几十年来，各种新的传媒形式不断涌现，外来西方文化和国内其他地域文化的冲击越来越强烈，北京地区人口流动日趋频繁，老北京人逐渐分散，老北京话已几近消失。清代以来各个重要历史时期早期北京话语料的保护整理和研究迫在眉睫。

　　"早期北京话珍本典籍校释与研究（暨早期北京话文献数字化工程）"是北京大学中国语言学研究中心研究成果，由"早期北京话珍稀文献集成""早期北京话数据库"和"早期北京话研究书系"三部分组成。"集成"收录从清中叶到民国末年反映早期北京话面貌的珍稀文献并对内容加以整理，"数据库"为研究者分析语料提供便利，"研究书系"是在上述文献和数据库基础上对早期北京话的集中研究，反映了当前相关研究的最新进展。

　　本丛书可以为语言学、历史学、社会学、民俗学、文化学等多方面的研究提供素材。

　　愿本丛书的出版为中华优秀文化的传承做出贡献！

王洪君、郭锐、刘云
2016年10月

"早期北京话珍稀文献集成"序

　　清民两代是北京话走向成熟的关键阶段。从汉语史的角度看，这是一个承前启后的重要时期，而成熟后的北京话又开始为当代汉民族共同语——普通话源源不断地提供着养分。蒋绍愚先生对此有着深刻的认识："特别是清初到19世纪末这一段的汉语，虽然按分期来说是属于现代汉语而不属于近代汉语，但这一段的语言（语法，尤其是词汇）和'五四'以后的语言（通常所说的'现代汉语'就是指'五四'以后的语言）还有若干不同，研究这一段语言对于研究近代汉语是如何发展到'五四'以后的语言是很有价值的。"（《近代汉语研究概要》，北京大学出版社，2005年）然而国内的早期北京话研究并不尽如人意，在重视程度和材料发掘力度上都要落后于日本同行。自1876年至1945年间，日本汉语教学的目的语转向当时的北京话，因此留下了大批的北京话教材，这为其早期北京话研究提供了材料支撑。作为日本北京话研究的奠基者，太田辰夫先生非常重视新语料的发掘，很早就利用了《小额》《北京》等京味儿小说材料。这种治学理念得到了很好的传承，之后，日本陆续影印出版了《中国语学资料丛刊》《中国语教本类集成》《清民语料》等资料汇编，给研究带来了便利。

　　新材料的发掘是学术研究的源头活水。陈寅恪《〈敦煌劫余录〉序》有云："一时代之学术，必有其新材料与新问题。取用此材料，以研求问题，则为此时代学术之新潮流。"我们的研究要想取得突破，必须打破材料桎梏。在具体思路上，一方面要拓展视野，关注"异族之故书"，深度利用好朝鲜、日本、泰西诸国作者所主导编纂的早期北京话教本；另一方面，更要利用本土优势，在"吾国之旧籍"中深入挖掘，官话正音教本、满汉合璧教本、京味儿小说、曲艺剧本等新类型语料大有文章可做。在明确了思路之后，我们从2004年开始了前期的准备工作，在北京大学中国语言学研究中心的大力支持下，早期北京话的挖掘整理工作于2007年正式启动。本次推出的"早期北京话珍稀文献集成"是阶段性成果之一，总体设计上"取异族之故书与吾国之旧籍互相补正"，共分"日本北京话教科书汇编""朝鲜日据时期汉语会话书汇编""西人北京话教科书汇编""清代满汉合璧文献萃编""清代官话正音文献""十全福""清末民初京味儿小说书系""清末民初京味儿时评书系"八个系列，胪列如下：

"日本北京话教科书汇编"于日本早期北京话会话书、综合教科书、改编读物和风俗纪闻读物中精选出《燕京妇语》《四声联珠》《华语跬步》《官话指南》《改订官话指南》《亚细亚言语集》《京华事略》《北京纪闻》《北京风土编》《北京风俗问答》《北京事情》《伊苏普喻言》《搜奇新编》《今古奇观》等二十余部作品。这些教材是日本早期北京话教学活动的缩影，也是研究早期北京方言、民俗、史地问题的宝贵资料。本系列的编纂得到了日本学界的大力帮助。冰野善宽、内田庆市、太田斋、鳟泽彰夫诸先生在书影拍摄方面给予了诸多帮助。书中日语例言、日语小引的翻译得到了竹越孝先生的悉心指导，在此深表谢忱。

"朝鲜日据时期汉语会话书汇编"由韩国著名汉学家朴在渊教授和金雅瑛博士校注，收入《改正增补汉语独学》《修正独习汉语指南》《高等官话华语精选》《官话华语教范》《速修汉语自通》《速修汉语大成》《无先生速修中国语自通》《官话标准：短期速修中国语自通》《中语大全》《"内鲜满"最速成中国语自通》等十余部日据时期（1910年至1945年）朝鲜教材。这批教材既是对《老乞大》《朴通事》的传承，又深受日本早期北京话教学活动的影响。在中韩语言史、文化史研究中，日据时期是近现代过渡的重要时期，这些资料具有多方面的研究价值。

"西人北京话教科书汇编"收录了《语言自迩集》《官话类编》等十余部西人主编教材。这些西方作者多受过语言学训练，他们用印欧语的眼光考量汉语，解释汉语语法现象，设计记音符号系统，对早期北京话语音、词汇、语法面貌的描写要比本土文献更为精准。感谢郭锐老师提供了《官话类编》《北京话语音读本》和《汉语口语初级读本》的底本，《寻津录》、《语言自迩集》（第一版、第二版）、《汉英北京官话词汇》、《华语入门》等底本由北京大学图书馆特藏部提供,谨致谢忱。《华英文义津逮》《言语声片》为笔者从海外购回,其中最为珍贵的是老舍先生在伦敦东方学院执教期间,与英国学者共同编写的教材——《言语声片》。教材共分两卷:第一卷为英文卷,用英语讲授汉语,用音标标注课文的读音;第二卷为汉字卷。《言语声片》采用先用英语导入,再学习汉字的教学方法讲授汉语口语,是世界上第一部有声汉语教材。书中汉字均由老舍先生亲笔书写,全书由老舍先生录音,共十六张唱片,京韵十足,殊为珍贵。

上述三类"异族之故书"经江蓝生、张卫东、汪维辉、张美兰、李无未、王顺洪、张西平、鲁健骥、王澧华诸先生介绍,已经进入学界视野,对北京话研究和对外汉语教学史研究产生了很大的推动作用。我们希望将更多的域外经典北京话教本引入进来,考虑到日本卷和朝鲜卷中很多抄本字迹潦草,难以辨认,而刻本、印本中也存在着大量的异体字和俗字,重排点校注释的出版形式更利于研究者利用,这也是前文"深度利用"的含义所在。

对"吾国之旧籍"挖掘整理的成果,则体现在下面五个系列中:

"清代满汉合璧文献萃编"收入《清文启蒙》《清话问答四十条》《清文指要》《续编兼汉清文指要》《庸言知旨》《满汉成语对待》《清文接字》《重刻清文虚字指南编》等十余部经典满汉合璧文献。入关以后,在汉语这一强势语言的影响下,熟习满语的满人越来越少,故雍正以降,出现了一批用当时的北京话注释翻译的满语会话书和语法书。这批教科书的目的本是教授旗人学习满语,却无意中成为了早期北京话的珍贵记录。"清代满汉合璧文献萃编"首次对这批文献进行了大规模整理,不仅对北京话溯源和满汉语言接触研究具有重要意义,也将为满语研究和满语教学创造极大便利。由于底本多为善本古籍,研究者不易见到,在北京大学图书馆古籍部和日本神户外国语大学竹越孝教授的大力协助下,"萃编"将以重排点校加影印的形式出版。

"清代官话正音文献"收入《正音撮要》(高静亭著)和《正音咀华》(莎彝尊著)两种代表著作。雍正六年(1728),雍正谕令福建、广东两省推行官话,福建为此还专门设立了正音书馆。这一"正音"运动的直接影响就是以《正音撮要》和《正音咀华》为代表的一批官话正音教材的问世。这些书的作者或为旗人,或寓居京城多年,书中保留着大量北京话词汇和口语材料,具有极高的研究价值。沈国威先生和侯兴泉先生对底本搜集助力良多,特此致谢。

《十全福》是北京大学图书馆藏《程砚秋玉霜簃戏曲珍本》之一种,为同治元年陈金雀抄本。陈晓博士发现该传奇虽为昆腔戏,念白却多为京话,较为罕见。

以上三个系列均为古籍,且不乏善本,研究者不容易接触到,因此我们提供了影印全文。

总体来说,由于言文不一,清代的本土北京话语料数量较少。而到了清末民初,风气渐开,情况有了很大变化。彭翼仲、文实权、蔡友梅等一批北京爱国知识分子通过开办白话报来"开启民智""改良社会"。著名爱国报人彭翼仲在《京话日报》的发刊词中这样写道:"本报为输进文明、改良风俗,以开通社会多数人之智识为宗旨。故通幅概用京话,以浅显之笔,达朴实之理,纪紧要之事,务令雅俗共赏,妇稚咸宜。"在当时北京白话报刊的诸多栏目中,最受市民欢迎的当属京味儿小说连载和《益世余谭》之类的评论栏目,语言极为地道。

"清末民初京味儿小说书系"首次对以蔡友梅、冷佛、徐剑胆、儒丐、勋锐为代表的晚清民国京味儿作家群及作品进行系统挖掘和整理,从千余部京味儿小说中萃取代表作家的代表作品,并加以点校注释。该作家群活跃于清末民初,以报纸为阵地,以小说为工具,开展了一场轰轰烈烈的底层启蒙运动,为新文化运动的兴起打下了一定的群众基础,他们的作品对老舍等京味儿小说大家的创作产生了积极影响。本系列的问世亦将为文学史和思想史研究提供议题。于润琦、方梅、陈清茹、雷晓彤诸先生为本系列提供了部分底本或馆藏线索,首都图书馆历史文献阅览室、天津图书馆、国家图书馆提供了极大便利,谨致谢意!

"清末民初京味儿时评书系"则收入《益世余谭》和《益世余墨》,均系著名京味儿小说家蔡友梅在民初报章上发表的专栏时评,由日本岐阜圣德学园大学刘一之教授、矢野贺子教授校注。

这一时期存世的报载北京话语料口语化程度高,且总量庞大,但发掘和整理却殊为不易,称得上"珍稀"二字。一方面,由于报载小说等栏目的流行,外地作者也加入了京味儿小说创作行列,五花八门的笔名背后还需考证作者是否为京籍，以蔡友梅为例，其真名为蔡松龄，查明的笔名还有损、损公、退化、亦我、梅蒐、老梅、今睿等。另一方面，这些作者的作品多为急就章，文字错讹很多，并且鲜有单行本存世，老报纸残损老化的情况日益严重，整理的难度可想而知。

上述八个系列在某种程度上填补了相关领域的空白。由于各个系列在内容、体例、出版年代和出版形式上都存在较大的差异，我们在整理时借鉴《朝鲜时代汉语教科书丛刊续编》《〈清文指要〉汇校与语言研究》等语言类古籍的整理体例，结合各个系列自身特点和读者需求，灵活制定体例。"清末民初京味儿小说书系"和"清末民初京味儿时评书系"年代较近，读者群体更为广泛，经过多方调研和反复讨论，我们决定在整理时使用简体横排的形式，尽可能同时满足专业研究者和普通读者的需求。"清代满汉合璧文献萃编""清代官话正音文献"等系列整理时则采用繁体。"早期北京话珍稀文献集成"总计六十余册，总字数近千万字，称得上是工程浩大，由于我们能力有限，体例和校注中难免会有疏漏，加之受客观条件所限，一些拟定的重要书目本次无法收入，还望读者多多谅解。

"早期北京话珍稀文献集成"可以说是中日韩三国学者通力合作的结晶，得到了方方面面的帮助，我们还要感谢陆俭明、马真、蒋绍愚、江蓝生、崔希亮、方梅、张美兰、陈前瑞、赵日新、陈跃红、徐大军、张世方、李明、邓如冰、王强、陈保新诸先生的大力支持，感谢北京大学图书馆的协助以及萧群书记的热心协调。"集成"的编纂队伍以青年学者为主，经验不足，两位丛书总主编倾注了大量心血。王洪君老师不仅在经费和资料上提供保障，还积极扶掖新进，"我们搭台，你们年轻人唱戏"的话语令人倍感温暖和鼓舞。郭锐老师在经费和人员上也予以了大力支持，不仅对体例制定、底本选定等具体工作进行了细致指导，还无私地将自己发现的新材料和新课题与大家分享，令人钦佩。"集成"能够顺利出版还要特别感谢国家出版基金规划管理办公室的支持以及北京大学出版社王明舟社长、张凤珠副总编的精心策划，感谢汉语编辑室杜若明、邓晓霞、张弘泓、宋立文等老师所付出的辛劳。需要感谢的师友还有很多，在此一并致以诚挚的谢意。

"上穷碧落下黄泉，动手动脚找东西"，我们不奢望引领"时代学术之新潮流",惟愿能给研究者带来一些便利,免去一些奔波之苦,这也是我们向所有关心帮助过"早期北京话珍稀文献集成"的人士致以的最诚挚的谢意。

刘 云
2015年6月23日
于对外经贸大学求索楼
2016年4月19日
改定于润泽公馆

A COURSE OF
COLLOQUIAL CHINESE

BY

S. N. USOFF

HENRI VETCH
PEKING 1937

USOFF'S COLLOQUIAL CHINESE

A COURSE OF COLLOQUIAL CHINESE

BY

S. N. USOFF

Assistant Professor of the Harbin Law Faculty

BOOK I — ENGLISH EDITION

Adapted from the Sixth Russian Edition
of *Kitaiskii Razgavornii Yazik*,
in collaboration with

C. TYRWHITT

(Provisional Issue)

HENRI VETCH
PEKING 1937

Copyright by HENRI VETCH, Peking 1937

中 國 印
Printed in China
By the IMPRIMERIE DES LAZARISTES. Peking.
北京西什庫遣使會印字館印

TABLE OF CONTENTS

Preface	vii
Author's Note	viii
Hints to the Student on How to read the Text	ix
Wade Romanization System	xii

LESSON	page	LESSON	page
1	1	14	143
2	8	15	155
3	15	16	167
4	24	17	176
5	32	18	187
6	46	19	200
7	55	20	211
8	68	21	224
9	80	22	237
10	92	23	246
11	105	24	258
12	118	25	271
13	129		

EXERCISES FOR REVISION

I.	The Family (i)	282
II.	Shopping (i)	284
III.	Clothes	286
IV.	The Restaurant (i)	289
V.	The House	292
VI.	At School (i)	294
VII.	At School (ii)	297

VIII.	The Family (ii)	299
IX.	Shopping (ii)	302
X.	The Post Office	304
XI.	The Telegraph Office	306
XII.	The Cinema	308
XIII.	The Hospital	310
XIV.	The Restaurant (ii)	312
XV.	The Hotel	314
XVI.	Tradesmen	316
Index to Notes		319
Romanization Index		322
English Index		337
Tone Table		354

PREFACE

The present volume is the first of a series of four books, originally published in Russian for the use of Russian students of the Chinese language.

This textbook, which is intended for the beginner, is based on what is known as the "direct" method of theaching, i. e. an attempt is made to place before the student the Chinese language *in Chinese,* as far as possible.

The bases upon which the method has been constructed are as follows :

(a) It is assumed that a Chinese teacher is essential. He should speak Chinese only. This should not complicate matters as the English volume consists of both romanized and translated texts of each lesson, in addition to grammatical notes.

(b) The lessons are conversational in character in order that the simpler colloquial constructions may be grasped at an early stage.

(c) Notes on grammer will be found at the end of each lesson. These are so arranged that the student is introduced to the grammatical features of the language gradually, and is at the same time spared all unnecessary details.

(d) The complete course aims to take the student from the first stages of elementary conversation as far as the final lessons of Book Four on economics, politics and law.

(e) It will be found that even though the student may have no knowledge of Chinese, he will be able to prepare the lessons by himself. By virtue of methodical and constant repetition of the material learnt, however, any revision by the student should be unnecessary.

AUTHOR'S NOTE

This book being the first of my publications to appear in the English language, I feel that I should perhaps give the student a few details as to its origin. The material of the whole course, which will consist of four books, has been selected from the twenty-four books which comprised my « Colloquial Chinese » *(Kitaiskii Razgavornii Yazik)*, published in the Russian language by Messrs Tchurin and Company, Harbin, now in its sixth edition.

I take this opportunity to thank Mr. C. Tyrwhitt, who has done much of the work of translating and proof correcting and who is in fact largely responsible for the publication of the present version in its English form. I should also like to express my gratitude to Mr. Ho Hua-ch'ien 何化黔, who has assisted in the correction of the Chinese text and proofs, and finally to Mr. C. Crowe for his help in connection with the English proofs.

Since this edition is a provisional issue of a limited number of copies, any suggestions or criticisms would be very welcome.

SERGE N. USOFF
Peiping, October 1937.

HINTS

TO THE STUDENT ON HOW TO READ THE TEXT

Assuming that the student has obtained the services of a Chinese teacher, and preferably one who understands no English, I would suggest that he proceed on the following lines :

1. The student should prepare the lesson beforehand. This should be done by merely reading over the romanized text of the lesson in conjunction with the English translation. When he has accustomed himself to the romanization he should attempt to translate from Chinese into English, covering over the English text. Finally, after he has read through the grammatical notes for the lesson, he should attempt to *write* the romanized text, thus translating unseen from English into Chinese. No attempt should be made to do any of this preparation out loud, as by doing so the student is liable to make his own pronunciation fit the romanizations, which at best are only approximate.

2. It is suggested that the lesson now be conducted on the following lines :

   (a) The teacher reads out the introductory characters and phrases, slowly and distinctly.

   (b) The teacher then indicates by gestures that the student repeat them after him, correcting his pronunciation as necessary.

   (c) The teacher now turns to the illustrations at the end of the Chinese volume and points to the objects in the lesson, so that the student may again repeat them by name.

(d) The teacher then reads the text of the lesson from the Chinese volume, the student following the romanized text.

(e) The student now reads the romanized text out loud in unison with the teacher.

(f) Finally the student reads the romanized text out loud by himself while the teacher listens.

(g) The reading finished, the teacher questions the student and an attempt is made to discuss the material in the current and previous lessons.

(h) The last few minutes are spent in practicing tones. At the end of the English volume a table of phonetic exercises will be found. The characters shown are for the use of the teacher, who pronounces each character in each of the four tones, in the order indicated in the table. The student then repeats them with the teacher and finally he says them by himself.

(i) The next lesson should always begin with a brief revision of the previous one.

3. No attempt is made here to describe the four tones of the Mandarin Dialect as it is considered that these can only be explained by the teacher. With the help of the tone table mentioned above and with constant practice with a good teacher the tones will soon be mastered.

4. It will be noticed that some of the words in the romanized text are printed in **black type** as opposed to *italics*.

These black type words should be stressed. Provided that the tone of the stressed or accentuated word or words in the sentence is correct, the remaining words in the sentence may be regarded as toneless, in order to convey the sense intended. It should be understood however, that the accentuations as given are in many cases purely arbitrary, and a change in the arrangement of stresses in any sentence is often perfectly permissible, though the sense may be altered somewhat by doing so. There is a certain characteristic rhythm in spoken Chinese, and it is hoped that this method of accentuation will assist the student to grasp this quickly and easily.

5. It should be realized that one of the peculiarities of the Chinese language is that certain characters have more than one meaning. In order that the student may not be unduly confused at such an early stage, all the possible translations of any particular character are *not* given when that character is first introduced. As the student proceeds he will find that other meanings gradually occur for characters that he has already met. Thus his vocabulary will be built up with the minimum of effort and the maximum of usefulness.

WADE ROMANIZATION SYSTEM

Sir Thomas Wade's system of transliteration has been employed in this book for many reasons, the main one being that it is the only system of romanization which has so far attained any widespread and lasting recognition. The great majority of Chinese dictionaries use Wade and although much has been said and written against the system it is considered that it is still essential for the student of Chinese to have a working knowledge of it.

It is not possible to find exact, or in some cases even approximate equivalents in English to many of the sounds in the Chinese language, and these can only be learnt from a Chinese. The following table is merely an attempted list of approximations which may assist the student in mastering the Wade system.

It will be noticed that the following letters are not included in the system : b, d, g, q, r, v, x.

C. T.

WADE ROMANIZATION TABLE

Wade		English		
a	as	a	in	far
ai	«	ie	«	lie
ao	«	ow	«	how
ch	«	j	«	jerk
ch'	«	ch	«	chin (aspirated)
e	«	ear	«	earth and sometimes as 'e' in lens
ei	«	ay	«	say
en	«	un	«	sun
erh	«	err	«	erring
f	«	f	«	fall
h	«	ch	«	the Scottish 'loch'
hs	«	hsh		no equivalent in English. A aspirate followed by a strong sibilant
i	«	ee		in see, when by itself or as a final. Otherwise pronounced as 'i' in thing
ia	«	ya	in	yard
ieh	«	ye	«	yell
ien	«	ien	«	alien
ih	«	ir	«	bird, but there is no equivalent in English to this sound
iu	«	yeo		in yeoman and sometimes as 'yu' in yule
j	«	s		in fusion, but this is really the French 'j'
k	«	g	in	go
k'	«	k	«	key (aspirated)
l	«	l	«	low
m	«	m	«	man
n	«	n	«	not

Wade		English	
ng	as	hng	no equivalent in English. It is partly a nasal and partly a guttural
o	«	aw	in saw
ou	«	ow	« know
p	«	b	« bad
p'	«	p	« park (aspirated)
s	«	s	« son
sh	«	sh	« shop
ssu	«	ssz-ur	but it is impossible to represent this sound. A long 'ss' followed by a slight sound from the back of the throat.
t	«	d	in dear
t'	«	t	« take (aspirated)
ts	«	ds	« tweeds
ts'	«	ts	« bats (aspirated)
tz	«	ts	« jetsam
tz'	«	tz	« chintz (aspirated)
u	«	oo	« boot
ua	«	wa	« wash
uai	«	whi	« while
uei	«	way	« way
ui	«	ay	« lay, but sometimes as 'we' in week.
un	«		the German 'un'. There is no equivalent in English.
uo	«	war	in war
ü	«		the French 'u'. Here again there is no English equivalent.
w	«	w	in want, but very faint before 'u'
y	«	y	« yellow, but very faint before 'i' or 'ü'

LESSON 1

I

書 **shu¹** book(s)   紙 **chih³** paper   本子 **pen³**-*tzu¹* note-book(s)

1. *Shu¹, chih³,* **pen³**-*tzu¹*. — Book, paper, note-book.
2. *Chih³,* **pen³**-*tzu¹, shu¹*. — Paper, note-book, book.
3. **Pen³**-*tzu¹, shu¹, chih³*. — Note-book, book, paper.
4. *Chih³, shu¹,* **pen³**-*tzu¹*. — Paper, book, note-book.
5. *Shu¹,* **pen³**-*tzu¹, chih³*. — Book, note-book, paper.
6. **Pen³**-*tzu¹, chih³, shu¹*. — Note-book, paper, book.

II

我 **wo³** I, me.   您 **nin²** you (polite form).

他 **t'a¹** he, him, she, her, it   (你) **ni³** you (usual form).

1. *Wo³, nin², t'a¹.* — I, you, he.
2. *Nin², t'a¹, wo³.* — You, he, I.
3. *T'a¹, wo³, nin².* — He, I, you.
4. *Wo³, t'a¹, nin².* — I, he, you.
5. *Nin², wo³, t'a¹.* — You, I, he.
6. *T'a¹, nin², wo³.* — He, you, I.

III

有 yu³
have, has, have got, has got.

1. *Wo³ yu³* **shu¹**. — I have a book.
2. *Nin² yu³* **chih³**. — You have some paper.
3. *T'a¹ yu³* **pen³**-*tzu¹*. — He has a note-book.
4. *Wo³ yu³* **pen³**-*tzu¹*. — I have a note-book.
5. *Nin² yu³* **shu¹**. — You have a book.
6. *T'a¹ yu³* **chih³**. — He has some paper.
7. *Wo³ yu³* **chih³**. — I have some paper.
8. *Nin² yu³* **pen³**-*tzu¹*. — You have a note-book.
9. *T'a¹ yu³* **shu¹**. — He has a book.

IV

沒有 mei² yu³
have not, has not, have not got, has not got.

1. *T'a¹* **mei²** *yu³ pen³-tzu¹*.
2. *Wo³* **mei²** *yu³ shu¹*.
3. *Nin²* **mei²** *yu³ chih³*.
4. *T'a¹* **mei²** *yu³ shu¹, t'a yu³ chih³*.
5. *Nin²* **mei²** *yu³ pen³-tzu¹, nin² yu³ shu¹*.
6. *Wo³* **mei²** *yu³ chih³, wo³ yu³ pen³-tzu¹*.
7. *Nin² yu³ shu¹,* **mei²** *yu³ pen³-tzu¹*.
8. *T'a¹ yu³ chih³,* **mei²** *yu³ shu¹*.
9. *Wo³ yu³ pen³-tzu¹,* **mei²** *yu² chih³*.

1. He has not got a note-book.
2. I have not got a book.

LESSON 1

3. You have not got any paper.
4. He has not got a book, he has some paper.
5. You have not got a note-book, you have a book.
6. I have not got any paper, I have a note-book.
7. You have a book, (you) have not got a note-book.
8. He has some paper, (he) has not got a book.
9. I have a note-book, (I) have not got any paper.

V

(○ 有 ○ 沒 有?) — yu^3 — mei² yu^3?

(— have — not have ?) i. e.: have — got — or not ?

1. Wo^2 yu^3 chih³ mei² yu^3? Nin² yu³ chih³.
2. $T'a^1$ yu³ pen³-tzu¹ mei² yu³? $T'a^1$ mei² yu³ pen³-tzu¹.
3. Nin² yu³ shu¹ mei² yu³? Wo³ yu³ shu¹.
4. $T'a^1$ yu³ chih³ mei² yu³? $T'a^1$ mei² yu³ chih³, t'a¹ yu³ pen³-tzu¹.
5. Nin² yu³ pen³-tzu¹ mei² yu³? Wo³ mei² yu³ pen³-tzu¹, wo³ yu³ chih³.
6. $T'a^1$ yu³ shu¹ mei² yu³? $T'a^1$ yu³ shu¹.
7. $T'a^1$ yu³ shu¹, yu³ pen³-tzu¹ mei² yu³? $T'a^1$ yu³ shu¹ mei² yu³ pen³-tzu¹.

1. Have I got any paper or not? You have some paper.
2. Has he got a note-book or not? He has not got a note-book.
3. Have you got a book or not? I have a book.
4. Has he got any paper? He has not got any paper, he has a note-book.

5. Have you got a note-book ? I have not got a note-book, I have some paper.
6. Has he got a book ? He has a book.
7. He has a book, has (he) got a note-book or not ? He has a book, (he) has not got a note-book.

VI

鉛筆 ch'ien¹-*pi*³ pencil(s)   鋼筆 kang¹-*pi*³ pen(s)

1. *Nin*² *yu*³ ch'ien¹-*pi*³.
2. *T'a*¹ *yu*³ kang¹-*pi*³.
3. *Wo*³ mei² *yu*³ *ch'ien*¹-*pi*³, *wo*³ *yu*³ kang¹-*pi*³.
4. *Nin*² *yu*³ kang¹-*pi*¹, mei² *yu*³ *ch'ien*¹-*pi*³.
5. *T'a*¹ *yu*³ ch'ien¹-*pi*³ mei² *yu*³ ? *T'a*¹ *yu*³ *ch'ien*¹-*pi*³.
6. *Wo*³ mei² *yu*³ kang¹-*pi*³, *wo*³ *yu*³ ch'ien¹-*pi*³ mei² *yu*³? *Nin*² mei² *yu*³ kang¹-*pi*³, *nin*² *yu*³ *ch'ien*¹-*pi*³.

1. You have a pencil.
2. He has a pen.
3. I have not got a pencil, I have a pen.
4. You have a pen, (you) have not got a pencil.
5. Has he got a pencil or not ? He has a pencil.
6. I have not got a pen, have I got a pencil or not ? You have not got a pen, you have a pencil.

LESSON 1

VII

麼 ma¹?
an interrogative particle, i. e. : ?

1. *Nin² yu³* shu¹ *ma¹? Wo³ yu³* shu¹.
2. *T'a¹ yu³* pen³-*tzu¹-ma¹? T'a¹* mei² *yu³ pen³-tzu¹.*
3. *Wo³ yu³ ch'ien¹-pi³ ma¹? Nin² yu³ ch'ien¹-pi³.*
4. *T'a¹ yu³* kang¹-*pi³ ma¹? T'a¹* mei² *yu³ kang¹-pi³, t'a¹ yu³ ch'ien¹-pi³.*
5. *Nin² mei² yu³* shu¹, *nin² yu³* chih³ *ma¹? Wo³ mei² yu³* shu¹, *wo³* yu³ *chih³.*
6. *T'a¹ mei² yu³* pen³-*tzu¹ ma¹? T'a¹* mei² *yu³ pen³-tzu¹.*
7. *Nin² mei² yu³* shu¹ *ma¹? Wo³* yu³ shu¹.

1. Have you got a book? I have a book.
2. Has he got a note-book? He has not got a note-book.
3. Have I got a pencil? You have a pencil.
4. Has he got a pen? He has not got a pen, he has a pencil.
5. You have not got a book, have you got any paper? I have not got a book, I have some paper.
6. Has he not got a note-book? He has not got a note-book.
7. Have you not got a book? I have a book.

NOTES

1. Affirmative Sentence.

The sequence is : subject—verb—object.

我 有 紙 | I have paper.
wo^3 yu^3 chih^3 | (I have got some paper.)

2. Negative Sentence.

The sequence is : subject—negative—verb—object.

我 沒 有 紙 | I not have paper.
wo^3 mei^2 yu^3 chih^3 | (I have not got any paper).

3. Interrogative Sentence.

There are many forms of construction :

(a) Subject—verb—object—verb repeated with negative.

我 有 紙 沒 有 | I have paper not have ?
wo^3 yu^3 chih^3 mei^2 yu^3 ? | (Have I got any paper or not ?)
| (Have I any paper ?)

(b) The addition of the interrogative particle 麼 ma^1 ? at the end of the sentence.

我 有 紙 麼? | I have paper ?
wo^3 yu^3 chih^3 ma^1 ? | (Have I got any paper ?)
| (Have I any paper ?)

4. The Verb is not inflected, i. e., it is used in the same form for all persons and numbers. When it is required to indicate person or number, the verb is preceded by a pronoun (or noun).

LESSON 1

Affirmative.		Negative.	
我 有 wo^3 yu^3	I have.	我 沒 有 wo^3 mei^2 yu^3	I have not.
您 有 nin^2 yu^3	You have.	您 沒 有 nin^2 mei^2 yu^3	You have not.
他 有 $t'a^1$ yu^3	He has.	他 沒 有 $t'a^1$ mei^2 yu^3	He has not.

Interrogative.

我 有 沒 有? wo^3 yu^3 mei^2 yu^3?	Have I ?
您 有 沒 有? nin^2 yu^3 mei^2 yu^3?	Have you ?
他 有 沒 有? $t'a^1$ yu^3 mei^2 yu^3?	Has he ?

5. **Personal Pronouns**: he, him, she, her, it, are all expressed by the character 他 $t'a^1$.
Recently, the following characters have also been introduced: 她 $t'a^1$—she, her; and 牠 $t'a^1$—it.
The pronunciation is the same in each case.

6. 沒 mei^2 is a negative character. Used with verbs it usually denotes the negative PAST tense. With 有 yu^3— have, however, it forms the negative PRESENT tense.

7. All the pronouns in this lesson are singular in number.

8. **Articles: the** and **a**, are not expressed in Chinese. The character 書 shu^1, for example, may be translated as: book, a book, the book, books.

LESSON 2

I

一 **i¹** one 　　兩 **liang³** two 　　三 **san¹** three

四 **ssu⁴** four 　　五 **wu³** five

1. *I¹, liang³, san¹, ssu⁴, wu³.*
2. *Ssu⁴, san¹, wu³, liang³, i¹.*
3. *San¹, wu³, i¹, ssu⁴, liang³.*
4. *Wu³, san¹, i¹, liang³, ssu⁴.*
5. *Liang³, ssu⁴, i¹, wu³, san¹.*

1. One, two, three, four, five.
2. Four, three, five, two, one.
3. Three, five, one, four, two.
4. Five, three, one, two, four.
5. Two, four, one, five, three.

II

個 **ke⁴** general classifier　　(本子) **pen³-*tzu*¹** note-book(s)

1. *I¹* **ke⁴** *pen³-tzu¹.*
2. *San¹* **ke⁴** *pen³-tzu¹.*
3. *Nin² yu³* **ssu⁴ ke⁴** *pen³-tzu¹.*
4. *T'a¹ yu³* **wu³ ke⁴** *pen³-tzu¹.*

LESSON 2

5. *Wo³ yu³ liang³ ke⁴ pen³-tzu¹*, **mei²** *yu³ san¹ ke⁴ pen³-tzu¹*.
6. *Nin² yu³* **ssu⁴** *ke⁴ pen³-tzu¹ ma¹?*
   Wo³ mei² yu³ ssu⁴ ke⁴ pen³-tzu¹, wo³ yu³ liang³ ke⁴ pen³-tzu¹.

1. One note-book.
2. Three note-books.
3. You have four note-books.
4. He has five note-books.
5. I have two note-books, (I) have not got three note-books.
6. Have you got four note-books?
   I have not got four note-books, I have two note-books.

III

張 **chang¹** classifier for paper, tables, banknotes, documents, skins, tickets.

(紙) **chih³** paper

1. *Liang³ chang¹ chih³.*
2. **Wu³** *chang¹ chih³.*
3. *Nin² yu³ i⁴ chang¹ chih³.*
4. *Wo³ yu³ san¹ chang¹ chih³.*
5. *T'a¹ mei² yu³ ssu⁴ chang¹ chih³, t'a¹ yu³ i⁴ chang¹ chih³.*
6. *Nin² yu³* **wu³** *chang¹ chih³ ma¹? Wo³ yu³ wu³ chang¹ chih³.*
7. *Wo³ mei² yu³ san¹ chang¹ chih³ ma¹?*
   Nin² mei² yu³ san¹ chang¹ chih³, **t'a¹** *yu³ san¹ chang¹ chih³.*

1. Two sheets of paper.
2. Five sheets of paper.
3. You have one sheet of paper.
4. I have three sheets of paper.
5. He has not got four sheets of paper, he has one sheet of paper.
6. Have you five sheets of paper ? I have five sheets of paper.
7. Have I not got three sheets of paper ?
   You have not got three sheets of paper, he has three sheets of paper.

IV

本 pen³ classifier for books   (書) shu¹ book(s)

1. Ssu⁴ pen³ shu¹.   2. Wu³ pen³ shu¹.
3. Wo³ yu³ I⁴ pen³ shu¹.   4. T'a¹ yu³ san¹ pen³ shu¹.
5. Nin² yu³ liang³ pen³ shu¹, mei² yu³ wu³ pen³ shu¹.
6. Wo³ yu³ I⁴ pen³ shu¹ ma¹ ? Nin² yu³ i⁴ pen³ shu¹.
7. T'a¹ mei² yu³ san¹ pen³ shu¹ ma¹ ?
   T'a¹ mei³ yu³ san¹ pen³ shu¹, t'a¹ yu³ I⁴ liang³ pen³ shu¹.

1. Four books.   2. Five books.
3. I have one book.   4. He has three books.
5. You have two books, (you) have not got five books
6. Have I one book ? You have one book.
7. Has he not got three books ?
   He has not got three books, he has one (or) two books.

LESSON 2

V

枝 chih¹
classifier for pens, flowers and other long things.

(鋼筆) kang¹-*pi*³ pen(s)   (鉛筆) ch'ien¹-*pi*³ pencil(s)

1. I⁴ chih¹ *kang*¹-*pi*³
2. Liang³ chih¹ *ch'ien*¹-*pi*³.
3. *Wo*³ *yu*³ san¹ *chih*¹ *kang*¹-*pi*³
4. *T'a*¹ *yu*³ *ssu*⁴ *chih*¹ *ch'ien*¹-*pi*³.
5. *Nin*² mei² *yu*³ *wu*³ *chih*¹ *ch'ien*¹-*pi*³, *wo*³ *yu*³ *wu*³ *chih*¹ *ch'ien*¹-*pi*³.
6. *T'a*¹ *yu*³ *ssu*⁴ *chih*¹ kang¹-*pi*³ ma¹ ?
   *T'a*¹ *mei*² *yu*³ *ssu*⁴ *chih*¹ *kang*¹-*pi*³, *t'a*¹ *yu*³ *san*¹ *chih*¹ *kang*¹-*pi*³.
7. *Nin*² *mei*² *yu*³ *liang*³ *san*¹ *chih*¹ ch'ien¹-*pi*³ ma¹ ?
   *Wo*³ *yu*³ *liang*³ *san*¹ *chih*¹ *ch'ien*¹-*pi*³.

1. One pen.
2. Two pencils.
3. I have three pens.
4. He has four pencils.
5. You have not got five pencils, I have five pencils.
6. Has he four pens ?
   He has not got four pens, he has three pens.
7. Have you not got two (or) three pencils ?
   I have two (or) three pencils.

VI

幾? chi³?
how many? how much?

1. Chi³ ke⁴ pen³-tzu¹? I² ke⁴ pen³-tzu¹.
2. Chi³ chang¹ chih³? Liang³ chang¹ chih³.
3. Wo³ yu³ chi³ pen³ s'hu¹? Nin² yu³ ssu⁴ wu³ pen³ shu¹.
4. T'a¹ yu³ chi³ chih¹ ch'ien¹-pi³? T'a¹ yu³ san¹ chih¹ ch'ien¹-pi³.
5. Nin² yu³ i⁴ chih¹ kang¹-pi³, t'a¹ yu³ chi³ chih¹? T'a¹ yu³ wu³ chih¹.
6. T'a¹ yu³ i⁴ pen³ shu¹, yu³ chi³ ke⁴ pen³-tzu¹? T'a¹ yu³ i⁴ pen³ shu¹, ssu⁴ ke⁴ pen³-tzu¹.
7. Nin² yu³ chi³ chang¹ chih³? Wo³ mei² yu³ chih³, wo³ yu³ pen³-tzu¹.
8. T'a¹ yu³ chi³ chih¹ ch'ien¹-pi³, chi³ chih¹ kang¹-pi³? T'a¹ yu³ wu³ chih¹ ch'ien¹-pi³, san¹ ssu⁴ chih¹ kang¹-pi³.

1. How many note-books? One note-book.
2. How many sheets of paper? Two sheets of paper.
3. How many books have I? You have four (or) five books.
4. How many pencils has he? He has three pencils.
5. You have one pen; how many has he? He has five.
6. He has one book, how many note-books has he? He has one book (and) four note-books.
7. How many sheets of paper have you? I have no paper, I have a note-book.

LESSON 2

8. How many pencils (and) how many pens has he?
He has five pencils (and) three (or) four pens.

NOTES

9. **Interrogative Sentence,** Also formed by introduction of the character 幾? *chi³?* — how many? how much?
10. **Classifiers** are peculiar to the Chinese language. Nearest equivalent is the word 'piece', but this is usually omitted in English.

   (a) To denote a definite quantity of things, the appropriate classifier (or numerator) is always inserted between numeral and noun.

   一 個 本 子 | one piece note-book
   I² ke⁴ pen³-tzu¹ | (one note-book)

   兩 張 紙 | two pieces paper
   liang³ chang¹ chih³ | (two sheets of paper)

   三 本 書 | three pieces books
   san¹ pen³ shu¹ | (three books)

   四 枝 鉛 筆 | four pieces pencils
   ssu⁴ chih¹ ch'ien¹-pi³ | (four pencils)

   五 枝 鋼 筆 | five pieces pens
   wu³ chih¹ kang¹-pi³ | (five pens)

   (b) When answering an interrogation, the classifier is often used by itself, to represent the noun.

您 有 幾 個 本 子？ You have how many pieces note-books?
*nin*² *yu*³ **chi**³ *ke*⁴ *pen*³-*tzu*¹ ? (How many note-books have you?)

我 有 兩 個 I have two pieces
*wo*² *yu*³ **liang**³ *ke*⁴ (I have two)

您 有 幾 張 紙？ You have how many pieces paper?
*nin*² *yu*³ **chi**³ *chang*¹ *chih*³ ? (How many sheets of paper have you?)

我 有 四 張 I have four pieces
*wo*² *yu*³ **ssu**⁴ *chang*¹ (I have four sheets)

LESSON 3

I

這	che⁴ this, these	那	na⁴ that, those
是	shih⁴ is, are	不	pu⁴ ⁽²⁾ no, not

(這是) che⁴ shih⁴ this is, these are

(那是) na⁴ shih⁴ that is, those are

(這不是) che⁴ pu² shih⁴ this is not, these are not

(那不是) na⁴ pu² shih⁴ that is not, those are not

1. *Che⁴ shih⁴* **shu¹**.
2. *Na⁴ shih⁴* **chih³**.
3. *Che⁴ shih⁴* **san¹** *ke⁴ pen³-tzu¹*.
4. *Na⁴ shih⁴* **wu³** *ke⁴ pen³-tzu¹*.
5. *Che⁴ pu² shih⁴ kang¹-pi³, na⁴ shih⁴ kang¹-pi³*.
6. *Na⁴ pu² shih⁴ ssu⁴ pen³ shu¹, na⁴ shih⁴* **liang³** *pen³ shu⁴*.
7. *Che⁴ shih⁴ pen³-tzu¹, pu² shih⁴ chih³*.
8. *Na⁴ shih⁴ i⁴ pen³ shu¹, pu² shih⁴ san¹ pen³ shu¹*.

1. This is a book.
2. That is paper.

3. These are three note-books.
4. Those are five note-books.
5. This is not a pen, that is a pen.
6. Those are not four books, those are two books.
7. That is a note-book, not paper.
8. That is one book, not three books.

II

是 shih⁴ yes   不是 pu² shih⁴ no

1. Che⁴ shih⁴ ch'ien¹-pi³ ma¹? Shih⁴, che⁴ shih⁴ ch'ien¹-pi³.
2. Che⁴ shih⁴ chih³ ma¹? Pu² shih⁴, che⁴ shih⁴ pen³-tzu¹.
3. Na⁴ shih⁴ pen³-tzu¹ ma¹? Na⁴ pu² shih⁴ pen³-tzu¹, che⁴ shih⁴ pen³-tzu¹.
4. Che⁴ pu² shih⁴ kang¹-pi³ ma¹? Shih⁴, che⁴ pu² shih⁴, kang¹-pi³.
5. Na⁴ pu² shih⁴ shu¹ ma¹? Pu² shih⁴, na⁴ pu² shih⁴ shu¹, che⁴ shih⁴ shu¹.
6. Na⁴ pu² shih⁴ kang¹-pi³ ma¹? Pu² shih⁴, na⁴ shih⁴ ch'ien¹-pi³.

1. Is this a pencil? Yes, this is a pencil.
2. Is this paper? No, this is a note-book.
3. Is that a note-book? That is not a note-book, this is a note-book.
4. Isn't this a pen? (No), this is not a pen.
5. Isn't that a book? No, that is not a book, this is a book.
6. Isn't that a pen? No, that is a pencil.

LESSON 3

III

(這是〇不是) *che⁴* **shih⁴** — *pu² shih⁴?*
(this is — not is?) i. e. : this is — isn't it?

(那是〇不是) *na⁴* **shih⁴** — *pu² shih⁴?*
(that is — not is?) i. e. : that is—isn't it?

1. *Che⁴* **shih⁴** *chih³ pu² shih⁴?* *Che⁴* **shih⁴** *chih³.*
2. *Na⁴* **shih⁴** **kang¹**-*pi³ pu² shih⁴?*
   Na⁴ pu² shih⁴ **kang¹**-*pi³, na⁴* **shih⁴** **ch'ien¹**-*pi³.*
3. *Che⁴* **shih⁴** **shu¹** *pu² shih⁴?* **Shih⁴**, *che⁴* **shih⁴** **shu¹**.
4. *Na⁴* **shih⁴** **pen³**-*tzu¹ pu² shih⁴?*
   Pu² shih⁴, na⁴ **shih⁴** **chih³**.

1. This is paper, isn't it? This is paper.
2. That is a pen, isn't it? That isn't a pen, that is a pencil.
3. This is a book, isn't it? Yes, this is a book.
4. That is a note-book, isn't it? No, that is paper.

IV

(這是幾〇〇) *che⁴* **shih⁴** **chi³** — —?
(these are how many— ?) i. e. : how many—are there here?

(那是幾〇〇) *na⁴* **shih⁴** **chi³** — —?
(those are how many—?) i. e. : how many—are there there?

1. *Che⁴ shih⁴* **chi³** *chih¹ kang¹-pi³* ?
   Che⁴ shih⁴ **liang³** *chih¹ kang¹-pi³*.
2. *Na⁴ shih⁴* **chi³** *ke⁴ pen³-tzu¹* ?
   Na⁴ shih⁴ **wu³** *ke⁴ pen³-tzu¹*.
3. *Che⁴ shih⁴* **san¹** *pen³ shu¹, na⁴ shih⁴* **chi³** *pen³* ?
   Na⁴ shih⁴ **ssu⁴** *pen³*.
4. *Na⁴ shih⁴* **i⁴** *chih¹ ch'ien¹-pi³, che⁴ shih⁴* **chi³** *chih¹*?
   Che⁴ shih⁴ **liang³** *chih¹*.
5. *Na⁴ shih⁴* **chi³** *ke⁴ pen³-tzu,* **chi³** *chang¹ chih³* ?
   Na⁴ shih⁴ **wu³** *ke⁴ pen³-tzu¹, ssu⁴ chang¹ chih³.*

1. How many pens are there here ?
   There are two pens here.
2. How many note-books are there there ?
   There are five note-books there.
3. There are three books here, how many are there there ?
   There are four.
4. That is one pencil, how many is this ? This is two.
5. How many note-books (and) sheets of paper are there there ? There are five note-books (and) four sheets of paper there.

V

出 yeh³
also, even

1. *Che⁴ shih⁴ shu¹, na⁴ yeh³ shih⁴ shu¹.*
2. *Wo³ yu³ pen³-tzu¹, t'a¹ yeh³ yu³ pen³-tzu¹.*
3. *Che⁴ pu² shih⁴ chih³, na⁴ yeh³ pu² shih⁴ chih³.*

LESSON 3

4. Nin² mei² yu³ kang¹-pi³, t'a¹ yeh³ mei² yu³ kang¹-pi³.
5. Na⁴ shih⁴ ch'ien¹-pi³, che⁴ yeh³ shih⁴ ch'ien¹-pi³ ma¹?
   Shih⁴, che⁴ yeh³ shih⁴ ch'ien¹-pi³.
6. T'a¹ yu³ pen³-tzu¹, nin² yeh³ yu³ pen³-tzu¹ ma¹?
   T'a¹ yu³ pen³-tzu¹, wo³ mei² yu³ pen³-tzu¹.
7. Che⁴ shih⁴ wu³ chang¹ chih³, na⁴ yeh³ shih¹ wu³ chang¹ chih³ ma¹?
   Pu² shih⁴, na⁴ shih⁴ ssu⁴ chang¹.
8. Wo³ yu³ i⁴ chih¹ kang¹-pi³, t'a¹ yeh³ yu³ i⁴ chih¹ ma¹?
   T'a¹ yeh³ yu³ i⁴ chih¹.
9. Na⁴ shih⁴ liang³ pen³ shu¹, che⁴ shih⁴ chi³ pen³?
   Che⁴ yeh³ shih⁴ liang³ pen³.
10. T'a¹ yu³ san¹ ke⁴ pen³-tzu¹, nin² yu³ chi³ ke⁴?
    Wo³ yeh³ yu³ san¹ ke⁴.
11. Nin² yu³ pen³-tzu¹, nin² yeh³ yu³ chih³ ma¹?
    Shih⁴ wo³ yeh³ yu³ chih³.
12. T'a¹ yu³ ch'ien¹-pi³, t'a¹ mei² yu³ kang¹-pi³ ma¹?
    T'a¹ yu³ ch'ien¹-pi³, yeh³ yu³ kang¹-pi³.

1. This is a book, that is also a book.
2. I have a note-book, he also has a note-book.
3. This is not paper, that also is not paper.
4. You have not got a pen, he also has not got a pen.
5. That is a pencil, is this also a pencil?
   Yes, this is also a pencil.
6. He has a note-book, have you also got a note-book?
   He has a note-book, I have not got a note-book.
7. There are five sheets of paper here, are there also five sheets of paper there?

No, there are four sheets there.
8. I have one pen, has he also got one ?
He also has one.
9. There are two books there, how many are there here ?
There are also two here.
10. He has three note-books, how many have you got ?
I also have three.
11. You have a note-book, have you also got some paper ?
Yes, I have some paper also.
12. He has a pencil, has he not got a pen ?
He has a pencil, (he) also has a pen.

VI

棹子 cho¹-*tzu*¹ table(s)   椅子 I³-*tzu*¹ chair(s)

1. *Wo*³ *yu*³ **cho**¹-*tzu*¹, *t'a*¹ *yu*³ I³-*tzu*¹.
2. *Na*⁴ *shih*⁴ **cho**¹-*tzu*¹, **che**⁴ **yeh**³ *shih*⁴ **cho**¹-*tzu*¹.
3. *Nin*² *yu*³ I³-*tzu*¹ *mei*² *yu*³ ?
   *Wo*³ **mei**² *yu*³ *i*³ *tzu*¹, *wo*³ *yu*³ **cho**¹-*tzu*¹.
4. *Na*⁴ *shih*⁴ I³-*tzu*¹ *pu*² *shih*⁴ ?
   *Pu*² *shih*⁴, *na*⁴ *shih*⁴ **cho**¹-*tzu*¹.
5. *T'a*¹ *yu*³ *cho*¹ *tzu*¹, **yeh**³ *yu*³ I³-*tzu*¹ *ma*¹ ?
   T'a **yeh**³ *yu*³ *i*³-*tzu*¹.

1. I have a table, he has a chair.
2. That is a table, this is also a table.
3. Have you a chair ?   I have not got a chair, I have a table.
4. That is a chair isn't it ?   No, that is a table.

LESSON 3

5. He has a table, has (he) also got a chair?
   He also has a chair.

VII

六 liu⁴ six   七 ch'i¹ ⁽²⁾ seven   八 pa¹ ⁽²⁾ eight   九 chiu³ nine
十 shih² ten   把 pa³ ⁽²⁾ classifier for chairs, knives

(〇 張棹子) — chang¹ cho¹-tzu¹
             — table(s)
(〇 把椅子) — pa² i³-tzu¹
             — chair(s)

1. Liu⁴ chang¹ chih³.
2. Ch'i² ke⁴ pen³-tzu¹.
3. Che⁴ shih⁴ pa¹ pen³ shu¹, na⁴ shih⁴ chiu³ chih¹ ch'ien¹-
   [pi³.
4. Nin² yu³ chi³ chang¹ chih³?
   Wo³ yu³ shih² chang¹ chih³.
5. T'a¹ yu³ liu⁴ chang¹ cho¹-tzu¹, nin² yu³ ch'i¹ pa² i³-tzu¹.
6. Na⁴ shih⁴ chi³ pa² i³-tzu¹? Na⁴ shih⁴ pa¹ pa² i³tzu¹.
7. Nin² yu³ shih² chang¹ cho¹-tzu¹ ma¹?
   Wo³ mei² yu³ shih² chang¹ cho¹-tzu¹, wo² yu³ chiu³
   chang¹.
8. Che⁴ shih⁴ liu⁴ pa² i³-tzu¹, na⁴ yeh³ shih⁴ liu⁴ pa² i³-
   tzu¹ ma¹?
   Pu² shih⁴, na⁴ shih⁴ pa¹ pa³.

1. Six sheets of paper.
2. Seven note-books.

3. There are eight books here, there are nine pencils there.
4. How many sheets of paper have you?
   I have ten sheets of paper.
5. He has six tables, you have seven chairs.
6. How many chairs are there there?
   There are eight chairs there.
7. Have you ten tables?
   I have not got ten tables, I have nine.
8. There are six chairs here, are there also six chairs there?
   No, there are eight there.

LESSON 3

NOTES

11. 這是 **che⁴ shih⁴** — this is, 那是 **na⁴ shih⁴** — that is. When these phrases are followed by a noun, the thing spoken of may be either singular or plural in number.

    這 是 書 | this is a book
    che⁴ shih⁴ shu¹ | these are books

12. 不 **pu⁴** is a negative character. Used with verbs it usually denotes the negative present or future tense.

13. **Negatives.** 沒 **mei²** is used to negate 有 **yu³** — have, while 不 **pu⁴** is used to negate 是 **shih⁴** — is; NEVER vice versa.

    沒 有 | have not, has not, 　　不 是 | no, is not,
    mei² yu³ | there is not 　　**pu² shih⁴** | is not so

    沒 有 書 | have not a book
    mei² yu³ shu¹ | have not got a book
    　　　　　　　 | there is not a book

    不 是 書 | not a book
    pu² shih⁴ shu¹ | is not a book

LESSON 4

I

毛筆 mao²-pi³
Chinese writing-brush(es), brush-pen(s)

(○枝毛筆) — chih¹ mao²-pi³
— writing-brush(es)

1. *Nin² yu³* **mao²-pi³** *mei² yu³?*   *Wo³* **yu³** *mao²-pi³*
2. *Nin² yu³* **chi³** *chih¹ mao²-pi³?*
   Wo³ yu³ **ch'i¹** *chih¹ mao²-pi³.*
3. *T'a¹ yeh³ yu³ mao²-pi³ ma¹?*
   Shih⁴, t'a¹ yeh³ yu³ mao²-pi³.
4. **Na⁴ shih⁴ mao²-pi³** *pu² shih⁴?*
   Pu² shih⁴, na⁴ shih⁴ ch'ien¹-pi³, che⁴ shih⁴ mao²-pi³.
5. *Che⁴ shih⁴ chi³ chih¹ mao²-pi³? Che⁴ shih⁴ pa¹ chih¹.*

1. Have you got a writing-brush? I have a writing-brush.
2. How many writing-brushes have you?
   I have seven writing-brushes.
3. Has he also got a writing-brush?
   Yes, he also has a writing-brush.
4. That is a writing-brush isn't it?
   No, that is a pencil, this is a writing-brush.
5. How many writing-brushes are there here?
   There are eight here.

LESSON 4

II

甚麼？ shen²-ma¹?
what?, what sort of?

1. Che⁴ shih⁴ shen²-ma¹? Che⁴ shih⁴ cho¹-tzu¹.
2. Na⁴ shih⁴ shen²-ma¹? Na⁴ shih⁴ i³-tzu.
3. Nin² yu³ shen²-ma? Wo³ yu³ mao²-pi³.
4. T'a¹ yu³ shen²-ma¹? T'a¹ yu³ kang¹-pi³.
5. Che⁴ shih⁴ pen³-tzu¹, na⁴ shih⁴ shen²-ma¹?
   Che⁴ shih⁴ pen³-tzu¹, na⁴ yeh³ shih⁴ pen³-tzu¹.
6. Wo³ yu³ chih³, t'a¹ yu³ shen²-ma¹? T'a¹ yu³ ch'ien¹-pi³.

1. What is this? This is a table.
2. What is that? That is a chair.
3. What have you got? I have a writing-brush.
4. What has he got? He has a pen.
5. This is a note-book, what is that?
   This is a note-book, that is also a note-book.
6. I have some paper, what has he got? He has a pencil.

III

人 jen²
man, men, person(s), people.

東西 tung¹-hsi¹
thing(s)

(○個人) 一 ke⁴ jen²
— man, (men)

(○個東西) 一 ke⁴ tung¹-hsi¹
— thing(s)

1. Che⁴ shih⁴ liu⁴ ke⁴ jen², na⁴ yeh³ shih⁴ liu⁴ ke⁴ jen².
2. Na⁴ shih⁴ chiu³ ke⁴, che⁴ shih⁴ ch'i² ke⁴.

3. Chi³ ke⁴ jen² yu³ cho¹-tzu¹?
   Shih² ke⁴ jen² yu³ cho¹-tzu¹.
4. Chi³ ke⁴ jen² yu³ i³-tzu¹? Ssu⁴ ke⁴ jen² yu³ i³-tzu¹.
5. I² ke⁴ jen² yu³ liang³ chih¹ mao²-pi³, wu³ ke⁴ jen² yu³ chi³ chih¹? Wu³ ke⁴ jen² yu³ shih² chih¹.
6. San¹ ke⁴ jen² yu³ san¹ ke⁴, liu⁴ ke⁴ jen² yu³ chi³ ke⁴? Liu⁴ ke⁴ jen² yu³ liu⁴ ke⁴.
7. Che⁴ shih⁴ shen²-ma¹ tung¹-hsi¹? Che⁴ shih⁴ shu¹.
8. Na⁴ shih⁴ shen²-ma¹ tung¹-hsi¹? Na⁴ shih⁴ pen³-tzu¹.
9. Nin² yu³ shen²-ma¹ tung¹ hsi¹? Wo³ yu³ cho¹-tzu¹.
10. T'a¹ yu³ shen²-ma¹ tung¹-hsi¹? T'a¹ yeh³ yu³ cho¹-tzu¹.
11. Na⁴ shih⁴ kang¹-pi³, che⁴ shih⁴ shen²-ma¹ tung¹-hsi¹? Na⁴ shih⁴ kang¹-pi³, che⁴ shih⁴ mao²-pi³.
12. Wo³ yu³ ch'ien¹-pi³, nin² yu³ shen²-ma¹ tung¹-hsi¹? Wo³ yu³ mao²-pi³, yu³ kang¹-pi³.

1. There are six men here, there are also six men there.
2. There are nine there, there are seven here.
3. How many people have tables?
   Ten people have tables.
4. How many people have chairs?
   Four people have chairs.
5. One person has got two writing-brushes, how many have five people got? Five people have ten.
6. Three men have three pieces, how many have six men got? Six men have six pieces.
7. What is this thing? This is a book.
8. What is that thing? That is a note-book.

LESSON 4

9. What (thing) have you got ?   I have a table.
10. What (thing) has he got ?   He also has a table.
11. That is a pen, what is this thing ?
    That is a pen, this is a writing-brush.
12. I have a pencil, what (thing) have you got ?
    I have a writing-brush (and) a pen.

IV

先生 hsien¹-sheng¹ teacher(s), Mr.

學生 hsüeh²-sheng¹ student(s), pupil(s)

位 wei⁴ classifier for persons (polite form)

1. *Wo³ shih⁴* **hsien¹-sheng¹**.
2. *T'a¹ shih⁴* **hsüeh²-sheng¹**.
3. *Na⁴ shih⁴* **liu⁴ wei⁴ hsüeh²-sheng¹**.
4. *Che⁴ shih⁴* **liang³ wei⁴ hsien¹-sheng¹**.
5. *Nin² yu³* **chi³ wei⁴ hsien¹-sheng¹** *?*
   Wo³ yu³ **i² wei⁴ hsien¹-sheng¹**.
6. *T'a¹ yu³* **chi³ wei⁴ hsüeh²-sheng¹** *?*
   T'a¹ yu³ **shih² wei⁴ hsüeh²-sheng¹**.
7. *Hsien¹-sheng¹ yu³* **shen²-ma¹ tung¹-hsi¹** *?*
   Hsien¹-sheng¹ yu³ **shu¹**, *yu³* **kang¹-pi³**.
8. *Hsüeh²-sheng¹ yu³* **shen²-ma¹ tung¹-hsi¹** *?*
   Hsüeh²-sheng¹ yu³ **mao²-pi³**, *yu³* **ch'ien¹-pi³**.
9. *T'a¹ shih⁴* **hsien¹-sheng¹** *pu² shih⁴ ?*
   Pu² shih⁴, t'a¹ shih⁴ **hsüeh²-sheng¹**.

10. *Che⁴ shih⁴* **chi³** *wei³ hsüeh²-sheng¹?*
    Na⁴ shih⁴ **pa²** *wei⁴.*

1. I am a teacher.
2. He is a pupil.
3. There are six pupils there.
4. There are two teachers here.
5. How many teachers have you ? I have one teacher.
6. How many students has he ? He has ten students.
7. What (things) has the teacher got ?
   The teacher has a book (and) a pen.
8. What has the pupil got ?
   The student has a writing-brush and a pencil.
9. He is a teacher, isn't he ? No, he is a student.
10. How many students are there here ?
    There are eight there.

V

誰? **shui?**
who ? which ?

1. **Shui²** *shih⁴ hsien¹-sheng¹?* T'a¹ *shih⁴ hsien¹-sheng¹.*
2. **Shui²** *shih⁴ hsüeh²-sheng¹?* Wo³ *shih¹ hsüeh²-sheng¹*
3. **Shui²** *yu³ hsien¹-sheng¹?* T'a¹ *yu³ hsien¹-sheng¹.*
4. **Shui²** *yu³* **liang³** *pa² i³-tzu¹?* Wo³ *yu³ liang³ pa² i³-*
5. **Shui²** *mei² yu³ chih³?* T'a¹ *mei² yu³ chih³.*   [*tzu¹.*
6. **Shui²** *yu³ cho¹-tzu¹, mei² yu³ i³-tzu¹?*
   Wo³ *yu³ cho¹-tzu¹, mei² yu³ i³-tzu¹.*

1. Who is a teacher ? He is a teacher.

LESSON 4

2. Who is a student ?   I am a student.
3. Who has a teacher ?   He has a teacher.
4. Who has two chairs ?   I have two chairs.
5. Who has not got any paper ?   He has no paper.
6. Who has a table (but) has not got a chair ?
   I have a table (but) no chair.

VI

的 ti¹
possessive particle

我的 wo³-ti¹
my, mine

你的 ni³-ti¹
your, yours (usual form)

他的 t'a¹-ti¹
his, her, hers, its

您的 nin²-ti¹
your, yours (polite form)

1. Wo³-ti¹ kang¹-pi³
2. Nin²-ti¹ pen³-tzu¹.
3. T'a¹-ti¹ hsüeh²-sheng¹.
4. Nin² shih⁴ t'a¹-ti¹ hsüeh²-sheng¹ ma¹ ?
   Wo³ shih⁴ t'a¹-ti¹ hsüeh²-sheng¹.
5. T'a¹ shih⁴ nin²-ti¹ hsien¹-sheng¹ ma¹ ?
   Pu² shih⁴, t'a¹ pu² shih⁴ wo³-ti¹ hsien¹-sheng¹.
6. Na⁴ shih⁴ wo³-ti¹ mao²-pi³ ma¹ ?
   Na⁴ shih⁴ nin²-ti¹ mao²-pi³.
7. Che⁴ pu² shih⁴ nin²-ti¹ ch'ien¹-pi³ ma¹ ?
   Na⁴ pu² shih⁴ wo³-ti¹ ch'ien¹-pi³, na⁴ shih⁴ t'a¹-ti¹ ch'ien¹-pi³.

1. My pen.
2. Your note-book.
3. His pupil.
4. Are you his pupil ?   I am his pupil.
5. Is he your teacher ?   No, he is not my teacher.
6. Is that my writing-brush ?   That is your writing-brush.
7. Isn't this your pencil ?
   That is not my pencil, that is his pencil.

VII

誰 的 ?   shui²-ti¹ ?
          whose ?

1. Che⁴ shih⁴ shui²-ti¹ cho¹-tzu¹ ?
   Na⁴ shih⁴ t'a¹-ti¹ cho¹-tzu¹.
2. Na⁴ shih⁴ shui²-ti¹ i³-tzu¹ ?   Che⁴ shih⁴ wo³-ti¹ i³-tzu¹.
3. Nin² shih⁴ shui²-ti¹ hsüeh²-sheng¹ ?
   Wo³ shih⁴ t'a¹-ti¹ hsüeh²-sheng¹.
4. T'a¹ shih⁴ shui²-ti¹ hsien¹-sheng¹ ?
   T'a¹ shih⁴ wo³-ti¹ hsien¹-sheng¹.

1. Whose table is this ?   That is his table.
2. Whose chair is that ?   This is my chair.
3. Whose pupil are you ?   I am his pupil.
4. Whose teacher is he ?   He is my teacher.

LESSON 4

NOTES

14. Possessive Pronouns are formed by the addition of the particle 的 ti¹ to the personal pronouns, as a suffix:

我 wo³ } I, me   你 ni³ } you (usual form)   您 nin² } you (polite form)

我的 wo³-ti¹ } my, mine   你的 ni³-ti¹ } your, yours   您的 nin²-ti¹ } your, yours

他 t'a¹ } he, him, she, her, it   他的 t'a¹-ti¹ } his, her, hers, its

15. Interrogative Pronoun 誰的 shui²-ti¹? — whose? is formed from 誰 shui²? — who? and the particle 的 ti¹.

LESSON 5

I

先生的 hsien¹-sheng¹-ti¹ teacher's
學生的 hsüeh²-sheng¹-ti¹ pupil's

1. *Che⁴ shih⁴* **shui²***-ti¹ shu¹?*
   Che⁴ shih⁴ **hsien¹***-sheng¹-ti¹ shu¹.*
2. *Na⁴ shih⁴* **hsüeh²***-sheng¹-ti¹ ch'ien¹-pi³ ma¹?*
   Na⁴ **shih⁴** *hsüeh²-sheng¹-ti¹ ch'ien¹-pi³*
3. *Che⁴ shih⁴* **nin²** *hsien¹-sheng¹-ti¹ cho¹-tzu¹ ma¹?*
   Shih⁴, che⁴ **shih⁴** *wo³ hsien¹-sheng¹-ti¹ cho¹-tzu¹.*
4. *Na⁴ shih⁴* **nin²** *hsüeh²-sheng¹-ti¹ mao²-pi³ ma¹?*
   Pu⁴ shih⁴, na⁴ **pu²** *shih⁴ wo³ hsüeh²-sheng¹-ti¹ mao²-pi³.*

1. Whose book is this? This is the teacher's book.
2. Is that the pupil's pencil? That is the pupil's pencil.
3. Is this your teacher's table? Yes, this is my teacher's table.
4. Is that your pupil's writing-brush? No, that is not my pupil's writing-brush.

II

這 本 書	che⁴ pen³ shu¹	this book
那 本 書	na⁴ pen³ shu¹	that book
這張桌子	che⁴ chang¹ cho¹-tzu¹	this table
那張桌子	na⁴ chang¹ cho¹-tzu¹	that table

LESSON 5

這 張 紙	che⁴ chang¹ chih³	this sheet of paper
那 張 紙	na⁴ chang¹ chih³	that sheet of paper
這 個 本子	che⁴ ke⁴ pen³-tzu¹	this note-book
那 個 本子	na⁴ ke⁴ pen³-tzu¹	that note-book
這 個 人	che⁴ ke⁴ jen²	this man
那 個 人	na⁴ ke⁴ jen²	that man
這 個 東西	che⁴ ke⁴ tung¹-hsi¹	this thing
那 個 東西	na⁴ ke⁴ tung¹-hsi¹	that thing
這 把 椅子	che⁴ pa² i³-tzu¹	this chair
那 把 椅子	na⁴ pa² i³-tzu¹	that chair
這 枝 毛筆	che⁴ chih¹ mao²-pi³	this writing-brush
那 枝 毛筆	na⁴ chih¹ mao²-pi³	that writing-brush
這 枝 鉛筆	che⁴ chih¹ ch'ien¹-pi³	this pencil
那 枝 鉛筆	na⁴ chih¹ ch'ien¹-pi³	that pencil
這 枝 鋼筆	che⁴ chih¹ kang¹-pi³	this pen
那 枝 鋼筆	na⁴ chih¹ kang¹-pi³	that pen
這 位 先生	che⁴ wei⁴ hsien¹-sheng¹	this teacher
那 位 先生	na⁴ wei⁴ hsien¹-sheng¹	that teacher
這 位 學生	che⁴ wei⁴ hsüeh²-sheng¹	this student
那 位 學生	na⁴ wei⁴ hsüeh²-sheng¹	that student

這／那 {幾 : 本, 張, 個, 枝, 位 : ○

che⁴/na⁴ {chi³ : pen³, chang¹, ke⁴, chih¹, wei⁴ : —

(this/that {several, some : —) = here are / = there are {several, some : —

1. Che⁴ pen³ shu¹ shih⁴ wo³-ti¹, na⁴ chang¹ chih³ shih⁴ t'a¹-ti¹.
2. Che⁴ pa² i³-tzu¹ shih⁴ hsien¹-sheng¹-ti¹, na⁴ chang¹ cho¹-tzu¹ shih⁴ hsüeh²-sheng¹-ti¹.

3. *Che⁴ ke⁴ pen³-tzu¹ shih⁴* **shui²**-*ti¹?*
   Che⁴ ke⁴ pen³-tzu¹ shih⁴ **na⁴** *wei⁴ hsüeh²-sheng¹-ti¹.*
4. *Che⁴ liang³ chih¹ ch'ien¹-pi³* **shih⁴** *t'a¹-ti¹ pu² shih⁴?*
   Pu² shih⁴, shih⁴ **che⁴** *wei⁴ hsien¹-sheng¹-ti¹.*
5. *Che⁴ chi³ chih¹ mao²-pi³ shih⁴* **nin²**-*ti¹ ma¹?*
   Shih⁴, che⁴ chi³ chih¹ mao²-pi³ **shih⁴** *wo³-ti¹.*
6. *Na⁴ chi³ chih¹ kang¹-pi³ yeh³ shih⁴ nin²-ti¹ ma¹?*
   Pu² shih⁴, shih⁴ **na⁴** *wei⁴ hsüeh²-sheng¹-ti¹.*
7. **Shui²** *shih⁴ nin²-ti¹ hsien¹-sheng¹?*
   Na⁴ *wei⁴ shih⁴ wo³-ti¹ hsien¹-sheng¹,*
8. *Che⁴ wei⁴ shih⁴* **shui²**? *Che⁴ wei⁴ shih⁴ t'a¹-ti¹ hsüeh²-*
   ⌊*sheng¹.*
9. *Na⁴ wei⁴ hsien¹-sheng¹ yu³* **chi³** *wei⁴ hsüeh²-sheng¹?*
   Na⁴ wei⁴ hsien¹-sheng¹ yu³ **shih²** *wei⁴ hsüeh²-sheng¹.*

1. This book is mine, that sheet of paper is his.
2. This chair is the teacher's, that table is the pupil's.
3. Whose is this note-book? This note-book is that pupil's.
4. These two pencils are his, aren't they?
   No, (they) are this teacher's.
5. Here are some writing-brushes, are they yours?
   Yes, these writing-brushes are mine.
6. There are some pens, are they also yours?
   No, (they) are that pupil's.
7. Who is your teacher?
   That is my teacher. (That person is my teacher.)
8. Who is this person?
   This is his pupil. (This person is his pupil.)

LESSON 5

9. How many pupils has that teacher got?
That teacher has ten pupils.

III

(是 ○ 是 ○ ?) shih⁴ — shih⁴ — ?
— or — ?

1. Che⁴ shih⁴ chih³ shih⁴ pen³-tzu¹? Che⁴ shih⁴ pen³-tzu¹.
2. Na⁴ wei⁴ shih⁴ hsien¹-sheng⁴ shih⁴ hsüeh²-sheng¹?
Na⁴ wei⁴ shih⁴ hsüeh²-sheng¹.
3. Che⁴ chang¹ cho¹-tzu¹ shih⁴ nin²-ti¹ shih⁴ t'a¹-ti¹?
Che⁴ chang¹ cho¹-tzu¹ shih⁴ t'a¹-ti¹.
4. Na⁴ pa² i³-tzu¹ shih⁴ hsien¹-sheng¹-ti¹ shih⁴ hsüeh²-sheng¹-ti¹?
Na⁴ pa² i³-tzu¹ pu² shih⁴ hsien¹-sheng¹-ti¹, shih⁴ hsüeh²-sheng¹-ti¹.
5. Na⁴ shih⁴ san¹ ke⁴ shih⁴ ssu⁴ ke⁴?
Na⁴ pu² shih⁴ san¹ ke⁴, yeh³ pu² shih⁴ ssu⁴ ke⁴, na⁴ shih⁴ wu³ ke⁴.

1. Is this paper or a note-book? This is a note-book.
2. Is that a teacher or a student? That is a student.
3. Is this table yours or his? This table is his.
4. Is that chair the teacher's or the student's?
That chair is not the teacher's (it) is the student's.
5. Are there three pieces or four pieces there?
There are neither three pieces nor four pieces, there are five pieces there.

IV

大 ta⁴ large, great, big, tall   小 hsiao³ small, mean, little, short

1. *Che⁴ chang⁴ cho¹-tzu¹ ta⁴, na⁴ chang¹ cho¹-tzu¹* **hsiao³**.
2. *Wo³-ti¹ shu¹* **ta⁴**, *nin²-ti¹ shu¹* **hsiao³**.
3. *Na⁴ ke⁴ pen³-tzu¹ ta⁴ hsiao³? Na⁴ ke⁴ pen³-tzu¹* **hsiao³**.
4. *Che⁴ pen³ shu¹ ta⁴ hsiao³ ? Che⁴ pen³ shu¹* **pu⁴** *hsiao³*.
5. *Hsien¹-sheng¹-ti¹ pen³-tzu¹ shih⁴* **ta⁴**-*ti¹ shih⁴* **hsiao³**-*ti¹?*
   Hsien¹-sheng¹-ti¹ pen³-tzu¹ shih⁴ **ta⁴**-*ti¹*.
6. *Shih⁴ che⁴ pen³ shu¹ ta⁴ shih⁴ na⁴ pen³ shu¹* **ta⁴** *?*
   Che⁴ *pen³ shu¹ ta⁴, na⁴ pen³ shu¹ hsiao³*.
7. *Shih⁴* **nin²**-*ti¹ hsüeh²-sheng¹ ta⁴, shih⁴ t'a¹-ti¹ hsüeh²-sheng¹ ta⁴ ?*
   Wo³-ti¹ hsüeh²-sheng¹ **mei²** *yu³ t'a¹-ti¹ hsüeh²-sheng¹ ta⁴*.
8. *Che⁴ liang³ chang¹ chih³ shih⁴* **shui²**-*ti¹*.
   Ta⁴-*ti¹ shih⁴ t'a¹-ti¹,* **hsiao³**-*ti¹ shih⁴* **wo³**-*ti¹,*
9. *Che⁴ pa² i³-tzu¹, ta⁴ pu² ta⁴ ? Che⁴ pa² i³-tzu¹ pu² ta⁴*.
10. *Na⁴ chang¹ cho¹-tzu¹.* **hsiao³** *pu⁴ hsiao³ ?*
    Na⁴ chang¹ cho¹-tzu¹ **pu²** *ta⁴ pu⁴ hsiao³*.

1. This table (is) large, that table (is) small.
2. My book (is) big, your book (is) small.
3. (Is) that note-book large (or) small ?
   That note-book (is) small.
4. (Is) this book large (or) small ?
   This book (is) not small (i. e. : is large).
5. Is the teacher's note-book large or small ?
   The teacher's note-book is large.

6. Is this book larger than that book?
   This book (is) larger than that book.
7. Who is the taller, your pupil or his pupil?
       (Is your pupil big, is his pupil big?)
   My pupil is not as tall as his pupil.
       (My pupil has not his pupil big.)
8. Whose are these two sheets of paper?
   The big (one) is his, the small (one) is mine.
9. Is this chair large? (This chair, large not large?)
   This chair (is) not large.
10. Is that table small?
    That table is neither large, nor is it small.
        (That table not large, not small.)

V

長 **ch'ang²** long   短 **tuan³** short

1. *Che⁴ chih¹ ch'ien¹-pi³* **ch'ang²**, *na⁴ chih¹ mao²-pi³* **tuan³**.
2. *Che⁴ chih¹ kang¹-pi³* **ch'ang²** *tuan³* ?
   Che⁴ chih¹ kang¹-pi³ pu⁴ ch'ang².
3. *Nin²-ti¹ ch'ien¹-pi³* **ch'ang²** *tuan³* ?
   Wo³-ti¹ ch'ien¹-pi³ **tuan³**.
4. *Shih⁴* **nin²**-*ti¹ ch'ien¹-pi³* **ch'ang²** *shih⁴ t'a¹-ti¹ ch'ien¹-pi³ ch'ang²* ?
   Wo³-ti¹ ch'ien¹-pi³ mei² yu³ t'a¹-ti¹ ch'ien¹-pi³ ch'ang².
5. *Hsüeh²-sheng¹-ti¹ ch'ien¹-pi³ shih⁴* **ch'ang²**-*ti¹ shih⁴* *tuan³-ti¹* ? *Hsüeh²-sheng¹-ti¹ shih⁴* **ch'ang²**-*ti¹*.

1. This pencil (is) long, that writing-brush (is) short.

2. (Is) this pen long (or) short ? This pen (is) not long.
3. (Is) your pencil long (or) short ? My pencil (is) short.
4. Which is the longer, your pencil or his pencil ?
    (Is your pencil long, is his pencil long ?)
   My pencil is not as long as his pencil.
    (My pencil has not his pencil long.)
5. Is the student's pencil long or short ?
   The student's is long.

VI

知道 chih¹-tao⁴
to know

1. Nin² chih¹-tao⁴ t'a¹ shih⁴ shui² ma¹? Wo³ chih¹-tao⁴, t'a¹ shih⁴ hsien¹-sheng¹.
2. Nin² chih¹-tao⁴ t'a¹ yu³ chi³ wei⁴ hsüeh²-sheng¹? T'a¹ yu³ ssu⁴ wei⁴ hsüeh²-sheng¹.
3. Na⁴ ke⁴ jen² shih⁴ shui², nin² chih¹-tao⁴ pu⁴ chih¹-tao⁴? Wo³ chih¹-tao⁴, na⁴ ke⁴ jen² shih⁴ shui², na⁴ ke⁴ jen² shih⁴ hsüeh²-sheng¹.
4. Nin² chih¹-tao⁴ na⁴ chang¹ ta⁴ cho¹-tzu¹ shih⁴ shui²-ti¹ pu⁴ chih¹-tao¹? Wo³ chih¹-tao⁴, na⁴ chang¹ ta⁴ cho¹-tzu¹ shih⁴ hsien¹-sheng¹-ti¹. [tao⁴?
5. Nin² chih¹-tao⁴ t'a¹ yu³ shen²-ma¹ tung¹-hsi¹ pu⁴ chih¹- Wo³ pu⁴ chih¹-tao⁴ t'a¹ yu³ shen²-ma¹ tung¹-hsi¹.
6. Nin² chih¹-tao⁴ na⁴ liang³ chih¹ kang¹-pi³ shih⁴ shui²-ti¹? Wo³ chih¹-tao⁴, ch'ang²-ti¹ shih⁴ hsien¹-sheng¹-ti¹ tuan³-ti¹ shih⁴ hsüeh²-sheng¹-ti¹.

LESSON 5

1. Do you know who he is? I know he is a teacher.
2. Do you know how many pupils he has?
   He has four pupils.
3. Do you know who that man is?
   (That man is who, you know not know?)
   I know who that man is, that man is a pupil.
4. Do you know whose that big table is?
   I know that big table is the teacher's.
5. Do you know what (things) he has got?
   I don't know what (things) he has got.
6. Do you know whose those two pens are?
   I know the long one is the teacher's (and) the short one is the student's

VII

茶 ch'a² tea   水 shui³ water   飯 fan⁴ food, cooked rice.

(○個茶) — ke⁴ ch'a² tea   (○個水) — ke⁴ shui³ water
(○個飯) — ke⁴ fan⁴ food

1. Che⁴ shih⁴ ch'a² na⁴ shih⁴ shui³.
2. Nin² yu³ ch'a² mei² yu³? Wo³ mei² yu³ ch'a², wo³ yu³
3. Shui² mei² yu³ ch'a²? T'a¹ mei² yu³ ch'a². [shui³.
4. Che⁴ shih⁴ shen²-ma¹? Che⁴ shih⁴ fan⁴.
5. Na⁴ yeh³ shih⁴ fan⁴ ma¹?
   Na⁴ pu² shih⁴ fan⁴, na⁴ shih⁴ ch'a².

6. *Che⁴ ke⁴ fan⁴ shih⁴ nin²-ti¹, na⁴ ke⁴ ch'a² shih⁴ shui²-
  Na⁴ ke⁴ ch'a² shih⁴ t'a¹-ti¹.* [*ti¹?*
7. *Che⁴ shih⁴ nin² hsüeh²-sheng¹-ti¹ ch'a² ma¹?
  Shih⁴, che⁴ shih⁴ wo³ hsüeh²-sheng¹-ti¹ ch'a².*

1. This is tea, that is water.
2. Have you any tea?
  I haven't any tea, I have some water.
3. Who has no tea? He has no tea.
4. What is this? This is food.
5. Is that also food? That isn't food, that is tea.
6. This food is yours, whose tea is that? That tea is his.
7. Is this your student's tea? Yes, this is my student's tea.

VIII

碗 wan³ bowl(s), cup(s)

(〇個碗) — ke⁴ wan³ bowl(s)

茶碗 ch'a²-wan³ tea-cup(s)

飯碗 fan⁴-wan³ rice-bowl(s)

玻璃盃 po¹-li²-pei¹ glass(es), tumbler(s)

(〇個玻璃盃) — ke⁴ po¹-li²-pei¹ glass(es)

1. *Na⁴ shih⁴ shen²-ma¹ tung¹-hsi¹? Na⁴ shih⁴ wan³.*
2. *Na⁴ shih⁴ chi³ ke⁴ wan³? Na⁴ shih⁴ i² ke⁴ wan³.*
3. *Hsien¹-sheng¹ yu³ ch'a²-wan³, hsüeh²-sheng¹ yu³ fan⁴-wan³.*

LESSON 5

4. *Che⁴ shih⁴* **shen²-ma¹** *wan³? Che⁴ shih⁴* **fan⁴**-*wan³*.
5. *Na⁴ shih⁴* **po¹-li²-pei¹** *ma¹?*
   Shih⁴, na⁴ **shih⁴** *po¹-li²-pei¹*.
6. *Shih⁴ ch'a²-wan³* **ta⁴** *shih⁴ fan⁴-wan³* **ta⁴**?
   Fan⁴-*wan³ ta⁴,* **ch'a²**-*wan³ hsiao³*.
7. *Nin² yu³ ch'a²-wan³,* **yeh³** *yu³ po¹-li²-pei¹ ma¹?*
   Shih⁴, wo³ **yeh³** *yu³ po¹-li²-pei¹*.
8. *Che⁴ san¹ ke⁴ fan⁴-wan³ shih⁴* **nin²**-*ti¹ ma¹?*
   Pu² *shih⁴ wo³-ti¹, na⁴* **pa²** *ke⁴ ch'a²-wan³ shih⁴ wo³-ti¹*.
9. *Nin² yu³* **chi³** *ke⁴ po¹-li²-pei¹?*
   Wo³ yu³ **chiu³** *ke⁴ po¹-li²-pei¹*.
10. *Na⁴ shih⁴* **shen²-ma¹** *wan³? Na⁴ shih⁴* **fan⁴**-*wan³*.

1. What is that (thing)? That is a cup.
2. How many bowls are there there? There is one bowl.
3. The teacher has a tea-cup, the pupil has a rice-bowl.
4. What bowl is this? This is a rice-bowl.
5. Is that a glass? Yes, that is a glass.
6. Which is the larger, a tea-cup or a rice-bowl?
   (Is tea-cup large, is rice-bowl large?)
   A rice-bowl (is) larger than a tea-cup.
7. You have a tea-cup, have (you) also got a glass?
   Yes, I also have a glass.
8. Are these three rice-bowls yours?
   (They) are not mine, those eight tea-cups are mine.
9. How many tumblers have you? I have nine tumblers.
10. What sort of bowl is that? That is a rice-bowl.

NOTES

16. Possessive Case is indicated by the particle 的 **ti¹**, which is added to the noun or pronoun. 的 **ti¹** is equivalent to the apostrophe s in English.

先 生 的 椅 子
hsien¹-*sheng¹*-*ti¹* *i³*-*tzu¹*   } the teacher's chair

學 生 的 椅 子
hsüeh²-*sheng¹*-*ti¹* *cho¹*-*tzu¹*   } the student's table

17. 這 **che⁴**—this, **na⁴**—that. When a classifier is inserted between these pronouns and a noun, the thing spoken of is singular in number.

那 張 紙 是 我 的
na⁴ *chang¹* *chih³* *shih⁴* **wo³**-*ti¹*   } that sheet of paper is mine

這 張 桌 子 是 他 的
che⁴ *chang¹* *cho¹*-*tzu¹* *shih⁴* **t'a¹**-*ti¹*   } this table is his

那 把 椅 子 是 您 的
na⁴ *pa²* *i³*-*tzu¹* *shih⁴* **nin²**-*ti¹*   } that chair is yours

這 枝 毛 筆 是 先 生 的
che⁴ *chih¹* *mao²*-*pi³* *shih⁴* **hsien¹**-*sheng¹*-*ti¹*   } this writing-brush is the teacher's

這 位 學 生 是 我 的
che⁴ *wei⁴* *hsüeh²*-*sheng¹* *shih⁴* **wo³**-*ti¹*   } this pupil is mine

18. Interrogative Sentence. Another form of construction. Repetition of the character 是 **shih⁴** — is.

這 位 是 先 生 是 學 生?
che⁴ *wei⁴* *shih⁴* **hsien¹**-*sheng¹* *shih⁴* **hsüeh²**-*sheng¹*?
This (man) is teacher is pupil?
(Is this man a teacher OR a pupil?)

LESSON 5

那 個 東 西 是 先 生 的 是
na⁴ ke⁴ tung¹-hsi¹ shih⁴ hsien¹-sheng¹-ti¹ shih⁴

學 生 的
hsüeh²-sheng¹-ti¹? That thing is teacher's is pupil's?

(Is that thing the teacher's OR the pupil's?)

19. 的 ti¹. When such adjectives as: 大 ta⁴—big, 小 hsiao — small, 長 ch'ang²— long, 短 tuan³— short, substitute nouns, the particle 的 ti¹ is added to them. In these cases 的 ti¹ is equivalent to the English word 'one'.

這 兩 把 椅 子 是 誰 的?
che⁴ liang³ pa² i³-tzu¹ shih⁴ shui²-ti¹?
These two chairs are whose?
(Whose are these two chairs?)

大 的 是 他 的, 小 的 是 我 的
ta⁴-ti¹ shih⁴ t'a¹-ti¹, hsiao³-ti¹ shih⁴ wo³-ti¹
The big one is his, the small one is mine.

那 兩 枝 鉛 筆 是 誰 的
na⁴ liang³ chih¹ ch'ien¹-pi³ shih⁴ shui²-ti¹?
Those two pencils are whose?
(Whose are those two pencils?)

長 的 是 先 生 的 短 的 是
ch'ang²-ti¹ shih⁴ hsien¹-sheng¹-ti¹, tuan³-ti¹ shih⁴

學 生 的
hsüeh²-sheng¹-ti¹ The long one is the teacher's, the short one is the pupil's.

20. Comparative Degree may be expressed in many ways.

(a) Repetition of 是 **shih**⁴ — is, as the first character of the phrase, combined with repetition of an adjective as the last character of the phrase. This will form an interrogative sentence (see § 18).

是 這 本 書 大 是 那 本 書 大？
*shih*⁴ **che**⁴ *pen*³ *shu*¹ **ta**⁴ *shih*⁴ **na**⁴ *pen*³ *shu*¹ **ta**⁴？
Is this book big is that book big?
(Which is bigger, this book or that book?)

是 這 枝 毛 筆 長 是 那 枝
*shih*⁴ **che**⁴ *chih*¹ *mao*²-*pi*³ **ch'ang**² *shih*⁴ **na**⁴ *chih*¹
毛 筆 長？
*mao*²-*pi*³ **ch'ang**²？
Is this writing-brush long is that writing-brush long?
(Which is longer, this writing-brush or that writing-brush?)

(b) Use of a negative expression, such as 沒有 **mei**² *yu*³ — has not. This will form a negative sentence and may be translated as: not as — as, or: not so — as.

我 的 棹 子 沒 有 他 的 棹 子 大
*wo*³-*ti*¹ *cho*¹-*tzu*¹ **mei**² *yu*³ *t'a*¹-*ti*¹ *cho*¹-*tzu*¹ **ta**⁴
My table has not his table big.
(My table is not as big as his table.)

我 的 鉛 筆 沒 有 他 的 鉛 筆 長
*wo*³-*ti*¹ *ch'ien*¹-*pi*³ **mei**² *yu*³ *t'a*¹-*ti*¹ *ch'ien*¹-*pi*³ **ch'ang**²
My pencil has not his pencil long.
(My pencil is not as long as his pencil.)

LESSON 5

這 個 茶 碗 沒 有 那 個 茶 碗 大
*che*⁴ *ke*⁴ *ch'a*²-*wan*³ *mei*² *yu*³ *na*⁴ *ke*⁴ *ch'a*²-*wan*³ *ta*⁴
This tea-cup has not that tea-cup big.
(This tea-cup is not so big as that tea-cup.)

他 的 學 生 沒 有 我 的 學 生 大
*T'a*¹-*ti*¹ *hsüeh*²-*sheng*¹ *mei*² *yu*³ *wo*²-*ti*¹ *hsüeh*²-*sheng*¹ *ta*⁴
His student has not my student big.
(His student is not as tall as my student.)

21. **Compound Nouns.** There are many examples in Chinese, as in English.

茶 **ch'a²**	tea	碗 **wan³**	bowl, cup	茶 碗 **ch'a²-*wan*³**	tea-cup
飯 **fan⁴**	food, cooked rice	碗 **wan³**	bowl, cup	飯 碗 **fan⁴-*wan*³**	rice-bowl
書 **shu¹**	book, writings, to write	桌 子 **cho¹-*tzu*¹**	table	書 桌 子 **shu¹-*cho*¹-*tzu*¹**	writing-table, desk

LESSON 6

I

書棹子 shu¹-*cho¹-tzu¹*
writing-table(s), desk(s)

飯棹子 fan⁴-*cho¹-tzu¹*
dining-table(s), dinner-table(s)

1. Che⁴ *skih*⁴ shen²-*ma¹ cho¹-tzu¹?*
   Che⁴ *shih*⁴ shu¹-*cho¹- tzu¹.*
2. ShuI² *yu³* fan⁴-*cho¹-tzu¹ ?*
   Na⁴ *ke*⁴ *jen²* yu³ *fan*⁴-*cho¹-tzu¹.*
3. Che⁴ *chang¹* ta⁴ shu¹-*cho¹-tzu¹* shih⁴ shuI²-*ti¹ ?*
   Wo³ pu⁴ *chih¹-tao*⁴ shih⁴ *shui²-ti¹.*
4. Shih⁴ fan⁴-*cho¹-tzu¹* ta¹ shih⁴ shu¹-*cho¹-tzu¹* ta⁴?
   Shu¹-*cho¹-tzu¹* mei² *yu³ fan*⁴-*cho¹-tzu¹ ta*⁴.
5. Na⁴ wei⁴ *hsien¹-sheng¹* yu³ chi³ *chang¹* fan⁴-*cho¹-tzu¹,*
   chi³ *chang¹* shu¹-*cho¹-tzu¹,* nin² chih¹-*tao*⁴ pu⁴ *chih¹-*
   [*tao*⁴?
   Wo³ chih¹-*tao*⁴. *T'a¹* yu³ san¹ *ssu*⁴ *chang¹ shu¹-cho¹-*
   tzu¹, wu³ liu⁴ *chang¹ fan*⁴-*cho¹-tzu¹.*
6. Na⁴ *chang¹* shu¹-*cho¹-tzu¹* ta⁴ pu² ta⁴?
   Na⁴ *chang¹* shu¹-*cho¹-tzu¹* pu² ta⁴, che⁴ *chang¹* fan⁴-
   [*cho¹-tzu¹* ta⁴.

1. What table is this ? This is a writing table.
2. Who has a dining-table ? That man has a dining-table.

LESSON 6

3. Whose is this big desk ? I don't know whose (it) is.
4. Which is the bigger, the dining-table or the writing-table ?
    (Is dining-table big, is writing-table big ?)
   The writing-table is not as big as the dining-table.
    (Writing-table has not dining-table big.)
5. How many dining-tables (and) how many writing-tables has that teacher got, do you know ?
   I do know. He has three (or) four writing-tables (and) five (or) six dining-tables.
6. Is that writing-table big ?
   (That writing-table, big not big ?)
   That writing-table (is) not big, this dining-table (is) big.

II

父親 fu⁴-ch'in¹ father(s)   母親 mu³-ch'in¹ mother(s)

兒子 erh²-tzu¹ son(s), boy(s)   姑娘 ku¹-niang² daughter(s), girl(s), Miss

1. Che⁴ wei⁴ shih⁴ shui²?
   Che⁴ wei⁴ shih⁴ wo³-ti¹ fu⁴-ch'in¹.
2. T'a¹ shih⁴ shui²-ti¹ mu³-ch'in¹?
   T'a¹ shih⁴ na⁴ wei⁴ hsüeh²-sheng¹-ti¹ mu³-ch'in¹.
3. Ni³ fu⁴-ch'in¹ yu³ chi³ ke⁴ erh²-tzu¹?
   Wo³ fu⁴-ch'in¹ yu³ ssu⁴ ke⁴ erh²-tzu¹.
4. Na⁴ wei⁴ hsien¹-sheng¹ yu³ chi³ ke⁴ ku¹-niang²?
   T'a¹ yu³ liang³ ke⁴ ku¹-niang².

5. *Na⁴ wei⁴ ku¹-niang² yu³* **shen²-ma¹**?
   T'a¹ yu³ po¹-li²-pei¹.
6. **Ni³**-*ti¹ erh²-tzu¹ ta⁴ hsiao³*? *Wo³-ti¹ erh²-tzu¹* **pu² ta⁴.**
7. *Che⁴ ke⁴ ch'a²-wan³ shih⁴ wo³* **erh²-tzu¹-ti¹**, *na⁴ ke⁴ fan⁴-wan³ shih⁴ wo³ ku¹-niang²-ti¹.*
8. *Che⁴ chang¹ shu¹-cho¹-tzu¹ shih⁴* **shui²-ti¹**?
   Che⁴ chang¹ shu¹-cho¹-tzu¹ shih⁴ wo³ **fu⁴-ch'in¹-ti¹.**

1. Who is this? This is my father.
2. Whose mother is she? She is that student's mother.
3. How many sons has your father got?
   My father has four sons.
4. How many daughters has that teacher got?
   He has two daughters.
5. What has that girl? She has a glass.
6. Is your son tall? (Your son big, small?)
   My son (is) not tall.
7. This tea-cup is my son's, that rice-bowl is my daughter's.
8. Whose is this writing-table?
   This writing-table is my father's.

III

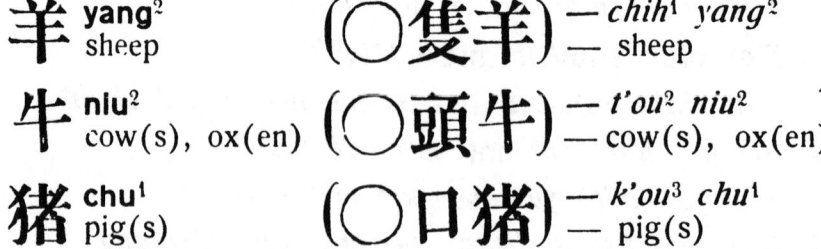

1. *Che⁴ shih⁴* **yang²** *pu² shih⁴*? *Shih⁴, che⁴ shih⁴* **yang².**

LESSON 6

2. *Na⁴ yeh³ shih⁴* **yang²** *ma¹?*
   Na⁴ **pu²** *shih⁴ yang², na⁴ shih⁴* **niu².**
3. *Che⁴ shih⁴ niu², na⁴ shih⁴* **shen²**-*ma¹? Na⁴ shih⁴* **chu¹.**
4. *Na⁴ shih⁴* **chi³** *k'ou³ chu¹? Na⁴ shih⁴* **wu³** *k'ou³ chu¹.*
5. *Che⁴ shih⁴* **chi³** *chih¹ yang²?*
   Che⁴ shih⁴ **ch'i¹** *chih¹ yang².*
6. *Na⁴* **pa¹** *t'ou² niu² shih⁴* **ni³ mu³**-*ch'in¹*-*ti¹ ma¹?*
   Shih⁴ *wo³ mu³*-*ch'in¹*-*ti¹.*
7. *T'a¹*-*ti¹ chu¹* **ta⁴** *hsiao³?*
   T'a¹ yu³ i⁴ k'ou³ ta⁴-*ti¹,* **ssu⁴** *k'ou³ hsiao³*-*ti¹.*

1. This is a sheep, isn't it? Yes, this is a sheep.
2. Is that also a sheep? That is not a sheep, that is a cow.
3. This is a cow, what is that? That is a pig.
4. How many pigs are there there?
   There are five pigs there.
5. How many sheep are there here?
   There are seven sheep here.
6. Are those eight cows your mother's?
   (They) are my mother's.
7. Is his pig a big one? (His pig large small?)
   He has one big (one) (and) four small (ones).

IV

肉 jou⁴ meat   羊肉 yang²-jou⁴ mutton   牛肉 niu²-jou⁴ beef

猪肉 chu¹-jou⁴ pork   斤 chin¹ catty (=1⅓ lbs.)

1. *Che⁴ shih⁴* **yang²**-*jou⁴, na⁴ shih⁴* **niu²**-*jou⁴.*

2. *Che⁴ shih⁴ chi³ chin¹ yang²-jou⁴?*
   Che⁴ shih⁴ san¹ chin¹ yang²-jou⁴.
3. *Na⁴ shih⁴ chi³ chin¹ niu²-jou⁴?*
   Na⁴ shih⁴ shih² chin¹ niu²-jou⁴.
4. *Che⁴ shih⁴ shen²-ma¹-jou⁴? Che⁴ shih⁴ chu¹-jou⁴.*

1. This is mutton, that is beef.
2. How many catties of mutton is this?
   This is three catties of mutton.
3. How many catties of beef is that?
   That is ten catties of beef.
4. What sort of meat is this?   This is pork.

V

魚　yü²
　　fish

條　t'iao²
　　classifier for fish, streets, dogs and long slender things

塊　k'uai⁴
　　classifier : bit(s), piece(s), lump(s)

1. *Che⁴ shih⁴ chi³ t'iao² yü²? Che⁴ shih⁴ liang³ t'iao² yü².*
2. *Na⁴ shih⁴ chi³ k'uai⁴ chu¹-jou⁴?*
   Na⁴ shih⁴ liu⁴ k'uai⁴ chu¹-jou⁴.
3. *Shih⁴ che⁴ t'iao² yü² ta⁴ shih⁴ na⁴ t'iao² yü² ta⁴?*
   Na⁴ tiao² yü² ta⁴, che⁴ t'iao² yü² hsiao³.
4. *Na⁴ k'uai⁴ jou⁴ yu³ chi³ chin¹?*
   Na⁴ k'uai⁴ jou⁴ yu³ pa¹ chin¹.

LESSON 6

5. *Che⁴ t'iao² yü² yu³* **chi³** *chin¹?*
   Che⁴ t'iao² yü² yu³ **liu⁴** *chin¹.*

1. How many fish are there here?   There are two fish here.
2. How many pieces of pork are there there?
   There are six pieces of pork.
3. Is this fish bigger than that fish?
   (Is this fish big, is that fish big?)
   That fish is bigger.
4. How many catties is (has) that piece of meat?
   That piece of meat is (has) eight catties.
5. How many catties is (has) this fish?
   This fish is (has) six catties.

VI

麵包 mien⁴-pao¹ bread   茶葉 ch'a²-yeh⁴ tea (in leaf)

咖啡 k'a¹-*fei*⁴ coffee

1. *T'a¹ yu³* **mien⁴**-*pao¹* **ma¹?**   *T'a¹* **mei²** *yu³ mien⁴-pao¹.*
2. *Che⁴ shih⁴* **shui²**-*ti¹ ch'a²-yeh⁴?*
   Che⁴ shih⁴ **hsien¹**-*sheng¹-ti¹ ch'a²-yeh⁴.*
3. *Che⁴ shih⁴ k'a¹-fei⁴ shih⁴ ch'a²-yeh⁴?*
   Che⁴ shih⁴ k'a¹-fei⁴.
4. *Na⁴ shih⁴* **chi³** *chin¹ mien⁴-pao¹?*
   Na⁴ shih⁴ liu⁴ chin¹ mien⁴-pao¹.

1. Has he any bread?   He has no bread.
2. Whose tea is this?   This is the teacher's tea.

3. Is this coffee or tea ? This is coffee.
4. How many catties of bread is that ?
That is six catties of bread.

VII

一　erh⁴
二　two

1. *Shih²-I¹, shih²-erh⁴, shih²-san¹, shih²-ssu⁴, shih²-wu³, shih²-liu⁴, shih²-ch'i¹, shih²-pa¹, shih²-chiu³.*
2. **Erh⁴**-*shih²,* **san¹**-*shih²,* **wu³**-*shih²,* **pa¹**-*shih².*
3. *Erh⁴-shih²-*I¹, *san¹-shih²-*erh⁴, *wu³-shih²-*ssu⁴, *liu⁴-shih²-*wu³, *ch'i¹-shih²-*pa¹, *pa¹-shih²-*chiu³, *chiu³-shih²-*chiu³.
4. *Ssu⁴-shih²-*ssu⁴ *ke⁴ jen², ch'i¹-shih²-*erh⁴ *chin¹ ch'a²-yeh⁴, pa¹-shih²-*wu³ *t'iao² yü². erh⁴-shih²-*san¹ *chih¹ yang², san¹-shih²-*wu³ *chin¹ yang²-jou⁴.*
5. *Ssu⁴-shih²-*liu⁴ *t'ou² niu², wu³-shih²-*erh⁴ *k'uai⁴ niu²-jou⁴, liu⁴-shih²-*ch'i¹ *chin¹ niu²-jou⁴.*
6. *Ch'i¹-shih²-*ssu⁴ *k'ou³ chu¹, pa¹-shih²-*I² *k'uai⁴ mien⁴-pao¹, chiu³-shih²-*erh⁴ *chin¹ ch'a²-yeh⁴, shih²-*pa¹ *chin¹ k'a¹-fei⁴, shih²-*ssu⁴ *chin¹ chu¹-jou⁴, ssu⁴-shih²-*wu³ *k'uai⁴ chu¹-jou⁴, wu³-shih²-*wu³ *chin¹ yü².*

1. Eleven, twelve, thirteen, fourteen, fifteen, sixteen, seventeen, eighteen, nineteen.
2. Twenty, thirty, fifty, eighty.
3. Twenty-one, thirty-two, fifty-four, sixty-five, seventy-eight, eighty-nine, ninety-nine.
4. Forty-four men, seventy-two catties of tea, eighty-five fish, twenty-three sheep, thirty-five catties of mutton.

LESSON 6

5. Forty-six cows, fifty-two pieces of beef, sixty-seven catties of beef.
6. Seventy-four pigs, eighty-one pieces of bread, ninety-two catties of tea, eighteen catties of coffee, fourteen catties of pork, forty-five pieces of pork, fifty-five catties of fish.

NOTES

22. Weights.

一 斤 i⁴ *chin*¹ — one catty (approx. 1⅓ lbs.) = 16 兩 = 596.816 grammes.

一 兩 i⁴ *liang*³ — one tael (approx. 1 oz.) = 37.30 grs.

23. Classifiers, (see § 10) introduced in this lesson are : -

六 隻 羊　　six sheep
liu⁴ *chih*¹ *yang*²

九 頭 牛　　nine cows
*chiu*³ *t'ou*² *niu*²

八 口 豬　　eight pigs
*pa*¹ *k'ou*³ *chu*¹

七 條 魚　　seven fish
*ch'i*¹ *t'iao*² *yü*²

十 塊 肉　　ten pieces of meat
*shih*² *k'uai*⁴ *jou*⁴

八 塊 麵 包　　eight pieces of bread
*pa*² *k'uai*⁴ *mien*⁴-*pao*¹

24. Cardinal Numbers one to ninety-nine are : -

一	i¹	1	六	liu⁴	6
二	erh⁴	2	七	ch'i¹	7
三	san¹	3	八	pa¹	8
四	ssu⁴	4	九	chiu³	9
五	wu³	5	十	shih²	10

十一	shih²-i¹	11	二十五	erh⁴-shih²-wu³	25
十二	shih²-erh⁴	12	二十六	erh⁴-shih²-liu⁴	26
十三	shih²-san¹	13	二十七	erh⁴-shih²-ch'i¹	27
十四	shih²-ssu⁴	14	二十八	erh⁴-shih¹-pa²	28
十五	shih²-wu³	15	二十九	erh⁴-shih²-chiu³	29
十六	shih²-liu⁴	16	三十	san¹-shih²	30
十七	shih²-ch'i¹	17	三十一	san¹-shih²-i¹	31
十八	shih²-pa¹	18	四十	ssu⁴-shih²	40
十九	shih²-chiu³	19	五十	wu³-shih²	50
二十	erh⁴-shih²	20	六十	liu⁴-shih²	60
二十一	erh⁴-shih²-i¹	21	七十	ch'i¹-shih²	70
二十二	erh⁴-shih²-erh⁴	22	八十	pa¹-shih²	80
二十三	erh⁴-shih²-san¹	23	九十	chiu³-shih²	90
二十四	erh⁴-shih²-ssu⁴	24	九十九	chiu³-shih²-chiu³	99

LESSON 7

I

多 to¹
many, much, more

少 shao³
few, little

1. *Yang²-jou⁴* to¹, *chu¹-jou⁴* shao³.
2. *Ch'a²-yeh⁴* to¹, *k'a¹-fei⁴* shao³.
3. *Nin²-ti¹ niu²* to¹, *wo³-ti¹ niu²* shao³.
4. *T'a¹-ti¹ niu²* to¹ shao³? *T'a¹-ti¹ niu²* to¹.
5. *Shih⁴* ch'a²-wan³ to¹, *shih⁴* fan⁴-wan³ to¹?
    Ch'a²-wan³ to¹, *fan⁴-wan³* shao³.
6. *Shih⁴* hsien¹-sheng¹-ti¹ shu¹ to¹, *shih⁴* hsüeh²-sheng¹-[ti¹ shu¹ to¹?
    Wo³ pu⁴ *chih¹-tao⁴* shui²-ti¹ shu¹ to¹, *shui²-ti¹ shu¹* [shao³.
7. *Nin²* shih⁴ hsien¹-sheng¹ ma¹?
    Shih⁴, wo³ shih⁴ hsien¹-sheng¹.
8. *Nin²* shih⁴ shui²-ti¹ hsien¹-sheng¹?
    Wo³ shih⁴ na⁴ wei⁴ hsüeh²-sheng¹-ti¹ hsien¹-sheng¹.

1. (There is) much mutton (and) little pork.
2. (There is) much tea (and) little coffee.
3. You have more cows than I have
   (Your cows many, my cows few.)
4. Has he many cows? (His cows many, few?)
   He has many cows. (His cows many.)
5. Are there more tea-cups than rice-bowls?

There are more tea-cups than rice-bowls.
6. Has the teacher more books than the student?
(Are the teacher's books many, are the student's books many?)
I don't know who has the most.
(I not know whose books many, whose books few.)
7. Are you a teacher? Yes, I am a teacher.
8. Whose teacher are you? I am that student's teacher.

II

多少？ to¹-shao³?
how many? how much?

1. Che⁴ shih⁴ to¹-shao³ chih¹ yang²?
   Che⁴ shih⁴ ssu⁴-shih²-erh⁴ chih¹ yang².
2. Na⁴ shih⁴ chi³ t'ou² niu²? Na⁴ shih⁴ liu⁴ t'ou² niu².
3. T'a¹ yu³ to¹-shao³ chin¹ ch'a²-yeh⁴, to¹-shao³ chin¹ k'a¹-
   [fei⁴?.
   T'a¹ yu³ erh²-shih²-wu³ chin¹ ch'a²-yeh⁴, san¹-shih²-pa¹ chin¹ k'a¹-fei⁴.
4. Nin²-ti¹ erh²-tzu¹ yu³ chi³ wei⁴ hsien¹-sheng¹?
   Wo³-ti¹ erh²-tzu¹ yu³ i² wei⁴ hsien¹-sheng¹.
5. Na⁴ shih⁴ to¹-shao³ wei⁴ hsüeh²-sheng¹, che⁴ shih⁴ chi³ wei⁴ hsien¹-sheng¹?
   Na⁴ shih⁴ ssu⁴-shih² wei⁴ hsüeh²-sheng¹, che⁴ shih⁴ liang³ wei⁴ hsien¹-sheng¹.

1. How many sheep are there here? There are forty-two sheep here.

LESSON 7

2. How many oxen are there there?
   There are six oxen there.
3. How many catties of tea (and) how many catties of coffee has he? He has twenty-five catties of tea (and) thirty-eight catties of coffee.
4. How many teachers has your son got?
   My son has one teacher.
5. How many students are there there (and) how many teachers are there here?
   There are forty students there (and) there are two teachers here.

III

十幾 **shih**² **chi**³
over ten, more than ten, ten odd

幾十 *chi*³ **shih**²
several tens, (dozens)

(二十幾) erh⁴-*shih*² **chi**³
over twenty, more than twenty, twenty [odd

(五十幾) wu³-*shih*² **chi**³
over fifty, more than fifty, fifty odd

1. *Na*⁴ *shih*⁴ *to*¹-*shao*³ *chin*¹ *yü*²?
   *Na*⁴ *shih*⁴ **shih**² **chi**³ *chin*¹ *yü*².
2. *Che*⁴ *shih*⁴ *to*¹-*shao*³ *chang*¹ *shu*¹-*cho*¹-*tzu*¹?
   *Che*⁴ *shih*⁴ **shih**²-**chi**³ *chang*¹ *shu*¹-*cho*¹-*tzu*¹.
3. *Che*⁴ *wei*⁴ *hsien*¹-*sheng*¹ *yu*³ *to*¹-*shao*³ *wei*⁴ *hsüeh*²-
   *T'a*¹ *yu*³ **chi**³ *shih*² *wei*⁴.   [*sheng*¹?
4. *Nin*² *yu*³ **chi**³ *shih*² *ke*⁴ *po*¹-*li*²-*pei*¹?
   *Wo*³ *yu*³ *erh*⁴-*shih*² *ke*⁴ *po*¹-*li*²-*pei*¹.

5. Na⁴ erh⁴-shih² chi³ chang¹ fan⁴-cho¹-tzu¹ shih⁴ shui²-
   Wo³ pu⁴ chih¹-tao⁴ shih⁴ shui²-ti¹.   [ti¹?
6. Che⁴ shih⁴ ch'i¹-shih² chi³ chih¹ mao²-pi³?
   Che⁴ shih⁴ ch'i¹-shih²-erh⁴ chih¹.

1. How many catties of fish is that?
   That is over ten catties of fish.
2. How many writing-tables is this?
   This is more than ten writing-tables.
3. How many pupils has this teacher?
   He has several dozen.
4. How many dozen glasses have you got?
   I have twenty glasses.
5. Whose are those twenty odd dining-tables?
   I don't know whose (they) are.
6. There are seventy and how many writing-brushes here?
   There are seventy-two here.

IV

字 tzu⁴
character(s), letters

1. Che⁴ shih⁴ chi³ ke⁴ tzu⁴? Che⁴ shih⁴ san¹ ke⁴ tzu⁴.
2. Na⁴ shih⁴ to¹-shao³ ke⁴ tzu⁴?
   Na⁴ shih⁴ pa¹-shih²-san¹ ke⁴ tzu⁴.
3. Che⁴ shih⁴ 'fan'⁴ tzu⁴ pu² shih⁴?
   Che⁴ pu² shih⁴ 'fan'⁴ tzu⁴, che⁴ shih⁴ 'ch'ien'¹ tzu⁴.
4. Shih⁴ che⁴ ke⁴ tzu⁴ shih⁴ 'shu'¹ tzu⁴, shih⁴ na⁴ ke⁴ tzu⁴
   shih⁴ 'shu'¹ tzu⁴?
   Che⁴ ke⁴ tzu⁴ shih⁴ 'pen'³ tzu⁴, na⁴ tzu⁴ shih⁴ 'shu'¹ tzu⁴.

LESSON 7

1. How many characters are there here?
   There are three characters here.
2. How many characters are there there?
   There are eighty-three characters there.
3. This is the character *fan* isn't it?
   This isn't the character *fan*, this is the character *ch'ien*.
4. Is this the character *shu* or is that the character *shu*?
   This is the character *pen*, that is the character *shu*.

V

們 men² plural particle (of persons)　　我們 wo³-men² we, us

你們 ni³-men² you (pl.)　　他們 t'a¹-men² they, them

1. Ni³-men² yu³ shen²-ma¹? Wo³-men² yu³ mao²-pi³.
2. Shui² yu³ shu¹-cho¹-tzu¹? T'a¹-men² yu³ shu¹-cho¹-tzu¹.
3. Shui² mei² yu³ fan⁴-cho¹-tzu¹?
   Wo³-men² mei² yu³ fan⁴-cho¹-tzu¹.
4. Hsien¹-sheng¹-men² yu³ to¹-shao³ chih¹ ch'ien¹-pi³?
   Hsien¹-sheng¹-men² yu³ shih²-chi³ chih¹ ch'ien¹-pi³.
5. Che⁴ chi³-shih² chang¹ shu¹-cho¹-tzu¹ shih⁴ hsüeh²-sheng¹-men²-ti¹ pu² shih⁴?
   Shih⁴ hsüeh²-sheng¹-men²-ti¹.

1. What have you got? We have some writing-brushes.
2. Who has some writing-tables?
   They have some writing-tables.
3. Who hasn't got any dining-tables?
   We haven't got any dining-tables.

4. How many pencils have the teachers got ?
   The teachers have more than ten pencils.
5. These dozens of writing-tables are the students', aren't they ? (They) are the students'.

VI

我們的 wo³-men²-ti¹
       our, ours

你們的 ni³-men²-ti¹
       your (pl.), yours (pl.)

他們的 t'a¹-men²-ti¹
       their, theirs

1. *Na⁴ t'iao² yü² shih⁴* **t'a¹-men²-ti¹** *ma¹ ?*
   Shih⁴, na⁴ t'iao² yü² shih⁴ t'a¹-men²-ti¹.
2. *Che⁴ k'ou³ chu¹ shih⁴* **nin²-ti¹** *ma¹ ?*
   Pu² shih⁴ wo³-ti¹, shih⁴ **wo³-men²-ti¹**.
3. *Na⁴ wu³-shih²-chiu³ chin¹ k'a¹-fei⁴ shih⁴* **shui²-ti¹** *?*
   Na⁴ wu³-shih²-chiu³ chin¹ k'a¹-fei⁴ shih⁴ **wo³-men²-ti¹**.
4. *Che⁴ ssu⁴-shih²-erh⁴ chang¹ shu¹-cho¹-tzu¹, shih⁴* **ni³-men²-ti¹** *shih⁴* **t'a¹-men²-ti¹** *?*
   Che⁴ ssu⁴-shih²-erh⁴ chang¹ shu¹-cho¹-tzu¹ shih⁴ t'a¹-men²-ti¹, na⁴ san¹-shih²-liu⁴ chang¹ **fan⁴-cho¹-tzu¹** *shih⁴* **wo³-men²-ti¹**.

1. Is that fish theirs ? Yes, that fish is theirs.
2. Is this pig yours ? (It) is not mine, (it) is ours.
3. Whose are those fifty-nine catties of coffee ?
   Those fifty-nine catties of coffee are ours.
4. Are these forty-two desks yours or theirs ?
   These forty-two desks are theirs, those thirty-six dining-tables are ours.

LESSON 7

VII

百 pai³
hundred

零 ling²
zero, nought

1. I⁴-pai³, erh⁴-pai³, liu⁴-pai³, chiu³-pai³.
2. I⁴-pai³-ling²-I¹, san¹-pai³-ling²-ssu⁴, ch'i¹-pai³-ling²-pa¹.
3. Pa¹-pai³-I¹-shih², chiu³-pai³-ssu⁴-shih², erh⁴-pai³-wu³-shih².
4. I⁴-pai³-i¹-shih²-chiu³, erh⁴-pai³-san¹-shih²-liu⁴, wu³-pai³-ssu⁴-shih²-I¹, chiu³-pai³-pa¹-shih²-erh⁴.
5. Ssu⁴-pai³ ke⁴ ch'a²-wan³.
6. Chiu³-pai³-erh⁴-shih²-I¹ chin¹ k'a¹-fei⁴.
7. Pa¹-pai³-chiu³-shih²-wu³ ke⁴ jen².
8. Ch'i¹-pai³-ling²-ch'i¹ chin¹ ch'a²-yeh⁴.
9. Wu³-pai³-I¹-shih²-wu³ ke⁴ po¹-li²-pei¹.
10. Liu⁴-pai³-ch'i¹-shih² k'uai⁴ mien⁴-pao¹.
11. Ch'i¹-pai³-pa¹-shih² pa² I³-tzu¹.
12. Chiu³-pai³ chiu³-shih² ke⁴ tzu⁴.
13. Erh⁴-pai³-ling²-wu³ chih¹ yang².
14. I⁴-pai³-pa¹-shih² k'ou³ chu¹.
15. Ssu⁴-pai³-ch'i¹-shih² t'ou² niu².

1. One hundred, two hundred, six hundred, nine hundred.
2. One hundred and one, three hundred and four, seven hundred and eight.
3. Eight hundred and ten, nine hundred and forty, two hundred and fifty.
4. One hundred and nineteen, two hundred and thirty-six, five hundred and forty-one, nine hundred and eighty-two.

5. Four hundred tea-cups.
6. Nine hundred and twenty-one catties of coffee.
7. Eight hundred and ninety-five men.
8. Seven hundred and seven catties of tea.
9. Five hundred and fifteen tumblers.
10. Six hundred and seventy pieces of bread.
11. Seven hundred and eighty chairs.
12. Nine hundred and ninety characters.
13. Two hundred and five sheep.
14. One hundred and eighty pigs.
15. Four hundred and seventy cows.

VIII

千 ch'ien¹
thousand

1. *I¹-ch'ien¹*, **erh⁴**-*ch'ien¹*, **pa¹**-*ch'ien¹*.
2. *I¹-ch'ien¹*-**chiu³**-*pai³-san¹-shih²*-**liu⁴**, *liang³-ch'ien¹*-**pa¹**-*pai³-erh⁴-shih²*-**wu³**, *pa¹-ch'ien¹*-**ssu⁴**-*pai³-ch'i¹-shih²-i¹*.
3. *San¹-ch'ien¹*-**ling²**-*erh⁴-shih²-pa¹*, *pa¹-ch'ien¹-ssu⁴-pai³-*ling²*-ch'i¹*, *liu⁴-ch'ien¹*-**ling²**-*wu³-shih²-ssu⁴*, *chiu³-ch'ien¹*-**ling²**-*san¹*, *pa¹-ch'ien¹*-**wu³**-*pai³*.
4. *San¹-ch'ien¹-ssu⁴-pai³ ke⁴* **ch'a²**-*wan³*.
5. *Ssu⁴-ch'ien¹-liu⁴-pai³-chiu³-shih²*-**san¹** *t'ou² niu²*.
6. *Chi¹-ch'ien¹-san¹-pai³-liu⁴-shih²*-**chiu³** *k'ou³* **chu¹**.
7. *Pa¹-ch'ien¹-erh⁴-pai³-wu³-shih²-pa¹ t'iao² yü²*.
8. *Ssu⁴-ch'ien¹-ling²-i² ke⁴* **pen³**-*tzu¹*, *wu³-ch'ien¹-san¹-pai³-erh⁴-shih²*-**ssu⁴** *ke⁴* **fan⁴**-*wan³*.

9. *Chiu³-ch'ien¹-chiu³-pai³-chiu³-shih²-*chiu³ *chih¹* mao²-[*pi³*.
10. *Liu⁴-ch'ien¹-san¹-pai³-ch'i¹-shih²-*pa¹ *chih¹* yang², *wu³-ch'ien¹-ssu⁴-pai³-san¹-shih²-*erh⁴ *chin¹* mien⁴-*pao¹*.

1. One thousand, two thousand, eight thousand.
2. One thousand nine hundred and thirty-six, two thousand eight hundred and twenty-five, eight thousand four hundred and seventy-one.
3. Three thousand and twenty-eight, eight thousand four hundred and seven, six thousand and fifty-four, nine thousand and three, eight thousand five hundred.
4. Three thousand four hundred tea-cups.
5. Four thousand six hundred and ninety-three oxen.
6. Seven thousand three hundred and sixty-nine pigs.
7. Eight thousand two hundred and fifty-eight fish.
8. Four thousand and one note-books, five thousand three hundred and twenty-four rice-bowls.
9. Nine thousand nine hundred and ninety-nine writing-brushes.
10. Six thousand three hundred and seventy-eight sheep, five thousand four hundred and thirty-two catties of bread.

NOTES

25. 您 **nin²** and 你 **ni³** are both translated as: you.

    您 **nin²** is the polite form, which is also used when addressing a superior. It is, however, extensively used in Peiping.

    你 **ni³** is the more usual form outside of Peiping. It is always used when addressing children, servants, coolies, etc. Chinese university students use it when talking amongst themselves.

    你們 **ni³-men²** is the only plural form.

26. **Comparison** may be expressed by employing adjectives (or adverbs) of opposite meanings, thus:

    先 生 大, 學 生 小
    hsien¹-sheng¹ **ta⁴**, *hsüeh²-sheng¹* **hsiao³**
    The teacher big, the pupil little
    (The teacher is taller than the pupil.)

    牛 大, 羊 小
    niu² **ta⁴**, *yang²* **hsiao³**
    The cow big, the sheep small
    (The cow is bigger than the sheep.)

    茶 碗 多, 飯 碗 少
    ch'a²-wan³ **to¹**, *fan⁴-wan³* **shao³**
    Tea-cups many, rice-bowls few
    (More tea-cups than rice-bowls.)

27. 幾? **chi³?** and 多少? **to¹-shao³?** are both translated as: how many? or: how much?

    幾? **chi³?** however is usually employed with numbers less than ten, while 多少? **to¹-shao³?** is usually employed with numbers greater than ten.

LESSON 7

28. 十幾 shih² chi³ denotes some number between ten and twenty, i. e. : more than ten, over ten, ten odd. Similarly 二十幾 erh⁴-shih² chi³ denotes some number between twenty and thirty, i. e. : more than twenty, over twenty, twenty odd. And so on.

幾十 chi³ shih² is translated as : several tens, dozens. It denotes a number of tens : twenty, thirty, forty, fifty, etc.

29. 們 men² is the plural particle of persons. As a suffix to a personal noun or pronoun it forms the plural, thus :

我 wo³ { I, me 我們 wo³-men² { we, us

你 ni³ { you 你們 ni³-men² { you (pl.)

他 t'a¹ { he, him, she, her 他們 t'a¹-men² { they, them

先生 hsien¹-sheng¹ { teacher, Mr. 先生們 hsien¹-sheng¹-men² { teachers, Messrs.

學生 hsüeh²-sheng¹ { student, pupil 學生們 hsüeh²-sheng¹-men² { students, pupils

30. 的 ti¹ added as a suffix to plural personal pronouns, forms plural possessive pronouns, thus :

我們 wo³-men² { we, us 我們的 wo³-men²-ti¹ { our, ours

你們 ni³-men² { you (pl.) 你們的 ni³-men²-ti¹ { your (pl.), yours (pl.)

| 他們
t'a¹-men² | } they, them | 他們的
t'a¹-men²-ti¹ | } their, theirs |

31. Cardinal numbers one hundred to nine thousand nine hundred and ninety-nine are :-

百	pai³	hundred
一百	i⁴-pai³	100
一百零一	i⁴-pai³-ling²-i¹	101
一百零二	i⁴-pai³-ling²-erh⁴	102
一百零三	i⁴-pai³-ling²-san¹	103
一百零四	i⁴-pai³-ling²-ssu⁴	104
一百零五	i⁴-pai³-ling²-wu³	105
一百零六	i⁴-pai³-ling²-liu⁴	106
一百零七	i⁴-pai³-ling²-ch'i¹	107
一百零八	i⁴-pai³-ling²-pa¹	108
一百零九	i⁴-pai³-ling²-chiu³	109
一百一十	i⁴-pai³-i¹-shih²	110
一百一十一	i⁴-pai³-i¹-shih²-i⁴	111
一百一十二	i⁴-pai³-i¹-shih²-erh⁴	112
一百一十三	i⁴-pai³-i¹-shih²-san¹	113
一百二十	i⁴-pai³-erh⁴-shih²	120
一百三十	i⁴-pai³-san¹-shih²	130
一百四十	i⁴-pai³-ssu⁴-shih²	140
一百五十	i⁴-pai³-wu³-shih²	150
二百	erh⁴-pai³	200
三百	san¹-pai³	300
四百	ssu⁴-pai³	400
五百	wu³-pai³	500

LESSON 7

六百	liu⁴-pai³	600
七百	ch'i¹-pai³	700
八百	pa¹-pai³	800
九百	chiu³-pai³	900
九百九十九	chiu³-pai³-chiu³-shih²-chiu³	999
千	ch'ien¹	thousand
一千	i⁴-ch'ien¹	1000
一千零一	i⁴-ch'ien¹-ling²-i¹	1001
一千零二	i⁴-ch'ien¹-ling²-erh⁴	1002
一千零三	i⁴-ch'ien¹-ling²-san¹	1003
一千零一十	i⁴-ch'ien¹-ling²-i¹-shih²	1010
一千零二十	i⁴-ch'ien¹-ling²-erh⁴-shih²	1020
一千零三十	i⁴-ch'ien¹-ling²-san¹-shih²	1030
一千零九十	i⁴-chien¹-ling²-chiu³-shih²	1090
二千	erh⁴-ch'ien¹	2000
兩千	liang³-ch'ien¹	2000
三千	san¹-ch'ien¹	3000
四千	ssu⁴-ch'ien¹	4000

五 千 七 百 二 十 六
wu³-ch'ien¹-ch'i¹-pai³-erh⁴-shih²-liu⁴   5726

九 千 九 百 九 十 九
chiu³-ch'ien¹-chiu³-pai³-chiu³-shih²-chiu³   9999

LESSON 8

I

都 tou¹ — all, both

甚麼的 shen²-ma¹-ti¹ — etc., and so on

〇百多 — pai³ to¹ — over — hundred, more than — hundred, [— hundred odd

〇千多 — ch'ien¹ to¹ — over — thousand, more than — thousand, [— thousand odd

幾百 chi³ pai³ — how many hundred ?, several hundred

幾千 chi³ ch'ien¹ — how many thousand ?, several thousand

1. Che⁴ tou¹ shih⁴ yang²-jou⁴, na⁴ tou¹ shih⁴ chu¹-jou⁴.
2. Ni³-men² tou¹ yu³ shen²-ma¹ tung¹-hsi¹ ?
   Wo³-men² yu³ pen³-tzu¹, yu³ ch'ien¹-pi³, yu³ shu¹-cho¹-tzu¹, yu³ i³-tzu¹, shen²-ma¹-ti¹.
3. Na⁴ san¹-pai³ to¹ chih¹ kang¹-pi³, che⁴ i⁴-ch'ien¹ to¹ chang¹ chih³, tou¹ shih⁴ na⁴ ke⁴ jen²-ti¹ ma¹ ?
   Shih⁴, tou¹ shih⁴ t'a¹-ti¹.
4. Ni³-men² yu³ chi³ pai³ chin¹ ch'a²-yeh⁴ ?
   Wo³-men² yu³ san¹-pai³ chin¹.
5. Che⁴ shih⁴ to¹-shao³ chin¹ k'a¹-fei¹ ?
   Che⁴ shih⁴ chi³ ch'ien¹ chin¹.

LESSON 8

1. All this is mutton, all that is pork.
2. What (things) have you all got?
    We have note-books, (have) pencils, (have) writing-tables, (have) chairs, etc.
3. Are all those three hundred odd pens (and) these one thousand odd sheets of paper, that man's?
    Yes, (they) are all his.
4. Wow many hundred catties of tea have you (pl.)?
    We have three hundred catties.
5. How many catties of coffee are there here?
    There are several thousand catties here.

II

這些 che⁴-hsieh¹ these   那些 na⁴-hsieh¹ those

1. *Che⁴-hsieh¹ ke⁴ pen³-tzu¹ tou¹ shih⁴ shui²-ti¹?*
    Che⁴-hsieh¹ ke⁴ pen³-tzu¹ tou¹ shih⁴ wo³ erh²-tzu¹-ti¹.
2. *Na⁴-hsieh¹ yang² tou¹ shih⁴ t'a¹-men²-ti¹ ma¹?*
    Pu² tou¹ shih⁴ t'a¹-men²-ti¹, yeh³ yu³ wo³-men²-ti¹.
3. *Che⁴-hsieh¹ k'ou³ chu¹ shih⁴ nin²-ti¹, na⁴-hsieh¹ t'ou² niu² yeh³ shih⁴ nin²-ti¹ ma¹?*
    Pu² shih⁴, na⁴-hsieh¹ t'ou² niu² shih⁴ na⁴ ke⁴ jen²-ti¹.

1. Whose are all these note-books?
    These note-books are all my son's.
2. Are all those sheep theirs?
    (They) are not all theirs, there are also (some of) ours.
3. These pigs are yours, are those cows also yours?
    No, those cows are that man's.

III

(問答) wen⁴-ta²
question and answer

Q. Che⁴ shih⁴ shen²-ma¹ tung¹-hsi¹ ?
A. Che⁴ shih⁴ cho¹-tzu¹.
Q. Che⁴ shih⁴ shen²-ma¹ cho¹-tzu¹ ?
A. Che⁴ shih⁴ shu¹-cho¹-tzu¹.
Q. Che⁴ shih⁴ chi³ chang¹ shu¹-cho¹-tzu¹.
A. Che⁴ shih⁴ liang³ chang¹ shu¹-cho¹-tzu¹.
Q. Che⁴ liang³ chang¹ shu¹-cho¹-tzu¹ tou¹ shih⁴ nin²-ti¹ ma¹ ?
A. Pu² tou¹ shih⁴ wo³-ti¹, che⁴ chang¹ ta⁴-ti¹ shih⁴ wo³-ti¹, na⁴ chang¹ hsiao³-ti¹ pu² shih⁴ wo³-ti¹.
Q. Na⁴ chang¹ hsiao³-ti¹ shih⁴ shui²-ti¹ ?
A. Na⁴ chang¹ hsiao³-ti¹ shih⁴ hsüeh²-sheng¹-ti¹.

Q. What is this thing ?
A. This is a table.
Q. What sort of table is this ?
A. This is a writing-table.
Q. How many writing-tables are there here ?
A. There are two writing-tables.
Q. Are both these two writing-tables yours ?
A. (They) aren't both mine, this big one is mine, that small small one isn't mine.
Q. Whose is that small one ?
A. That small one is the student's.

LESSON 8

IV

(問答) wen⁴-ta²
question and answer

Q. *Na⁴ wei⁴ ku¹-niang² tou¹ yu³ shen²-ma¹ tung¹-hsi¹?*
A. *Na⁴ wei⁴ ku¹-niang² yu³ shu¹, yu³ chih³, yu³ pen³-tzu¹, yu³ ch'ien¹-pi³, yu³ mao²-pi³, shen²-ma¹-ti¹.*
Q. *T'a¹ yu³ to¹-shao³ chih¹ ch'ien¹-pi³ to¹-shao³ chih¹ [mao²-pi³?*
A. *T'a¹ yu³ shih² chi³ chih¹ ch'ien¹-pi³ erh⁴-shih² chi³ chih¹ mao²-pi³.*
Q. *Nin²-ti¹ erh²-tzu¹ yu³ chi³ chang¹ chih³, chi³ pen³ shu¹, chi³ ke⁴ pen³-tzu¹?*
A. *Wo³ erh²-tzu¹ yu³ wu³ chang¹ chih³, pa² ke⁴ pen³-tzu¹, chiu³ pen³ shu¹.*

Q. What (things) have those girls got?
A. Those girls have books, paper, note-books, pencils, writing-brushes, and so on.
Q. How many pencils and how many writing-brushes has [he?
A. He has ten odd pencils and twenty odd writing-brushes.
Q. How many sheets of paper, books and note-books has your son got?
A. My son has five sheets of paper, eight note-books and nine books.

V

(問答) wen⁴-ta² question and answer

Q. *Na⁴ ke⁴ jen² shih⁴* shen²-ma¹ *jen², nin²* chih¹-tao⁴ *pu⁴ chih¹-tao⁴?*

A. *Wo³* chih¹-tao⁴, *na⁴ ke⁴ jen² shih⁴* hsien¹-sheng¹.

Q. *T'a¹ shih⁴* shui²-ti¹ *hsien¹-sheng¹?*

A. *T'a¹ shih⁴ wo³-men²-ti¹ hsien¹-sheng¹.*

Q. *Ni³-men² shih⁴* chi³ *wei⁴ hsüeh²-sheng¹?*

A. *Wo³-men² shih⁴* liu⁴ *ke⁴ hsüeh²-sheng¹.*

Q. *Ni³-men² liu⁴ wei⁴ yu³* chi³ *wei⁴ hsien¹-sheng¹?*

A. *Wo³-men² yu³* liang³ *wei⁴ hsien¹-sheng¹.*

Q. *Ni³-men²-ti¹ hsien¹-sheng¹ yu³* to¹-shao³ *wei⁴ hsüeh²-sheng¹?*

A. *I⁴ wei⁴ hsien¹-sheng¹ yu³* san¹-shih² to¹ *wei⁴, i⁴ wei⁴ hsien¹-sheng¹ yu³* ssu⁴-shih² chi³ *wei⁴.*

Q. Do you know what sort of man that person is?
A. I know that man is a teacher.
Q. Whose teacher is he?
A. He is our teacher.
Q. How many students are you?
A. We are six students.
Q. You six (students) have how many teachers?
A. We have two teachers.
Q. How many students have your teachers got?
A. One teacher has more than thirty, and one teacher has more than forty.

LESSON 8

VI

(問答) wen⁴-*ta*²
question and answer

Q. *Na⁴ shih⁴* shen²-ma¹?
A. *Na⁴ shih⁴* wan³.
Q. *Na⁴ shih⁴* shen²-ma¹ *wan*³?
A. *Na⁴ shih⁴ fan⁴-wan³.*
Q. *Na⁴ shih⁴* nin²-*ti*¹ *fan⁴-wan³* ma¹?
A. *Na⁴* pu² *shih⁴ wo³-ti*¹ *fan⁴-wan³, na⁴ shih⁴* t'a¹-*ti*¹
Q. Nin² yeh³ yu³ *fan⁴-wan³* ma¹? [*fan⁴-wan³.*
A. *Shih⁴, wo³* yeh³ yu³ *fan⁴-wan³.*
Q. Ni³-men² yu³ *fan⁴-wan³,* yeh³ yu³ ch'a²-*wan³* ma¹?
A. *Shih⁴, wo³-men²* yeh³ yu³ ch'a²-*wan³.*
Q. *Na⁴*-hsieh¹ ch'a²-*wan³ shih⁴* ni³-*men²-ti*¹ ma¹?
A. **Shih⁴** *wo³-men²-ti*¹.

Q. What is that?
A. That is a bowl.
Q. What sort of bowl is that?
A. That is a rice-bowl.
Q. Is that your rice-bowl?
A. That is not my rice-bowl, that is his rice-bowl.
Q. Have you also got a rice-bowl?
A. Yes, I also have a rice-bowl.
Q. You have (some) rice-bowls, have (you) also got (some)
A. Yes, we also have (some) tea-cups. [tea-cups?
Q. Are those tea-cups yours?
A. (They) are ours.

VII

(問答) wen⁴-ta²
question and answer

Q. Shui² yu³ i³-tzu¹ ?
A. Wo³-men² yu³ i³-tzu¹.
Q. Ni³-men² yu³ to¹-shao³ pa² i³-tzu¹ ?
A. Wo³-men² yu³ erh⁴-shih⁴ to¹ pa² i³-tzu¹.
Q. T'a¹-men² yeh³ yu³ i³-tzu¹ ma¹ ?
A. T'a¹-men² yeh³ yu³ i³-tzu¹.
Q. Shih⁴ ni³-men²-ti¹ i³-tzu¹ to¹ shih⁴ t'a¹-men²-ti¹ i³-tzu¹ ⌊to¹ ?
A. Wo³-men²-ti¹ i³-tzu¹ to¹, t'a¹-men²-ti¹ i³-tzu¹ shao³.
Q. T'a¹-men² yu³ to¹-shao³ pa² i³-tzu¹ ?
A. T'a¹-men² yu³ shih² chi³ pa² i³-tzu¹.
Q. Ni³-men²-ti¹ i³-tzu¹ ta⁴ pu² ta⁴ ?
A. Wo³-men²-ti¹ i³-tzu¹ pu² ta⁴ pu² hsiao³.
Q. Shih⁴ ni³-men²-ti¹ i³-tzu¹ ta⁴ shih⁴ t'a¹-men²-ti¹ i³-tzu¹ ⌊ta⁴ ?
A. Wo³-men²-ti¹ i³-tzu¹ mei² yu³ t'a¹-men²-ti¹ i³-tzu¹ ta⁴.

Q. Who has some chairs ?
A. We have some chairs.
Q. How many chairs have you got ?
A. We have twenty odd chairs.
Q. Have they also got some chairs ?
A. They also have chairs.
Q. Have you more chairs than they have ?
A. We have more chairs than they have.

Q. How many chairs have they?
A. They have over ten chairs.
Q. Are your chairs large?
A. Our chairs are not large nor are they small.
Q. Are your chairs larger than their chairs?
A. Our chairs are not as large as their chairs.

VIII

(問答) wen⁴-ta²
question and answer

Q. Na⁴ ke⁴ jen² yu³ **yang²** mei² yu³?
A. **Yu³ yang²**.
Q. T'a¹ yeh³ yu³ **niu²** ma¹?
A. Shih⁴, t'a¹ yeh³ yu³ niu².
Q. Shih⁴ **yang²** to¹ shih⁴ **niu²** to¹?
A. T'a¹-ti¹ yang² to¹, niu² **shao³**.
Q. T'a¹ yu³ to¹-shao³ chih¹ yang², **chi³** t'ou² niu²?
A. T'a¹ yu³ chi³ **pai³** chih¹ yang², pa¹ t'ou² niu².
Q. Na⁴-hsieh¹ k'ou³ chu¹ yeh³ shih⁴ t'a¹-ti¹ ma¹?
A. Pu² shih⁴, t'a¹ **mei²** yu³ chu¹.

Q. Has that man got any sheep?
A. He has some sheep.
Q. Has he also got some cows?
A. Yes, he also has some cows.
Q. Has he more sheep than cows?
A. He has more sheep than cows.

Q. How many sheep and how many cows has he?
A. He has several hundred sheep and eight cows.
Q. Are those pigs also his?
A. No, he has no pigs.

IX

(問答) **wen**^{4}-*ta*^{2}
question and answer

Q. *Che*^{4}-*hsieh*^{1} *k'uai*^{4} *jou*^{4}, **tou**^{1} **shih**^{4} **shen**^{2}-*ma*^{1} *jou*^{4}?
A. *Yu*^{3} **yang**^{2}-*jou*^{4}, *yu*^{3} **niu**^{2}-*jou*^{4}, *yeh*^{3} *yu*^{3} **chu**^{1}-*jou*^{4}.
Q. *Che*^{4}-*hsieh*^{1} *k'uai*^{4} *jou*^{4}, *na*^{4}-*hsieh*^{1} *t'iao*^{2} *yü*^{2}, **tou**^{1} **shih**^{4}
A. *Tou*^{1} *shih*^{4} **na**^{4} *ke*^{4} *jen*^{2}-*ti*^{1}. |**shui**^{2}-*ti*^{1}?
Q. *Che*^{4} *t'iao*^{2} *yü*^{2} **ta**^{4} *pu*^{2} *ta*^{4}?
A. *Che*^{4} *t'iao*^{2} *yü*^{2} **ta**^{4}.

Q. What sort of meat are all these pieces of meat?
A. There is mutton, beef and also pork.
Q. Whose are all these pieces of meat and those fish?
A. They are all that man's.
Q. Is this fish big?
A. This fish is big.

X

(問答) **wen**^{4}-*ta*^{2}
question and answer

Q. *Na*^{4} *wei*^{4} *shih*^{4} **shui**^{2}?
A. *Na*^{4} *wei*^{4} *shih*^{4} *wo*^{3} **fu**^{4}-*ch'in*^{1}.

LESSON 8

Q. *Na⁴ wei⁴ shih⁴ ni³ mu³-ch'in¹ ma¹?*
A. *Shih⁴, na⁴ wei⁴ shih⁴ wo³ mu³-ch'in¹.*   [*ma¹?*
Q. *Na⁴ chih¹ ch'ang² ch'ien¹-pi³ shih⁴ ni³ fu⁴-ch'in¹-ti¹*
A. *Pu² shih⁴, na⁴ chih¹ tuan³-ti¹ shih⁴ wo³ fu⁴-ch'in¹-ti¹, na⁴ chih¹ ch'ang²-ti¹ shih⁴ wo³ mu³-ch'in¹-ti¹.*
Q. *Na⁴ ke⁴ po¹-li²-pei¹ shih⁴ shui²-ti¹?*
A. *Na⁴ ke⁴ po¹-li²-pei¹ shih⁴ shui²-ti¹, wo³ pu⁴ chih¹-tao⁴.*
Q. *Na⁴ ke⁴ k'a¹-fei⁴ shih⁴ ni³ mu³-ch'in¹-ti¹ ma¹?*
A. *Shih⁴ wo³ mu³-ch'in¹-ti¹.*
Q. *Na⁴ shih⁴ chi³ chin¹ ch'a²-yeh⁴, chi³ chin¹ k'a¹-fei⁴?*
A. *Na⁴ shih⁴ san¹ chin¹ ch'a²-yeh⁴, wu³ chin¹ k'a¹-fei⁴.*

Q. Who is that?
A. That is my father.
Q. Is that your mother?
A. Yes, that is my mother.
Q. Is that long pencil your father's?
A. No, that short one is my father's, that long one is my
Q. Whose is that glass?   [mother's.
A. I don't know whose that glass is.
Q. Is that coffee your mother's?
A. It is my mother's.
Q. How many catties of tea and how many catties of coffee are there there?
A. There are three catties of tea and five catties of coffee there.

NOTES

32. Approximate Numbers are expressed:-

(a) By adding the character 多 **to¹**—more, much, many, after the tens and hundreds:

有 十 多 位 學 生　　have ten more
yu³ shih² to¹ wei⁴ hsüeh²-sheng¹　　students
(there are more than ten students)

有 一 百 多 把 椅 子　　have one hundred more
yu³ i⁴-pai³ to¹ pa² i³-tzu¹　　chairs
(there are one hundred odd chairs)

有 七 百 多 斤　　have seven hundred more
yu³ ch'i¹ pai³ to¹ chin¹　　catties
(there are over seven hundred catties)

(b) By adding the character 幾 **chi³**—several, before the numerals 百 **pai³**—hundred, and 千 **ch'ien¹**—thousand:

有 幾 百 張 桌 子　　have several hundred
yu³ chi³ pai³ chang¹ cho¹-tzu¹　　tables
(there are several hundred tables)

有 幾 千 口 猪　　have several thousand pigs
yu³ chi³ ch'ien¹ k'ou³ chu¹　　(there are several thousand pigs)

33. 都 **tou¹** may usually be translated as: all, but in some cases it is omitted in English, merely implying completeness.

LESSON 8

這 三 百 頭 牛 都 是 我 的
che⁴ san¹-pai³ t'ou² niu² tou¹ shih⁴ wo³-ti¹
These three hundred cows all are mine
(These three hundred cows are all mine)

這 都 是 學 生 | These all are students
che⁴ tou¹ shih⁴ hsüeh²-sheng¹ | (All these are students)

寫 字 念 書 他 都 不 會
hsieh³ tzu⁴ nien⁴ shu¹ t'a¹ tou¹ pu² hui⁴
Write characters read books he all not can
(He can neither read nor write)

34. 這 **che⁴**-this, 那 **na⁴**-that. The plural of these pronouns is formed by addition of the character 些 **hsieh¹**—some, several, as a suffix.

| 這 些 *che⁴-hsieh¹* | these | 這 些 人 *che⁴-hsieh¹ jen²* | these men, these people |
| 那 些 *na⁴-hsieh¹* | those | 那 些 東 西 *na⁴-hsieh¹ tung¹-hsi¹* | those things |

LESSON 9

I

作 **tso⁴** to make, to do   (做) **tso⁴** to make, to do

(棹子) **cho¹-tzu¹** table(s)   (椅子) **I³-tzu¹** chair(s)

1. Che⁴ ke⁴ jen² tso⁴ shu¹-cho¹-tzu¹, na⁴ ke⁴ jen² tso⁴ fan⁴-cho¹-tzu¹.
2. Ni³-men² tso⁴ I³-tzu¹ ma¹? Shih⁴, wo³-men² tso⁴ i³-tzu¹.
3. Nin² tso⁴ i³-tzu¹, yeh³ tso⁴ cho¹-tzu¹ ma¹?
   Wo³ yeh³ tso⁴ cho¹-tzu¹.
4. Na⁴ wei⁴ hsüeh²-sheng¹ tso⁴ shen²-ma¹?
   T'a¹ tso⁴ I³-tzu¹.
5. Na⁴ ke⁴ jen² tso⁴ shen²-ma¹ cho¹-tzu¹?
   Na⁴ ke⁴ jen² tso⁴ shu¹-tso¹-tzu¹, yeh³ tso⁴ fan⁴-cho¹-tzu¹.

1. This man is making a writing-table, that man is making a dining-table.
2. Are you making chairs? Yes, we are making chairs.
3. You are making a chair, are you also making a table? I am also making a table.
4. What is that pupil making? He is making a chair.
5. What sort of tables is that man making?
   That man is making a writing-table and (he) is also making a dining-table.

LESSON 9

II

作書　tso⁴ shu¹
to compose a book, to write a book

1. *Hsien¹-sheng¹ tso⁴ shu¹ pu² tso⁴?*
   Hsien¹-sheng¹ tso⁴ shu¹.
2. *Shih⁴ hsien¹-sheng¹ tso⁴ shu¹ shih⁴ hsüeh²-sheng¹ tso⁴*
   Shih⁴ hsien¹-sheng¹ tso⁴ shu¹.　　　　　　　　[*shu¹?*
3. *Ni³-men²-ti¹ hsien¹-sheng¹ tso⁴ shu¹ pu² tso⁴?*
   T'a¹ pu² tso⁴ shu⁴.

1. Does the teacher compose books?
   The teacher does compose books.
2. Does the teacher write books or does the pupil write
   The teacher writes books.　　　　　　　　[books?
3. Does your teacher compose books?
   He does not compose books.

III

做飯　tso⁴ fan⁴
to prepare food, to cook

1. *Nin² mu³-ch'in¹ tso⁴ shen²-ma¹?*
   Wo³ mu³-ch'in¹ tso⁴ fan⁴.
2. *Nin²-ti¹ ku¹-niang² tso⁴ fan⁴ pu² tso⁴?*
   T'a¹ pu² tso⁴ fan⁴.
3. *T'a¹ pu² tso⁴ fan⁴, t'a¹ tso⁴ shen²-ma¹?*
   T'a¹ pu² tso⁴ shen²-ma¹.

4. *Ni³-men²-ti¹ fan⁴ shih⁴* **shui²** *tso⁴?*
   Wo³-men²-ti¹ fan⁴ shih⁴ **na⁴** *ke⁴ jen² tso⁴.*

1. What is your mother doing ? My mother is cooking.
2. Does your daughter prepare the food ?
   She does not prepare the food.
3. She isn't cooking, what is she doing ?
   She isn't doing anything.
4. Who cooks your food ? That person cooks our food.

IV

寫　**hsieh³**
　　to write

1. **Shui²** *hsieh³ tzu⁴?* *Wo³ hsieh³ tzu⁴.*
2. *Hsien¹-sheng¹* **hsieh³** *tzu⁴ ma¹?*
   Hsien¹-sheng¹ yeh³ hsieh³ tzu⁴.
3. *Nin²-ti¹ erh²-tzu¹ hsieh³ tzu⁴ pu⁴ hsieh³?*
   T'a¹ pu⁴ hsieh³ tzu⁴.
4. *Nin²-ti¹ ku¹-niang² hsieh³ tzu⁴, t'a¹ yu³* **mao²-*pi³*** *ma¹?*
5. *T'a¹ mei² yu³ mao²-pi³, t'a¹ yu³* **kang¹-*pi³*.**

1. Who writes characters ? I write characters.
2. Does the teacher write characters ?
   The teacher also writes characters.
3. Is your son writing characters ?
   He is not writing characters.
4. Your daughter writes characters, has she a writing-brush ?
5. She has not got a writing-brush, she has a pen.

LESSON 9

V

念 nien⁴
to read, to study

1. *Na⁴ wei⁴ hsüeh²-sheng¹ nien⁴ shu¹ ma¹?*
   Na⁴ wei⁴ hsüeh²-sheng¹ nien⁴ shu¹.
2. *Nin² pu² nien⁴ shu¹, nin² tso⁴ shen²-ma¹?*
   Wo³ hsieh³ tzu⁴.
3. *Che⁴ ke⁴ tzu⁴ nien⁴ shen²-ma¹?*
   Che⁴ ke⁴ tzu⁴ nien⁴ 'chih'³.
4. *Na⁴ pen³ shu¹ nin² nien⁴ pu² nien⁴? Wo³ pu² nien⁴.*
5. *Na⁴ liang³ wei⁴ ku¹-niang² shih⁴ shui² nien⁴ shu¹?*
   Shih⁴ na⁴ wei⁴ ta⁴-ti¹ nien⁴ shu¹.
6. *Na⁴ wei⁴ hsien¹-sheng¹-ti¹ erh²-tzu¹ nien⁴ shu¹ pu² nien⁴? T'a¹ nien⁴ shu¹.*
7. *Ni³-men² yu³ shu¹ nien⁴ ma¹?*
   T'a¹ yu³ shu¹ nien⁴, wo³ mei² yu³ shu¹ nien⁴.

1. Is that pupil reading a book?
   That pupil is reading a book.
2. You are not reading a book, what are you doing?
   I am writing characters.
3. What does this character read?
   This character reads *chih*.
4. Are you reading that book? I am not reading (it).
5. Which of those two girls is studying?
   (Those two girls is who reading a book?)
   That tall one is studying.

6. Does that teacher's son study?
   He does study.
7. Have you got a book to read?
   He has a book to read, I haven't a book to read.

VI

 hui⁴
to be able, can

1. *Ni³* **hui⁴** *tso⁴ fan⁴ ma¹?* *Wo³* **hui⁴** *tso⁴ fan⁴*.
2. *T'a¹* **hui⁴** *tso⁴* **shen²-ma¹?**
   T'a¹ hui⁴ tso⁴ **cho¹-*tzu¹*,** *yeh³ hui⁴ tso⁴ i³-tzu¹*.
3. *Nin²-ti¹* **erh²-tzu¹** **hui⁴** *tso⁴* **shu¹** *pu² hui⁴?*
   T'a¹ pu² hui⁴ tso⁴ shu¹.
4. *Na⁴ wei⁴ hsüeh²-sheng¹* **hui⁴** *hsieh³* **to¹-shao³** *ke⁴ tzu⁴?*
   Na⁴ wei⁴ hsüeh²-sheng¹ hui⁴ hsieh³ **chi³ shih²** *ke⁴ tzu⁴*.

1. Can you cook? I can cook.
2. What can he make?
   He can make tables and also chairs.
3. Can your son write books?
   He cannot write books.
4. How many characters can that pupil write?
   That pupil can write dozens of characters.

VII

he¹
to drink

1. *T'a¹-men²* **he¹** *ch'a² ma¹?* *T'a¹-men²* **he¹** *ch'a²*.
2. **Shui²** *pu⁴* **he¹** *ch'a²?* *Wo³ pu⁴* **he¹** *ch'a²*.

LESSON 9

3. *Nin² he¹ shui³ ma¹? Wo³ he¹ shui³.*
4. *T'a¹ shih⁴ he¹ k'a¹-fei⁴ shih⁴ he¹ ch'a²? T'a¹ tou¹ pu⁴ he¹.*
5. *Na⁴ wei⁴ ku¹-niang² yu³ ch'a² he¹ mei² yu³?*
   T'a¹ yu³ ch'a² he¹.
6. *Wo³ yu³ ch'a², nin² he¹ pu⁴ he¹? Wo³ he¹.*

1. Are they drinking tea? They are drinking tea.
2. Who isn't drinking tea? I am not drinking tea.
3. Are you drinking water? I am drinking water.
4. Is he drinking coffee or tea?
   He isn't drinking anything.
5. Has that girl any tea to drink?
   She has some tea to drink.
6. I have some tea, (will) you drink? I (will) drink.

VIII

吃　ch'ih¹
　　to eat

1. *Ni³ ch'ih¹ shen²-ma¹? Wo³ ch'ih¹ mien⁴-pao¹.*
2. *Ni³-ti¹ erh²-tzu¹ ch'ih¹ yang²-jou⁴ pu⁴ ch'ih¹?*
   Wo³-ti¹ erh²-tzu¹ pu⁴ ch'ih¹ yang²-jou⁴.
3. *Ni³-ti¹ ku¹-niang² ch'ih¹ yü² pu⁴ ch'ih¹?*
   T'a¹ ch'ih¹ yü².
4. *Ni³ shih⁴ ch'ih¹ chu¹-jou⁴ shih⁴ ch'ih¹ niu²-jou⁴?*
   Wo³ ch'ih¹ chu¹-jou⁴.
5. *Na⁴ wei⁴ hsien¹-sheng¹ ch'ih¹ shen²-ma¹?*
   T'a¹ ch'ih¹ fan⁴.
6. *Nin² ch'ih¹ fan⁴ pu⁴ ch'ih¹ fan⁴? Wo³ pu⁴ ch'ih¹ fan⁴.*
7. *Nin² ch'ih¹ shen²-ma¹ jou⁴? Wo³ ch'ih¹ yang²-jou⁴.*

8. *Nin²-ti¹ fu⁴-ch'in¹ ch'ih¹* **shen²-ma¹ jou⁴?**
   Wo³-ti¹ fu⁴-ch'in¹ ch'ih¹ **chu¹-jou⁴.**
9. *Nin²-ti¹ mu³-ch'in¹ yeh³ ch'ih¹* **chu¹-jou⁴ ma¹?**
   Pu² shih⁴, t'a¹ ch'ih¹ **niu²-jou⁴.**
10. *Na⁴ ke⁴ jen² yu³* **fan⁴ ch'ih¹** *mei² yu³?*
    T'a¹ yu³ **fan⁴ ch'ih¹.**
11. *Na⁴ liang³ ke⁴ jen², shui² yu³ fan⁴ ch'ih¹,* **shui² mei²** *yu³ fan⁴ ch'ih¹? T'a¹ men²* **tou¹** *yu³ fan⁴ ch'ih¹.*

1. What are you eating? I am eating bread.
2. Is your son eating mutton?
   My son is not eating mutton.
3. Is your daughter eating fish? She is eating fish.
4. Are you eating pork or beef? I am eating pork.
5. What is that teacher eating? He is eating cooked rice.
6. Are you eating? I am not eating.
7. What sort of meat are you eating? I am eating mutton.
8. What sort of meat is your father eating?
   My father is eating pork.
9. Does your mother also eat pork? No, she eats beef.
10. Has that man any food to eat? He has food to eat.
11. Which of those two men has food to eat and which hasn't food to eat? They both have food to eat.

IX

要　yao⁴
　　to want, will, shall.

1. *Na⁴ wei⁴ hsien¹-sheng¹* **yao⁴ tso⁴ shen¹-ma¹?**
   T'a¹ yao⁴ **hsieh³ tzu⁴.**

LESSON 9

2. *Na⁴ wei⁴ hsüeh²-sheng¹* **yao⁴** *tso⁴* **shen²-ma¹**?
   T'a¹ yao⁴ **tso⁴** *i³-tzu¹*.
3. *Nin²-ti¹ erh²-tzu¹ yao⁴* **ch'ih¹ shen²-ma¹**?
   Wo³-ti¹ erh²-tzu¹ yao⁴ ch'ih¹ yü².
4. *Nin²-ti¹ fu⁴-ch'in¹ shih⁴ yao⁴ hsieh³ ta⁴ tzu⁴ shih⁴ yao⁴ hsieh³* **hsiao³** *tzu⁴*?
   Wo³-ti¹ fu⁴-ch'in¹ yao⁴ hsieh³ **hsiao³** *tzu⁴*.
5. *Nin²-ti¹* **mu³** *ch'in¹ yao⁴ he¹ ch'a² shih⁴ yao⁴ he¹* **shui³**?
   T'a¹ yao⁴ he¹ **ch'a²**.
6. *Na⁴ chi³ ke⁴ ku¹-niang² shih⁴ yao⁴ nien⁴ shu¹ pu² shih⁴*?
   Shih⁴, t'a¹-men² shih⁴ yao⁴ nien⁴ shu¹.
7. *Nin² yao⁴ he¹ k'a¹-fei⁴ ma¹*?
   Wo³ pu⁴ he¹ k'a¹-fei⁴, wo³ yao⁴ he¹ ch'a².
8. *T'a¹ yao⁴ tso⁴ cho¹-tzu¹ ma¹*?
   Pu² shih⁴, t'a¹ yao⁴ tso⁴ i³-tzu¹.
9. *Ni³* **yao⁴** *nien⁴* **che⁴** *pen³ shu¹ ma¹*?
   Shih⁴, wo³ **yao⁴** *nien⁴ che⁴ pen³ shu¹*.
10. *Nin² yao⁴ ch'ih¹ niu²-jou⁴ ma¹*?
    Pu² shih⁴, wo³ yao⁴ ch'ih¹ chu¹-jou⁴.
11. *Nin² pu⁴ ch'ih¹ yang²-jou⁴, nin² yao⁴ ch'ih¹ shen²-ma¹*?
    Wo³ yao⁴ ch'ih¹ mien⁴-pao¹.
12. *Nin² yao⁴ ch'ih¹ fan⁴ ma¹*? *Shih⁴, wo³ yao⁴ ch'ih¹ fan⁴*.

1. What does that teacher want to do?
   He wants to write characters.
2. What does that student want to do?
   He wants to make a chair.
3. What does your son want to eat?
   My son wants to eat fish.

4. Does your father want to write large characters or small characters?
   My father wants to write small characters.
5. Does your mother want to drink tea or water?
   She wants to drink tea.
6. Do those girls want to study?
   Yes, they want to study.
7. Do you want to drink coffee?
   I will not drink coffee, I want to drink tea.
8. Does he want to make a table?
   No, he wants to make a chair.
9. Do you want to read this book?
   Yes, I want to read this book.
10. Do you want to eat beef? No, I want to eat pork.
11. You don't eat mutton, what do you want to eat?
    I want to eat bread.
12. Do you want to eat? Yes, I want to eat.

LESSON 9

NOTES

35. Verbs. Some verbs consist of only one character, while some have two or more characters, e. g.:

念 nien⁴ — to read, to study

寫 hsieh³ — to write

作 tso⁴ — to make, to do

知道 chih¹-tao⁴ — to know, consists of 知 chih¹ — to know, to perceive, and 道 tao⁴ — way, road.

36. Compound Verbs are often formed by combining a simple verb with a noun:

念 書 nien⁴ shu⁴ — to read a book aloud (to study) (to learn)

寫 字 hsieh³ tzu⁴ — to write characters (to write)

吃 飯 ch'ih¹ fan⁴ — to eat food, to eat cooked rice (to eat)

37. 作 tso⁴, 做 tso⁴. Both these characters may be translated as: to do, to make. They are pronounced the same. Strictly speaking, 作 implies: to do, to act, to make, with the use of the brain. 做 implies the use of the hands in making or doing. 作 is used throughout this book.

Some compound verbs from 作 are:

作 書 tso⁴ shu¹ — to make a book (to write a book) (to compose a book)

作 飯 { to make food, to make rice
tso⁴ fan⁴ (to prepare food) (to cook)

作 甚 麼 { to do what
tso⁴ shen²-ma¹ (for what)

This last phrase has two translations, depending on the context, e. g. :

你 要 作 甚 麼? { You want to do what ?
ni³ yao⁴ tso⁴ shen²-ma¹? (What do you want to do ?)

你 寫 字 作 甚 麼? { you write characters
ni³ hsieh³ tzu⁴ tso⁴ shen²-ma¹? to do what ?
(What are you writing characters for ?)
(What do you write characters for ?)

38. **Word Order.** The object usually follows the verb in the sentence (see § 36), but sometimes precedes it. This order is found with the verb 有 **yu³** — to have, e. g. :

我 有 飯 吃 { I have food to eat
wo³ yu³ fan⁴ ch'ih¹ (I have some food to eat)

我 有 書 念 { I have a book to read
wo³ yu³ shu¹ nien⁴

我 有 茶 喝 { I have tea to drink
wo³ yu³ ch'a² he¹ (I have some tea to drink)

LESSON 9

similarly in the negative:

我 沒 有 飯 吃　(I have not food to eat
wo³ mei² yu³ fan⁴ ch'ih¹　(I have no food to eat)

我 沒 有 書 念　(I have not a book to read
wo³ mei² yu³ shu¹ nien⁴　(I have no book to read)

我 沒 有 茶 喝　(I have not tea to drink
wo³ mei² yu³ ch'a² he¹　(I have no tea to drink)

39. **Future Time** is indicated by the use of the character 要 yao⁴— to want, which may often be translated as: will, shall.

我 要 寫 字　(I want to write characters
wo³ yao⁴ hsieh³ tzu⁴　(I shall write characters

我 要 念 書　(I want to study
wo³ yao⁴ nien⁴ shu¹　(I shall study

我 要 吃 飯　(I want to eat
wo³ yao⁴ ch'ih¹ fan⁴　(I shall eat

similarly in the negative:

我 不 要 寫 字　(I don't want to write characters
wo³ pu² yao⁴ hsieh³ tzu⁴　I shall not write characters

我 不 要 念 書　(I don't want to study
wo³ pu² yao⁴ nien⁴ shu¹　I shall not study

我 不 要 吃 飯　(I don't want to eat
wo³ pu² yao⁴ ch'ih¹ fan⁴　I shall not eat

LESSON 10

I

今天 chin¹-t'ien¹ to-day

昨天 tso²-t'ien¹ yesterday

明天 ming²-t'ien¹ to-morrow

了 la¹ particle denoting the past tense

1. Chin¹-t'ien¹ ni³-men² nien⁴ shu¹ pu² nien⁴?
   Chin¹-t'ien¹ wo³-men² nien⁴ shu¹.
2. Tso²-t'ien¹ ni³-men² nien⁴ shu¹ la¹ ma¹?
   Tso²-t'ien¹ wo³-men² mei² nien⁴ shu¹.
3. Ming²-t'ien¹ ni³-men² yao⁴ nien⁴ shu¹ ma¹?
   Ming²-t'ien¹ wo³-men² pu² nien⁴ shu¹.
4. Nin² chin¹-t'ien¹ yao⁴ tso⁴ shen²-ma¹?
   Wo³ chin¹-t'ien¹ yao⁴ tso⁴ fan⁴-cho¹-tzu¹.
5. Nin² chin¹-t'ien¹ hsieh³ tzu⁴ la¹ ma¹?
   Wo³ chin¹-t'ien¹ hsieh³ tzu⁴ la¹.
   Hsieh³-la¹ to¹-shao³ ke⁴ tzu⁴?
   Hsieh³-la¹ erh⁴-pai³ to¹ ke⁴ tzu⁴.
6. Na⁴ wei⁴ hsüeh²-sheng¹ ming²-t'ien¹ tso⁴ shu¹-cho¹-tzu¹ pu² tso⁴?
   T'a¹ ming²-t'ien¹ pu² tso⁴.
7. Tso²-t'ien¹ nin² tso⁴ shen²-ma¹ mei² tso⁴?
   Tso²-t'ien¹ wo³ mei² tso⁴ shen²-ma¹.
8. T'a¹-ti¹ ku¹-niang² he¹ ch'a² pu⁴ he¹?
   T'a¹ pu⁴ he¹, t'a¹ he¹-la¹.

LESSON 10

9. *T'a*¹ *he*¹-*la*¹ **chi**³ *wan*³ *ch'a*² ?
   *T'a*¹ *he*¹-*la*¹ **liang**³ *wan*³ *ch'a*².
10. *Nin*²-*ti*¹ *erh*²-*tzu*¹ **ch'ih**¹ *fan*⁴ *la*¹ *ma*¹ ?
    *T'a*¹ *mei*² *chih*¹ *fan*⁴.
11. *T'a*¹ **yeh**³ *mei*² *he*¹ *ch'a*² *ma*¹ ? [*k'a*¹-*fei*⁴.
    *T'a*¹ **yeh**³ *mei*² *he*¹ *ch'a*², *t'a*¹ *he*¹-*la*¹ *l*⁴ *po*¹-*li*²-*pei*¹
12. *Na*⁴ *ke*⁴ *jen*² *ch'ih*¹-*la*¹ **chi**³ *wan*³ *fan*⁴ ?
    *Na*⁴ *ke*⁴ *jen*² *ch'ih*¹-*la*¹ *l*⁴ *wan*³ *fan*⁴.
13. *Nin*² *he*¹-*la*¹ *l*⁴ *wan*³ **ch'a**² *ma*¹ ?
    *Pu*² *shih*⁴, *wo*³ *he*¹-*la*¹ **liang**³ *wan*³.
14. *Nin*² *ch'ih*¹-*la*¹ *l*⁴ *wan*³ *fan*⁴ *ma*¹ ?
    *Shih*⁴, *wo*³ *ch'ih*¹-*la*¹ *l*⁴ *wan*³ *fan*⁴.

1. Are you studying to-day ? To-day we are studying.
2. Did you study yesterday ? Yesterday we did not study.
3. Will you study to-morrow ?
   To-morrow we shall not study.
4. What will you do to-day ?
   To-day I shall make a dining-table.
5. Have you written any characters to-day ?
   I have written some characters to-day.
   How many characters have you written ?
   I have written more than two hundred characters.
6. Will that pupil make a writing-table to-morrow ?
   He will not make one to-morrow.
7. Did you do anything yesterday ?
   I did not do anything yesterday.
8. Is his daughter drinking tea ?
   She is not drinking, she has drunk (some tea).

9. How many cups of tea has he drunk?
   He has drunk two cups of tea.
10. Has your son eaten? He has not eaten.
11. Hasn't he drunk some tea either?
   He hasn't drunk any tea either (but) he has drunk a glass of coffee.
12. How many bowls of rice has that man eaten?
   That man has eaten one bowl of rice.
13. Did you drink one cup of tea? No, I drank two cups.
14. Did you eat one bowl of rice?
   Yes, I ate one bowl of rice.

II

的 ti[1]
particle denoting the past participle

1. *Che⁴ chang¹* **fan⁴-cho¹-tzu¹** *shih⁴* **shui²** *tso⁴-ti¹?*
   Che⁴ chang¹ fan⁴-cho¹-tzu¹ shih⁴ **t'a¹** *tso⁴-ti¹.*
2. *Na⁴ ke⁴ fan⁴ shih⁴ nin²* **mu³-ch'in¹** *tso⁴-ti¹ ma¹?*
   Shih⁴ *t'a¹ tso⁴-ti¹.*
3. *Na⁴ chang¹ shu¹-cho¹-tzu¹ shih⁴ nin²-ti¹ erh²-tzu¹ tso⁴-*
   Shih⁴ *wo³ erh²-tzu¹ tso⁴-ti¹.*   ⌊ *ti¹ ma¹?*
4. *Che⁴-***hsieh¹** *pen³ shu¹ shih⁴* **shui²** *tso⁴-ti¹?*
   Che⁴-hsieh¹ shu¹ shih⁴ na⁴ wei⁴ hsien¹-sheng¹ tso⁴-ti¹.
5. *Na⁴ i⁴ po¹-li²-pei¹* **ch'a²** *shih⁴* **shui²** *he¹·ti¹?*
   Shih⁴ *wo³* **ku¹-***niang² he¹-ti¹.*
6. *Na⁴-***hsieh¹** *k'uai⁴ yü² tou¹ shih⁴* **shui²** *ch'ih¹-ti¹?*
   Tou¹ shih⁴ **t'a¹-***men² ch'ih¹-ti¹.*
7. *Na⁴ ke⁴ tzu⁴ shih⁴ nin² hsieh³-ti¹ ma¹?*
   Pu² *shih⁴ wo³ hsieh³-ti¹, shih⁴ hsien¹-sheng¹ hsieh³-ti¹.*

LESSON 10

8. *Na⁴ pen³ shu¹ shih⁴* **nin² nien⁴-***ti¹ ma¹?*
   Shih⁴ *wo³ nien⁴-ti¹*

1. By whom was this dining-table made?
   This dining-table was made by him.
2. Was that food prepared by your mother?
   It was prepared by her.
3. Was that writing-table made by your son?
   It was made by my son.
4. By whom were these books composed?
   These books were composed by that teacher.
5. By whom was that glass of tea drunk?
   It was drunk by my daughter.
6. By whom were all those pieces of fish eaten?
   They were all eaten by them.
7. Was that character written by you?
   It was not written by me, it was written by the teacher.
8. Was that book read by you? It was read by me.

III

還 **hai²**
still more, besides, still, yet, also

1. *Na⁴ wei⁴ hsüeh²-sheng¹ yu³ shu¹,* **hai²** *yu³ shen²-ma¹?*
   T'a¹ hai² yu³ **pen³**-*tzu¹.*
2. *Na⁴ wei⁴ hsien¹-sheng¹ yu³ erh²-tzu¹,* **hai²** *yu³* **ku¹-niang²** *ma¹?*
   T'a¹ hai² yu³ **ku¹**-*niang².*
3. *Che⁴ wei⁴ yao⁴ nien⁴ shu¹,* **hai²** **yao⁴** *tso⁴ shen²-ma¹?*
   T'a¹ hai² yao⁴ **hsieh³** *tzu⁴.*

4. *Nin² chin¹-t'ien¹ tso⁴ fan⁴, nin² ming²-t'ien¹ hai² tso⁴*
   Wo³ ming²-t'ien¹ hai² tso⁴ fan⁴. [*fan⁴ ma¹?*

1. That student has a book, what else has he got?
   He also has a note-book.
2. That teacher has a son, has he a daughter besides?
   He also has a daughter.
3. This (person) wants to read a book, what else does he want to do? He also wants to write characters.
4. You are cooking to-day, will you still be cooking to-morrow? To-morrow I shall still be cooking.

IV

哪 na¹
final particle (sometimes interrogative)

1. *Ni³-men²-ti¹* **hsien¹-sheng¹ tso⁴ shen²**-*ma¹ na¹?*
   T'a¹ **tso⁴ shu¹** *na¹.*
2. *Nin²* **mu³-*ch'in¹* tso⁴ shen²**-*ma¹ na¹? T'a¹* **tso⁴ fan⁴** *na¹.*
3. *Na⁴ wei⁴ hsüeh²-sheng¹* **nien⁴ shu¹** *na¹ ma¹?*
   Shih⁴, t'a¹ **nien⁴ shu¹** *na¹.*
4. *Na⁴ ke⁴ ku¹-niang²* **tso⁴ shen²**-*ma¹ na¹?*
   T'a¹ **hsieh³ tzu⁴** *na¹.*

1. What is your teacher doing? He is composing a book.
2. What is your mother doing? She is cooking.
3. Is that student studying? Yes, he is studying.
4. What is that girl doing? She is writing characters.

LESSON 10

V

(還 ○ ○ 哪) hai² — — na¹
yet, still

1. *Nin²-ti¹* **fu⁴-ch'in¹** **he¹** *k'a¹-fei⁴ la¹ mei² yu³?*
   Hai² **mei²** **he¹** *na¹.*
2. *Ni³-men²* **ch'ih¹** **fan⁴** *la¹ ma¹?*
   Wo³-men² **hai²** **mei²** *ch'ih¹ na¹.*
3. *T'a¹-men²* **tou¹** **yu³** **ch'a²** *la¹ ma¹?*
   T'a¹-men² **hai²** **mei²** *yu³ na¹.*
4. *Nin² erh²-tzu¹* **nien⁴** **shu¹** *la¹ mei² yu³?*
   T'a¹ **hai²** **mei²** *nien⁴ na¹*
5. *Nin² yu³-la¹* **kang¹-pi³** *la¹ ma¹?*
   Wo³ **hai²** **mei²** *yu³ na¹.*
6. *Nin²* **hai²** *nien⁴* **shu¹** *na¹ ma¹?*
   Shih⁴, wo³ **hai²** *nien⁴* **shu¹***.*
7. *Na⁴ wei⁴ hsüeh²-sheng¹* **hai²** **hsieh³** **tzu⁴** *na¹ ma¹?*
   T'a¹ **hai²** *hsieh³ tzu⁴ na¹.*

1. Has your father drunk any coffee?
   (He) has not drunk any yet.
2. Have you eaten? We have not eaten yet.
3. Have they all got some tea? They have not got any yet.
4. Has your son studied? He has not studied yet.
5. Have you got a pen? I have not got (one) yet.
6. Are you still studying? Yes, I am still studying.
7. Is that student still writing characters?
   He is still writing characters.

VI

好 hao³ good, well, all right 不好 pu⁴ hao³ bad, not well, badly

1. *Na⁴ chang¹ cho¹-tzu¹ tso⁴-ti¹* **hao³**.
2. *Che⁴ pa² i³-tzu¹ tso⁴-ti¹* **pu⁴ hao³**.
3. *Na⁴*-**hsieh¹** *ke⁴* **pen³**-*tzu¹ tso⁴-ti¹* **hao³** *pu⁴ hao³* ?
   Yu³ *hao³-ti¹*, *yu³ pu⁴ hao³-ti¹*.
4. *Na⁴ wei⁴ hsüeh²-sheng¹* **hsieh³**-*ti¹ na⁴ chi³ ke⁴* **tzu⁴**, **hao³** *pu⁴ hao³* ?
   Ta⁴ tzu⁴ hsieh³-ti¹ **hao³**, **hsiao³** *tzu⁴ hsieh³-ti¹ pu⁴ hao³*.
5. *Ni³-men² ssu⁴ wei⁴* **shu¹²** *hsieh³-ti¹ tzu⁴* **hao³** ?
   Wo³-men² tou¹ hsieh³-ti¹ **hao³**.
6. *Che⁴ pen³* **shu¹** *tso⁴-ti¹* **hao³** *pu⁴ hao³* ?
   Che⁴ pen³ **shu¹** *tso⁴-ti¹* **hao³**.
7. *Na⁴ ke⁴ fan⁴ tso⁴-ti¹* **hao³** *pu⁴ hao³* ?
   Na⁴ ke⁴ fan⁴ tso⁴-ti¹ **pu⁴ hao³**.
8. *Na⁴ wei⁴ hsüeh²-sheng¹ nien⁴-ti¹* **shu¹** **hao³** *pu⁴ hao³* ?
   T'a¹ nien⁴-ti¹ **hao³**.

1. That table is well made.
2. This chair is badly made.
3. Are those note-books well made ?
   Some are good ones and some are bad ones.
   (Have good ones, have bad ones.)
4. Did that student write those (numerous) characters well ?
   The large characters are well written, the small characters are badly written.

LESSON 10

5. Which of you four writes characters well?
    We all write well.
6. Is this book well written? This book is well written.
7. Is that food cooked well? That food is badly cooked.
8. Does that student read well? He reads well.

VII

還是 hai² shih⁴ or   啊 a¹? interrogative particle

呢 ni¹? interrogative final particle

1. *Na⁴ wei⁴ shih⁴ hsien¹-sheng¹ a¹, hai² shih⁴ hsüeh²-sheng¹ ni¹?*
    T'a¹ shih⁴ hsüeh²-sheng¹, pu² shih⁴ hsien¹-sheng¹.
2. *Na⁴ chang¹ cho¹-tzu¹ shih⁴ shu¹-cho¹-tzu¹ a¹, hai² shih⁴ fan⁴-cho¹-tzu¹ ni¹?*
    Na⁴ shih⁴ shu¹-cho¹-tzu¹.
3. *Che⁴-hsieh¹ ke⁴ tzu⁴ shih⁴ ni³ hsieh³-ti¹ a¹, hai² shih⁴ t'a¹ hsieh³-ti¹ ni¹?*
    Tou¹ shih⁴ t'a¹ hsieh³-ti¹.
4. *Ni³ shih⁴ chin¹-t'ien¹ nien⁴ shu¹ a¹, hai² shih⁴ ming²-t'ien¹ nien⁴ shu¹ ni¹?*
    Wo³ chin¹-t'ien¹ pu² nien⁴, ming²-t'ien¹ nien⁴.
5. *Che⁴ pa² i³-tzu¹ shih⁴ ni³-men² liang³ ke⁴ jen² tso⁴-ti¹ a¹, hai² shih⁴ ni³ i² ke⁴ jen² tso⁴-ti¹ ni¹?*
    Shih⁴ wo³-men² liang³ ke⁴ jen² tso⁴-ti¹.

1. Is that (person) a teacher or a student?
    He is a student, not a teacher.

2. Is that table a writing-table or a dining-table?
That is a writing-table.
3. Were these characters written by you or by him?
(They) were all written by him.
4. Are you studying to-day or will you study to-morrow?
I shall not study to-day, (I) shall study to-morrow.
5. Was this chair made by you two or was it made by you alone?   It was made by us two.

VIII

還是 hai² shih⁴
denotes comparison

好吃 hao³ ch'ih¹
good to eat, tasty

1. *Shih*⁴ **niu**²-*jou*⁴ **hao**³ **ch'ih**¹ *shih*⁴ **yang**²-*jou*⁴ **hao**³ **ch'ih**¹?
   Hai² **shih**⁴ **yang**²-*jou*⁴ **hao**³ **ch'ih**¹.
2. *Che*⁴ *liang*³ **chang**¹ *cho*¹-*tzu*¹, *shih*⁴ **che**⁴ **chang**¹ **ta**⁴ *shih*⁴ **na**⁴ **chang**¹ **ta**⁴?
   Hai² *shih*⁴ **che**⁴ **chang**¹ **ta**⁴.
3. *Shih*⁴ **ni**³ **fu**⁴-*ch'in*¹ *ti*¹ **shu**¹ **to**¹ *shih*⁴ **ni**³ **mu**³-*ch'in*¹-*ti*¹ **shu**¹ **to**¹?
   Hai² *shih*⁴ **wo**³ **fu**⁴-*ch'in*¹-*ti*¹ **to**¹. **mu**³-*ch'in*¹-*ti*¹ **shao**³.
4. *Shih*⁴ **nin**² **ku**¹-*niang*²-*ti*¹ **ch'ien**¹-*pi*³ **ch'ang**² *shih*⁴ **nin**² **erh**²-*tzu*¹-*ti*¹ **ch'ien**¹-*pi*³ **ch'ang**²?
   Hai² *shih*⁴ **wo**³ **ku**¹-*niang*²-*ti*¹ **ch'ien**¹-*pi*³ **ch'ang**².
5. *Shih*⁴ **ch'a**²-*wan*³ **ta**⁴ *shih*⁴ **fan**⁴-*wan*³ **ta**⁴?
   Hai² *shih*⁴ **fan**⁴-*wan*³ **ta**⁴, **ch'a**²-*wan*³ **hsiao**³.

6. *Shih⁴ na⁴ wei⁴ ta⁴ hsüeh²-sheng¹ hsieh³-ti¹ tzu⁴ hao³, hai² shih⁴ che⁴ wei⁴ hsiao³ hsüeh²-sheng¹ hsieh³-ti¹ tzu⁴ hao³ ni¹?*
Hai² shih⁴ na⁴ wei⁴ ta⁴ hsüeh²-sheng¹ hsieh³-ti¹ hao³.

1. Which is better to eat, beef or mutton?
   (Is beef good to eat, is mutton good to eat?)
   Mutton is better to eat.
2. Which of these two tables is the bigger?
   This one is the bigger.
3. Has your father more books than your mother?
   My father has more than my mother.
4. Which is the longer, your daughter's pencil or your son's pencil?   My daughter's pencil is the longer.
5. Which is the larger, the tea-cup or the rice-bowl?
   The rice-bowl is larger than the tea-cup.
6. Who writes characters better, that tall pupil or this short pupil?   That tall pupil writes better.

NOTES

40. Present Time is indicated by the simple form of sentence. No particles are necessary.

我 寫 字 | I write, I write characters
wo³ hsieh³ tzu⁴ | I am writing, I am writing characters

先 生 吃 飯 | The teacher eats, the teacher
hsien¹-sheng¹ ch'ih¹ fan⁴ | eats food
The teacher is eating, the teacher is eating food

Negative, with 不 pu⁴ ⁽²⁾ — no, not :

我 不 念 書 | I do not study
wo³ pu² nien⁴ shu¹ | I am not studying

學 生 不 作 書 | The student does not
hsüeh²-sheng¹ pu² tso⁴ shu¹ | compose (write) books
The student is not composing (writing) a book

41. Past Time is indicated by :

(a) Addition of the particle 了 la¹ to the verb, as a suffix.

我 寫 字 了 | I wrote, I wrote characters
wo³ hsieh³ tzu⁴ la¹ | I have written, I have written characters

先 生 吃 飯 了 | The teacher ate
hsien¹-sheng¹ ch'ih¹ fan⁴ la¹ | (some food)
The teacher has eaten (some food)

Negative, with 沒 mei² — no, not :

我 沒 念 書 了 | I did not study
wo³ mei² nien⁴ shu¹ la¹ | I have not studied

LESSON 10

學 生 沒 作 書 了
hsüeh²-sheng¹ **mei²** *tso⁴ shu¹la¹*
The student did not compose a book
The student has not composed a book

(b) Addition of the particle 的 *ti¹* to the verb, as a suffix. This forms the past participle.

那 個 字 是 我 寫 的
na⁴ ke⁴ tzu⁴ shih⁴ wo³ **hsieh³**-*ti¹*
That character was I written
(That character was written by me)

那 個 飯 是 先 生 吃 的
na⁴ ke⁴ fan⁴ shih⁴ **hsien¹**-*sheng¹* **ch'ih¹**-*ti¹*
That food was teacher eaten
(That food was eaten by the teacher)

Negative, with 不 是 *pu² shih⁴* — is not, isn't:

那 張 桌 子 不 是 我 作 的
na⁴ chang¹ cho¹-tzu¹ pu² shih⁴ wo³ tso⁴-ti¹
That table was not I made
(That table was not made by me)

那 個 咖 啡 不 是 我 喝 的
na⁴ ke⁴ k'a¹-fei⁴ pu² shih⁴ wo³ he¹-ti¹
That coffee was not I drank
(That coffee was not drunk by me)

42. 哪 *na¹* is a final particle which usually denotes PRESENT time. (It is sometimes interrogative.)

他 寫 字 哪
t'a¹ hsieh³ tzu⁴ na¹
he (she) is writing

他 不 念 書 哪
t'a¹ **pu²** *nien⁴ shu¹ na¹*
he (she) is not studying

43. 還 ○ ○ 哪 **hai**² — — *na*¹. This combination suggests that the action has not taken place yet, but will soon be completed.

他 還 沒 喝 哪 } He has not drunk any yet
*t'a*¹ **hai**² *mei*² *he*¹ *na*¹ } Still he has not drunk any

我 還 沒 念 哪 } I have not read (it) yet
*wo*³ **hai**² *mei*² *nien*⁴ *na*¹ } Still I haven't read (it)

44. 還 是 **hai**² *shih*⁴ may be translated as : or, but in some cases it merely denotes comparison and is not translated.

是 你 寫 的 還 是 他 寫 的?
*shih*⁴ *ni*³ *hsieh*³-*ti*¹ **hai**² *shih*⁴ *t'a*¹ *hsieh*³-*ti*¹?
Did you write (it) or did he write (it) ?
Was (it) written by you or by him ?

還 是 這 個 大 } This one is larger
hai² *shih*⁴ *che*⁴ *ke*⁴ *ta*⁴ } This is larger

45. 啊 **a**¹?, 呢 **ni**¹? are both interrogative particles. They are used :

   (a) As the final syllable to a phrase which is a question by virtue of its meaning, irrespective of whether 麼 **ma**¹? is also used or not.

   (b) As a final particle to any phrase, which, to the Chinese ear, would sound too abrupt without one or the other.

   See examples in this lesson, para. VII.

LESSON 11

I

甚麼○也不○ shen²-ma¹ — yeh³ pu⁴ —
甚麼○也沒○ shen²-ma¹ — yeh³ mei² —
not — any —, — nothing

誰也不○ shui² yeh³ pu⁴ —
誰也沒○ shui² yeh³ mei² —
no one —, nobody —

甚麼○都○ shen²-ma¹ — tou¹ —
— any kind of —, — all kinds of —, — everything

誰都○ shui² tou¹ —
everyone —, everybody —

1. Na⁴ wei⁴ hsüeh²-sheng¹ yu³ shen²-ma¹ tung¹-hsi¹?
   T'a¹ shen²-ma¹ yeh³ mei² yu³.
2. Nin²-ti¹ hsien¹-sheng¹ yu³ shen²-ma¹ shu¹?
   T'a¹ shen²-ma¹ shu¹ yeh³ mei² yu³.
3. Na⁴ ke⁴ jen² hui⁴ hsieh³ shen²-ma¹ tzu⁴?
   T'a¹ shen²-ma¹ yeh³ pu² hui⁴ hsieh³.
4. Ni³ ch'ih¹ shen²-ma¹? Wo³ shen²-ma¹ yeh³ mei² ch'ih¹.

5. *T'a*¹ hui⁴ *tso*⁴ shen²-*ma*¹ *?* *T'a*¹ shen²-*ma*¹ yeh³ *pu*² *hui*⁴.
6. *Nin*² *yu*³ shen²-*ma*¹ chih³ ?   [*tso*⁴.
   *Wo*³ shen²-*ma*¹ chih³ yeh³ *mei*² *yu*³.
7. *Ni*³-*men*² shui² *tso*⁴ *fan*⁴ ?
   *Wo*³-*men*² shui² yeh³ *pu*² *tso*⁴ *fan*⁴.
8. *T'a*¹-*men*² shui² *he*¹ *ch'a*² ?
   *T'a*¹-*men*² shui² yeh³ *pu*⁴ *he*¹ *ch'a*².
9. Shui² *yu*³ ch'ien¹-*pi*³ *?* Shui² yeh³ *mei*² *yu*³ ch'ien¹-*pi*³.
10. Shui² *yu*³ shu¹ ? Shui² yeh³ *mei*² *yu*³ shu¹.
11. T'a¹ *shih*⁴ shui² ?
    Shui² yeh³ *pu*⁴ *chih*¹-*tao*⁴ t'a¹ *shih*⁴ shui².
12. *Ni*³ hui⁴ *tso*⁴ shen²-*ma*¹ *cho*¹-*tzu*¹ *?*
    *Wo*³ shen²-*ma*¹ *cho*¹-*tzu*¹ tou¹ *hui*⁴ *tso*⁴.
13. *Ni*³-*men*² *yu*³ shen²-*ma*¹ shu¹ *?*
    *Wo*³-*men*² shen²-*ma*¹ shu¹ tou¹ *yu*³.
14. *Na*⁴ *ke*⁴ *jen*² hui⁴ *tso*⁴ shen²-*ma*¹ *?*
    *T'a*¹ shen²-*ma*¹ tou¹ *hui*⁴ *tso*⁴.
15. Shen²-*ma*¹ *jen*² tou¹ *yu*³.
16. Shui² *yao*⁴ *ch'ih*¹ *fan*⁴ *?* Shui² tou¹ *yao*⁴ *ch'ih*¹ *fan*⁴.
17. Shui² *yao*⁴ *nien*⁴ shu¹ *?* Shui² tou¹ *yao*⁴ *nien*⁴ shu¹.

1. What (thing) has that student got ?   He has nothing.
2. What books has your teacher got ?
   He hasn't got any books.
3. What characters can that man write ?
   He can't write any characters.
4. What are you eating ?   I have eaten nothing.
5. What can he do ?   He can't do anything.
6. What sort of paper have you got ?

I haven't got any paper.
7. Which of you cooks ? No one (of us) cooks.
8. Which of them is drinking tea ?
   No one (of them) is drinking tea.
9. Who has a pencil ? Nobody has a pencil.
10. Who has some books ? Nobody has any books.
11. Who is he ? No one knows who he is.
12. What sort of table can you make ?
    I can make any kind of table.
13. What sort of books have you got ?
    We have all kinds of books.
14. What can that man do ? He can do everything.
15. There are all kinds of people.
16. Who wants to eat ? Everbody wants to eat.
17. Who wants to study ? Everyone wants to study.

II

(問答) wen⁴-ta²
question and answer

Q. *Ni³-men² tso⁴ shen²-ma¹ ?*
A. *Wo³-men² tso⁴ cho¹-tzu¹.*
Q. *Ni³-men² tso⁴ shen²-ma¹ cho¹-tzu¹ ?*
A. *Wo³-men² tso⁴ shu¹-cho¹-tzu¹, tso⁴ fan⁴-cho¹-tzu¹, shen²-*
Q. *Ni³-men² hui⁴ tso⁴ i³-tzu¹ ma¹ ?*   [*ma¹-ti¹.*
A. *Wo³-men² yeh³ hui⁴ tso⁴ i³-tzu¹.*
Q. *Ni³-men² tso⁴-ti¹ cho¹-tzu¹ i³-tzu¹ hao³ pu⁴ hao³ ?*
A. *Wo³-men² tso⁴-ti¹ cho¹-tzu¹ i³-tzu¹ hao³.*

Q. What are you making?
A. We are making tables.
Q. What sort of tables do you make?
A. We make writing-tables, dining-tables and so on.
Q. Can you make chairs?
A. We can also make chairs.
Q. Are the tables and chairs which are made by you good (ones)?
A. The tables and chairs made by us are good (ones).

III

(問答) wen⁴-ta²
question and answer

Q. Nin² fu⁴-ch'in¹ tso⁴ shen²-ma¹ na¹?
A. T'a¹ tso⁴ shu¹ na¹.
Q. Nin²-ti¹ mu³-ch'in¹ tso⁴ shen²-ma¹ na¹?
A. T'a¹ tso⁴ fan⁴ na¹.
Q. Nin²-ti¹ erh²-tzu¹ hai² nien⁴ shu¹ na¹ ma¹?
A. T'a¹ pu² nien⁴ shu¹.
Q. Nin²-ti¹ ku¹-niang² hui⁴ hsieh³ tzu⁴ pu² hui⁴?
A. T'a¹ hai² hsiao³ na¹, hai² pu² hui⁴ hsieh³ na¹.

Q. What is your father doing?
A. He is writing a book.
Q. What is your mother doing?
A. She is cooking.
Q. Does your son still study?
A. He does not study.

Q. Can your daughter write characters?
A. She is still small and can't write yet.

IV

(問答) wen⁴-ta²
question and answer

Q. Nin² chin¹-t'ien¹ nien⁴ shu¹ la¹ mei² yu³?
A. Wo³ chin¹-t'ien¹ nien⁴ shu¹ la¹.
Q. Yeh³ hsieh³ tzu⁴ la¹ ma¹?
A. Mei² hsieh³ tzu⁴.
Q. Nin² chin¹-t'ien¹ hai² yao⁴ hsieh³ tzu⁴ ma¹?
A. Wo³ chin¹-t'ien¹ pu⁴ hsieh³ tzu⁴ la¹, wo³ ming²-t'ien¹
[hsieh³ tzu⁴.
Q. Na⁴-hsieh¹ ke⁴ tzu⁴ shih⁴ nin² hsieh³-ti¹ ma¹?
A. Pu² shih⁴ wo³ hsieh³-ti¹
Q. Shih⁴ shui² hsieh³-ti¹, nin² chih¹-tao⁴ ma¹?
A. Wo³ chih¹-tao⁴, shih⁴ hsien¹-sheng¹ hsieh³-ti¹.
Q. Na⁴ pen³ shu¹ shih⁴ nin² nien⁴-ti¹ pu² shih⁴?
A. Shih⁴ wo³ nien⁴-ti¹.

Q. Have you studied today?
A. I have studied today.
Q. (Have you) also written any characters?
A. (I) have not written any characters.
Q. Will you write any more characters today?
A. I shall not write characters today, I shall write tomorrow.
Q. Were those characters written by you?
A. (They) were not written by me.

Q. By whom were (they) written, do you know?
A. I do know, (they) were written by the teacher.
Q. Did you read that book?
A. I did read it.

V

(問答) wen⁴-ta²
question and answer

Q. *Hsien¹-sheng¹! Nin² yao⁴* **he¹ ch'a²** *ma¹?*
A. *Wo³* **pu⁴ he¹** *ch'a², wo³* **he¹** *k'a¹-fei⁴ la¹.*
Q. *Nin² yao⁴* **ch'ih¹ fan¹** *ma¹?*
A. *Wo³ yao⁴ ch'ih¹ fan⁴.*
Q. *Nin² yao⁴* **ch'ih¹ shen²-ma¹?**
A. *Nin² yu³ shen²-ma¹, wo³ ch'ih¹ shen²-ma¹.*
Q. *Wo³ yu³ yū², nlu²-jou⁴, yang²-jou⁴, chu¹-jou⁴, nin²*
A. *Wo³ yao⁴ ch'ih¹ yū².*   [**ch'ih¹ shen²-ma¹?**

Q. Teacher! Do you want to drink some tea?
A. I shall not drink tea, I have drunk some coffee.
Q. Do you want to eat?
A. I want to eat.
Q. What do you want to eat?
A. I shall eat whatever you have.
Q. I have fish, beef, mutton and pork, what will you eat?
A. I shall eat some fish.

LESSON 11

VI

來 lai² to come   去 ch'ü⁴ to go, to go away, to go out

1. *Lai² la¹* san¹ ke⁴ *hsüeh²-sheng¹*.
2. *Ch'ü⁴-la¹* pa² ke⁴ *hsüeh²-sheng¹*.
3. *Nin² chin¹-t'ien¹* lai² *pu⁴ lai²? Wo³ chin¹-t'ien¹* lai².
4. *Hsüeh²-sheng¹* tou¹ *lai²-la¹ ma¹?*
   Hsüeh²-sheng¹ tou¹ *lai²-la¹.*
5. *Hsien¹-sheng¹ lai²-la¹ mei² yu³?*
   Hsien¹-sheng¹ hai² *mei² lai² na¹.*
6. *Tso²-t'ien¹ lai²-ti¹ na⁴ ke⁴ jen² shih⁴* shui²?
   Na⁴ shih⁴ wo³ fu⁴-ch'in¹.
7. *Nin²* tso⁴ *shen²-ma¹ ch'ü⁴? Wo³ ch'ih¹ fan⁴ ch'ü⁴.*
8. *T'a¹ tso²-t'ien¹* tso⁴ *shen²-ma¹ ch'ü⁴-la¹?*
   T'a¹ nien⁴ shu¹ *ch'ü⁴-la¹.*
9. *Na⁴ wei⁴ hsüeh²-sheng¹ ch'ü⁴-la¹ ma¹?*
   T'a¹ hai² mei² ch'ü⁴ na¹.
10. *Ni³-men² shih² wei⁴ chi³ ke⁴ jen² ch'ü⁴, chi³ ke⁴ jen²* Liu⁴ *ke⁴ jen² ch'ü⁴,* ssu⁴ *ke⁴ jen² pu² ch'ü⁴.* [pu² *ch'ü⁴?*
11. *Lai²-la¹ chi³ wei⁴ la¹? Lai²-la¹ ch'i² wei⁴ la¹.*
12. Shui² hai² *mei² lai² na¹?* Tou¹ *lai²-la¹.*
13. Chang¹ *hsien¹-sheng¹ lai²-la¹ mei² yu³?*
    Chang¹ *hsien¹-sheng¹ lai²-la¹.*
14. Shu¹ *hsien¹-sheng¹ lai²-la¹ mei² yu³?*
    Shu¹ *hsien-sheng¹* hai² *mei² lai² na¹.*

1. Three pupils have come.
2. Eight pupils have gone away.

3. Will you come today ? I'll come to-day.
4. Have the pupils all come ? The pupils have all come.
5. Has the teacher come ? The teacher has not come yet.
6. Who was that man who came yesterday?
   That was my father.
7. What are you going out for (to do) ?
   I am going out to eat.
8. What did he go out for yesterday ? He went to study.
9. Has that pupil gone ? He has not gone yet.
10. Of you ten, how many (men) are going and how many will not go ?
    Six (men) are going and four (men) will not go.
11. How many (people) have come ?
    Seven (people) have come.
12. Who has not come yet ? All have come.
13. Has Mr. Chang come ? Mr. Chang has come.
14. Has Mr. Shu come ? Mr. Shu has not come yet.

VII

您好啊？ nin^2 hao^3 a^1? how are you ? are you well ?

謝謝 $hsieh^4$-$hsieh^4$ thanks, thank you

請 $ch'ing^3$ please

請坐 $ch'ing^3$ tso^4 please sit down

再見 $tsai^4$-$chien^4$ we shall meet again, good-bye

1. $Chang^1$ $hsien^1$-$sheng^1$, nin^2 hao^3 a^1? Hao^3 hao^3.
   Nin^2 na^1? $Hsieh^4$-$hsieh^4$ yeh^3 hao^3.

2. *Chang¹ hsien¹-sheng¹, ch'ing³ nin² he¹ ch'a²?*
   Hsieh⁴-*hsieh⁴, wo³* he¹ *i⁴ wan³ la¹. Ch'ing³ nin²* ch'ih¹ jou⁴. Hsieh⁴-*hsieh⁴, wo³* pu⁴ *ch'ih¹, wo³* ch'ih¹-*la¹.*
3. *Pao¹ hsien¹-sheng¹, nin² lai²-la¹,* ch'ing³ tso⁴, *ch'ing³ tso⁴.*
   Hsieh⁴-*hsieh⁴,* nin² *ch'ing³ tso⁴.*
4. *Pao¹ hsien¹-sheng¹ nin² yao⁴* ch'ü⁴ ma¹?
   Shih⁴, tsai⁴-chien⁴, tsai⁴-chien⁴.

1. Mr. Chang, how are you? Well, and you?
   Thank you, (I am) also well.
2. Mr. Chang, please drink some tea?
   Thank you, I'll drink a cup.
   Please eat some meat?
   Thank you, I won't eat, I have eaten.
3. Mr. Pao, (so) you have come, please sit down.
   Thank you, you sit down.
4. Mr. Pao, must you go? Yes, good-bye.

VIII

請 ch'ing³
to invite, to request, to ask (polite form)

1. *Nin² ming²-t'ien¹* ch'ing³ *Chang¹ hsien¹-sheng¹* ch'ih¹ fan⁴ ma¹? Shih⁴, *wo³ ming²-t'ien¹* ch'ing³ t'a¹ *ch'ih¹ fan⁴.*
2. *Nin² yao⁴ ch'ing³ Pao¹ hsien¹-sheng¹* tso⁴ shen²-*ma¹?*
   Wo³ yao⁴ ch'ing³ t'a¹ hsieh³ tzu⁴.
3. *Ni³* ch'ing³-la¹ chi³ ke⁴ jen²? *Wo³* ch'ing³-la¹ pa² ke⁴ jen².
4. Shih⁴ nin² yao⁴ *ch'ing³* t'a¹, shih⁴ t'a¹ yao⁴ *ch'ing³* nin²?
   Shih⁴ t'a¹ yao⁴ *ch'ing³ wo³,* pu² shih⁴ *wo³ yao⁴ ch'ing³* t'a¹.

1. Will you invite Mr. Chang to eat to-morrow?
   Yes, I'll invite him to eat to-morrow.
2. What do you want to ask Mr. Pao to do?
   I want to ask him to write some characters.
3. How many people have you invited?
   I have invited eight people.
4. Do you want to invite him, or does he want to invite you?
   It is he (who) wants to invite me, it isn't I (who) want to invite him.

NOTES

46. 先 生 hsien¹-sheng¹, may be translated as: teacher, or: Mr. It is the usual form of polite address. The position of this title is the reverse of the English usage, i. e.: 先 生 hsien¹-sheng¹ ALWAYS follows the name.

    張　先　生
    Chang¹ hsien¹-sheng¹ } Mr. Chang

    錢　先　生
    Ch'ien² hsien¹-sheng¹ } Mr. Ch'ien

    A Chinese surname is generally one character only.

47. 甚 麽 ○ 也 沒 (不) ○: shen²-ma¹ — yeh³ mei² (pu⁴) —. Expresses the fact that: there are not any things, have not any things, had not any things. If a verb and a noun are inserted in the blank spaces, the sense implied is still: not — any —

LESSON 11

甚 麽 書 也 沒 有 | What books even
shen²-*ma*¹ *shu*¹ *yeh*³ *mei*² *yu*³ | not have
(There are not any books)
(— haven't got any books)

甚 麽 書 也 沒 念 | What books even
shen²-*ma*¹ *shu*¹ *yeh*³ *mei*² *nien*⁴ | not read
(— haven't read any books)
(— didn't read any book)

甚 麽 飯 也 沒 吃 | What food even
shen²-*ma*¹ *fan*⁴ *yeh*³ *mei*² *ch'ih*¹ | not eat
(— haven't eaten any food)
(— didn't eat any food)

甚 麽 飯 也 不 吃 | What food even
shen²-*ma*¹ *fan*⁴ *yeh*³ *pu*⁴ *ch'ih*¹ | not eat
(— do not eat any food)
(— will not eat any food)

48. 甚麽 ○ 都 ○ : **shen**²-*ma*¹ — **tou**¹ —. Expresses the fact that : there are all kinds of things, have every kind of thing, have any kind of thing. If a noun and a verb are inserted in the black spaces the sense implied is still : — all kinds of —

甚 麽 碗 都 有 | What bowls all have
shen²-*ma*¹ *wan*³ **tou**¹ *yu*³ |
(There are all kinds of bowls)
(— have every kind of bowl)

甚 麼 學 生 都 有 | What students all
shen²-ma¹ hsüeh²-sheng¹ tou¹ yu³ | have
(There are all kinds of students)
(— has every kind of student)

甚 麼 字 都 會 寫 | What characters all
shen²-ma¹ tzu⁴ tou¹ hui⁴ hsieh³ | can write
(— can write every kind of character)
(— can write any character)

甚 麼 棹 子 都 會 作 | What tables all
shen²-ma¹ cho¹-tzu¹ tou¹ hui⁴ tso⁴ | can make
(— can make every kind of table)
(— can make any table)

49. 來 lai² — to come, 去 ch'ü⁴ — to go. It is not possible to translate these characters exactly. As will be seen from the text 來 lai² implies motion to, towards; while 去 ch'ü⁴ implies motion from, away from.

50. **Forms of Greeting.** The more usual form is 您 好 啊? nin² hao³ a¹? or 您 好? nin² hao³? — how are you? are you well? This is an equivalent to the English: good morning, good day, how do you do?, etc.

51. 謝 謝 hsieh⁴-hsieh⁴ — thanks, thank you. 謝 hsieh⁴ means: to thank, to be grateful. The character is repeated for euphonic reasons.

52. 請 ch'ing³ — please, to invite, to request, to ask (polite form). The meaning implied is immediately understood from the context.

請 坐 } Please sit
ch'ing³ tso⁴ } (Please sit down)

我 請 了 先 生 } I invited the teacher
wo³ ch'ing³-la¹ hsien¹-sheng¹

我 請 他 給 我 寫 字 } I asked him give me
wo³ ch'ing³ t'a¹ kei³ wo³ hsieh³ tzu⁴ } write characters.
(I asked him to write some characters for me.)

53. 再 見 tsai⁴-chien⁴ —good-bye. 再 tsai⁴ means: again, and 見 chien⁴ means: to see. Thus 再 見 tsai⁴-chien⁴ implies: until we meet again, until we see each other again, au revoir.

LESSON 12

I

問 **wen⁴**
to ask

1. *T'a¹* **wen⁴ shui² na¹?**
   T'a¹ wen⁴ **Chang¹** *hsien¹-sheng¹ na¹?*
2. *Hsien¹sheng¹* **wen⁴ hsüeh²-sheng¹ pu² wen⁴?**
   Hsien¹-sheng¹ wen⁴ hsüeh²-sheng¹.
3. *Nin² wen⁴ t'a¹* **shen²-ma¹ la¹?**
   Wo³ wen⁴ t'a¹ **yu³ shu¹ mei² yu³.**
4. *Ni³* **yao⁴** *wen⁴* **shui²?** *Wo³* **yao⁴** *wen⁴* **hsien¹-**sheng¹.

1. Whom is he asking ?   He is asking Mr. Chang.
2. Does the teacher ask the pupil ?
   The teacher asks the pupil.
3. What did you ask him ?   I asked him (if) he had a book.
4. Whom do you want to ask ?   I want to ask the teacher.

II

回答 **hui²-ta²**
to answer, to reply

1. *Hsien¹-sheng¹ wen⁴ hsüeh²-sheng¹, hsüeh²-sheng¹* **hui²-**
   Hsüeh²-sheng¹ **hui²-ta².**   **ta² ma¹?**
2. *Hsien¹-sheng¹ wen⁴* **nin²,** *nin²* **hui²-ta² pu⁴ hui²-ta²?**
   Wo³ **hui²-ta².**   **ta².**
3. *Nin² wen⁴* **t'a¹,** *t'a¹* **hui²-ta²-la¹ ma¹?** *T'a¹* **mei² hui²-**

LESSON 12

1. The teacher asks the pupil, does the pupil reply?
   The pupil replies.
2. The teacher asks you, do you answer? I answer.
3. You asked him, did he answer? He did not answer.

III

說話 shuo¹-hua⁴
(to speak words), to speak, to say

跟 ken¹
with

句 chü⁴
sentence(s), phrase(s)

1. I² ke⁴ jen² wen⁴, i² ke⁴ jen² hui²-ta²;
   na⁴ shih⁴ liang³ ke⁴ jen² shuo¹-hua⁴.
2. Nin² shuo¹ shen²-ma¹ na¹? Wo³ shuo¹ t'a¹ lai²-la¹.
3. T'a¹ yao⁴ ken¹ shui² shuo¹-hua⁴?
   T'a¹ yao⁴ ken¹ nin²-ti¹ ku¹-niang² shuo¹-hua⁴.
4. Che⁴ chü⁴ hua⁴ shih⁴ t'a¹ shuo¹-ti¹ ma¹?
   Pu² shih⁴ t'a¹ shuo¹-ti¹.
5. Nin² yao⁴ ken¹ shui² nien⁴ shu¹?
   Wo³ yao⁴ ken¹ Chang¹ hsien¹-sheng¹ nien⁴ shu¹.
6. T'a¹ shih⁴ ken¹ shui² lai²-ti¹?
   T'a¹ shih⁴ ken¹ t'a¹ mu³-ch'in¹ lai²-ti¹.
7. Nin²-ti¹ erh²-tzu¹ shih⁴ ken¹ shui² ch'ü⁴-ti¹?
   Shih⁴ ken¹ t'a¹ fu⁴-ch'in¹ ch'ü⁴-ti¹.
8. Ni³ shuo¹-la¹ chi³ chü⁴ hua⁴?
   Wo³ i² chü⁴ hua⁴ yeh³ mei² shuo¹.
9. Ni³ yu³ hua⁴ shuo¹? Wo³ mei² yu³ hua⁴ shuo¹.

10. *Che¹ chü⁴ hua⁴* **shih⁴ shul²** *shuo¹-ti¹?*
    Shih⁴ **wo³** *shuo¹-ti¹.*

1. One man asks (and) one man answers; that is two men speaking.
2. What are you saying?
   I am saying (that) he has come.
3. With whom does he want to speak?
   He wants to speak with your daughter.
4. Was this sentence said by him?
   It was not said by him.
5. With whom do you want to study?
   I want to study with Mr. Chang.
6. With whom did he come? He came with his mother.
7. With whom did your son go? He went with his father.
8. How many sentences did you say?
   I did not say (even) one sentence.
9. Have you anything to say?
   I haven't anything to say.
10. Who said this? I said it.

IV

明白 ming²-pai² to understand   跟 ken¹ and

1. *Wo³ shuo¹-ti¹ hua⁴ ni³ ming²-pal² ma¹?*
   Wo³ ming²-pai².
2. *Shu¹ hsien¹-sheng¹ shuo¹-ti¹ hua⁴ ni³ ming²-pai² pu⁴ ming²-pai²? T'a¹ shuo¹-ti¹ hua⁴ wo³ pu⁴ ming²-pai².*

3. *Hsüeh²-sheng¹ yu³* **pu⁴** *ming²-pai²-ti¹,* **yao⁴ wen⁴ shui²** *?*
   Yao⁴ wen⁴ **hsien¹-sheng¹**.
4. *Na⁴ chih¹ kang¹-pi³ ken¹ che⁴ chih¹ kang¹-pi³, tou¹ shih⁴* **nin²-ti¹ ma¹** *?*
   Pu² tou¹ shih⁴ wo³-ti¹, na⁴ i⁴ chih¹ ch'ang²-ti¹ shih⁴ wo³-ti¹, na⁴ chih¹ tuan³-ti¹ pu² shih⁴ wo³-ti¹.
5. *Che⁴ wei⁴ hsüeh²-sheng¹ ken¹ na⁴ wei⁴ hsüeh²-sheng¹, tou¹ hui⁴ hsieh³ tzu⁴ ma¹ ?* **Tou¹ hui⁴**.
6. *Nin² yu³* **shen²-ma¹** *tung¹-hsi¹ ?*
   Wo³ yu³ **shu¹ ken¹ pen³-tzu¹**.

1. Do you understand what I say? I do understand.
2. Do you understand what Mr. Shu says?
   I don't understand what he says.
3. Whom will the student ask if he has something that he does not understand?
   (The student has not understand will ask who?)
   (He) will ask the teacher.
4. That pen and this pen, are they both yours?
   (They) are not both mine, that long one is mine, that short one is not mine.
5. Can both this pupil and that pupil write characters?
   (They) both can.
6. What have you got? I have a book and a note-book.

V

對 **tui⁴**
correct, right

不對 **pu² tui⁴**
incorrect, wrong

1. *Na⁴ ke⁴ tzu⁴ hsieh³-ti¹ tui⁴ ma¹ ?*
   Na⁴ ke⁴ tzu⁴ hsieh³-ti¹ tui⁴.

2. *T'a*¹ **hui**²-*ta*²-*ti*¹ **tui**⁴ *pu*² *tui*⁴ ?
   *T'a*¹ *hui*²-*ta*²-*ti*¹ **tui**⁴.
3. *Nin*² *yao*⁴ **ch'ing**³ **hsien**¹-*sheng*¹ *ma*¹ ?
   Tui⁴-*la*¹, *wo*³ *yao*⁴ **ch'ing**³ **hsien**¹-*sheng*¹.
4. *T'a*¹ **shuo**¹-*ti*¹ **na**⁴ **chü**⁴ **hua**⁴ **tui**⁴ *pu*² *tui*⁴ ?
   *T'a*¹ **shuo**¹-*ti*¹ **na**⁴ **chü**⁴ **hua**⁴ **pu**² *tui*⁴.

1. Is that character written correctly ?
   That character is written correctly.
2. Did he answer correctly ?   He answered correctly.
3. Do you want to invite the teacher ?
   Right, I want to invite the teacher.
4. Did he say that sentence correctly ?
   He said that sentence wrong.

VI

(我說) *wo*³ *shuo*¹   (你說) *ni*³ *shuo*¹
       I say   you say

(他說) *t'a*¹ *shuo*¹   (您說) *nin*² *shuo*¹
       he says   you say

1. *Nin*² *shuo*¹ **shih**⁴ **che**⁴ **ke**⁴ **ta**⁴ **shih**⁴ **na**⁴ **ke**⁴ **ta**⁴ ?
   *Wo*³ *shuo*¹ **shih**⁴ **che**⁴ **ke**⁴ **ta**⁴.
2. *T'a*¹ *shuo*¹ **shih**⁴ **chin**¹-*t'ien*¹ *tso*⁴ **hao**³ *a*¹, **shih**⁴ **ming**²-*t'ien*¹ *tso*⁴ **hao**³ *ni*¹ ?   *hao*³.
   *T'a*¹ *shuo*¹ **ming**²-*t'ien*¹ *tso*⁴ **mei**² *yu*³ **chin**¹-*t'ien*¹ *tso*⁴
3. *Na*⁴ *wei*⁴ **hsüeh**¹-*sheng*¹ *shuo*¹, **ch'ien**¹-*pi*³ **shih**⁴ **ch'ang**²-*ti*¹ **hao**³ *a*¹, **shih**⁴ **tuan**³-*ti*¹ **hao**³ *ni*¹ ?
   *T'a*¹ *shuo*¹ **shih**⁴ **ch'ang**²-*ti*¹ **hao**³.

4. *Nin² shuo¹ t'a¹-men² liang³ ke⁴ jen² shui² tso⁴-ti¹ hao³?*
   T'a¹-men² tou¹ tso⁴-ti¹ hao³.
5. *Hsien¹-sheng¹ shuo¹ shih⁴ che⁴ ke⁴ hsüeh²-sheng¹ nien⁴-ti¹ shu¹ hao³ a¹, shih⁴ na⁴ ke⁴ hsüeh²-sheng¹ nien⁴-ti¹ shu¹ hao³ ni¹?*
   Hsien¹-sheng¹ shuo¹ t'a¹-men² tou¹ nien⁴-ti¹ pu⁴ hao³.

1. Do you say (that) this is larger than that?
   I say that this is larger.
2. Does he say that it is better to do it today or tomorrow?
   (He says is today do good, is tomorrow do good?)
   He says that it is not as good to do it tomorrow as today.
   (He says tomorrow do, has not today do good.)
3. Does that pupil say (that) long pencils are better than short ones? He says (that) long ones are better.
4. Which of those two men do you say does it well?
   (You say they two men, which does well?)
   They both do it well.
5. Does the teacher say (that) this student studies better than that student?
   The teacher says (that) they both study badly.

VII

再 **tsai⁴**
again, a second time, more

回 **hui²**
a time

1. *Hsien¹-sheng¹, ch'ing³ nin² tsai⁴ hsieh³ i² ke⁴ tzu⁴.*
   Hao³, wo³ tsai⁴ hsieh³ i² ke⁴.

2. *Na⁴ ke⁴ tzu⁴ nin² hsieh³-la¹ mei² yu³?*
   Wo³ hsieh³-la¹ liang³ hui² la¹.
3. *Nin² ch'ing³ t'a¹ tsai⁴ lai² i⁴ hui² ma¹?*
   Wo³ ch'ing³ t'a¹ tsai⁴ lai² i⁴ hui²
4. *Che⁴ chü⁴ hua⁴ hsien¹-sheng¹ shuo¹-la¹ chi³ hui² la¹?*
   T'a¹ shuo¹-la¹ san¹ ssu⁴ hui² la¹?
5. *Nin² shuo¹-ti¹ hua⁴ wo³ pu⁴ ming²-pai², ch'ing³ nin² tsai⁴ shuo¹ i⁴ hui².*
   Hao³ hao³, wo³ tsai⁴ shuo¹ i⁴ hui².
6. *Na⁴ ke⁴ tzu⁴ wo³ hai² pu² hui⁴ hsieh³ na¹, ch'ing³ nin² tsai⁴ hsieh³ i⁴ hui².*
   Hao³ hao³, wo³ tsai⁴ hsieh³ i⁴ hui².

1. Teacher, please write one character more.
   All right, I will write one more.
2. Have you written that character?
   I have written it twice.
3. Will you invite him to come once again?
   I will invite him to come once again.
4. How many times did the teacher say this phrase?
   He said (it) three (or) four times.
5. I don't understand (what) you say, please say (it) once more.   All right, I will say (it) once more.
6. I still can't write that character, please write (it) once again.   All right, I will write (it) once again.

LESSON 12

VIII

(請問您哪)? *ch'ing³ wen⁴ nin² na¹?* may I ask you?, will you please tell me?

好些個 *hao³-hsieh¹-ke⁴* a great many, a good many

一點兒 *i⁴-tien³-erh², i⁴-tien-'rh³* a little

1. *Ch'ing³ wen⁴ nin² na¹, che⁴ wan³ ch'a² shih⁴ shui² he¹-ti¹?*
   Che⁴ wan³ ch'a² shih⁴ Chang¹ hsien¹-sheng¹ he¹-ti¹.
2. *Ch'ing³ wen⁴ nin² na¹, na⁴ ke⁴ jen² shih⁴ shui²?*
   Na⁴ ke⁴ jen² shih⁴ Chang¹ hsien¹-sheng¹.
3. *Na⁴ hao³-hsieh¹-ke⁴ jen² tso⁴ shen²-ma¹?*
   T'a¹-men² shuo¹-hua⁴ na¹.
4. *Hsüeh²-sheng¹ tou¹ lai²-la¹ ma¹?*
   Hai² yu³ hao³-hsieh¹-ke⁴ jen² mei² lai² na¹.
5. *Nin² he¹ k'a¹-fei⁴ pu⁴ he¹? Wo³ he¹ i⁴-tien-'rh³.*
6. *Ch'ing³ nin² tsai⁴ he¹ i⁴-tien-'rh³.*
   Hsieh⁴-hsieh⁴, wo³ pu⁴ he¹-la¹.
7. *T'a¹ shuo¹-ti¹ hua⁴ nin² tou¹ ming²-pai²-la¹ ma¹?*
   Wo³ i⁴-tien-'rh³ yeh³ pu⁴ ming²-pai².

1. Will you please tell me who drank this cup of tea?
   Mr. Chang drank this cup of tea.
2. May I ask you, who is that person?
   That man is Mr. Chang.
3. What are all those (many) men doing?
   They are talking.

4. Have all the students come ?
    There are still a great many people (who) have not come.
5. (Will) you drink some coffee ? I (will) drink a little.
6. Please drink a little more. Thank you, I (will) not drink.
7. Did you understand everything that he said ?
    I understood nothing.
    (I a little even not understand.)

NOTES

54. 回答 **huí**²-*ta*² — to answer. 回 **huí**² means: to return, and 答 **ta**² means: to reply, to answer. The usual colloquial form is 回答 **huí**²-*ta*².

55. 說話 **shuo**¹-**hua**⁴ — to speak, to say. 說 **shuo**¹ means to speak, and 話 **hua**⁴ means a word. The usual colloquial form is 說話 **shuo**¹-**hua**⁴, but note the following sentences for other combinations:

您 說 甚 麼 話? You speak what words?
nin² shuo¹ shen²-ma¹ hua⁴? (What are you saying?)

我 有 話 說 I have words to speak
wo³ yu³ hua⁴ shuo¹ (I have something to say)

我 沒 有 話 說 I not have words say
wo³ mei² yu³ hua⁴ shuo¹ (I have nothing to say)

56. 跟 **ken**¹ may be translated as: with, or: and, depending on its position in the sentence.

跟 誰 說 話? With whom speak?
ken¹ shui² shuo¹ hua⁴?
(With whom are you speaking?)
(With whom is he speaking?)

跟 我 說 話 With me speak
ken¹ wo³ shuo¹ hua⁴ (He is speaking with me)

這 個 碗 跟 那 個 碗 都 是 他 的
che⁴ ke⁴ wan³ ken¹ na⁴ ke⁴ wan³ tou¹ shih⁴ t'a¹-ti¹
This bowl and that bowl both are his
(Both this bowl and that bowl are his)

57. 明白 ming²-pai² — to understand. 明 ming² means bright, clear, and 白 pai² means white, obvious. The combination 明白 ming²-pai² is the usual colloquial form for : to understand.

58. 我說 wo³ shuo¹, 您（你）說 nin² (ni³) shuo¹, 他說 t'a¹ shuo¹, may be translated as: I say, You say, He (she) says, but the sense implied is : My opinion is, Your opinion is, His (her) opinion is.

59. 兒 erh² is introduced in this lesson in combination with 一點 i⁴-tien³ to form the expression 一點兒 i⁴-tien³-erh² or i⁴-tien-'rh³ — a little.

兒 erh² means a son, a child, but it is also frequently appended to nouns and adverbs as a euphonic colloquial ending. In these cases the final sound of the noun (or adverb) is elided with the 'e' of 兒 erh², resulting in a drawn-out slurred sound which is indicated in the romanization by -'rh.

As a colloquial ending 兒 erh² is generally equivalent to 子 tzu³,⁽¹⁾ although the former is a decided characteristic of the Peiping dialect where it is used excessively, while it is rarely heard in other parts of China.

LESSON 13

I

姓 hsing⁴ surname

名子 ming²-tzu¹ name, personal name

叫 chiao⁴ to call, to call by name

1. Nin² hsing⁴ shen²-ma¹? Wo³ hsing⁴ Shu¹.
2. Nin² chiao⁴ shen²-ma¹ ming²-tzu¹?
   Wo³ ming²-tzu¹ chiao⁴ Tao⁴-Ming².
3. Chang¹ hsien¹-sheng¹-ti¹ ming²-tzu¹ chiao⁴ shen²-ma¹?
   Chang¹ hsien¹-sheng¹-ti¹ ming²-tzu² chiao⁴ Chih¹-Sheng¹.
4. Jen² yu³ ming²-tzu¹, tung¹-hsi¹ yeh³ yu³ ming²-tzu¹
   Tung¹-hsi¹ yeh³ yu³ ming²-tzu¹.   [ma¹?
5. Ch'ing³ wen⁴ nin² na¹, na⁴ ke⁴ tung¹-hsi¹ chiao⁴ shen²-ma¹ ming²-tzu¹?
   Na⁴ ke⁴ tung¹-hsi¹ ming²-tzu¹ chiao⁴ mao²-pi³.
6. Che⁴ ke⁴ wan³ ming²-tzu¹ chiao⁴ ch'a²-wan³, na⁴ ke⁴ wan³ ming²-tzu¹ chiao⁴ shen²-ma¹?
   Na⁴ ke⁴ wan³ ming²-tzu¹ chiao⁴ fan⁴-wan³.

1. What (is) your surname? My surname (is) Shu.
2. What is your name? My name is Tao-Ming.
3. What is Mr. Chang's name?
   Mr. Chang's name is Chih-Sheng.
4. People have names, have things also got names?
   Things also have names.

5. Will you please tell me, what is that thing called?
   (That thing is called what name?)
   That thing is called a writing-brush.
   (That thing name called writing-brush.)
6. This cup is called a tea-cup, what is that bowl called?
   That bowl is called a rice-bowl.

II

完 wan² to finish, to complete

就 chiu⁴ then, when, thereupon, just, immediately

叫 chiao⁴ to call, to summon, to order

1. Che⁴ pen³ shu¹ nin² nien⁴ wan²-la¹ ma¹?
   Nien⁴ wan²-la¹.
2. Nin² he¹ wan²-la¹ ch'a² la¹ ma¹?
   Hai² mei² he¹ wan² na¹.
3. Na⁴ wei⁴ hsüeh²-sheng¹ hsieh³ wan²-la¹ tzu⁴ la¹ ma¹?
   Na⁴ chi³ ke⁴ ta⁴ tzu⁴ hsieh³ wan²-la¹, na⁴ chi³ shih² ke⁴ hsiao³ tzu-'rh⁴ hai² mei² hsieh³ na¹.
4. Nin² ch'ih¹ wan² fan⁴ chiu⁴ he¹ k'a¹-fei⁴ ma¹?
   Shih⁴, wo³ ch'ih¹ wan² fan⁴ chiu⁴ he¹ k'a¹-fei⁴.
5. Hsien¹-sheng¹ wen⁴ nin², nin² chiu⁴ hui²-ta² ma¹?
   Shih⁴, t'a¹ wen⁴ wo³, wo³ chiu⁴ hui²-ta².
6. T'a¹ chiao⁴ nin² tso⁴ shen²-ma¹?
   T'a¹ chiao⁴ wo³ nien⁴ shu¹
7. Hsien¹-sheng¹ chiao⁴ hsüeh²-sheng¹ tso⁴ shen²-ma¹?
   Hsien¹-sheng¹ chiao⁴ hsüeh²-sheng¹ hsieh³ tzu⁴.

LESSON 13

8. *Wo³ mu³-ch'in¹* chiao⁴ *wo³ tso⁴ shen²-ma¹, wo³* chiu⁴ *tso⁴ shen²-ma¹.*
9. *T'a¹* chiao⁴ *wo³ lai² wo³* chiu⁴ *lai², t'a¹* chiao⁴ *wo³ ch'ü⁴, wo³* chiu⁴ *ch'ü⁴.*
10. *Wo³ ken¹ t'a¹ shuo¹ wan²-la¹ hua⁴,* chiu⁴ *ch'ü⁴.*

1. Have you finished reading this book? I have finished reading. (This book you reading finished? Reading finished.)
2. Have you finished drinking tea?
   (I) have not finished drinking yet.
3. Has that student finished writing characters?
   (He) has finished writing those (several) large characters, (he) has not yet written those (dozens of) small characters.
4. Will you drink some coffee when you have finished eating?
   (You eating finished food, then will drink coffee?)
   Yes, when I have finished eating I will drink some coffee.
   (Yes, I eating finished food, then will drink coffee.)
5. Do you reply when the teacher asks you?
   (The teacher asks you, you then reply?)
   Yes, when he asks me I reply.
   (Yes, he asks me, I then reply.)
6. What is he calling you for? He is calling me to study.
7. What does the teacher summon the students for?
   The teacher summons the students to write characters.
8. I just do what my mother tells me to do.
   (My mother summons me to do what, I thereupon do what.)

9. He summons me to come (and) thereupon I come.
He orders me to go (and) I just go.
10. (When) I have finished speaking with him, then (I) will go.

III

錢 ch'ien² money

○塊錢 — k'uai⁴-ch'ien² — dollar(s)

○毛錢 — mao²-ch'ien² — ten-cents

○分錢 — fen¹-ch'ien² — cent(s)

1. Ch'ing³ wen⁴ nin² na¹, che⁴ shih⁴ shen²-ma¹ tung¹-hsi? Na⁴ shih⁴ ch'ien².
2. Nin² yu³ ch'ien² ma¹? Wo³ yu³ ch'ien².
3. Nin² yu³ to¹-shao³ ch'ien²? Wo³ yu³ i² k'uai⁴-ch'ien².
4. I² k'uai⁴-ch'ien² shih⁴ chi³ mao²-ch'ien²? I² k'uai⁴-ch'ien² shih⁴ shih² mao²-ch'ien².
5. I⁴ mao²-ch'ien² shih⁴ chi³ fen¹-ch'ien²? I⁴ mao²-ch'ien² shih⁴ shih² fen¹-ch'ien².
6. Che⁴ shih⁴ to¹-shao³ ch'ien²? Che⁴ shih⁴ i² k'uai⁴ ssu⁴ mao²-ch'ien².
7. Na⁴ shih⁴ chi³ mao²-ch'ien²? Na⁴ shih⁴ wu³ mao² wu³ fen¹-ch'ien².
8. Che⁴ liang³ k'uai⁴ wu³ shih⁴ shui²-ti¹? Che⁴ liang³ k'uai⁴ wu³ shih⁴ t'a¹-ti¹.

LESSON 13

9. *Che⁴ ssu⁴ mao² wu³ shih⁴ nin²-ti¹ ma¹?*
   Pu² shih⁴ wo³-ti¹, shih⁴ na⁴ ke⁴ jen²-ti¹.
10. *T'a¹ yu³ chi³ k'uai⁴-ch'ien²?*
    T'a¹ yu³ wu³ k'uai⁴-ch'ien².

1. Will you please tell me what this (thing) is?
   That is money.
2. Have you any money? I have some money.
3. How much money have you got? I have one dollar.
4. One dollar is how many ten-cents?
   One dollar is ten ten-cents.
5. One ten-cents is how many cents?
   One ten-cents is ten cents.
6. How much money is this?
   This is one dollar (and) four ten-cents (forty cents.)
7. How much money is that? That is fifty-five cents.
8. Whose is this two dollars fifty?
   This two dollars fifty is his.
9. Is this forty-five cents yours?
   (It) isn't mine, (it) is that man's.
10. How many dollars has he got? He has five dollars.

IV

要 **yao⁴**
to want, to require

1. *Nin² yao⁴ shen²-ma¹? Wo³ yao⁴ chih³.*
2. *T'a¹ tso⁴ shen²-ma¹ lai²-la¹? T'a¹ yao⁴ ch'ien² lai²-la¹.*
3. *T'a¹ yao⁴ pen³-tzu¹ tso⁴ shen²-ma¹?*
   T'a¹ yao⁴ hsieh³ tzu⁴.

4. *Na⁴* **liang³** *chang¹ cho¹-tzu¹,* *nin²* **shih⁴ yao⁴ ta¹-*ti¹***
   shih⁴ yao⁴ *hsiao³-ti¹ ?*
   Wo³ yu³ cho¹-tzu¹, wo³ tou¹ pu⁴ yao⁴.
5. *Che⁴ chang¹* **fan¹**-*cho¹-tzu¹, t'a¹ yao⁴* **to¹**-*shao³ ch'ien² ?*
   T'a¹ yao⁴ wu³ k'uai⁴ wu³ mao²-ch'ien².
6. *T'a¹ tso⁴ shen²-ma¹ ch'ü⁴-la¹ ?*
   T'a¹ yao⁴ ch'ien² ch'ü⁴-la¹.

1. What do you want ? I want some paper.
2. What has he come for ? (He to do what, has come ?)
   He wants money, that is why he has come.
3. What does he want a note-book for ?
   He wants to write characters.
4. Do you want the larger or the smaller of these two tables ?
   I have a table, I don't want either.
5. How much money does he want (for) this table ?
   He wants five dollars and fifty cents.
6. What has he gone for ? (He to do what, has gone ?)
   He wants money, that is why he has gone. (He wants money has gone.)

V

給 kei³
  to give

1. *Nin² kei³ t'a¹ to¹-shao³ ch'ien² ?*
   Wo³ kei³ t'a¹ ssu⁴ k'uai⁴ erh⁴ mao²-ch'ien².
2. *Hsien¹-sheng¹* **kei³** *nin² shu¹ la¹ ma¹ ?*
   Hsien¹-sheng¹ hai² mei² kei³ wo³ shu¹ na¹.

LESSON 13

3. *Nin² fu⁴-ch'in¹* kei³-*la¹ nin² chi³ chih¹* kang¹-*pi³?*
   T'a¹ kei³-*la¹ wo³ i⁴ chih¹.*
4. *Che⁴ pen³ shu¹ shih⁴* shui² *kei³ nin²-ti¹?*
   Na⁴ pen³ shu¹ shih⁴ Ch'ien² hsien¹-sheng¹ *kei³ wo³-ti¹.*
5. *Nin² yao⁴ kei³ t'a¹* shen²-*ma¹ tung¹-hsi¹?*
   T'a¹ yao⁴ shen²-ma¹, wo³ kei³ t'a¹ shen²-ma¹.
6. *T'a¹ mu³-ch'in¹* kei³-*la¹ t'a¹ chi³ mao²-ch'ien²?*
   Kei³-*la¹ t'a¹ liang³ mao²-ch'ien².*

1. How much money are you giving him?
   I am giving him four dollars twenty cents.
2. Has teacher given you the book?
   Teacher has not given me the book yet.
3. How many pens did your father give you?
   He gave me one.
4. Who gave you this book? Mr. Ch'ien gave me that book.
5. What (thing) will you give him?
   I will give him whatever he wants. (He wants what, I give him what.)
6. How much money has his mother given him?
   (She) has given him twenty cents.

VI

給 kei³
for, on behalf of, to

1. *Na⁴ ke⁴ tzu⁴ shih⁴ shui² kei³ ni³ hsieh³-ti¹?*
   Na⁴ ke⁴ tzu⁴ shih⁴ Ch'ien² hsien¹-sheng¹ *kei³ wo³*
2. *Nin² kei³ shui² tso⁴ fan⁴?*   [hsieh³-ti¹.
   Wo³ kei³ wo³ mu³-ch'in¹ tso⁴ fan⁴.

3. Shui² kei³ hsüeh²-sheng¹ tso⁴ shu¹?
   Hsien¹-sheng¹ kei³ hsüeh²-sheng¹ tso⁴ shu¹.
4. Na⁴ pa² i³-tzu¹ shih⁴ kei³ shui² tso⁴-ti¹?
   Na⁴ pa² i³-tzu¹ shih⁴ kei³ Chang¹ hsien¹-sheng¹ tso⁴-ti¹.
5. Nin² kei³ shui² nien⁴ shu¹ na¹?
   Wo³ kei³ wo³-ti¹ ku¹-niang² nien⁴ shu¹ na¹.

1. Who wrote that character for you?
   Mr. Ch'ien wrote that character for me.
2. Whom are you cooking for? I am cooking for my mother.
3. Who is composing books for the students?
   The teacher is composing books for the students.
4. For whom was that chair made?
   That chair was made for Mr. Chang.
5. To whom are you reading a book?
   I am reading a book to my daughter.

VII

買 mai³ to buy   賣 mai⁴ to sell

1. Wo³ kei³ t'a¹ ch'ien², t'a¹ kei³ wo³ tung¹-hsi¹; wo³ shih⁴ mai³ tung¹-hsi¹.
2. Wo³ kei³ t'a¹ tung¹-hsi¹, t'a¹ kei³ wo³ ch'ien²; wo³ shih⁴ mai⁴ tung¹-hsi¹.
3. T'a¹ tso⁴ shen²-ma¹ ch'ü⁴-la¹?
   T'a¹ mai³ tung¹-hsi¹ ch'ü⁴-la¹.
   T'a¹ mai³ shen²-ma¹ ch'ü⁴-la¹?
   T'a¹ mai³ ch'a²-yeh⁴ ch'ü⁴-la¹.

4. *T'a¹-men² mai³ ch'a²-yeh⁴,* yeh³ mai³ *k'a¹-fei⁴ ma¹?*
 Shih⁴, *t'a¹-men²* yeh³ mai³ *k'a¹-fei⁴.* [*jou⁴?*
5. *Nin² mai³-la¹* chi³ chin¹ yang²-*jou⁴,* chi³ chin¹ chu¹-
 Wo³ *mai³-la¹* i⁴ chin¹ yang²-*jou⁴,* erh⁴ chin¹ *chu¹-jou⁴.*
6. *Ni³-men²* mai⁴ shen²-*ma¹* jou⁴?
 Wo³-men² mai⁴ *niu²,* yang², chu¹ *jou⁴.*
7. *T'a¹-men²* mai⁴ shen²-*ma¹* tung¹-*hsi¹?*
 T'a¹-men² mai⁴ mien⁴-*pao¹.*
8. *Che⁴ ke⁴ mien⁴-pao¹ to¹-shao³ ch'ien² i⁴* chin¹?
 Che⁴ ke⁴ mien⁴-pao¹ i⁴ mao²-ch'ien² i⁴ chin¹.
9. *Che⁴ t'iao² yü² shih⁴ to¹-shao³ ch'ien²* mai³-*ti¹?*
 Shih⁴ i² *k'uai⁴* to¹ *ch'ien² mai³-ti¹.*
10. *Na⁴ ke⁴ ch'a²-wan³ shih⁴* kei³ shui² *mai³-ti¹?*
 Shih⁴ kei³ wo³ ku¹-*ni ıng² mai³-ti¹.*
11. *Na⁴ chang¹* fan⁴-*cho¹-tzu¹* mai⁴ *to¹-shao³ ch'ien²?*
 Mai⁴ shih² *k'uai⁴* ling² wu³ *mao²-ch'ien².*
12. *Na⁴* chih¹ hsiao³ *yang-'rh²* ni³ mai⁴ kei³ shui² la¹?
 Mai⁴ kei³ Chang¹ hsien¹-*sheng¹ la¹.*

1. I give him some money. he gives me something ; I am buying things.
2. I give him something, he gives me money ; I am selling things.
3. What has he gone for ? He has gone to buy things. What has he gone to buy ? He has gone to buy tea.
4. They are buying tea, are (they) also buying coffee ? Yes, they are also buying coffee.
5. How many catties of mutton and how many catties of pork have you bought ?

    I have bought one catty of mutton and two catties of pork.
 6. What meat do you sell ?   We sell beef, mutton and pork.
 7. What (things) do they sell ?   They sell bread.
 8. How much (money) (is) one catty of this bread ?
    This bread (is) ten cents a catty.
 9. How much was this fish ?
    (This fish was how much money bought ?)
    It was bought (for) more than one dollar.
10. For whom was that tea-cup bought ?
    (It) was bought for my daughter.
11. How much is that dining-table ?
    (That dining-table to sell, how much money ?)
    It is ten dollars fifty cents.
    (To sell, ten dollars zero five ten-cents.)
12. To whom did you sell that little lamb ?
    (That little sheep you sold to whom ?)
    (I) sold (it) to Mr. Chang.

LESSON 13

NOTES

60. 叫 **chiao**⁴ as used in this lesson, has two distinct translations :

   (a) to call, to call by name :

   我 的 名 字 叫 道 明
   *wo*³-*ti*¹ *ming*²-*tzu*¹ **chiao**⁴ *Tao*⁴-*ming*²
   My name is called Tao-Ming
   (My name is Tao-Ming)

   (b) to summon, to order :

   我 叫 他 寫 字 I order him to write
   *wo*³ **chiao**⁴ *t'a*¹ *hsieh*³ *tzu*⁴ (characters)

61. 完 **wan**² is translated as : to finish, to complete. When it follows directly after a verb however, it denotes completion of the action, or, past time. In this case the particle 了 **la**¹, is added as a suffix.

   我 喝 完 了   I have drunk (it)
   *wo*³ *he*¹ **wan**²-*la*¹   I have finished drinking

   寫 完 了 Written
   *hsieh*³ **wan**²-*la*¹ Finished writing

   念 完 了 Read
   *nien*⁴ **wan**²-*la*¹ Finished reading

62. 就 **chiu**⁴ has no equivalent in English, but is used frequently in colloquial Mandarin. As introduced in this lesson it may be translated as : then, when, thereupon,

immediately, just, according to the context. It usually indicates immediate future time.

你 叫 我 去 我 就 去
ni³ chiao⁴ wo³ ch'ü⁴, wo³ chiu⁴ ch'ü⁴
You order me to go, I thereupon go
(You order me to go and I go immediately)

他 就 來 ｜ He immediately comes
t'a¹ chiu⁴ lai² ｜ (He is just coming)
(He will come immediately)

我 們 就 吃 飯 ｜ We then eat
wo³-men² chiu⁴ ch'ih¹ fan⁴ ｜ (We will eat immediately)
(We are just going to eat)

我 寫 完 了 字 就 念 書
wo³ hsieh³ wan²-la¹ tzu⁴ chiu⁴ nien⁴ shu¹
I writing finished characters thereupon read a book
(When I have finished writing I shall read)

說 完 了 話 他 就 來
shuo¹ wan²-la¹ hua⁴ t'a¹ chiu⁴ lai²
Speaking finished words he thereupon comes
(When he has finished speaking he will come)

63. Money.

(a) 一塊錢 i² k'uai⁴-ch'ien² is translated as: one dollar. This phrase is a combination of: 一 i²⁽¹⁾ one, 塊 k'uai⁴ — piece, and 錢 ch'ien² — money. Direct translation would be: one piece money.

五 塊 錢 ｜ Five pieces money
wu³ k'uai⁴-ch'ien² ｜ (Five dollars)

LESSON 13

(b) 一毛錢 I⁴ *mao²-ch'ien²* is translated as : one ten-cents. This phrase is a combination of : 一 I⁴⁽¹⁾ — one, 毛 **mao²** — hair, and 錢 **ch'ien²** — money. Direct translation would be : one hair money.

三 毛 錢　　｜ Three hairs money
san¹ *mao²-ch'ien²*　｜ (Three ten-cents)
　　　　　　　｜ (Thirty cents)

(c) 一分錢 I⁴ *fen¹-ch'ien²* is translated as : one cent. This phrase is a combination of : 一 I⁴⁽¹⁾ — one, 分 **fen¹** — to divide, one tenth, and 錢 **ch'ien²** — money. Direct translation would be : one tenth money.

七 分 錢　　｜ Seven tenths money
ch'i¹ *fen¹-ch'ien²*　｜ (Seven cents).

64. 要 **yao⁴**. This character may be translated as : to want, or : to require. See also § 39 above.

你 要 問 誰　　　　｜ You want to ask who ?
ni³ **yao⁴** *wen⁴ shui²* ?　｜ (Whom do you want to ask ?)

他 要 錢 來 了　　　　　｜ He wants money came
t'a¹ **yao⁴** *ch'ien² lai²-la¹*　｜ (He requires money, that is
　　　　　　　　　　　｜ why he has come)

我 要 跟 他 說 話　　　　　　｜ I want with him
wo³ **yao⁴** *ken¹ t'a¹ shuo¹ hua⁴*　｜ to speak
(I want to speak with him)

65. 給 **kei³** indicates the dative case. In some cases it may be translated as : to give, in others as : to, for, on behalf of.

那 個 錢 我 給 了 他 了 } That money
na⁴ ke⁴ ch'ien² wo³ kei³-la¹ t'a¹ la¹ } I gave him
(I gave him that money)

父 親 給 了 兒 子 三 塊 錢 了
fu⁴-ch'in¹ kei³-la¹ erh²-tzu¹ san¹ k'uai⁴-ch'ien² la¹
Father gave son three dollars
(The father gave three dollars to his son)

那 個 字 我 給 他 寫 了 } That character I
na⁴ ke⁴ tzu⁴ wo³ kei³ t'a¹ hsieh³-la¹ } for him wrote
(I wrote that character for him)

那 個 飯 是 誰 給 你 作 的
na⁴ ke⁴ fan⁴ shih⁴ shui² kei³ ni³ tso⁴-ti¹?
That food was who for you cooked?
(Who cooked that food for you?)

LESSON 14

I

貴 kuei⁴ dear, expensive 賤 chien⁴ cheap 很 hen³⁽²⁾ very

不大好 pu² ta⁴ hao³ not very good, not very well

1. *Mai³ tung¹-hsi¹ ch'ien² to¹ shih⁴ kuei⁴, ch'ien² shao³ shih⁴ chien⁴.*
2. *Che⁴ wei⁴ hsieh³-ti¹ tzu⁴ pu² ta⁴ hao³, na⁴ wei⁴ hsieh³-ti¹ hen² hao³.*
3. *Na⁴ chang¹ cho¹-tzu¹ kuei⁴, che⁴ pa² i³-tzu¹ chien⁴.*
4. *Che⁴ t'ou² niu² shih⁴ wu³-shih² k'uai⁴-ch'ien² mai³-ti¹, nin² shuo¹ kuei⁴ pu² kuei⁴? Wo³ shuo¹ hen³ kuei⁴.*
5. *Na⁴ chih¹ mao²-pi³ i⁴ mao²-ch'ien², chien⁴ pu² chien⁴? I⁴ mao²-ch'ien² pu² kuei⁴.*
6. *Che⁴ ke⁴ ta⁴ pen³-tzu¹ kuei⁴ chien⁴? Che⁴ ke⁴ ta⁴ pen³-tzu¹ hen³ kuei⁴.*
7. *Na⁴ ke⁴ jen² mai⁴-ti¹ tung¹-hsi¹ hen³ chien⁴.*
8. *Kuei⁴-ti¹ pu² kuei⁴, chien⁴-ti¹ pu² chien⁴.*

1. When buying things if we pay much, it is expensive; if we pay a little, it is cheap.
   (To buy things money much, is expensive; money little, is cheap.)
2. This (person) writes characters not very well, that (person) writes very well.
3. That table (is) expensive, this chair (is) cheap.

4. Fifty dollars were paid for this cow, (This cow was fifty dollars sold,) do you say (it is) expensive?
I (should) say very expensive.
5. That writing-brush (is) ten cents; (is it) cheap?
Ten cents (is) not expensive.
6. (Is) this big note-book expensive or cheap?
This big note-book (is) very expensive.
7. The things that man sells are very cheap.
8. The expensive things are not dear and the cheap things are not cheap.
(Expensive not expensive, cheap not cheap.)

II

貴 姓 kuei⁴ hsing⁴
honourable name, what is your honourable [name?

賤 姓 chien⁴ hsing⁴
humble name, my humble name is —

1. *Nin² yao⁴ wen⁴ t'a¹* hsing⁴ shen²-*ma¹, nin² chiu⁴ shuo¹* 'kuei⁴ hsing⁴'.
2. *T'a¹ wen⁴ nin² kuei² hsing⁴, nin² yao⁴* hui²-*ta²* 'chien⁴ [hsing⁴'.
3. *Nin²* kuei⁴ *hsing⁴? Chien⁴ hsing⁴* Ch'ien².
4. Na⁴ *wei⁴* kuei⁴ *hsing⁴? T'a¹ hsing⁴* Chang¹.

1. (If) you want to ask him what (his) surname (is), you just say *kuei hsing*.
2. (If) he asks you *kuei hsing*, you will reply *chien hsing*.
3. What is your honourable name?
My humble name is Ch'ien.

LESSON 14

4. What is that man's honourable name?
   His name is Chang.

III

講 **chiang³** to explain, to expound

功課 **kung¹-k'e⁴** lesson(s)

1. *Nin² chin¹-t'ien¹ yu³ kung¹-k'e⁴ ma¹?*
   Chin¹-t'ien¹ wo³ mei² yu³ kung¹-k'e⁴, ming²-t'ien¹ yu³ kung¹-k'e⁴.
2. *Tso²-t'ien¹ nin² yu³ kung¹-k'e⁴ ma¹?*
   Tso²-t'ien¹ wo³ yu³ kung¹-k'e⁴.
3. *Chin¹-t'ien¹ shui² kei³ ni³-men² chiang³-ti¹ kung¹-k'e⁴?*
   Pai² hsien¹-sheng¹ chin¹-t'ien¹ kei³ wo³-men² chiang³-ti¹ kung¹-k'e⁴.
4. *Tso²-t'ien¹ Pao¹ hsien¹-sheng¹ chiang³-ti¹ kung¹-k'e⁴, nin² tou¹ ming²-pai²-la¹ ma¹?*
   Wo³ tou¹ ming²-pai²-la¹.
5. *Che⁴ pen³ shu¹ hsien¹-sheng¹ kei³ nin² chiang³ wan²-la¹ ma¹?*
   Hai² mei² chiang³ wan² na¹.
6. *Chin¹-t'ien¹-ti¹ kung¹-k'e⁴ wo³ pu⁴ hen³ ming²-pai², ch'ing³ nin² tsai⁴ kei³ wo³ chiang³ i⁴ hui².*

1. Have you a lesson today?
   I haven't a lesson today, (I) have a lesson to-morrow.
2. Did you have a lesson yesterday?
   Yesterday I had a lesson.
3. Who explained the lesson to you (pl.) today?
   Mr. Pai explained the lesson to us today.

4. Did you understand all the lesson (which) Mr. Pao explained yesterday ?   I understood all (of it).
5. Has the teacher finished explaining this book to you ? (He) has not finished explaining (it) yet.
6. I don't quite understand today's lesson, please explain (it) to me once again.

IV

意思 I⁴-ssu¹
meaning(s), idea(s), intention(s)

1. *Ch'ing³ wen⁴* **nin²** *na¹, pu² kuei⁴ shih⁴* **shen²-ma¹** *i⁴-* *Pu² kuei⁴ shih⁴* **chien⁴**.   [*ssu¹?*
2. *Che⁴ ke⁴ tzu⁴ yu³* **chi³** *ke⁴ i⁴-ssu¹?*
   Yu³ **liang³** *ke⁴ i⁴-ssu¹*.
3. *Nin²* **ming²-pai²** *wo³-ti¹* **I⁴-ssu¹** *ma¹?*
   Wo³ **ming²-pai²** *nin²-ti¹ i⁴-ssu¹*.
4. *T'a¹-men² liang³ ke⁴ jen² yu³* **liang³** *ke⁴ i⁴-ssu¹*. *Che⁴ ke⁴ jen²-ti¹ i⁴-ssu¹ shih⁴ yao⁴* **nien⁴ shu¹**, *na⁴ ke⁴ jen²-ti¹ i⁴-ssu¹ shih⁴ yao⁴* **hsieh³** *tzu⁴*.

1. Will you please tell me, what is the meaning (of) *pu kuei* ? *Pu kuei* is cheap.
2. How many meanings has this character ?
   (It) has two meanings.
3. Do you understand my idea ?   I do understand your idea.
4. (Those) two men have two intentions.
   This man's intention is to study, that man's intention is to write characters.

LESSON 14

V

告訴 kao⁴-su⁴
to tell

1. *Ch'ing³ nin² kao⁴-su⁴ wo³, chin¹-t'ien¹ hsien¹-sheng¹ lai²*
   Chin¹-t'ien¹ hsien¹-sheng¹ pu⁴ lai².   [*pu⁴ lai²?*
2. *Nin² wen⁴ t'a¹ tso⁴ shen²-ma¹ ch'ü⁴, t'a¹ kao⁴-su⁴ nin²*
   T'a¹ mei² kao⁴-su⁴ wo³.   [*la¹ ma¹?*
3. *T'a¹ yu³ shen²-ma¹ i⁴-ssu¹, mei² kao⁴-su⁴ nin² ma¹?*
   Mei² kao⁴-su⁴ wo³.
4. *Wo³ ken¹ nin² shuo¹-ti¹ hua⁴, ch'ing³ nin² pu² yao⁴*
   Shih⁴, wo³ pu² kao⁴-su⁴ t'a¹.   [*kao⁴-su⁴ t'a¹.*
5. *Che⁴ chü⁴ hua⁴ shih⁴ shui² kao⁴-su⁴ nin²-ti¹?*
   Shih⁴ na⁴ wei⁴ ku¹-niang² kao⁴-su⁴ wo³-ti¹

1. Please tell me, will the teacher come to-day?
   The teacher will not come to-day.
2. You asked him what (he) went to do, did he tell you?
   He did not tell me.
3. Didn't (he) tell you what idea he had?
   (He) didn't tell me.
4. Please don't tell him (what) I have said with you.
   Yes, I won't tell him.
5. Who told you this phrase?
   (It) was that girl (who) told me.

VI

太 t'ai⁴
too, very

1. *Che⁴ k'ou³ chu¹* **mai⁴** *shih²-wu³ k'uai⁴-ch'ien²,* *nin² shuo¹* **kuei⁴** *pu² kuei⁴?*
   Shih²-wu³ k'uai⁴-ch'ien² t'ai⁴ kuei⁴ la¹.
2. *Che⁴ chih¹ ch'ien¹-pi³ t'ai⁴* **ch'ang²**, *hai² yu³ tuan³ i⁴-tien-'rh³-ti¹ ma¹?* **Hai²** *yu³ tuan³-ti¹.*
3. *T'a¹ shuo¹-ti¹ hua⁴ t'ai⁴* **to¹** *la¹, chiao⁴ t'a¹* **shao³** *shuo¹ chi³ chü⁴.*
4. *T'a¹ hsieh³-ti¹ na⁴ ke⁴ tzu⁴ t'ai⁴* **hsiao³** *la¹, chiao⁴ t'a¹ hsieh³* **ta⁴** *i⁴-tien-'rh³.*

1. This pig costs fifteen dollars, do you say (it) is expensive? Fifteen dollars (is) too expensive.
2. This pencil (is) too long, have (you) also got one a little shorter ? (We) also have a short one.
3. He talks too much, order him to talk less.
   (He says speech too much, order him less speak several sentences.)
4. He has written that character too small, order him to write (it) a little bigger.

VII

丈夫 chang⁴-fu¹
husband(s)

太太 t'ai⁴-t'ai⁴
wife, wives, lady, ladies, Mrs., Madam

1. *Che⁴ wei⁴ shih⁴* **shui²**? *Shih⁴ wo³ chang⁴-fu¹.*

2. *Nin² shih⁴ t'a¹ t'ai⁴-t'ai⁴ ma¹?*
   Tui⁴-*la¹, wo³* **shih⁴** *t'a¹ t'ai⁴-t'ai⁴.*
3. *T'a¹ shih⁴ ku¹-niang² shih⁴ t'ai⁴-t'ai⁴?*
   T'a¹ shih⁴ t'ai⁴-t'ai⁴.
4. *Na⁴ wei⁴ t'ai⁴-t'ai⁴ hsing⁴ shen²-ma¹?*
   Na⁴ wei⁴ t'ai⁴-t'ai⁴ hsing⁴ Ch'ien².
5. *Chang¹ t'ai⁴-t'ai⁴ tso²-t'ien¹ tso⁴ shen²-ma¹ ch'ü⁴-la¹?*
   T'a¹ **mai³** *tung¹-hsi¹ ch'ü⁴-la¹.*
6. *Nin² chang⁴-fu¹* **mai³** *shen²-ma¹ tung¹-hsi¹ ch'ü⁴-la¹?*
   T'a¹ kei³ wo³-men²-ti¹ ku¹-niang², **erh²**-*tzu¹-men², mai⁴* **shu¹** *ch'ü⁴-la¹?*

1. Who is this person? (He) is my husband.
2. Are you his wife? Right, I am his wife.
3. Is she a girl or a wife? She is a wife.
4. What is that lady's name? That lady's name is Ch'ien.
5. What did Mrs. Chang go (out) for yesterday?
   She went (out) to buy things.
6. What things has your husband gone (out) to buy?
   He has gone (out) to buy books for our daughter and sons.

VIII

(問答) wen⁴-*ta²*
question and answer

Q. *Hsien¹-sheng¹ ken¹* **shui²** *shuo¹-hua⁴ na¹?*
A. *Hsien¹-sheng¹ ken¹ hsüeh²-sheng¹ shuo¹-hua⁴ na¹.*
Q. *Hsien¹-sheng¹ ken¹ t'a¹-men² shuo¹ shen²-ma¹ na¹?*
A. *Hsien¹-sheng¹* **wen⁴** *hsüeh²-sheng¹ na¹.*

Q. *Hsien¹-sheng¹ wen⁴ hsüeh²-sheng¹, hsüeh²-sheng¹* **hui²-ta²-la¹** *mei² yu³?*
A. *Hsüeh²-sheng¹* **hui²-ta²-la¹**.
Q. *Hui²-ta²-ti¹* **tui⁴** *pu² tui⁴?*
A. *Hui²-ta²-ti¹* **hen³** *tui⁴*
Q. *Na⁴ wei⁴ hsien¹-sheng¹* **kuei⁴ hsing⁴?**
A. *Hsing⁴* **Pai²**.
Q. *T'a¹ chiao⁴* **shen²-ma¹ ming²-tzu¹?**
A. *Wo³ pu⁴ chih¹-tao⁴ t'a¹ chiao⁴ shen²-ma¹ ming²-tzu¹.*
Q. *Pai² hsien¹-sheng¹* **yeh³** *kei³* **ni³-men²** *chiang³ kung¹-[k'e⁴?*
A. **Tui⁴-la¹**, *yeh³ kei³ wo³-men² chiang³ kung¹-k'e⁴.*
Q. *T'a¹ chiang³-ti¹ kung¹-k'e⁴* **hao³** *pu⁴ hao³?*
A. *T'a¹ chiang³-ti¹ kung¹-k'e⁴ t'ai⁴ hao³ la¹, wo³-men²* **mei² yu³ i⁴-tien-'rh³** *pu⁴ ming²-pai²-ti¹.*

Q. With whom is the teacher talking?
A. The teacher is talking with the pupils.
Q. What is the teacher talking (about)?
A. The teacher is asking the pupils.
Q. The teacher asked the pupils, did the pupils reply?
A. The pupils replied.
Q. Did (they) reply correctly?
A. (They) replied quite correctly.
Q. What is that teacher's honourable surname?
A. (His) surname (is) Pai.
Q. What is his name?
A. I do not know what his name is.

Q. Does Mr. Pai also explain lessons to you (pl.) ?
A. Right, (he) also explains lessons to us.
Q. Does he explain the lessons well ?
A. He explains the lessons very well; we have nothing which we don't understand. (We do not have a little not understood.)

IX

(問答) wen⁴-ta²
question and answer

Q. *Nin²* **hao³** *a¹?* **Ch'ing³** *tso⁴,* **ch'ing³** *tso⁴.*
A. **Ch'ing³** *tso⁴,* **ch'ing³** *tso⁴.*
Q. *Ch'ing³ nin²* **he¹** *ch'a².*
A. **Hsieh⁴-hsieh⁴.**
Q. *Nin² tso²-t'ien¹ tso⁴ shen²-ma¹ ch'ü⁴-la¹?*
A. *Wo³ tso²-t'ien¹* **mai³** *tung¹-hsi¹ ch'ü⁴-la¹.*
Q. *Nin²* **mai³** *shen²-ma¹ ch'ü⁴-la¹.*
A. *Wo³* **mai³ shu¹** *ch'ü⁴-la¹.*
Q. *Nin²-ti¹* **shu¹** *shih⁴ to¹-shao³ ch'ien² mai³-ti¹?*
A. **San¹** *k'uai⁴* **ssu⁴** *mao²-ch'ien² mai³-ti¹.*
Q. *T'a¹-men²* **mai³ shu¹,** *hai² mai⁴* **shen²-ma¹** *tung¹-hsi¹?*
A. *T'a¹-men² hai² mai⁴* **pen³-tzu¹, kang¹-pi³, ch'ien¹-/.i³,** *shen²-ma¹-ti¹.*
Q. *T'a¹-men²-ti¹ tung¹-hsi¹* **mai⁴-ti¹ kuei⁴ chien⁴** ?
A. *T'a¹-men²-ti¹ tung¹-hsi¹ pu² kuei⁴.*
Q. *Ch'ing³ wen⁴ nin² na¹, che⁴ pen³ shu¹ nin² shih⁴ kei³ shui² mai³-ti¹?*
A. *Shih⁴ kei³ wo³ t'ai⁴-t'ai⁴ mai³-ti¹.*

Q. *Kei³ shu¹² mai³-ti¹ ? Ch'ing³ nin² tsai⁴ shuo¹ i⁴ hui².*
A. *Shih⁴ kei³ wo³ t'ai⁴-t'ai⁴ mai³-ti¹.*
Q. *Nin²-ti¹ t'ai⁴-t'ai⁴ nien⁴ shu¹ na¹ ma¹ ?*
A. **Tui⁴**-*la¹, nien⁴ shu¹ na¹.*

Q. How are you ? Please sit down.
A. Please sit down.
Q. Please drink some tea.
A. Thank you.
Q. What did you go (out) for yesterday ?
A. Yesterday I went (out) to buy things.
Q. What did you go to buy ?
A. I went to buy a book.
Q. How much did your book cost ?
A. It cost three dollars forty cents.
Q. They sell books, what else do they sell ?
A. They also sell note-books, pens, pencils, etc.
Q. Are their things expensive or cheap ?
A. Their things are not expensive.
Q. May I ask you, for whom did you buy this book ?
A. (I) bought it for my wife.
Q. Bought it for whom ? Please say (it) once again.
A. (I) bought it for my wife.
Q. Is your wife studying ?
A. Right, (she) is studying.

LESSON 14

X

(問答) wen⁴-ta²
question and answer

Q. *Kuei⁴ hsing⁴?*
A. *Chien⁴ hsing⁴ Pao¹. Nin² kuei⁴ hsing⁴?*
Q. *Chien⁴ hsing⁴ Pai². Pao¹ hsien¹-sheng¹, nin² tso⁴ shen²-ma¹ lai²-la¹?*
A. *Wo³ yao⁴ ch'ing³ nin² kei³ wo³-men² chiang³ kung¹-k'e⁴.*
Q. *Ni³-men² chi³ ke⁴ jen² nien⁴ shu¹?*
A. *Wo³-men² san¹ ke⁴ jen² nien⁴ shu¹.*
Q. *Na⁴ liang³ ke⁴ jen² shih⁴ shui²?*
A. *Na⁴ liang³ ke⁴ jen², i² wei⁴ shih⁴ Chang¹ t'ai⁴-t'ai⁴, i² wei⁴ shih⁴ Chang¹ t'ai⁴-t'ai⁴-ti¹ chang⁴-fu¹.*
Q. *T'a¹-men² lai²-la¹ ma¹?*
A. *Mei² lai², t'a¹-men² ming²-t'ien¹ lai².*
Q. *Hao³, ch'ing³ t'a¹-men² ming²-t'ien¹ lai².*
A. **Tsai⁴-chien⁴, tsai⁴-chien⁴.**
Q. **Tsai⁴-chien⁴, tsai⁴-chien⁴.**

Q. What is your honourable name?
A. My humble name is Pao. What is your honourable name?
Q. My humble name is Pai. Mr. Pao, what have you come for?
A. I want to ask you to explain the lesson for us.
Q. How many of you are studying?
A. We are three persons studying.
Q. Who are those two people?
A. Those two people, one is Mrs. Chang and one is Mrs. Chang's husband.

Q. Have they come?
A. (They have) not come, they will come to-morrow.
Q. All right, invite them to come to-morrow.
A. Good-bye, good-bye.
Q. Good-bye, good-bye.

NOTES

66. 貴姓 **kuei⁴ hsing⁴?** literally means Expensive name? It is the polite and more general term used when asking an individual's name. 貴 **kuei⁴** is an honorific in this case, and a more correct rendering is: What is your honourable name? or simply: What is your name?

您姓甚麼?
nin² hsing⁴ shen²-m:¹? } What is your surname?

is grammatically correct, but is rarely used.

賤姓 **chien⁴ hsing⁴** literally means Cheap name. It is the polite answer to 貴姓 **kuei⁴ hsing⁴?** and may be translated as: My humble name is —, or simply: My name is —.

67. **Superlative Degree** is formed by inserting an adverb of quantity immediately before the adjective to be governed. In this lesson 很 **hen³** — very, is introduced.

這很大了
che⁴ hen³ ta⁴ la¹ } This very big
(This is very big)
(This is the largest)

這很貴了
che⁴ hen³ kuei⁴ la¹ } This very expensive
(This is very dear)
(This is the most expensive)

LESSON 15

I

屋子 wu¹-tzu¹ room(s)   間 chien¹ classifier for rooms

1. Che⁴ shih⁴ shen²-ma¹? Che⁴ shih⁴ wu¹-tzu¹.
2. Na⁴ shih⁴ chi³ chien¹ wu¹-tzu¹?
   Na⁴ shih⁴ i⁴ chien¹ wu¹-tzu¹.
3. Na⁴ chien¹ wu¹-tzu¹ ta⁴ hsiao³?
   Na⁴ chien¹ wu¹-tzu¹ pu⁴ hen³ ta⁴.
4. Che⁴ chien¹ wu¹-tzu¹ shih⁴ nin²-ti¹ ma¹?
   Shih⁴ wo³-ti¹.

1. What is this? This is a room.
2. How many rooms are there there?
   There is one room there.
3. (Is) that room large or small?
   That room (is) not very large.
4. Is this room yours? (It) is mine.

II

裡 li³ in, inside   在 tsai⁴ in, at

(在 ○ 裡) tsai⁴ — li³ in, at

1. Na⁴ chien¹ wu¹-tzu¹ li³ yu³ shen²-ma¹ tung¹-hsi?
   Na⁴ chien¹ wu¹-tzu¹ li³ yu³ cho¹-tzu¹, yu³ i³-tzu¹.

2. *Nin²-ti¹* **chang⁴-fu¹** *tsai⁴* **na⁴** *chien¹* **wu¹-tzu¹**. *li³* **tso⁴** **shen²-ma¹** *na¹*?
   T'a¹ tsai⁴ na⁴ chien¹ wu¹-tzu¹ li³ ken¹ **Ch'ien²** *hsien¹-sheng¹* **shuo¹-hua⁴** *na¹*.
3. *Ch'ing³ wen⁴* **nin²** *na¹*, **Pao¹** *t'ai¹-t'ai⁴ mai³-ti¹ ch'a²-yeh⁴* **tsai⁴** *na⁴ chien¹ wu¹-tzu¹ li³ na¹ ma¹?*
   Tui⁴-la¹, *tsai⁴ na⁴ chien¹ wu¹-tzu¹ li³ na¹.*
4. *Hsien¹-sheng¹ hsieh³-ti¹* **na⁴** *ke⁴ tzu⁴, tsai⁴* **che⁴** *pen³ shu¹ li³* **yu³** *mei² yu³*?
   Tsai⁴ che⁴ pen³ shu¹ li³ **mei²** *yu³*.
5. *Tsai⁴* **che⁴** *ke⁴ ch'a²-wan³ li³* **yu³** *ch'a² ma¹?*
   Tsai⁴ che⁴ ke⁴ ch'a²-wan³ li³ **yu³** *ch'a²*.
6. *Tsai⁴* **na⁴** *ke⁴ fan⁴-wan³ li³* **yu³** *fan⁴ ma¹?*
   Tsai⁴ na⁴ ke⁴ fan⁴-wan³ li³ **mei²** *yu³ fan⁴*.
7. *Che⁴ ke⁴ po¹-li²-pei¹ li³* **yu³** *k'a¹-fei⁴ ma¹?*
   Na⁴ ke⁴ po¹-li²-pei¹ li³ **mei²** *yu³ k'a¹-fei⁴, yu³* **shui³**.
8. *Tsai⁴ fan⁴-wan³ li³ yu³* **fan⁴***, shih⁴ i⁴ wan³ fan⁴; tsai⁴ fan⁴-wan³ li³* **mei²** *yu³ fan⁴, shih⁴ i² ke⁴* **fan⁴-wan³**.
9. *Tsai⁴ ch'a²-wan³ li³ yu³* **ch'a²***, shih⁴ i⁴ wan³ ch'a²; tsai⁴ ch'a²-wan³ li³* **mei²** *yu³ ch'a², shih⁴ i² ke⁴* **ch'a²-wan³**.
10. *Tsai⁴* **che⁴** *chien¹ wu¹-tzu¹ li³ yu³* **to¹-shao³** *jen²?*
    Yu³ **san¹-shih²** *to¹ ke⁴ jen²*.
11. *Tsai⁴* **na⁴** *chien¹ wu¹-tzu¹ li³* **mei²** *yu³ jen² ma¹?*
    Shih⁴, *tsai⁴ na⁴ chien¹ wu¹-tzu¹ li³* **mei²** *yu³ jen²*.

1. What things are there in that room?
   In that room there are tables and chairs.

LESSON 15   157

2. What is your husband doing in that room?
He is talking with Mr. Ch'ien in that room.
3. Will you please tell me, is the tea that Mrs. Pao bought in that room?   Right, it is in that room.
4. Are those characters written by the teacher in this book or not?   They are not in this book.
5. Is there any tea in this tea-cup?
There is some tea in this tea-cup.
6. Is there any food in that rice-bowl?
There is no food in that rice-bowl.
7. Is there any coffee in this glass?
There is no coffee in that glass, there is some water.
8. (If) there is food in a rice-bowl, it is one bowl of food;
(if) there is no food in a rice-bowl, it is one rice-bowl.
9. (If) there is tea in a tea-cup, it is one cup of tea; (if) there is no tea in a tea-cup, it is one tea-cup.
10. How many people are there in this room?
There are more than thirty people.
11. Are there no people in that room?
Yes, there are no people in that room.

III

窗戶 ch'uang¹-hu⁴ window(s)   門 men² door(s)

1. *Ni³-men² ch'ih¹ fan⁴-ti¹ na⁴ chien¹ wu¹-tzu¹ yu³* **chi³** *ke⁴ ch'uang¹-hu⁴? Yu³* **liang³** *ke⁴ ch'uang¹-hu⁴.*

2. *Na⁴ ssu⁴ ke⁴ ch'uang¹-hu⁴ ta⁴ hsiao³?*
   Na⁴ ssu⁴ ke⁴ ch'uang¹-hu⁴ tou¹ pu⁴ hsiao³.
3. *Nin² nien⁴ shu¹-ti¹ na⁴ chien¹ wu¹-tzu¹ yu³ chi³ ke⁴ ch'uang¹-hu⁴, chi³ ke⁴ men²?*
   Yu³ wu³ ke⁴ ch'uang¹-hu⁴, liang³ ke⁴ men².
4. *Che⁴ liang³ chien¹ wu¹-tzu¹ tou¹ yu³ liang³ ke⁴ ch'uang¹-hu⁴ ma¹?*
   Pu² shih⁴, i⁴ chien¹ yu³ liang³ ke⁴ ch'uang¹-hu⁴, i⁴ chien¹ yu³ i² ke⁴ ch'uang¹-hu⁴.
5. *Che⁴ ke⁴ men² tso⁴-ti¹ hao³ pu⁴ hao³?*
   Che⁴ ke⁴ men² tso⁴-ti¹ pu⁴ hao³.
6. *Shih⁴ che⁴ ke⁴ men² ta⁴ shih⁴ na⁴ ke⁴ men² ta⁴?*
   Na⁴ ke⁴ men² ta⁴.

1. How many windows has that room (where) you eat?
   (It) has two windows.
2. (Are) those four windows large or small?
   Those four windows are not small (i. e.: large).
3. How many windows and how many doors has that room (where) you study? It has five windows and two doors.
4. Have these two rooms both got two windows?
   No, one has two windows and one has one window.
5. Is this door well made? This door is badly made.
6. Which is the larger, this door or that door?
   That door is larger.

IV

房子 **fang**²-*tzu*¹ house(s)　　所 **so**³ classifier for buildings

1. *Na*⁴ *shih*⁴ **nin**²-*ti*¹ **fang**²-*tzu*¹ *ma*¹?
   *Tui*⁴-*la*¹, *na*⁴ **shih**⁴ *wo*³-*ti*¹ **fang**²-*tzu*¹.
2. *Nin*² *yu*³ **chi**³ *so*³ **fang**²-*tzu*¹?
   *Wo*³ *yu*³ *i*⁴ *so*³ **fang**²-*tzu*¹.
3. *Na*⁴ *so*³ **fang**²-*tzu*¹ *yu*³ *to*¹-*shao*³ *chien*¹ **wu**¹-*tzu*¹?
   *Yu*³ **shih**² *chien*¹ *wu*¹-*tzu*¹.
4. *Na*⁴ *so*³ **fang**²-*tzu*¹ **hao**³ *pu*⁴ *hao*³?
   *Na*⁴ *so*³ **fang**²-*tzu*¹ *pu*² *ta*⁴ *hao*³.

1. Is that your house? Right, that is my house.
2. How many houses have you got? I have one house.
3. How many rooms has that house? It has ten rooms.
4. Is that a good house? That house is not very good.

V

住 **chu**⁴ to dwell, to live, to live in, to inhabit

1. *Nin*² *chu*⁴ **chi**³ *chien*¹ *wu*¹-*tzu*¹?
   *Wo*³ *chu*⁴ **liu**⁴ *chien*¹ *wu*¹-*tzu*¹.
2. *Shui*² *tsai*⁴ *che*⁴ *so*³ **fang**²-*tzu*¹ *li*³ **chu**⁴?
   *Ch'ien*² *t'ai*⁴-*t'ai*⁴ *tsai*⁴ *che*⁴ *so*³ **fang**²-*tzu*¹ *li*³ *chu*⁴.
3. *Che*⁴ *shih*⁴ *nin*² *chu*⁴-*ti*¹ **fang**²-*tzu*¹ *ma*¹?
   *Shih*⁴, *che*⁴ **shih**⁴ *wo*³ *chu*⁴-*ti*¹ **fang**²-*tzu*¹.
4. *Na*⁴ *chien*¹ *wu*¹-*tzu*¹ *shih*⁴ **shui**² *chu*⁴?
   *Na*⁴ *chien*¹ *wu*¹-*tzu*¹ *shih*⁴ *wo*³ *ken*¹ *wo*³ **chang**⁴-*fu*¹ *chu*⁴.

5. *T'a¹ chu⁴-ti¹* **na⁴** *chien¹ wu¹-tzu¹ yu³* **chi³** *ke⁴ men²,* **chi³** *ke⁴ ch'uang¹-hu⁴?*
   T'a¹ chu⁴-ti¹ **na⁴** *chien¹ wu¹-tzu¹ yu³* **i²** *ke⁴ men²,* **liang³** *ke⁴ ch'uang¹-hu⁴.*
6. *Che⁴ so³ fang²-tzu¹ shih⁴* **shui²-*ti¹*** *?*
   Shih⁴ **Pao¹** *t'ai⁴-t'ai⁴-ti¹.*

1. How many rooms do you live in ? I live in six rooms.
2. Who lives in this house ?
   Mrs. Ch'ien lives in this house.
3. Is this the house you live in ?
   Yes, this is the house I live in.
4. Who lives in that room ?
   I and my husband live in that room.
5. How many doors and windows has that room he lives in ?
   That room he lives in has one door and two windows.
6. Whose is this house ? It is Mrs. Pao's.

VI

家 chia¹
family, home

1. *Nin² chia¹ li³ yu³* **chi³** *k'ou-'rh³ jen²?*
   Wo³ chia¹ li³ yu³ **wu³** *k'ou-'rh³ jen².*
2. *Nin² chia¹ li³* **tou¹** *yu³ shen²-ma¹ jen²?*
   Wo³ yu³ **fu⁴-*ch'in¹*,** **mu³-*ch'in¹*,** **t'ai⁴-*t'ai⁴*,** **hai²** *yu³ i² ke⁴ erh²-tzu¹, i² ke⁴* **ku¹-*niang²*.**
3. *Nin² t'ai⁴-t'ai⁴ tsai⁴ chia¹ li³ tso⁴ shen²-ma¹?*
   T'a¹ tsai⁴ chia¹ li³ kei³ wo³-men² tso⁴ **fan⁴.**

LESSON 15

4. *Nin²-ti¹ hsien¹-sheng¹* **tsai⁴** *chia¹ na¹ ma¹?*
   T'a¹ **mei²** *tsai⁴ chia¹.*
5. *Nin²-ti¹ chang⁴-fu¹* **tsai⁴** *chia¹ li³ na¹ ma¹?*
   T'a¹ **tsai⁴** *chia¹ li³ na¹.*

1. How many people are there in your family?
   In my family there are five people.
2. Of whom does your family consist?
   (Your family in all has what persons?)
   I have a father, mother and wife, and also one son and one daughter.
3. What does your wife do at home?
   She cooks for us at home.
4. Is your teacher at home? He is not at home.
5. Is your husband at home? He is at home.

VII

學堂 hsüeh²-t'ang²
school(s)

(○個學堂) — ke⁴ hsüeh²-t'ang²
— school(s)

地方 ti⁴-fang¹
place(s)

(○塊地方) — k'uai⁴ ti⁴-fang¹
— place(s)

1. *Che⁴ so³ fang²-tzu¹ shih⁴ ni³-men² hsüeh²-t'ang² pu² shih⁴? Che⁴ so⁴ fang²-tzu¹ shih⁴ wo³-men² hsüeh²-t'ang².*

2. *Che⁴ ke⁴ ti⁴-fang¹ yu³ hsüeh²-t'ang² mei² yu³?*
   Yu³ *hsüeh²-t'ang².*
3. *Hsüeh²-t'ang² shih⁴* **tso⁴ shen²-ma¹-ti¹** *ti⁴-fang¹?*
   Hsüeh²-t'ang² shih⁴ **nien⁴ shu¹** *ti¹ ti⁴-fang¹.*
4. *T'a¹-men² hsüeh²-t'ang² li³ yu³* **to¹-shao³ wei⁴ hsien¹-sheng¹?** *Yu³* **shih² chi³** *wei⁴ hsien¹-sheng¹.*
5. *Nin²-ti¹* **ku¹-niang²** *tsai⁴ hsüeh²-t'ang² li³ nien⁴ shu¹ na¹ ma¹?*
   Pu² *shih⁴, t'a¹ hai² hsiao³ na¹, tsai⁴* **chia¹** *li³ nien⁴ shu¹.*
6. *Nin²-ti¹* **erh²-tzu¹** *tsai⁴* **chia¹** *li³ nien⁴ shu¹ ma¹?*
   Pu² *shih⁴, t'a¹ tsai⁴ hsüeh²-t'ang² nien⁴ shu¹.*
7. *Shih⁴ che⁴ ke⁴ hsüeh²-t'ang² hsüeh²-sheng¹ to¹, shih⁴* **na⁴** *ke⁴ hsüeh²-t'ang² hsüeh²-sheng¹ to¹?*
   Shih⁴ **na⁴** *ke⁴ hsüeh²-t'ang² hsüeh²-sheng¹ to¹, che⁴ ke⁴ hsüeh²-t'ang² hsüeh²-sheng¹ shao³.*
8. *Che⁴ i² k'uai⁴ ti⁴-fang¹ shih⁴* **wo³-ti¹**, *na⁴ i² k'uai⁴ ti⁴-fang¹ shih⁴* **t'a¹-ti¹**.

1. Is this house your school?
   This house is our school.
2. Has this place got a school?   It has a school.
3. What is done at school?   (School is do what place?)
   A school is a place to study.
4. How many teachers are there in their school?
   It has a dozen odd teachers.
5. Is your daughter studying at school?
   No, she is still young (little), she studies at home.
6. Does your son study at home?   No, he studies at school.
7. Which has the most pupils, this school or that school?

LESSON 15

(Is this school pupils more, is that school pupils more ?)
That school has the most pupils.
(Is that school pupils more, this school pupils few.)
8. This place is mine, that place is his.

VIII

舖子　p'u⁴-tzu¹
shop(s), store(s)

1. Mai⁴ tung¹-hsi¹-ti¹ ti⁴-fang¹ chiao⁴ shen²-ma¹ ming²-tzu¹ ? Mai⁴ tung¹-hsi¹-ti¹ ti⁴-fang¹ chiao⁴ p'u⁴-tzu¹.
2. Tsai⁴ che⁴ ke⁴ p'u⁴-tzu¹ li³ mai⁴ shen²-ma¹ tung¹-hsi ? Tsai⁴ che⁴ ke⁴ p'u⁴-tzu¹ li³ mai⁴ ch'a²-yeh⁴, k'a¹-fei⁴, mien⁴-pao¹, shen²-ma¹-ti¹.
3. Mai⁴ shu¹-ti¹ p'u⁴-tzu¹ shih⁴ shen²-ma¹ p'u⁴-tzu¹ ? Mai⁴ shu¹-ti¹ p'u⁴-tzu¹ shih⁴ shu¹-p'u⁴.
4. Shen²-ma¹ p'u⁴-tzu¹ mai⁴ cho¹-tzu¹, mai⁴ i³-tzu¹ ? Cho¹-i³-p'u⁴ mai⁴ cho¹-tzu¹, mai⁴ i³-tzu¹.
5. Mai⁴ niu², yang², chu¹-jou⁴-ti¹, che⁴ ke⁴ p'u⁴-tzu¹ chiao⁴ shen²-ma¹ ming²-tzu¹ ? Na⁴ chiao⁴ jou⁴-p'u⁴.
6. Tsai⁴ jou⁴-p'u⁴ li³ yeh³ mai⁴ yü² ma¹ ? Yeh³ mai⁴ yü².
7. Che⁴ ke⁴ mien⁴-pao¹-fang² shih⁴ nin²-ti¹ ma¹ ? Shih⁴ wo³-ti¹.
8. Che⁴ ke⁴ ti⁴-fang¹ yu³ shen²-ma¹ p'u⁴-tzu¹ ? Che⁴ ke⁴ ti⁴-fang¹ shen²-ma¹ p'u⁴-tzu¹ tou¹ yu³.
9. Shu¹-p'u⁴ li³ yeh³ mai⁴ chih³, kang¹-pi³, ch'ien¹-pi³, mao²-pi³ ma¹ ? Yeh³ mai⁴.
10. Nin²-ti¹ t'ai⁴-t'ai⁴ tsai⁴ na⁴ ke⁴ p'u⁴-tzu¹ li³ mai³ shen²-ma¹ ? T'a¹ tsai⁴ na⁴ ke⁴ p'u⁴-tzu¹ li³ mai³ po¹-li²-pei¹.

1. What is the place where things are sold called?
   (Sell things place called what name?)
   The place (where) things are sold is called a shop.
2. What (things) are sold in this shop?
   In this shop (they) sell tea, coffee, bread and so on.
3. What sort of shop is a shop (where) books are sold?
   A shop (where) books are sold is a book-shop.
4. What sort of shop sells tables and chairs?
   A furniture shop sells tables and chairs.
5. What is a shop where beef, mutton and pork are sold called?
   (Sell beef, mutton, pork, this shop called what name?)
   That is called a butcher's shop.
6. (Is) fish also sold at the butcher's?
   (They) also sell fish.
7. Is this baker's shop yours? It is mine.
8. What sort of shops has this place got?
   This place has all kinds of shops.
9. Does a book-store also sell paper, pens, pencils and writing-brushes? Yes. (Also sell.)
10. What is your wife buying in that shop?
    She is buying tumblers in that shop.

LESSON 15

NOTES

68. In, inside, at, are expressed in two ways:

(a) Addition of character 裡 li³ after the noun.

茶 碗 裡 | Tea-cup inside
ch'a²-*wan*³ **li**³ | (In the tea-cup)

玻 璃 盃 裡 | Glass inside   書 裡 | Book inside
po¹-**li**²-**pei**¹ **li**³ | (In the glass)   **shu**¹ **li**³ | (In the book)

(b) Use of the two characters 在 **tsai**⁴ — in, at, and 裡 **li**³, where 在 *tsai*⁴ precedes the noun and 裡 *li*³ follows it.

在 學 堂 裡 | At school inside
tsai⁴ *hsüeh*²-*t'ang*² **li**³ | (At school) (In school)

在 家 裡 | At home inside
tsai⁴ *chia*¹ **li**³ | (At home)

在 飯 碗 裡 | At rice-bowl inside
tsai⁴ *fan*⁴-*wan*³ **li**³ | (In the rice-bowl)

69. 家 **chia**¹ has two meanings: home (house) and family.

張 家 | Chang home
Chang¹ **chia**¹ | (Mr. Chang's home) (Mr. Chang's family)

這 是 包 家 的 房 子 | This is Pao
*Che*⁴ *shih*⁴ **Pao**¹ *chia*¹-*ti*¹ **fang**²-*tzu*¹ | family's house
(This is the house of the Pao family)
(This is the Pao home)

70 舖子 **p'u⁴-tzu¹** — shop, store, in the general sense. Various varieties of shops are denoted by the addition of appropriate characters as prefixes to 舖 **p'u⁴**.

書 *shu¹* — book,   舖 *p'u⁴* — shop,
書舖 **shu¹-*p'u⁴*** — book-shop.

肉 *jou⁴* — meat,   舖 *p'u⁴* — shop,
肉舖 **jou⁴-*p'u⁴*** — butcher's shop.

筆 *pi³* — pen,   舖 *p'u⁴* — shop,
筆舖 **pi³-*p'u⁴*** — pen shop.

紙 *chih³* — paper,   舖 *p'u⁴* — shop,
紙舖 **chih³-*p'u⁴*** — paper shop.

飯 *fan⁴* — food,   舖 *p'u⁴* — shop,
飯舖 **fan⁴-*p'u⁴*** — restaurant.

棹椅 *cho¹-i³* — furniture,   舖 *p'u⁴* — shop,
棹椅舖 **cho¹-i³-*p'u⁴*** — furniture shop.

The following is an exception, 房 *fang²* — house, taking the place of 舖 *p'u⁴*.

麪包 *mien⁴-pao¹* — bread, 房 *fang²* — house,
麪包房 **mien⁴-pao¹-fang²** — baker's shop.

LESSON 16

I

紅 hung² red   黃 huang² yellow   綠 lü⁴ green   白 pai² white

黑 hei¹ black   藍 lan² blue   顏色 yen²-se⁴ colour

1. Na⁴ so³ hung² fang²-tzu¹ shih⁴ hsüeh²-t'ang² ma¹?
   Tui⁴-la¹, shih⁴ hsüeh²-t'ang².
2. Che⁴ liang³ ke⁴ lü⁴ ch'uang¹-hu⁴ ta⁴ hsiao³?
   Che⁴ liang³ ke⁴ lü⁴ ch'uang¹-hu⁴ ta⁴-ti¹ hen³.
3. Na⁴ chang¹ cho¹-tzu¹ shih⁴ huang²-ti¹ pu² shih⁴?
   Shih⁴ huang²-ti¹.
4. Nin² mai³-la¹ chi³ chin¹ hei¹ mien⁴-pao¹?
   Wo³ mai³-la¹ erh⁴ chin¹ hei¹ mien⁴-pao¹.
5. Pai² mien⁴-pao¹ kuei⁴ chien⁴?
   Pai² mien⁴-pao¹ kuei⁴ i⁴-tien-'rh³.
6. Che⁴ chi³ chang¹ chih³ shih⁴ lü⁴-ti¹ pu² shih⁴?
   Che⁴ chi³ chang¹ chih³ pu² shih⁴ lü⁴-ti¹, shih⁴ lan²-ti¹.
7. Che⁴ chih¹ ch'ien¹-pi³ shih⁴ shen²-ma¹ yen²-se⁴-ti¹?
   Che⁴ chih¹ ch'ien¹-pi³ shih⁴ hei¹ yen²-se⁴-ti¹.
8. Ch'a²-wan³ yu³ hung² yen²-se⁴-ti¹ mei² yu³?
   Ch'a²-wan³ shen²-ma¹ yen²-se⁴ tou¹ yu³

1. Is that red house a school? Right, it is a school.
2. Are these two green windows large or small?
   These two green windows are very large.

3. That table is yellow isn't it ? It is yellow.
4. How many catties of black bread have you bought ?
   I have bought two catties of black bread.
5. Is white bread expensive or cheap ?
   White bread is a little expensive.
6. These sheets of paper are green aren't they ?
   These sheets of paper are not green, they are blue.
7. What colour is this pencil ? This pencil is black (colour).
8. Have (you) red coloured tea-cups ?
   (We) have tea-cups of all kinds of colours.

II

地板 ti⁴-pan³
floor(s), wooden floor(s)

頂棚 ting³-p'eng²
ceiling(s)

1. *Na⁴ chien¹ wu¹-tzu¹-ti¹* **ti⁴-pan³** *shih⁴* **shen²-ma¹** *yen²-se⁴-ti¹ ?* *Shih⁴* **huang²** *yen²-se⁴-ti¹.*
2. *Ti⁴-pan³ shih⁴* **shen²-ma¹** *yen²-se⁴-ti¹ to¹ ?*
   Ti⁴-pan³ shih⁴ **huang²** *yen²-se⁴-ti¹ to¹.*
3. *Che⁴ chi³ chien¹ wu¹-tzu¹* **ting³-p'eng²** *shih⁴* **shen²-ma¹** *yen²-se⁴-ti¹ ?*
   Che⁴ chi³ chien¹ wu¹-tzu¹-ti¹ ting³-p'eng² shih⁴ **pai²-ti¹.**
4. **Che⁴** *chien¹ wu¹-tzu¹-ti¹ ting³-p'eng² shih⁴* **pai²-*ti¹ ma¹ ?***
   Che⁴ wu¹-tzu¹-ti¹ ting³-p'eng² pu² shih⁴ **pai²-*ti¹,*** *shih⁴* **lan²-*ti¹.***

LESSON 16

169

1. What colour is the floor of that room?
   It is yellow (colour).
2. What colour are most floors.
   Most floors are yellow in colour.
3. What colour are the ceilings of these numerous rooms?
   The ceilings of these rooms are white.
4. Is the ceiling of this room white?
   The ceiling of this room isn't white, it is blue.

III

牆 ch'iang² wall(s)   (○ 面 牆) — mien⁴ ch'iang² — walls

1. *Na⁴ chien¹ wu¹-tzu¹-ti¹* **ch'iang²** *shih⁴ shen²-ma¹ yen²-se⁴-ti¹? Shih⁴ lü⁴ yen²-se⁴-ti.*
2. *Che⁴ chien¹ wu¹-tzu¹ yu³* **chi³** *mien⁴ ch'iang²? Che⁴ chien¹ wu¹-tzu¹ yu³ ssu⁴ mien⁴ ch'iang².*
3. *Che⁴ mien⁴ ch'iang²* **ken¹** *na⁴ mien⁴ ch'iang² shih⁴ i² ke⁴ yen²-se⁴ ma¹? Shih⁴ i² ke⁴ yen²-se⁴.*
4. *Che⁴ mien⁴ ch'iang² yu³* **men²**, *na⁴ mien⁴ ch'iang² yu³ ch'uang¹-hu⁴.*
5. *Che⁴ mien⁴ ch'iang² yu³ chi³ ke⁴ men², chi³ ke⁴ ch'uang¹-hu⁴? Che⁴ mien⁴ ch'iang² yu³ i² ke⁴ men², i² ke⁴ ch'uang¹-hu⁴.*

1. What colour are the walls of that room?
   They are green coloured.
2. How many walls has this room?
   This room has four walls.

3. Are this wall and that wall the same colour?
   They are the same colour.
4. This wall has a door, that wall has a window.
5. How many doors and how many windows has this wall?
   This wall has one door and one window.

IV

墨水兒 mo⁴-shui-'rh³ ink(s)   粉筆 fen³⁽²⁾-pi³ chalk(s), crayon(s)

黑板 hei¹-pan³ blackboard(s)

1. Nin² yao⁴ mai³ kang¹-pi³, hai² yao⁴ mai³ **shen²-ma¹**?
   Hai² yao⁴ mai³ **mo⁴-shui-'rh³**.
2. Nin² yao⁴ mai³ **shen²-ma¹** yen²-se⁴-ti¹ mo⁴-shui-'rh³?
   Wo³ yao⁴ mai³ **lan²** yen²-se⁴-ti¹.
3. Che⁴ ke⁴ mo⁴-shui-'rh³ shih⁴ **shen²-ma¹** yen²-se⁴-ti¹?
   Che⁴ ke⁴ mo⁴-shui-'rh³ shih⁴ **hung²-ti¹**.
4. Che⁴ liang³ chih¹ fen²-pi³ shih⁴ **shui²-ti¹**?
   Na⁴ liang³ chih¹ fen²-pi³ shih⁴ **hsien¹-sheng¹-ti¹**.
5. Fen²-pi³ yu³ **pai²-ti¹**, yeh³ yu³ hung²-ti¹ ma¹?
   Fen²-pi³ yeh³ yu³ hung²-ti¹.
6. Che⁴ shih⁴ **shen²-ma¹** tung¹-hsi¹?
   Che⁴ shih⁴ **hei¹-pan³**.
7. Che⁴ k'uai⁴ hei¹-pan³ ta⁴ hsiao³?
   Che⁴ k'uai⁴ hei¹-pan³ **pu² ta⁴**.
8. Tsai⁴ ni³-men² na⁴ chien¹ wu¹-tzu¹ li³ yu³ chi³ k'uai⁴ [hei¹-pan³?
   Yu³ **liang³** k'uai⁴ hei¹-pan³.

LESSON 16

9. *Che⁴ chien¹ wu¹-tzu¹ li³* **yu³ hei¹**-*pan³ mei² yu³ ?*
   Che⁴ chien¹ wu¹-tzu¹ li³ **mei²** *yu³.*

1. You want to buy a pen, what else do you want to buy ?
   I also want to buy some ink.
2. What colour ink do you want to buy ?
   I want to buy blue (colour).
3. What colour is this ink ?   This ink is red.
4. Whose are these two chalks ?
   Those two chalks are the teacher's.
5. There are some white chalks, are there also some red ones?
   There are also some red chalks.
6. What is this thing ?   This is a blackboard.
7. Is this blackboard large or small ?
   This blackboard is not large.
8. How many blackboards have you in that room ?
   (We) have two blackboards.
9. Is there a blackboard in this room ?
   There is not (one) in this room.

V

畫兒 **hua-'rh⁴** drawing(s), picture(s)   畫 **hua⁴** to draw, to paint

1. *Na⁴ chang¹* **hua-'rh⁴** *shih⁴* **shui²**-*ti¹ ?*
   Che⁴ chang¹ hua-'rh⁴ shih⁴ Huang² hsien¹-sheng¹-ti¹.
2. *Che⁴ pen³ shu¹ li³ yu³* **hua-'rh⁴** *mei² ｊu³ ?*
   Che⁴ pen³ shu¹ li³ yu³ hua-'rh⁴.

3. *Nin² hui⁴ hua⁴* hua-'rh⁴ *ma¹?* *Wo³* hui⁴ hua⁴ hua-'rh⁴.
4. *Nin² hui⁴ hua⁴* shen²-*ma¹?*
   Wo³ shen²-ma¹ tou¹ hui⁴ hua⁴.
5. *Na⁴ liang³ chang¹ hua-'rh⁴* hua⁴-*ti¹* hao³ pu⁴ hao³?
   Na⁴ liang³ chang¹ hua-'rh⁴ hua⁴-ti¹ t'ai⁴ hao³ la¹.
6. *Che⁴ chang¹ hua-'rh⁴ shih⁴* nin² hua⁴-*ti¹* ma¹?
   Shih⁴ *wo³ hua⁴-ti¹.*

1. Whose is that picture ? This picture is Mr. Huang's.
2. Has this book any pictures in (it) ?
   This book has some pictures in (it).
3. Can you draw pictures ? I can draw pictures.
4. What can you draw ? I can draw anything.
5. Are those two pictures well drawn ?
   Those two pictures are drawn very well.
6. Did you draw this picture ?   I did draw it.

VI

筆 pi³
pen(s)

拿 na²
to take, to grasp, to take hold of

拿筆 na² pi³
to hold a pen, to use a pen (to write with)

1. *Che⁴ shih⁴* shen²-*ma¹* pi³? *Che⁴ shih⁴* mao²-*pi³.*
2. *Na⁴ shih⁴* shen²-*ma¹* pi³? *Na⁴ shih⁴* ch'ien¹-*pi³.*
3. *Che⁴ chih¹ pi³ shih⁴* nin²-*ti¹ pu² shih⁴?*
   Che⁴ chih¹ pi³ shih⁴ wo³-ti¹.
4. *Nin² yao⁴ na² shen²-ma¹ pi³?*
   Wo³ yao⁴ na² kang¹-*pi³.*

LESSON 16

5. *Nin² yao⁴ na² shih⁴ fen²-pi³ ma¹?*
   Shih⁴, *wo³ yao⁴ na² shih⁴ fen²-pi³.*
6. *Ni³-ti¹ erh²-tzu¹ yao⁴ na² shen²-ma¹?*
   Wo³-ti¹ erh²-tzu¹ yao⁴ na² ch'a²-wan³.
7. *Nin² ti¹ ku¹-niang² yao⁴ na² hung² ch'ien¹-pi³ shih⁴ yao⁴ na² lü⁴ ch'ien¹-pi³?*
   Wo³-ti¹ ku¹-niang² yao⁴ na² lü⁴ ch'ien¹-pi³.
8. *Wo³ yao⁴ na² shen²-ma¹ tung¹-hsi¹?*
   Ni³ yao⁴ na² fan⁴-wan³.
9. *Nin² na² ch'ien¹-pi³ tso⁴ shen²-ma¹?*
   Wo³ yao⁴ hsieh³ chi³ ke⁴ tzu⁴.
10. *Hsien¹-sheng¹ na² shen²-ma¹ pi³ hsieh³ tzu⁴?*
    Hsien¹-sheng¹ na² fen²-pi³ hsieh³ tzu⁴.
11. *Hsien¹-sheng¹ na² fen²-pi³ hsieh³ tzu⁴, hsüeh²-sheng¹ na² shen²-ma¹ pi³ hsieh³ tzu⁴?*
    Hsüeh²-sheng¹ na² kang¹-pi³ hsieh³ tzu⁴.
12. *Che⁴ chi³ ke⁴ tzu⁴ shih⁴ na² shen²-ma¹ pi³ hsieh³-ti¹?*
    Che⁴ chi³ ke⁴ tzu⁴ shih⁴ na² mao²-pi³ hsieh³-ti¹.
13. *Nin² hui⁴ na² mao²-pi³ hsieh³ tzu⁴ ma¹?*
    Wo³ hui⁴ na² mao²-pi³ hsieh³ tzu⁴.
14. *Nin² shuo¹ shih⁴ na² kang¹-pi³ hsieh³-ti¹ tzu⁴ hao³ a¹, hai² shih⁴ na² ch'ien¹-pi³ hsieh³-ti¹ tzu⁴ hao³ ni¹?*
    Wo³ shuo¹ hai² shih⁴ na² kang¹-pi³ hsieh³-ti¹ tzu⁴
    [*hao³.*

1. What sort of pen is this? This is a brush-pen.
2. What sort of pen is that? That is a pencil.
3. Is this pen yours? This pen is mine.
4. What sort of pen do you want to use?
   I want to use a steel pen.

5. Do you want to use the chalks?
    Yes, I want to use the chalks.
6. What does your son want to take?
    My son wants to take a tea-cup.
7. Does your daughter want to use a red pencil or a green
    My daughter wants to use a green pencil.   [pencil?
8. What do I want to take?   You want to take a rice-bowl.
9. What are you holding a pencil for?
    I want to write several characters.
10. What sort of pen does the teacher use to write charac-
    The teacher uses a chalk to write characters.   [ters?
11. The teacher uses a chalk to write characters, what does the student use to write characters?
    The student uses a pen to write.
12. With what sort of pen were these (several) characters written?   These (several) characters were written with a writing-brush.
13. Can you use a writing-brush to write characters?
    I can use a writing-brush to write characters.
14. Would you say that it is better to use a pen to write with than a pencil?
    I should say that it is better to use a pen to write with.

LESSON 16

NOTES

71. 筆 **pi³** — pen. To the Chinese this character originally implied 毛筆 **mao²-pi³** — a writing-brush or brush-pen. We may translate it as: an instrument for writing. From it we have the compound nouns:

鉛筆 **ch'ien¹-pi³** | lead pen (a pencil)

鋼筆 **kang¹-pi³** | steel pen (a pen)

毛筆 **mao²-pi³** | hair pen (a writing-brush, a brush-pen)

粉筆 **fen²-pi³** | chalk pen (a chalk, a crayon)

72. 拿筆 **na² pi³**. 拿 **na²** in this combination means to hold and suggests the instrumental case. Hence the phrase may be translated as: to hold a pen, to use a pen to write with, or merely: with a pen.

拿甚麼筆？ **na² shen²-ma¹ pi³?** | Hold what pen? (Use what sort of a pen?) (With what pen?)

拿鋼筆寫字 **na² kang¹-pi³ hsieh³ tzu⁴** | Hold steel pen to write characters
(Use a steel pen to write with)
(Write with a steel pen)

LESSON 17

I

上 shang⁴ on　　在 ○ 上 tsai⁴ — shang⁴ on

掛 kua⁴ to hang up, to suspend

1. *Tsai⁴ che⁴ chang¹ hua-'rh⁴ shang⁴* **hua⁴-ti¹ shih¹ shen²-ma¹**? *Tsai⁴ che⁴ chang¹ hua-'rh⁴ shang⁴ hua⁴-ti¹ shih¹* **hsüeh²-t'ang².**
2. *Hsien¹-sheng¹ tsai⁴ hei¹-pan³ shang⁴ hsieh³-la¹ chi³ ke⁴ tzu⁴*? *Hsien¹-sheng¹ tsai⁴ hei¹-pan³ shang⁴ hsieh³-la¹ liang³ ke⁴ tzu⁴.*
3. *Na⁴ chang¹ cho¹-tzu¹ shang⁴ yu³* **shen²-ma¹ tung¹-hsi¹**? *Na⁴ chang¹ cho¹-tzu¹ shang⁴ yu³ kang¹-pi³, hai² yu³ mo⁴-shui-'rh³.*
4. *'Huang'² tzu⁴ tsai⁴ wo³-men²-ti¹ shu¹ shang⁴ yu³ mei² yu³*? *'Huang'² tzu⁴ tsai⁴ wo³-men²-ti¹ shu¹ shang⁴ yu³.*
5. *Tsai⁴ na⁴ chang¹ hua-'rh⁴ shang⁴, hua⁴-ti¹ na⁴ liang³ ke⁴ jen², shih⁴* **hsien¹-sheng¹ shih¹ hsüeh²-sheng¹**? *I² wei⁴ shih¹ hsien¹-sheng¹, i² wei⁴ shih¹ hsüeh²-sheng¹.*
6. *Tsai⁴ che⁴ mien⁴ ch'iang² shang⁴ kua⁴-ti¹ shih¹ chi³ chang¹ hua-'rh⁴*? *Tsai⁴ che⁴ mien⁴ ch'iang² shang⁴ kua⁴-ti¹ shih⁴ liang³ chang¹ hua-rh⁴.*

LESSON 17

7. *Na⁴ mien⁴ ch'iang' shang¹* **kua⁴-ti¹ na⁴** *chang¹ hua-'rh⁴ shih⁴* **shul²** *hua⁴-ti¹ ?*
  Shih⁴ **Pai²** *hsien¹-sheng¹ hua⁴-ti¹.*

1. What is drawn on this picture?
  A school is drawn on this picture.
2. How many characters has the teacher written on the blackboard?
  The teacher has written two characters on the blackboard.
3. What things are there on that table?
  There is a pen and some ink on that table.
4. Is the character *huang* (written) on our book?
  The character *huang* is on our book.
5. Are those two people drawn on that picture teachers or students?
  One is a teacher and one is a student.
6. How many pictures are hanging up on this wall?
  There are two pictures hanging up on this wall.
7. Who painted that picture hanging on that wall?
  It was painted by Mr. Pai.

II

把 pa³
to take hold of

1. *Ch'ing³ nin² pa³ na⁴ chang¹ hua-'rh⁴ kei³ wo³.*
  Hao³, kei³ nin²
2. *Ch'ing³ pa³ na⁴ chih¹ fen²-pi³ kei³ t'a¹.*
  Wo³ kei³ t'a¹ la¹. *Hsieh⁴-hsieh⁴.*

3. Shul² pa³ na⁴ chang¹ hua-'rh⁴ kei³ Pao¹ hsien¹-sheng¹ la¹? Wo³ pa³ na⁴ chang¹ hua-'rh⁴ kei³ t'a¹ la¹.
4. Shul² pa³ che⁴ wan³ k'a¹-fei⁴ he¹-la¹? T'a¹ pa³ che⁴ wan³ k'a¹-fei⁴ tou¹ he¹-la¹.
5. Shul² pa³ na⁴ t'iao² yü² tou¹ ch'ih¹-la¹? Nin²-ti¹ erh²-tzu¹ pa³ na⁴ t'iao² yü² tou¹ ch'ih¹-la¹.

1. Please give me that picture.
   (Please you take hold of that picture give me.)
   All right, I (will) give (it to) you.
2. Please give him that chalk.
   I have given (it to) him. Thank you.
3. Who gave that picture to Mr. Pao?
   I gave that picture to him.
4. Who drank this cup of coffee?
   He drank (all) this cup of coffee.
5. Who ate all that fish? Your son ate all that fish.

III

拿來 na²-lai²
to bring here, to bring

拿去 na²-ch'ü⁴
to take away, to take

1. Ch'ing³ nin² pa³ na⁴ chi³ ke⁴ po¹-li²-pei¹ na²-ch'ü⁴.
2. Ch'ing³ nin² pa³ na⁴ chi³ k'uai⁴ pai² mien⁴-pao¹ kei³ wo³ na²-lai².
3. Na⁴ chang¹ shu¹-cho¹-tzu¹ na²-lai²-la¹ mei² yu³? Na²-lai²-la¹.

LESSON 17

4. Shui² pa³ na⁴ chang¹ fan⁴-cho¹-tzu¹ na²-ch'ü⁴-la¹?
   Ch'ien² hsien¹-sheng¹-ti¹ erh²-tzu¹ na²-ch'ü⁴-la¹.
5. Na⁴ pa³ i³-tzu¹ shih⁴ kei³ shui² na²-lai²-ti¹?
   Shih⁴ kei³ nin² na²-lai²-ti¹.
6. Che⁴ hsieh¹-ke⁴ mao²-ch'ien-'rh² shih⁴ shui² na²-ch'ü⁴-ti¹? Shih⁴ Huang² hsien¹-sheng¹ na²-ch'ü⁴-ti¹.
7. Nin² pa³ na⁴ san¹ chin¹ ch'a²-yeh⁴ kei³ wo³ na²-lai², pa³ na⁴ wu³ chin¹ k'a¹-fei⁴ kei³ t'a¹ na²-ch'ü⁴.
8. Ch'ing³ ni³ pa³ na⁴ i⁴ wan³ ch'a² kei³ wo³ na²-lai².
9. Ch'ing³ ni³ pa³ na⁴ wan³ k'a¹-fei⁴ kei³ t'a¹ na²-ch'ü⁴.
10. Na⁴ chang¹ hua-'rh⁴ kei³ shui² na²-ch'ü⁴-ti¹?
    Kei³ nin²-ti¹ t'ai⁴-t'ai⁴ na²-ch'ü⁴-ti¹.

1. Please take away those several glasses.
   (Please you take hold of those many glasses take away.)
2. Please bring those several pieces of bread here (and) give (them to) me.
3. Has that writing-table been brought here?
   (That writing-table brought here not has?)
   (It) has been brought here.
4. Who took away that dining-table?
   Mr. Ch'ien's son took (it) away.
5. To whom was that chair brought?
   (It) was brought to you.
6. Who took away these (many) ten-cents?
   Mr. Huang took (them) away.
7. Bring those three catties of tea to me and take those five catties of coffee to him.
8. Please bring me that cup of tea.

9. Please take him that cup of coffee.
10. For whom was that picture taken away?
    (It) was taken away for your wife.

IV

(拿 ○ 來) na² — lai²
to take, to bring

(拿 ○ 去) na² — ch'ü⁴
to take, to take away

1. *T'a¹* na² shen²-ma¹ lai²-la¹?
   T'a¹ na² fen²-pi³ lai²-la¹.
2. *Ch'ing³* ni³ kei³ wo³ na² i⁴ wan³ ch'a² lai².
3. *Ch'ing³* ni³ kei³ t'a¹ na² mo⁴-shui-'rh³ ch'ü⁴.
4. *T'a¹* yao⁴ na² shen²-ma¹ lai²?
   T'a¹ yao⁴ na² po¹-li²-pei¹ lai².
5. *Nin²* tso⁴ shen²-ma¹ lai²-la¹? Wo³ na² shu¹ lai²-la¹.
6. *Huang²* hsien¹-sheng¹ yao⁴ na² shen²-ma¹ ch'ü⁴?
   T'a¹ yao⁴ na² hei¹-pan³ ch'ü⁴.
7. *Nin²* yao⁴ na² mo⁴-shui-'rh³ ch'ü⁴-la¹ ma¹?
   Shih⁴, wo³ na² mo⁴-shui-'rh³ ch'ü⁴-la¹.
8. *Nin²* yao⁴ na² fan⁴-wan³ ch'ü⁴ ma¹?
   Pu² shih⁴, wo³ yao⁴ na² ch'a²-wan³ lai².
9. *Ch'ien²* hsien¹-sheng¹ na²-la¹ chi³ chih¹ pi³ lai²?
   T'a¹ na²-la¹ liang³ san¹ chih¹ lai².

1. What has he brought? He has brought some chalks.
2. Please bring me that cup of tea.
3. Please take him that ink.

LESSON 17

4. What will he bring? He will bring a glass.
5. What have you come for? I have come to take a book.
6. What will Mr. Huang take away?
   He will take the blackboard away.
7. Did you want to take away the ink?
   Yes, I wanted to take away the ink.
8. Do you want to take a rice-bowl?
   No, I want to take a tea-cup.
9. How many pens has Mr. Ch'ien brought?
   He has brought two or three.

V

大學堂 ta⁴-hsüeh²-t'ang² High School(s), University

中學堂 chung¹-hsüeh²-t'ang² Middle School(s)

小學堂 hsiao³-hsüeh²-t'ang² Primary School(s)

1. *Ch'ing³ wen⁴ nin² na¹, che⁴ ke⁴ ti⁴-fang¹ yu³ ta⁴-hsüeh²-t'ang² mei² yu³?*
   Che⁴ ke⁴ ti⁴-fang¹ yu³ ta⁴-hsüeh²-t'ang².
2. *Na⁴ liang³ wei⁴ hsüeh²-sheng¹ shih⁴ ta⁴-hsüeh²-t'ang²-ti¹ hsüeh²-sheng¹ ma¹?*
   T'a¹-men² shih⁴ ta⁴-hsüeh²-t'ang²-ti¹ hsüeh²-sheng¹.
3. *Na⁴ wei⁴ ku¹-niang² tsai⁴ shen²-ma¹ hsüeh²-t'ang² nien⁴ shu¹? T'a¹ tsai⁴ chung¹-hsüeh²-t'ang² nien⁴ shu¹.*
4. *Na⁴ ke⁴ chung¹-hsüeh²-t'ang² yu³ to¹-shao³ hsüeh²-sheng¹? Yu³ erh⁴-pai³ to¹ wei⁴ hsüeh²-sheng¹.*

5. *Nin² erh²-tzu¹ tsai⁴* **shen²-ma¹** *hsüeh²-t'ang² nien⁴ shu¹ na¹?   T'a¹ tsai⁴* **hsiao³-hsüeh²-t'ang²** *nien⁴ shu¹ na¹*.
6. *Lan² hsien¹-sheng¹ shih⁴* **chung¹-hsüeh²-t'ang²-ti¹ hsien¹-sheng¹ ma¹?**
   Pu² shih⁴, t'a¹ shih⁴ **ta⁴-hsüeh²-t'ang²-ti¹** *hsien¹-sheng¹*.

1. May I ask you, has this place got a university?
   This place has a university.
2. Are those two students university students?
   They are university students.
3. In what school does that girl study?
   She studies in the Middle School.
4. How many students has that Middle School?
   It has over two hundred students.
5. In what school does your son study?
   He studies in the Primary School.
6. Is Mr. Lan a Middle School teacher?
   No, he is a High School teacher.

VI

吃墨紙   ch'ih¹-mo⁴-chih³
blotting-paper

1. *Che⁴ liang³ chang¹ ch'ih¹-mo⁴-chih³ ni³ shih⁴ kei³ shui² mai³-ti¹?*
   Shih⁴ kei³ wo³ ku¹-niang², erh²-tzu¹, i² ke⁴ jen² i⁴ chang¹.
2. *Na⁴ ch'ih¹-mo⁴-chih³ tou¹ yu³ shen²-ma¹ yen²-se⁴-ti¹?*
   Hung², huang², lan², lü⁴, pai², tou¹ yu³.
3. *Na² mao²-pi³ hsieh³ tzu⁴ yao⁴ ch'ih¹-mo⁴-chih³ pu² yao⁴?*
   Na² mao²-pi³ hsieh³ tzu⁴ pu² yao⁴ ch'ih¹-mo⁴-chih³.

4. *Na*⁴ **kang**¹-*pi*³ *hsieh*³ *tzu*⁴ **mei**² *yu*³ *ch'ih*¹-*mo*⁴-*chih*³ *hao*³ *pu*⁴ *hao*³ ? *Mei*² *yu*³ *ch'ih*¹-*mo*⁴-*chih*³ *pu*⁴ *hao*³.
5. *Na*⁴ *ch'ih*¹-*mo*⁴-*chih*³ *ta*⁴ *chang*¹-*ti*¹ *to*¹-*shao*³ *ch'ien*², *hsiao*³ *chang*¹-*ti*¹ *to*¹-*shao*³ *ch'ien*² ?
*Ta*⁴ *chang*¹-*ti*¹ **liang**³ *mao*² *wu*³, *hsiao*³ *chang*¹-*ti*¹ *i*⁴ *mao*² **erh**⁴.

1. For whom did you buy these two sheets of blotting-paper? They are for my daughter and son, one sheet each.
2. What colours are all those (sheets of) blotting-paper ? (They are) all (colours), red, yellow, blue, green and white.
3. When writing with that writing-brush, is it necessary to have blotting-paper ?
(That writing-brush write characters want blotting-paper not want ?)
When writing with that writing-brush it is not necessary to have blotting-paper.
(That writing-brush write characters not want blotting-paper.)
4. When writing with that pen is it all right if there is no blotting-paper ?
(That pen write characters not have blotting-paper good not good ?)
(If) there is no blotting-paper (it is) bad.
5. How much is a large sheet of that blotting-paper, and how much is a small sheet ?
A large sheet is twenty-five cents, a small sheet is twelve cents.

NOTES

73. On, In, are expressed in two ways:—

(a) Addition of the character 上 **shang⁴** after the noun.

椅 子　上　　Chair on
I³-tzu¹ *shang⁴*　(On the chair)

畫 兒　上　　Picture on
hua-'rh⁴ *shang⁴*　(In the picture)

黑 板　上　　Blackboard on
hei¹-pan³ *shang⁴*　(On the blackboard)

(b) Use of the two characters 在 **tsai⁴** — in, at, and 上 **shang⁴**, where 在 *tsai⁴* precedes the noun and 上 *shang⁴* follows it.

在　棹 子　上　　At table on
tsai⁴ *cho¹-tzu¹* **shang⁴**　(On the table)

在　畫 兒　上　　At picture on
tsai⁴ *hua-'rh⁴* **shang⁴**　(In the picture)

在　牆　上　　At wall on
tsai⁴ *ch'iang²* **shang⁴**　(On the wall)

74. 把 **pa³** — to take hold of. This character is used to emphasise the object of the sentence, and, more often than not it is omitted in the English translation. Although frequently used together with verbs of motion, 把 **pa³** does not itself express motion. It simply implies the action of taking hold of something with the hand(s).

LESSON 17

誰 把 那 碗 咖 啡 喝 了?
shui² pa³ na⁴ wan³ k'a¹-fei⁴ he¹-la¹?
Who took hold of that cup coffee drank?
(Who drank that cup of coffee?)

你 把 那 個 錢 給 我 ｜ You take hold of that
ni³ pa³ na⁴ ke⁴ ch'ien² kei³ wo³ ｜ money give me
(Give me that money)

你 把 他 請 來 ｜ You take hold of him invite
ni³ pa³ t'a¹ ch'ing³ lai² ｜   ⌊ come
(Invite him to come)

75. 拿 na², 把 pa³. Both these characters are translated as: to take hold of, but they have different implications and uses.

拿 na² implies: to grasp, to seize, to apprehend. While 把 pa³ has the milder sense of: to lay (place) the hand(s) in contact with (on).

76. 拿 來 na²-lai², 拿 去 na²-ch'ü⁴.

(a) These two verbs of motion are in common use and may be translated as: to bring here and to take away.

Literally translated their characters imply:

拿 ｜   來 ｜
na² ｜ to take hold of   lai² ｜ motion towards

拿 來 ｜ to take hold of — motion towards,
na²-lai² ｜ (to bring here)

拿 | to take hold of　去 | motion away from
na^2 　　　　　　　　　 $ch'ü^4$

拿去 | To take hold of — motion away from,
$na^2\text{-}ch'ü^4$ | (to take away)

(b) Sometimes these verbs are split, that is, the first character stands at the beginning of the phrase and the second character at the end.

拿 那 個 東 西 來 | Take hold of that thing
na^2 **na**^{4} ke^4 $tung^1\text{-}hsi^1$ lai^2 | motion towards
(Bring that thing here)

拿 這 個 茶 碗 去 | Take hold of this
na^2 **che**^{4} ke^4 $ch'a^2\text{-}wan^3$ $ch'ü^4$ | tea-cup motion away
(Take this tea-cup away)

(c) When 把 **pa**^{3} is used together with one of these verbs, it precedes (governs) the object of the sentence, while 拿來 $na^2\text{-}$**lai**^{2} or 拿去 $na^2\text{-}$**ch'ü**^{4} stands at the end of the sentence. Moreover it is not translated.

把 那 張 桌 子 拿 來
pa^3 **na**^{4} $chang^1$ **cho**$^1\text{-}tzu^1$ $na^2\text{-}lai^2$

Lay your hands on that table, take hold of, motion
(Bring that table here)　　　　　　　　　[towards.

把 這 條 魚 拿 去
pa^3 **che**^{4} $t'iao^2$ $yü^2$ $na^2\text{-}ch'ü^4$

Lay your hands on this fish, take hold of, motion
(Take this fish away)　　　　　　　　　[away.

LESSON 18

I

(問答) wen⁴-ta²
question and answer

Q. Na⁴ so³ fang²-tzu¹ shih⁴ **shui**²-ti¹?
A. Na⁴ so³ fang²-tzu¹ shih⁴ **Pai**² hsien¹-sheng¹-ti¹.
Q. Nin² chih¹-tao⁴ shih⁴ to¹-shao³ ch'ien² **mai**³-ti¹?
A. Shih⁴ **ch'i**¹-ch'ien¹ to¹ k'uai⁴-ch'ien² mai³-ti¹.
Q. Na⁴ so³ fang²-tzu¹ yu³ **chi**³ chien¹ wu¹-tzu¹?
A. Yu³ **pa**¹ chiu³ chien¹ wu¹-tzu¹.
Q. Na⁴ chi³ chien¹ wu¹-tzu¹-ti¹ ti⁴-pan³ shih⁴ **shen**²-**ma**¹ yen²-se⁴-ti¹?
A. Shih⁴ huang² yen²-se⁴-ti¹.
Q. **Ting**³-p'eng² yeh³ shih⁴ huang²-ti¹ ma¹?
A. Pu² shih⁴ huang²-ti¹, shih⁴ pai²-ti¹.
Q. Na⁴ ch'iang² shih⁴ shen²-ma¹ yen²-se⁴-ti¹?
A. Yu³ hung²-ti¹, yu³ lü⁴-ti¹, yeh³ yu³ lan²-ti¹.

Q. Whose is that house?
A. That is Mr. Pai's house.
Q. Do you know how much it cost?
A. It cost more than seven thousand dollars.
Q. How many rooms has that house?
A. It has eight or nine rooms.

Q. What is the colour of the floors of those (several) rooms?
A. They are yellow.
Q. Are the ceilings also yellow?
A. They are not yellow, they are white.
Q. What colour are those walls?
A. There are red ones, green ones and also blue ones.

II

(問答) wen⁴-ta²
question and answer

Q. Nin² na⁴ so³ fang²-tzu¹ shih⁴ nin² i⁴ chia-'rh¹ chu⁴ ma¹?
A. Pu² shih⁴ wo³ i⁴ chia-'rh¹ chu⁴, shih⁴ wo³-men² liang³ chia-'rh¹ chu⁴.
Q. Nin² chu⁴ chi³ chien¹?
A. Wo³ chu⁴ ssu⁴ chien¹.
Q. Na⁴ chi³ chien¹ shui² chu⁴?
A. Na⁴ chi³ chien¹ Lan² chia¹ chu⁴.

Q. Does your family only, live in your house?
 (You that house is you one family live?)
A. Not only my family lives there, our two families live there.
 (Not is my one family lives, is our two families live.)
Q. How many rooms do you live in?
A. I live in four rooms.
Q. Who lives in those (several) rooms?
A. The Lan family lives in those rooms.

LESSON 18

III

(問答) wen⁴-ta²
question and answer

Q. *Che⁴ shih⁴* **hsüeh²-t'ang²** *pu² shih⁴?*
A. *Che⁴ shih⁴ hsüeh²-t'ang².*
Q. *Che⁴ shih⁴* **chung¹-hsüeh²-t'ang²** *ma¹?*
A. *Che⁴ pu² shih⁴ chung¹-hsüeh²-t'ang², che⁴ shih⁴* **hsiao³-hsüeh²-t'ang².**
Q. *Tsai⁴ che⁴ ke⁴ hsüeh²-t'ang² li³ yu³ to¹-shao³ wei⁴* **hsüeh²-sheng¹?**
A. *Yu³* **san¹-pai³** *to¹ wei⁴ hsüeh²-sheng¹.*
Q. *Yu³ to¹-shao³ wei⁴* **hsien¹-sheng¹?**
A. *Yu³* **erh⁴-shih²** *to¹ wei⁴ hsien¹ sheng¹.*
Q. *Na⁴ shih⁴ ta⁴-hsüeh²-t'ang² ma¹?*
A. **Shih⁴,** *na⁴ shih⁴ ta⁴-hsüeh²-t'ang².*

Q. This is a school isn't it?
A. This is a school.
Q. Is this a Middle School?
A. This isn't a Middle School, this is a Primary School.
Q. How many students are there in this school?
A. It has over three hundred students.
Q. How many teachers has it?
A. It has more than twenty teachers.
Q. Is that a High School?
A. Yes, that is a High School.

IV

(問答) wen⁴-ta²
question and answer

Q. *Na⁴ ke⁴ p'u⁴-tzu¹ shih⁴* **shen²-ma¹** *p'u⁴-tzu¹?*
A. *Na⁴ shih⁴* **cho¹-I³-*p'u⁴.***
Q. *Cho¹-i³-p'u⁴* **mai⁴ shen²-ma¹** *tung¹-hsi¹?*
A. *Cho¹-i³-p'u⁴ mai⁴* **cho¹-tzu¹**, *I³-tzu¹, shen²-ma²-ti¹.*
Q. *T'a¹-men²* **tou¹ mai⁴ shen²-ma¹** *cho¹-tzu¹?*
A. *T'a¹-men² mai⁴* **shu¹-*cho¹-tzu¹*, yeh³ mai³ fan⁴-*cho¹-tzu¹.*
Q. *I³-tzu¹ t'a¹-men²* **yeh³** *mai⁴ ma¹?*
A. *I³-tzu¹ t'a¹-men²* **yeh³** *mai⁴.*

Q. What sort of shop is that shop?
A. That is a furniture-shop.
Q. What does a furniture-shop sell?
A. A furniture-shop sells tables, chairs and so on.
Q. What sort of tables do they sell?
A. They sell writing-tables and also sell dinner-tables.
Q. Do they also sell chairs?
A. They also sell chairs.

V

(問答) wen⁴-ta²
question and answer

Q. *Che⁴ chang¹ hua-'rh⁴ shih⁴* **shui²** *hua⁴-ti¹?*
A. *Che⁴ chang¹ hua-'rh⁴ shih⁴* **wo³** *hua⁴-ti¹.*

LESSON 18

Q. *Nin² chang⁴-fu¹ yeh³* **hui⁴ hua⁴** *hua-'rh⁴ ma¹ ?*
A. *T'a¹* **pu² hui⁴ hua⁴** *hua-'rh⁴.*
Q. *Tsai⁴ ch'iang² shang¹* **kua¹**-*ti¹ na⁴ chang¹ hua-'rh⁴ yeh³ shih⁴* **nin²** *hua⁴-ti¹ ma¹ ?*
A. **Tui⁴**-*la¹, yeh³ shih⁴ wo³ hua⁴-ti¹.*
Q. *Na⁴ chang¹ hua-'rh⁴ shih⁴ na²* **shen²-ma¹ pi³ hua⁴**-*ti¹ ?*
A. *Shih⁴ na²* **mao²-pi³** *hua⁴-ti¹.*
Q. *Nin² na² mao²-pi³ hua⁴ hua-'rh⁴, na²* **shen²-ma¹ pi³ hsieh³** *tzu⁴ ?*
A. *Na²* **kang¹**-*pi³* **ken¹ ch'ien¹**-*pi³ hsieh³ tzu⁴.*

Q. By whom was this picture drawn ?
A. This picture was drawn by me.
Q. Can your husband also draw pictures ?
A. He can't draw pictures.
Q. Is that picture hanging on the wall also drawn by you ?
A. Right, it is also drawn by me.
Q. What sort of pen was used to draw that picture?
A. It was drawn with a brush-pen.
Q. You use a brush-pen to draw pictures, what sort of pen (do you) use to write characters ?
A. (I) use a steel pen and a pencil to write characters.

VI

(問答) wen⁴-*ta²*
question and answer

A. *Ch'ing³ nin²* **pa³** *na⁴ chih¹* **kang¹**-*pi³ kei³ wo³ na²-lai².*
Q. *Nin² yao⁴* **kang¹**-*pi³ tso⁴* **shen²-ma¹** *?*

A. *Wo³ yao⁴* **hsieh³** *tzu⁴.*
Q. *Nin² na² kang¹-pi³ hsieh³ tzu⁴, nin² yu³* **mo⁴-shui-'rh³**
A. *Wo³ yu³* **mo⁴-shui-rh³**. [*ma¹ ?*
Q. *Nin² yu³* **shen²-ma¹** *yen²-se⁴-ti¹ mo⁴-shui-'rh³ ?*
A. *Wo³ yu³* **lan²** *yen²-se⁴-ti¹ mo⁴-shui-'rh³.*
Q. *Ch'ing³ nin² pa³ na⁴ chang¹* **pai²** *yen²-se⁴-ti¹* **ch'ih¹-mo⁴-chih³** *yeh³ kei³ wo³ na²-lai².*

A. Please bring me that pen.
Q. What do you want a pen for ?
A. I want to write.
Q. You use a pen to write with, (but) have you any ink ?
A. I have some ink.
Q. What colour ink have you got ?
A. I have blue ink.
Q. Please bring me that sheet of white blotting-paper.

VII

(問答) wen⁴-ta²
question and answer

Q. *Ni³ tsai⁴* **shen²-ma¹** *hsüeh²-t'ang² nien⁴ shu¹ na¹ ?*
A. *Wo³ tsai⁴* **ta⁴-hsüeh²-t'ang²** *nien⁴ shu¹ na¹.*
Q. *Ni³-men²-ti¹* **hsien¹-sheng¹** *kei³ ni³-men² chiang³* **kung¹-k'e⁴**, *yeh³ kei³ ni³-men² hsieh³ tzu⁴ ma¹.*
A. *Yeh³ kei³ wo³-men² hsieh³ tzu⁴.*
Q. *Ni³-men²-ti¹* **hsien¹-sheng¹** *na² shen²-ma¹* **pi³** *kei³ ni³-men² hsieh³ tzu⁴ ?*
A. *Na²* **fen²-pi³** *kei³ wo³-men² hsieh³ tzu⁴.*

LESSON 18

Q. *Na² fen²-pi³ tsai⁴* **shen²-ma¹ shang⁴** *hsieh³ tzu⁴?*
A. *Tsai⁴* **hei¹-*pan³** shang⁴ hsieh³ tzu⁴.*

Q. At what school are you studying?
A. I am studying at the University.
Q. Your teacher explains the lessons for you, does he also write characters for you?
A. He also writes characters for us.
Q. What sort of pen does the teacher use to write characters for you?
A. He uses a chalk to write characters for us.
Q. On what does he write characters with a chalk?
A. He writes characters on a blackboard.

VIII

那 na³?
which?

1. **Na³** *chih¹* **ch'ien¹-*pi³* shih⁴ ni³-*ti¹?*
   Na⁴ *chih¹* **ch'ang²-*ti¹ shih⁴ wo³-ti¹.*
2. **Na³** *chih¹* **kang¹-*pi³ shih⁴ t'a¹-ti¹?*
   Che⁴ *chih¹* **tuan³-*ti¹ shih⁴ t'a¹-ti¹.*
3. **Na³** *chang¹* **cho¹-*tzu¹ shih⁴* **fan⁴-*cho¹-tzu¹?*
   Na⁴ *chang¹* *ta⁴-ti¹ shih⁴* **fan⁴-*cho¹-tzu¹.*
4. *Che⁴ liang³ ke⁴ pen³-tzu¹, na³ ke⁴ pen³-tzu¹ shih⁴* **hao³-*ti¹?* *Che⁴ liang³ ke⁴ pen³-tzu¹ tou¹ shih⁴ hao³-ti¹.*
5. *Ch'ing³ wen⁴* **nin²** *na¹, na³ pa² i³-tzu¹ shih⁴* **nin²** *mai³-ti¹? Na⁴ liang³ pa³* **hsiao³-*ti¹ shih⁴ wo³ mai³-ti¹.*

6. *Na⁴ chi³ chien¹ wu¹-tzu¹*, *na³ chien¹ wu¹-tzu¹-ti¹* **ch'uang¹-hu⁴ shih⁴ lü⁴-ti¹?** *Na⁴ chien¹* **hsiao³-ti¹** *shih⁴ lü⁴-ti¹*.
7. *Na⁴ chi³ ke⁴ p'u⁴-tzu¹*, *na³ ke⁴ p'u⁴-tzu¹* **mai⁴-ti¹** *tung¹-hsi¹* **chien⁴?**
   Na⁴ chi³ ke⁴ p'u⁴-tzu¹-ti¹ tung¹-hsi¹ **tou¹** *pu² chien⁴*.
8. **Na³** *i⁴ chü⁴ hua⁴-ti¹ i⁴-ssu¹ nin²* **pu⁴** *ming²-pai²?*
   Che⁴ *i⁴ chü⁴ hua⁴-ti¹ i⁴-ssu¹ wo³ pu⁴ ming²-pai²*, *ch'ing³ nin²* **tsai⁴** *kei³ wo³* **chiang³** *i⁴ hui²*.

1. Which pencil is yours? That long one is mine.
2. Which pen is his? This short one is his.
3. Which table is a dining-table?
   That big one is a dining-table.
4. Which of these two note-books is a good one?
   (These two note-books, which note-book is a good one?)
   Both of these two note-books are good ones.
   (These two note-books, both are good ones.)
5. May I ask you, which chair was bought by you?
   The small one (of those two) was bought by me.
6. Of those several rooms, which room's windows are green?
   (The windows) of that small (room) are green.
7. Which of those several shops sells cheap things?
   All the things sold by those shops are not cheap (i. e.: expensive).
8. The meaning of which phrase is it that you don't understand?
   The meaning of this phrase I don't understand, please explain it for me once again.

IX

這兒(裡)	che-'rh⁴, che⁴-*li*³ here
那兒(裡)	na-'rh⁴, na⁴-*li*³ there
那兒(裡)？	na-'rh³? na²-*li*³? where?
在這兒(裡)	tsai⁴ che-'rh⁴, tsai⁴ che⁴-*li*³ here
在那兒(裡)	tsai⁴ na-'rh⁴, tsai⁴ na⁴-*li*³ there
在那兒(裡)？	tsai⁴ na-'rh³? tsai na²-*li*³? where?

1. Nin² tsai⁴ che-'rh⁴ (*li*³) tso⁴ shen²-ma¹ na¹?
   Wo³ tsai⁴ che-'rh⁴ (*li*³) hua⁴ hua-'rh⁴ na¹.
2. T'a¹-ti¹ shu¹ tsai⁴ che⁴-*li*³ na¹ ma¹?
   T'a¹-ti¹ shu¹ mei² tsai⁴ che-'rh⁴.
3. Shui² tsai⁴ na-'rh⁴ chiang³ kung¹-k'e⁴?
   Ch'ien² hsien¹-sheng¹ tsai⁴ na-'rh⁴ chiang³ kung¹-k'e⁴.
4. Na⁴ wei⁴ ku¹-niang² tsai⁴ Pao¹ hsien¹-sheng¹ na-'rh⁴ nien⁴ shu¹ ma¹? T'a¹ tsai⁴ na⁴-*li*³ nien⁴ shu¹.
5. Che⁴ ke⁴ mo⁴-shui-'rh³ shih⁴ tsai⁴ na-'rh³ mai³-ti¹?
   Shih⁴ tsai⁴ na⁴ ke⁴ p'u⁴-tzu¹ *li*³ mai³-ti¹
6. Ch'ing³ wen⁴ nin² na¹, na⁴ wei⁴ hsüeh²-sheng¹ tsai⁴ na-'rh³ nien⁴ shu¹ na¹?
   Wo³ hai² pu⁴ chih¹-tao⁴ t'a¹ tsai⁴ na²-*li*³ nien⁴ shu¹ na¹.

1. What are you doing here?
   I am drawing a picture (here).
2. (Is) his book here?
   His book (is) not here.
3. Who explains the lessons there?
   Mr. Ch'ien explains the lessons there.
4. Does that girl study at Mr. Pao's?
   She does study there.
5. Where was this ink bought?
   It was bought at that shop.
6. May I ask you, where is that pupil studying?
   I still don't know where he is studying.

X

講堂 chiang³-t'ang²
class-room(s), lecture hall(s)

課堂 k'e⁴-t'ang²
class-room(s)

1. Che⁴ chien¹ wu¹-tzu¹ shih⁴ chiang³-t'ang² pu² shih⁴?
   Shih⁴, che⁴ chien¹ wu¹-tzu¹ shih⁴ chiang³-t'ang².
2. Che⁴ ke⁴ chiang³-t'ang² li³ yu³ chi³ ke⁴ men², chi³ ke⁴ ch'uang¹-hu⁴?
   Che⁴ ke⁴ chiang³-t'ang² li³ yu³ san¹ ke⁴ ch'uang¹-hu⁴, i² ke⁴ men².
3. Chiang³-t'ang² shih⁴ tso⁴ shen²-ma¹-ti¹ ti⁴-fang¹?
   Chiang³-t'ang² shih⁴ chiang³ kung¹-k'e⁴-ti¹ ti⁴-fang¹.
4. Shih⁴ ta⁴-hsüeh²-t'ang²-ti¹ k'e⁴-t'ang² ta⁴, shih⁴ hsiao³-hsüeh²-t'ang²-ti¹ k'e⁴-t'ang² ta⁴?

LESSON 18

Ta⁴-hsüeh²-t'ang²-ti¹ *k'e⁴-t'ang²* **ta⁴**, *hsiao³-hsüeh²-t'ang²-ti¹* *k'e⁴-t'ang²* **hsiao³**.

5. *Che⁴ ke⁴ k'e⁴-t'ang² li³ ti¹* **ti⁴**-*pan³ shih⁴* **shen²-ma¹ yen²-se⁴-ti¹**?   [*se⁴-ti¹*.

   Che⁴ ke⁴ k'e⁴-t'ang² li³ ti¹ ti⁴-pan³ shih⁴ **huang² yen²-**

6. *Che⁴ ke⁴ k'e⁴-t'ang² li³ ti¹* **ch'iang² tou¹** *shih⁴* **shen²-ma¹ yen²-se⁴-ti¹**?

   Che⁴ ke⁴ k'e⁴-t'ang² li³ ti¹ ch'iang² tou¹ shih⁴ **lan² yen²-se⁴-ti¹**.

7. *Che⁴ ke⁴ chiang³-t'ang² li³ ti¹* **ting³-p'eng²** *shih⁴* **shen²-ma¹ yen²-se⁴-ti¹**?   [*se⁴-ti¹*.

   Che⁴ ke⁴ chiang³-t'ang²-ti¹ ting³-p'eng² shih⁴ **pai²** *yen²-*

8. *Chiang³-t'ang² shang⁴* **tou¹** *yu³* **hei¹-*pan³** *ma¹*?

   Shih⁴, *chiang³-t'ang² shang⁴* **tou¹** *yu³ hei¹-pan³*.

9. *Che⁴ ke⁴ k'e⁴-t'ang² li³* **kua⁴-ti¹** *na⁴ chang¹* **hua-'rh⁴** *shih⁴* **shui²** *hua⁴-ti¹*?

   Shih⁴ **Huang²** *hsien¹-sheng¹ hua⁴-ti¹*.

10. *Tsai⁴ na⁴ ke⁴ k'e⁴-t'ang² li³ yu³* **to¹-*shao³ chang¹* **shu¹-cho¹-tzu¹**?

    Na⁴ ke⁴ k'e⁴-t'ang² li³ yu³ **erh⁴-shih²** *to¹ chang¹ shu¹-cho¹-tzu¹*.

1. Is this room a class-room ?
   Yes, this room is a class-room.   [room ?
2. How many doors and how many windows has this class-
   This class-room has three windows and one door.
3. What is done in a class-room ?
   (Class-room is do what place ?)
   A class-room is a place (where) lessons are explained.

4. Are the class-rooms (in) the High School larger than the class-rooms (in) the Primary School ?
   The class-rooms (in) the High School are larger than the class-rooms (in) the Primary School.
5. What is the colour of the floor of this class-room ?
   The floor of this class-room is yellow.
6. What colour are all the walls of this class-room ?
   All the walls of this class-room are blue.
7. What colour is the ceiling of this class-room ?
   The ceiling of this class-room is white.
8. Have all the class-rooms got blackboards ?
   Yes, all the class-rooms have blackboards.
9. By whom was the picture hanging up in this class-room [drawn ?
   It was drawn by Mr. Huang.
10. How many desks has that class-room in it ?
    That class-room has over twenty desks in it.

NOTES

77. 那? na³? This character in the third tone is the general interrogative particle and is translated as : which ? but sometimes as : where ?, what ?, who ? The same character in the fourth tone means : that, (see § 17.)

78. (a) 兒 erh² or 裡 li³ when added to 這 che⁴, 那 na⁴ and 那? na³? as suffixes, form the following adverbs :

| 這 che⁴ } this | 兒 erh² } colloquial ending | 裡 li³ } within, inside |

| 這 兒 （裡） | here |
| che-'rh⁴ *(li³)* | |

| 那 | that | 兒 | colloquial | 裡 | within, |
| na⁴ | | erh² | ending | li³ | inside |

| 那 兒 （裡） | there |
| na-'rh⁴ *(li³)* | |

| 那？ | which? | 兒 | colloquial | 裡 | within, |
| na³? | | erh² | ending | li³ | inside |

| 那 兒 （裡）？ | where? |
| na-'rh³ *(li³)?* | |

Either form is correct, although the 兒 erh² termination is more usual in Peiping, (see § 59.)

(b) Alternative forms of these adverbs are composed by adding 在 tsai⁴ — in, at, before them, thus:

| 在 這 兒 （裡） | at here |
| tsai⁴ che-'rh⁴, tsai⁴ che⁴-li³ | (here) |

| 在 那 兒 （裡） | at there |
| tsai⁴ na-'rh⁴, tsai⁴ na⁴-li³ | (there) |

| 在 那 兒 （裡）？ | at where? |
| tsai⁴ na-'rh³? tsai⁴ na²-li²? | (where?) |

LESSON 19

I

一塊兒 I²-k'uai-'rh⁴
together

1. *T'a¹ ken¹ shui² I²-k'uai-'rh⁴ nien⁴ shu¹?*
   T'a¹ ken¹ na⁴ wei⁴ hsüeh²-sheng¹ i²-k'uai-'rh⁴ nien⁴ shu¹.
2. *Nin² ken¹ shui² I²-k'uai-'rh⁴ lai²-ti¹?*
   Wo³ ken¹ Huang² hsien¹-sheng¹ i²-k'uai-'rh⁴ lai²-ti¹.
3. *Nin²-ti¹ t'ai⁴-t'ai⁴ ken¹ shui² I²-k'uai-'rh⁴ ch'ü⁴-ti¹?*
   T'a¹ ken¹ t'a¹-ti¹ ku¹-niang² i²-k'uai-'rh⁴ ch'ü⁴-ti¹.
4. *Nin² ken¹ shui² I²-k'uai-'rh⁴ mai³ tung¹-hsi¹ ch'ü⁴-la¹?*
   Wo³ ken¹ Shu¹ hsien¹-sheng¹ i²-k'uai-'rh⁴ mai³ tung¹-hsi¹ ch'ü⁴-la¹.

1. With whom does he study (together)?
   He studies together with that pupil.
2. With whom did you come?
   I came together with Mr. Huang.
3. With whom did your wife go away?
   She went away together with her daughter.
4. With whom did you go out to buy things?
   I went together with Mr. Shu to buy things.

II

父母 fu⁴-mu³
parents

1. *Nin²-ti¹ fu⁴-mu³ tsai⁴ chia¹ na¹ ma¹?*   [*chia¹.*
   Wo³ fu⁴-ch'in¹ tsai⁴ chia¹ na¹, wo³ mu³-ch'in¹ mei² tsai⁴

LESSON 19

2. *Nin² ken¹ nin²-ti¹ fu⁴-mu³ tsai⁴ l²-k'uai-'rh⁴ chu⁴ ma¹?*
   Shih⁴, *wo³ ken¹ wo³ fu⁴-mu³ tsai⁴ i²-k'uai-'rh⁴ chu⁴.*

1. Are your parents at home?
   My father is at home, my mother is not at home.
2. Do you live together with your parents?
   Yes, I live together with my parents.

III

孩子 hai²-tzu¹
child, children

1. *Na⁴ wei⁴ hsien¹-sheng¹ yu³ chi³ ke⁴ hai²-tzu¹?*
   Na⁴ wei⁴ hsien¹-sheng¹ yu³ liang³ ke⁴ hai²-tzu¹.
2. *Na⁴ ke⁴ hai²-tzu¹ yao⁴ mai³ shen²-ma¹ tung¹-hsi¹?*
   Na⁴ ke⁴ hai²-tzu¹ yao⁴ mai³ chih³.
3. *Na⁴ liang³ ke⁴ hai²-tzu¹, na³ ke⁴ hai²-tzu¹ shih⁴ nin²-ti¹?*
   Na⁴ ke⁴ ta⁴-ti¹ shih⁴ wo³-ti¹.
4. *T'a¹ chia¹ li³ yu³ chi³ ke⁴ hai²-tzu¹?*
   T'a¹ chia¹ li³ yu³ ssu⁴ ke⁴ hai²-tzu¹.

1. How many children has that teacher got?
   That teacher has two children.
2. What does that child want to buy?
   That child wants to buy some paper.
3. Which of those two children is yours?
   That tall one is mine.
4. How many children are there in his house?
   There are four children in his house.

IV

街 chieh¹ street(s)　（○條街）— t'iao² chieh¹ — street(s)

1. Che⁴ t'iao² chieh¹ ch'ang² tuan³?
   Che⁴ t'iao² chieh¹ pu⁴ tuan³.
2. Tsai⁴ nin² chu⁴-ti¹ na⁴ t'iao² chieh¹ shang⁴, yu³ chi³ ke⁴ hsüeh²-t'ang²? Yu³ liang³ ke⁴ hsüeh²-t'ang².
3. Pao¹ hsien¹-sheng¹ tsai⁴ shen²-ma¹ ti⁴-fang¹ chu⁴?
   Tsai⁴ Mai³-mai⁴ chieh¹.
4. Che⁴ t'iao² chieh¹ chiao⁴ shen²-ma¹ ming²-tzu¹?
   Che⁴ t'iao² chieh¹ ming²-tzu¹ chiao⁴ hsüeh²-t'ang² chieh¹.

1. Is this street a long one? (This street long short?)
   This street isn't short (i. e.: is long).
2. How many schools are there in the street in which you live?
   There are two schools.
3. Where (at what place) does Mr. Pao live?
   In *Mai-mai* Street.
4. What is this street called?
   This street is called *Hsüeh-t'ang* Street.

V

衣裳 i¹-shang¹ clothes, clothing

（○件衣裳）— chien⁴ i¹-shang¹ — article(s) of clothing

穿 ch'uan¹ to put on, to wear (of clothes)

1. Che⁴ shih⁴ shui²-ti¹ i¹-shang¹?

Che⁴ shih⁴ **wo³** *ken¹ wo³* **chang⁴**-*fu¹-ti¹ i¹-shang¹*.
2. *Na⁴ shih⁴* **chi³** *chien⁴ i¹-shang¹?*
   Na⁴ shih⁴ **liang³** *chien⁴ i¹-shang¹*.
3. *Na⁴ chien⁴* **hung²** *i¹-shang¹ shih⁴* **shui²**-*ti¹?*
   Na⁴ shih⁴ **na⁴** *wei⁴ t'ai⁴-t'ai⁴-ti¹*.
4. *Nin² ch'uan¹-ti¹ i¹-shang¹ shih⁴* **shen²-ma¹ yen²-se⁴**-*ti¹?*
   Wo³ ch'uan¹-ti¹ i¹-shang¹ shih⁴ **lan²**-*ti¹*.
5. *Ni³ shuo¹ shih⁴ ch'uan¹* **ch'ang²** *i¹-shang¹ hao³, shih⁴ ch'uan¹* **tuan³** *i¹-shang¹ hao³?*
   Wo³ shuo¹ **hai²** *shih⁴ ch'uan¹ tuan³-ti¹ hao³*.
6. *Tso²-t'ien¹ Huang² hsien¹-sheng¹ ch'uan¹-ti¹ shih⁴* **shen²-ma¹ yen²-se⁴**-*ti¹ i¹-shang¹?*
   Tso²-t'ien¹ Huang² hsien¹-sheng¹ ch'uan¹-ti¹ shih⁴ **hei¹** *i¹-shang¹*.

1. Whose clothes are these?
   These are mine and my husband's clothes.
2. How many articles of clothing are there there?
   There are two articles of clothing there.
3. Whose is that red article of clothing?
   That is that lady's.
4. What colour are the clothes (that) you wear?
   The clothes (that) I wear are blue.
5. Would you say it is better to wear long clothes or short clothes?
   I should say it is better to wear short ones.
6. What colour were the clothes (that) Mr. Huang wore yesterday?
   The clothes (that) Mr. Huang wore yesterday were black.

VI

帽子 mao⁴-tzu¹ hat(s)

(○頂帽子) 一 ting³ mao⁴-tzu¹ hat(s)

戴 tai⁴ to wear (on the head)

1. Che⁴ ting³ mao⁴-tzu¹ shih⁴ shui²-ti¹?
   Che⁴ ting³ mao⁴-tzu¹ shih⁴ Chang¹ hsien¹-sheng¹-ti¹.
2. Nin² tai⁴-ti¹ na⁴ ting³ mao⁴-tzu¹ shih⁴ to¹-shao³ ch'ien² [mai³-ti¹?
   Che⁴ ting³ mao⁴-tzu¹ shih⁴ san¹ k'uai⁴ wu³ mai³-ti¹.
3. Nin² chin¹-t'ien¹ tai⁴ mao⁴-tzu¹ lai²-la¹ ma¹?
   Wo³ chin¹-t'ien¹ mei² tai⁴ mao⁴-tzu¹ lai².
4. Tai⁴ pai² mao⁴-tzu¹-ti¹ na⁴ wei⁴ ku¹-niang² hsing⁴ T'a¹ hsing⁴ Lan². [shen²-ma¹?

1. Whose is this hat? This hat is Mr. Chang's.
2. How much did that hat (that) you are wearing cost?
   This hat was three dollars fifty.
3. Did you come with a hat today?
   (You today wear a hat came?)
   I came without a hat today.
   (I today not wear a hat come.)
4. What is the surname of that girl wearing a white hat?
   Her surname is Lan.

LESSON 19

VII

鞋 hsieh² shoe(s), slipper(s)   雙 shuang¹ a pair (of)

1. *Liang³ chih¹ hsieh² shih⁴ i⁴ shuang¹ hsieh² ma¹?*
   Shih⁴, *liang³ chih¹ hsieh² shih⁴ i¹ shuang¹ hsieh².*
2. **Che⁴** *shuang¹ hsieh² shih⁴ nin²-ti¹ ma¹?*
   Che⁴ *shuang¹ hsieh² pu² shih⁴ wo³-ti¹.*
3. *Nin²* **ch'uan¹**-*ti¹ che⁴ shuang¹ hsieh² shih⁴ shen²-ma¹ yen²-se⁴-ti¹?*   [*se⁴-ti¹.*
   Wo³ ch'uan¹-ti¹ che⁴ shuang¹ hsieh² shih⁴ **huang²** *yen²-*
4. **Che⁴** *shuang¹ hsieh² shih⁴* **chi³** *k'uai⁴-ch'ien² mai³-ti¹?*
   Che⁴ *shuang¹ hsieh² shih⁴* **chiu³** *k'uai⁴-ch'ien² mai³-ti¹.*
5. **Che⁴** *shuang¹ hsieh² shih² k'uai⁴-ch'ien² nin² shuo¹* **kuei⁴**
   Wo³ shuo¹ **kuei⁴** *i⁴-tien-'rh³.*   [*chien⁴?*
6. **Che⁴** *shuang¹ hsieh² ta⁴ i⁴-tien-'rh³, ch'ing³ nin² kei³ wo³ i⁴ shuang¹* **hsiao³** *i⁴-tien-'rh³.*

1. Are two shoes one pair of shoes?
   Yes, two shoes are one pair of shoes.
2. Is this pair of shoes yours?
   This pair of shoes is not mine.
3. What colour is this pair of shoes (that) you are wearing?
   This pair of shoes (that) I am wearing is yellow.
4. How much was this pair of shoes?
   This pair of shoes was nine dollars.
5. This pair of shoes is ten dollars, would you say (they are) expensive?
   I should say (they are) a little expensive.

6. This pair of shoes (is) a little large, please give me a smaller pair.

VIII

瓶子 p'ing²-tzu¹ bottle(s)   酒 chiu³ wine

1. Che⁴ shih⁴ **shen²-ma¹** tung¹-hsi¹?
   Che⁴ shih⁴ **p'ing²-tzu¹**.
2. Tsai⁴ che⁴ ke⁴ p'ing²-tzu¹ yu³ **shen²-ma¹**?
   Tsai⁴ che⁴ ke⁴ p'ing²-tzu¹ li³ yu³ **chiu³**.
3. Nin² **hui⁴** he¹ **chiu³** ma¹? Wo³ **hui⁴** he¹ chiu³.
4. Che⁴ p'ing²-tzu¹ chiu³ shih⁴ **chi³** k'uai⁴-ch'ien² **mai³-ti¹**?
   Che⁴ p'ing²-tzu¹ chiu³ shih⁴ **ssu⁴** k'uai⁴-ch'ien² mai³-ti.
5. Che⁴ p'ing²-tzu¹ shih⁴ chiu³, na⁴ p'ing²-tzu¹ yeh³ shih⁴ chiu³ ma¹?
   Na⁴ p'ing²-tzu¹ pu² shih⁴ chiu³, shui⁴ **shui³**.
6. Na⁴ ke⁴ p'ing²-tzu¹ shih⁴ chiu³ p'ing²-tzu¹ ma¹?
   Shih⁴ chiu³ p'ing²-tzu¹.

1. What is this thing? This is a bottle.
2. What is in this bottle?
   There is some wine is this bottle.
3. Can you drink wine? I can drink wine.
4. How much was this bottle of wine?
   This bottle of wine was four dollars.
5. This bottle is wine, is that bottle also wine?
   That bottle isn't wine, it is water.
6. Is that bottle a wine-bottle? It is a wine-bottle.

LESSON 19

IX

酒盃 chiu³-pei¹
wine-glass(es)

1. *Na⁴ ke⁴ chiu³-pei¹ shih⁴ shui² na²-lai²-ti¹?*
   Na⁴ ke⁴ chiu³-pei¹ shih⁴ wo³ na²-lai²-ti¹.
2. *Nin² he¹-la¹ chi³ pei¹ chiu³?*
   Wo³ he¹-la¹ ssu⁴ pei¹ chiu³.
3. *Ch'ing³ nin² tsai⁴ he¹ i⁴ pei¹! Hsieh⁴-hsieh⁴ Pu⁴ he¹-la¹.*
4. *Che⁴ shih⁴ shen²-ma¹? Che⁴ shih⁴ po¹-li²-pei¹.*
5. *Shih⁴ po¹-li²-pei¹ ta⁴ shih⁴ chiu³-pei¹ ta⁴?*
   Po¹-li²-pei¹ ta⁴, chiu³-pei¹ hsiao³.

1. Who brought that wine-glass here?
   I brought that wine-glass here.
2. How many glasses of wine have you drunk?
   I have drunk four glasses of wine.
3. Please drink one more! Thanks (I) will not drink (any).
4. What is this? This is a tumbler.
5. Which is larger, a tumbler or a wine-glass?
   A tumbler is larger than a wine-glass.

X

牛奶 niu²-nai³
milk

奶油 nai³-yu²
butter

1. *Nin² shih⁴ he¹ ch'a² shih⁴ he¹ niu²-nai³?*
   Wo³ he¹ niu²-nai³.

2. *Niu²-nai³* **to¹**-*shao³ ch'ien² i⁴ p'ing²-tzu¹?*
   Niu²-nai³ i⁴ mao² wu³, i⁴ p'ing²-tzu¹.
3. *Nin² he¹ ch'a² yao⁴ niu²-nai³ pu² yao⁴? Yao⁴ niu²-nai³.*
4. *Nin² tso²-t'ien¹ mai³-la¹ chi³ p'ing²-tzu¹ niu²-nai³?*
   Wo³ tso²-t'ien¹ mai³-la¹ liang³ p'ing²-tzu¹ niu²-nai³.
5. *Che⁴ shih⁴ chi³ chin¹ nai³-yu²?*
   Che⁴ shih⁴ i⁴ chin¹ nai³-yu².
6. *Nin² ch'ih¹ mien⁴-pao¹, ch'ih¹ nai³-yu² pu⁴ ch'ih¹?*
   Yeh³ ch'ih¹ nai³-yu².
7. *Nin² ming²-t'ien¹ yao⁴ mai³ chi³ chin¹ nai³-yu²?*
   Wo³ ming²-t'ien¹ yao⁴ mai³ wu³ chin¹.
8. *Nai³-yu² to¹-shao³ ch'ien² i⁴ chin¹?*
   Ch'i¹ *mao²-ch'ien¹ i⁴ chin¹.*
9. *Niu²-nai³ shih⁴ shen²-ma¹ yen²-se⁴?*
   Shih⁴ pai² yen²-se⁴.
10. *Nai³-yu² yeh³ shih⁴ pai² yen²-se⁴-ti¹ ma¹?*
    Yu³ pai² yen²-se⁴-ti¹ yeh³ yu³ huang² yen²-se⁴-ti¹.

1. Do you drink tea or milk ? I drink milk.
2. How much is one bottle of milk ?
   One bottle of milk is fifteen cents.
3. Do you take milk in your tea ?
   (You drink tea want milk not want ?)
   Yes, I take milk. (Want milk.)
4. How many bottles of milk did you buy yesterday ?
   Yesterday I bought two bottles of milk.
5. How many catties of butter is this ?
   This is one catty of butter.
6. Do you eat butter (when you) eat bread ?

LESSON 19

(I) also eat butter.
7. How many catties of butter will you buy tomorrow?
I shall buy five catties tomorrow.
8. How much is butter a catty? Seventy cents a catty.
9. What colour is milk? Milk is white.
10. Is butter also white?
There is (some) white and also (some) yellow.

NOTES

79. 一塊兒 **i²-k'uai-'rh⁴**—together. This expression is built up from the three characters:

一 *i²⁽¹⁾* } one 塊 *k'uai⁴* } piece, bit 兒 *erh²* } colloquial ending

一塊兒 **i²-k'uai-'rh⁴** } one piece, (in one piece) (together)

不在一塊兒 **pu² tsai⁴ i²-k'uai-'rh⁴** } not in one piece (not together)

80. 父母 **fu⁴-mu³** — parents, is a combination of the two characters 父 **fu⁴** — father and 母 **mu³** — mother. The character 親 *ch'in¹* in the combinations 父親 **fu⁴-ch'in¹** — father and 母親 **mu³ ch'in¹** — mother, means related, relatives.

81. **Street names.** As with names of people, the name is placed before the title. (see § 46.)

買賣街 *mai³-mai⁴ chieh¹* } Mai-mai (Trade) Street

82. 穿 **ch'uan¹**, 戴 **tai⁴**. 穿 **ch'uan¹** is the general verb for: to put on, to wear clothes while 戴 **tai⁴** is only used when speaking of putting on or wearing things on the head, the nose or the wrist (e. g. spectacles, watch, etc.)

穿衣裳 **ch'uan¹ i¹-shang¹** } to put on (wear) clothes

戴帽子 **tai⁴ mao⁴-tzu¹** } to put on (wear) a hat

LESSON 20

I

牛 **pan⁴**
half, ½

兩 **liang³**
ounce (Chinese), oz, tael

1. *Che⁴ so³ fang²-tzu¹ i² pan⁴ shih⁴ wo³-ti¹, i² pan⁴ shih⁴ t'a¹-ti¹.*
2. *I⁴ chin¹ shih⁴ shih²-liu⁴ liang³, pan⁴ chin¹ shih⁴ pa¹ liang³.*
3. *Ch'a²-yeh⁴ to¹-shao³ ch'ien² pan⁴ chin¹?*
   Che⁴ ke⁴ ch'a²-yeh⁴ ch'i¹ mao²-chien² pan⁴ chin¹, na⁴ ke⁴ ch'a²-yeh⁴ i² k'uai⁴.ch'ien² pan⁴ chin¹.
4. *Nin² mai³-la¹ chi³ chin¹ k'a⁴-fei¹?*
   Wo³ mai³-la¹ i⁴ chin¹ pan⁴.
5. *Che⁴ pan⁴ p'ing²-tzu¹ chiu³ yu³ chi³ liang³?*
   Che⁴ pan⁴ p'ing²-tzu¹ chiu³ yu³ shih²-erh⁴ liang³.
6. *Nin² yao⁴ mai³ chi³ p'ing²-tzu¹ niu²-nai³?*
   Wo³ yao⁴ mai³ pan⁴ p'ing²-tzu¹ niu²-nai³.
7. *T'a¹ tso²-t'ien¹ mai³-la¹ i⁴ chin¹ niu²-jou⁴, pan⁴ chin¹ chu¹-jou⁴, ssu⁴ liang³ yang²-jou⁴.*
8. *Che⁴ i¹ t'iao² yü² yu³ i⁴ chin¹ san¹ liang³.*
9. *Che⁴ i² pan⁴ shih⁴ wo³-ti¹ na⁴ i² pan⁴, na⁴ i² pan⁴ shih⁴ nin²-ti¹.*

1. One half of this house is mine, one half is his.
2. One catty is sixteen ounces, half a catty is eight ounces.

3. How much is half a catty of tea?
    This tea is seventy cents (for) half a catty, that tea is one dollar (for) half a catty.
4. How many catties of coffee have you bought?
    I have bought one and a half catties.
5. How many ounces is this half bottle of wine?
    This half bottle of wine is twelve ounces.
6. How many bottles of milk will you buy?
    I will buy half a bottle of milk.
7. Yesterday he bought one catty of beef, half a catty of pork and four ounces of mutton.
8. This fish is one catty and three ounces.
9. This half is my half, that half is yours.

II

倒 tao⁴
to pour, to pour out

1. *Ch'ing³ nin² kei³ wo³* **tao⁴** *i⁴ wan³ ch'a² lai².*
2. *Wo³ kei³ nin² **tao⁴** i⁴ pei¹ chiu³ lai², nin² he¹ pu⁴ he¹?* **Hsieh⁴-hsieh⁴**, *wo³ pu⁴ he¹.*
3. *Na⁴ wan³ k'a⁴-fei¹ shih⁴ shui² kei³ nin² **tao⁴**-ti¹? Shih⁴ t'a¹ kei³ wo³ **tao⁴**-ti¹.*
4. *Na⁴ po¹-li²-pei¹ niu²-nai³ shih⁴ kei³ shui² **tao⁴**-ti¹? Shih⁴ kei³ ni³ **tao⁴**-ti¹*
5. *Ch'ing³ nin² tsai⁴ kei³ wo³ **tao⁴** i⁴ pei¹ chiu³ lai².*

LESSON 20

1. Please pour me out a cup of tea.
2. I will pour you out a glass of wine, will you drink (it) ?
   Thank you, I will not drink (any).
3. Who poured out that cup of coffee for you ?
   He poured it out for me.
4. For whom was that glass of milk poured out ?
   It was poured out for you.
5. Please pour me out one more glass of wine.

III

新 hsin¹
new, recent, recently

舊 chiu⁴
old (of time, persons, places and things)

1. Che⁴ chien⁴ i¹-shang¹ shih⁴ hsin¹-ti¹ ma¹?
   Che⁴ chien⁴ i¹-shang¹ shih⁴ hsin¹-ti¹.
2. Che⁴ ting³ mao⁴-tzu¹ yeh³ shih⁴ hsin¹-ti¹ ma¹?
   Pu² shih⁴, che⁴ ting³ mao⁴-tzu¹ shih⁴ chiu⁴-ti¹.
3. Na⁴ wei⁴ hsüeh²-sheng¹ shih⁴ hsin¹ lai²-ti¹ pu² shih⁴?
   Tui⁴-la¹, t'a¹ shih⁴ hsin¹ lai²-ti¹.
4. Na⁴ chien⁴ i¹-shang¹ t'ai⁴ chiu⁴-la¹, ch'ing³ nin² kei³ wo³ mai³ i² chien⁴ hsin¹-ti¹ lai².
5. Ni³ hsin¹ mai³-ti¹ na⁴ so³ fang²-tzu¹ yu³ chi³ chien¹ wu¹-tzu¹? Yu³ pa¹ chien¹ wu¹-tzu¹.

1. Is this article of clothing new ?
   This article of clothing is new.

2. Is this hat also new? No, this hat is old.
3. Is that student a new-comer (recently come)?
   Right, he is a new-comer. [one.
4. That article of clothing is too old, please bring me a new
5. How many rooms has that house (that) you bought re-
   It has eight rooms. [cently?

IV

課本 k'e⁴-pen³
text-book(s)

1. Ch'ien² hsüeh²-sheng¹ mai³ shen²-ma¹ ch'ü⁴-la¹?
   T'a¹ mai³ k'e⁴-pen³ ch'ü⁴-a¹.
2. Che⁴ ke⁴ k'e⁴-pen³ shih⁴ hsin¹-ti¹ shih⁴ chiu⁴-ti¹?
   Che⁴ shih⁴ chiu⁴ k'e⁴-pen³.
3. Wo³-men² tso²-t'ien¹ ken¹ chin¹-t'ien¹ nien¹-ti¹ tou¹ shih⁴
   chiu⁴ k'e⁴-pen³, ming²-t'ien¹ yao⁴ nien⁴ hsin¹-ti¹.
4. Che⁴ ke⁴ k'e⁴-pen³ li³ ti¹ hua-'rh⁴ shih⁴ Huang² hsien¹-
   sheng¹ hua⁴-ti¹.

1. What has the student Ch'ien gone out to buy?
   He has gone out to buy a text-book.
2. Is this text-book a new one or an old one?
   This is an old text-book.
3. Yesterday and today we read the old text-book, tomorrow
   (we) shall read the new one.
4. The pictures in this text-book were drawn by Mr. Huang.

LESSON 20

V

中國 **chung¹-*kuo²***
China, Chinese

外國 **wai⁴-*kuo²***
a foreign country, foreign countries, abroad, foreign

國 **kuo²**
country

1. **Che⁴ shih⁴ na³ i⁴ kuo²? Che⁴ shih⁴ chung¹-kuo².**
2. **Na⁴ yeh³ shih⁴ chung¹-kuo² ma¹?**
   Na⁴ pu² shih⁴ chung¹-kuo², shih⁴ wai⁴-kuo².
3. **Wo³-men² shih⁴ tsai⁴ chung¹-kuo² chu⁴ ma¹?**
   Shih⁴, *wo³-men²* **shih⁴ tsai⁴ chung¹-kuo² chu⁴.**
4. **Che⁴ kuo² ta⁴ pu² ta⁴? Che⁴ kuo² hen³ ta⁴.**
5. **Chung¹-kuo²-ti¹ ti⁴-fang¹ ta⁴ pu² ta⁴?**
   Chung¹-kuo²-ti¹ ti⁴-fang¹ ta⁴-ti¹ hen³.

1. What country is this? This is China.
2. Is that also China?
   That isn't China, (that) is a foreign country.
3. Are we living in China?
   Yes, we are living in China.
4. Is this country big? This country is very big.
5. Is China a big place? (Chinese place big not big?)
   China is a very big place.

VI

中國人 chung¹-*kuo*² *jen*²
Chinese (person), The Chinese (people)

外國人 wai⁴-*kuo*² *jen*²
foreigner(s)

1. *Nin*² *shih*⁴ na³ *kuo*² *jen*²? Wo³ *shih*⁴ chung¹-*kuo*² *jen*².
2. *Nin*²-*ti*¹ hsien¹-*sheng*¹ shih⁴ wai⁴-*kuo*² *jen*² ma¹?
   Wo³-*ti*¹ hsien¹-*sheng*¹ shih⁴ *wai*⁴-*kuo*² *jen*².
3. *Ni*³-*men*² *hsüeh*²-*t'ang*²-*ti*¹ *hsüeh*²-*sheng*¹ tou¹ shih⁴ chung¹-*kuo*² hsüeh²-*sheng*¹ ma¹?
   Pu² tou¹ shih⁴ chung¹-*kuo*² hsüeh²-*sheng*¹, yeh³ yu³ wai⁴-*kuo*² hsüeh²-*sheng*¹.
4. *Chung*¹-*kuo*² *jen*² ch'uan¹-*ti*¹ i¹-*shang*¹ ch'ang² tuan³?
   Yu³ *ch'ang*²-*ti*¹, yeh³ yu³ *tuan*³-*ti*¹.
5. Pao¹ hsien¹-*sheng*¹! Na⁴ liang³ wei⁴ hsüeh²-*sheng*¹ shih⁴ wai⁴-*kuo*² *jen*² ma¹?
   Tui⁴-*la*¹, shih⁴ *wai*⁴-*kuo*² *jen*².
6. *Na*⁴ *ke*⁴ *p'u*⁴-*tzu*¹ *mai*⁴ chung¹-*kuo*² *tung*¹-*hsi*¹, yeh³ mai⁴ wai⁴-*kuo*² *tung*¹-*hsi*¹ ma¹?
   Yeh³ mai⁴ *wai*⁴-*kuo*² *tung*¹-*hsi*¹.

1. What is your nationality? (You are where country man?)
   I am Chinese.
2. Is your teacher a foreigner?
   My teacher is a foreigner.
3. Are all your school pupils Chinese pupils?
   They are not all Chinese pupils, there are also some foreign pupils.

LESSON 20

4. Are the clothes (that) the Chinese wear long or short?
Some are long and some are short.
5. Mr. Pao! Are those two pupils foreigners?
Right, (they) are foreigners.
6. That shop sells Chinese things, does it also sell foreign
It also sells foreign things.   [things?

VII

中國話 chung¹-kuo² hua⁴
Chinese language, Chinese

外國話 wai⁴-kuo² hua⁴
foreign language(s)

1. *Chung¹-kuo² jen² shuo¹ chung¹-kuo² hua⁴, wai⁴-kuo² jen² shuo¹ wai⁴-kuo² hua⁴.*
2. *Nin² hui⁴ shuo¹ wai⁴-kuo² hua⁴ ma¹?*
Shih⁴, wo³ hui⁴ shuo¹ i⁴-tien-'rh³ wai⁴-kuo² hua⁴.
3. *T'a¹-ti¹ ku¹-niang² hui⁴ shuo¹ na³ kuo² hua⁴?*
T'a¹-ti¹ ku¹-niang² hui⁴ shuo¹ chung¹-kuo² hua⁴.
4. *Na⁴ ke⁴ chung¹-kuo² jen² shuo¹-ti¹ wai⁴-kuo² hua⁴ hao³ pu⁴ hao³? T'a¹ shuo¹-ti¹ wai⁴-kuo² hua⁴ hen² hao³ la¹.*
5. *Wo³ shuo¹-ti¹ wai⁴-kuo² hua⁴ nin² ming²-pai² pu⁴ ming²-pai²? Nin² shuo¹-ti¹ wai⁴ kuo² hua⁴ wo³ ming²-pai².*
6. *Che⁴ san¹ ke⁴ k'e⁴-pen³ tou¹ shih⁴ na³ kuo² k'e⁴-pen³? Che⁴ liang³ ke⁴ k'e⁴-pen³ shih⁴ wai⁴-kuo² k'e⁴-pen³, na⁴ i² ke⁴ k'e⁴-pen³ shih⁴ chung¹-kuo² k'e⁴-pen³.*

1. Chinese speak the Chinese language, foreigners speak foreign languages.

2. Can you speak foreign languages?
   Yes, I can speak a little (of foreign languages).
3. What language can his daughter speak?
   His daughter can speak Chinese.
4. Does that Chinese speak foreign languages well?
   He speaks foreign languages very well.
5. Do you understand the foreign language that I speak?
   I do understand the foreign language you speak.
6. (In) what language are these three text-books?
   These two text-books are foreign text-books, that one (text-book) is a Chinese text-book.

VIII

中國字   chung¹-*kuo*² *tzu*⁴
Chinese character(s)

外國字   wai⁴-*kuo*² *tzu*⁴
foreign word(s), foreign letter(s)

(中國書)   chung¹-*kuo*² *shu*¹
Chinese book(s)

(外國書)   wai⁴-*kuo*² *shu*¹
foreign book(s)

(中國飯)   chung¹-*kuo*² *fan*⁴
Chinese food

(外國飯)   wai⁴-*kuo*² *fan*⁴
foreign food

1. *Na*⁴ *pen*³ *shu*¹ *shang*⁴ **yu**³ *wai*⁴-*kuo*² *tzu*⁴ *mei*² *yu*³?
   *Na*⁴ *pen*³ *shu*¹ *shang*⁴ **yu**³ *wai*⁴-*kuo*² *tzu*⁴.

LESSON 20

2. *Nin² hsieh³-ti¹* **na⁴ ke⁴ tzu⁴ shih⁴ na³ i⁴ kuo²-ti¹ tzu⁴?**
 Na⁴ shih⁴ **chung¹-kuo² tzu⁴.**
3. *Che⁴ ke⁴ chung¹-kuo² k'e⁴-pen³ shih⁴ na³ ke⁴ p'u⁴-tzu¹ mai³-ti¹?*
 Shih⁴ tsai⁴ na⁴ ke⁴ **chung¹-kuo² shu¹-p'u⁴ mai³-ti¹.**
4. *Che⁴ chi³ wei⁴ chung¹-kuo² hsüeh²-sheng¹* **nien⁴ wai⁴-kuo² shu¹ pu² nien⁴?** *T'a¹-men²* **nien⁴ wai⁴-kuo² shu¹.**
5. *Na⁴ ke⁴ jen² hui⁴ tso⁴ chung¹-kuo² fan⁴ ma¹?*
 T'a¹ hui⁴ tso⁴ chung¹-kuo² fan⁴.
6. *Nin² ch'ih¹-la¹ chi³ hui² chung¹-kuo² fan⁴ la¹?*
 Wo³ ch'ih¹-la¹ liang³ san¹ hui² la¹.
7. *Ch'ing³ wen⁴ nin² na¹, chin¹-t'ien¹ ni³ shih⁴ ch'ih¹* **wai⁴-kuo² fan⁴ shih⁴ ch'ih¹ chung¹-kuo² fan⁴?**
 Chin¹-t'ien¹ wo³ ch'ih¹ **wai⁴-kuo² fan⁴.**
8. *Chung¹-kuo² fan⁴ hao³ ch'ih¹ ma¹?*
 Chung¹-kuo² fan⁴ **hen² hao³ ch'ih¹.**

1. Has that book got foreign words on it?
 That book has got foreign words on it.
2. What language are those characters you have written?
 Those are Chinese characters.
3. At which shop were these Chinese text-books bought?
 They were bought at that Chinese book-shop.
4. Are these (several) Chinese students studying foreign
 They are studying foreign books. [books?
5. Can that man cook Chinese food?
 He can cook Chinese food.
6. How many times have you eaten Chinese food?
 I have eaten it two or three times.

7. May I ask you, are you eating foreign food or Chinese food today ? Today I am eating foreign food.
8. Is Chinese food good to eat ?
Chinese food is very good to eat.

IX

旗子 ch'i²-*tzu*¹
flag(s)

(○ 面 旗 子) — mien⁴ ch'i²-*tzu*¹
— flag(s)

1. *Che*⁴ mien⁴ ch'i²-*tzu*¹ shih⁴ ni³-*ti*¹ ma¹ ?
   *Che*⁴ mien⁴ ch'i²-*tzu*¹ shih⁴ wo³-*ti*¹.
2. *Na*⁴ shih⁴ na³ i⁴ kuo²-ti¹ ch'i²-*tzu*¹ ?
   *Na*⁴ shih⁴ chung¹-kuo² ch'i²-*tzu*¹.
3. *Chung*¹-kuo² ch'i²-*tzu*¹ yu³ chi³ ke⁴ yen²-se⁴ ?
   *Chung*¹-kuo² ch'i²-*tzu*¹ yu³ san¹ ke⁴ yen²-se⁴.
   *Tou*¹ shih⁴ shen²-ma¹ yen²-se⁴ ?
   *Hung*², pai², lan², che⁴ san¹ ke⁴ yen²-se⁴.
4. *Che*⁴ mien⁴ ch'i²-*tzu*¹ shih⁴ hsin¹-*ti*¹ shih⁴ chiu⁴-*ti*¹ ?
   *Che*⁴ mien⁴ ch'i²-*tzu*¹ shih⁴ chiu⁴-*ti*¹.
5. *Tsai*⁴ ch'iang² shang⁴ kua⁴-*ti*¹ ch'i²-*tzu*¹ shih⁴ shen²-ma¹ yen²-se⁴-*ti*¹ ?
   *Tsai*⁴ ch'iang² shang⁴ kua⁴-*ti*¹ ch'i²-*tzu*¹ shih⁴ lü⁴ yen²-se⁴-*ti*¹ ch'i²-*tzu*¹.
6. *Tsai*⁴ chiang³-*t'ang*² shang⁴, chin¹-*t'ien*¹ kua⁴ ch'i²-*tzu*¹ pu² kua⁴ ?
   *Chin*¹-*t'ien*¹ pu² kua⁴, ming²-*t'ien*¹ yao⁴ kua⁴.

LESSON 20

7. *Na⁴ shih⁴* **wai⁴-*kuo*²** **ch'i²-*tzu*¹** **ma¹**?
   Tui⁴-*la*¹, *na⁴* **shih⁴** *wai⁴-kuo² ch'i²-tzu¹*.
8. *Wai⁴-kuo² ch'i²-tzu¹* **tou¹** *ju³* **shen²-*ma*¹ yen²-*se*⁴**?
   Wai⁴-kuo² ch'i²-tzu¹ **shen²-*ma*¹** *yen²-se⁴* **tou¹** *yu³*.

1. Is this flag yours? This flag is mine.
2. What nationality is that flag?
   That is the Chinese flag.
3. How many colours has the Chinese flag?
   The Chinese flag has three colours.
   What colours are they?
   Red, white, blue — it has these three colours.
4. Is this flag a new one or an old one?
   This flag is an old one.
5. What colour is the flag hanging on the wall?
   The flag hanging on the wall is a green coloured flag.
6. Will (they) hang up a flag in the class-room today?
   (They) will not hang (one) up today, tomorrow (they) will hang (one) up.
7. Is that a foreign flag?
   Right, that is a foreign flag.
8. What colours have foreign flags?
   Foreign flags have all kinds of colours.

NOTES

83. 倒 **tao**⁴ — to pour, to pour out. When the character 來 **lai**² is added after the object, the sense of: hand it to me, hand it round, is implied.

倒 一 碗 茶 來
tao⁴ *i*¹ **wan**³ **ch'a**² *lai*² — pour out one cup. tea come (pour me out a cup of tea and hand it to me)

See examples in this lesson, para. II.

84. 中國 **chung**¹-*kuo*² — China. There are many expressions for the country of China. This is the more usual one. It consists of the two characters:

中 *chung*¹ { middle
國 *kuo*² { kingdom, country
中國 **chung**¹-*kuo*² { Middle kingdom, (China)

85. 外國 **wai**⁴-*kuo*² — foreign countries, is a combination of:

外 *wai*⁴ { outside, beyond
國 *kuo*² { kingdom, country
外國 **wai**⁴-*kuo*² { outside countries (foreign countries)

86. **Foreign Nations.**

澳大利亞 **ao**⁴-*ta*⁴-*li*⁴-**ya**³ } Australia
比國 **pi**³-*kuo*² } Belgium
坎拿大 **k'an**³-*na*²-**ta**⁴ } Canada
丹麥國 **tan**¹-*mai*⁴-*kuo*² } Denmark
英國 **ying**¹-*kuo*² } England
法國 **fa**⁴-*kuo*² } France
德國 **te**²-*kuo*² } Germany

LESSON 20

荷 蘭 國 } Holland
he²-lan²-*kuo*²

印 度 } India
yin⁴-*tu*⁴

意 國 } Italy
I⁴-*kuo*²

日 本 } Japan
jih⁴-*pen*³

那 威 國 } Norway
na¹-wei¹-*kuo*²

俄 國 } Russia
e⁴-*kuo*²

西 班 牙 國 } Spain
hsi¹-*pan*¹-ya²-*kuo*²

瑞 典 國 } Sweden
jui⁴-tien³-*kuo*²

美 國 } United States of America
mei³-*kuo*²

87. **National Adjectives** are the same as the proper nouns (in § 86.)

英 國 人 } Englishman
ying¹-*kuo*² *jen*²

中 國 書 } Chinese book
chung¹-*kuo*² *shu*¹

美 國 姑 娘 } American girl
mei³-*kuo*² *ku*¹-*niang*²

俄 國 飯 } Russian food
e⁴-*kuo*² *fan*⁴

LESSON 21

I

學 hsüeh²
to learn, to study

1. *Nin² ken¹* **shui²** *hsüeh² chung¹-kuo² hua⁴ na¹?*
   Wo³ ken¹ **Ch'ien²** *hsien¹-sheng¹ hsüeh² chung¹-kuo² hua⁴.*
2. *Nin² yeh³ hsüeh² hsieh³ chung¹-kuo² tzu⁴ ma¹?* [*na¹*.
   Wo³ yeh³ hsüeh² hsieh³ chung¹-kuo² tzu⁴.
3. *Na⁴ ke⁴ ku¹-niang² ken¹ t'a¹ mu³-ch'in¹ hsüeh² shen²-*
   [*ma¹ na¹?*
   Ken¹ t'a¹ mu³-ch'in¹ hsüeh² tso⁴ i¹-shang¹ na¹.
4. *Ni³-men² hsüeh²-t'ang² li³ ti¹ hsüeh²-sheng¹ yeh³ hsüeh²*
   wai⁴-*kuo² hua⁴ ma¹?*
   T'a¹-men² yeh³ hsüeh² wai⁴-kuo² hua⁴.

1. With whom are you learning Chinese?
   I am learning Chinese with Mr. Ch'ien.
2. Are you also learning to write Chinese characters?
   I am also learning to write Chinese characters.
3. What is that girl learning with her mother?
   (She) is learning to make clothes with her mother.
4. Do the pupils in your school also learn foreign languages?
   They also learn foreign languages.

LESSON 21

II

多喒 to¹-tsan² ?
when ?

1. **Huang²** hsien¹-sheng¹ kao⁴-su⁴ nin² to¹-tsan² lai² ?
 T'a¹ kao⁴-su⁴ wo³ **ming**²-t'ien¹ lai².
2. Na⁴ chang¹ hua-'rh⁴ shih⁴ to¹-tsan² hua⁴-ti¹ ?
 Shih⁴ tso²-t'ien¹ hua⁴-ti¹.
3. Nin² to¹-tsan² shang⁴ t'a¹ chia¹ li³ ch'ü⁴ ?
 Wo³ chin¹-t'ien¹ chiu⁴ yao⁴ ch'ü⁴.
4. T'a¹ che⁴ chien⁴ i¹-shang¹ shih⁴ to¹-tsan² mai³-ti¹ ?
 Wo³ pu⁴ chih¹-tao⁴ shih⁴ to¹-tsan² mai³-ti¹.

1. When did Mr. Huang tell you to come ?
 He told me to come tomorrow.
2. When was that picture drawn ? It was drawn yesterday.
3. When will you go to his home ? I will go today.
4. When was this article of his clothing bought ?
 I don't know when it was bought.

III

開 k'ai¹
to open

關 kuan¹
to close, to shut

1. Nin² shih⁴ yao⁴ k'ai¹ ch'uang¹-hu⁴ shih⁴ yao⁴ k'ai¹ men² ?
 Wo³ shih⁴ yao⁴ k'ai¹ ch'uang¹-hu⁴.
2. Na⁴ ke⁴ men² shih⁴ shui² k'ai¹-k'ai¹-ti¹ ?
 Shih⁴ na⁴ wei⁴ t'ai⁴-t'ai⁴ k'ai¹-k'ai¹-ti¹.

3. *Ch'ing*³ *nin*² **pa**³ **na**⁴ *ke*⁴ *ch'uang*¹-*hu*⁴ **k'ai**¹-*k'ai*¹.
   Hao³ *hao*³, *wo*³ *hsieh*³ **wan**²-*la*¹ *tzu*⁴ **chiu**⁴ *k'ai*¹-*k'ai*¹.
4. *Na*⁴ *ke*⁴ *men*² **k'ai**¹-*k'ai*¹-*la*¹ *ma*¹ ?
   *Na*⁴ *ke*⁴ *men*² *hai*² **mei**² *k'ai*¹-*k'ai*¹ *na*¹.
5. *Ch'ing*³ *wen*⁴ *nin*² *na*¹, *che*⁴ *ke*⁴ *men*² **kuan**¹ *pu*⁴ *kuan*¹ ?
   *Che*⁴ *ke*⁴ *men*² **pu**⁴ *kuan*¹.
6. **Shui**² *pa*³ *men*² **kuan**¹-*shang*⁴-*la*¹ ?
   Hsien¹-*sheng*¹ *pa*³ *men*² *kuan*¹-*shang*⁴-*la*¹.
7. *Ch'ing*³ *nin*² *pa*³ **men**² **k'ai**¹-*k'ai*¹, *pa*³ **ch'uang**¹-*hu*⁴ **kuan**¹-*shang*⁴.   ⌊*hu*⁴ *la*¹.
   *Wo*³ **k'ai**¹-*k'ai*¹ *men*² *la*¹, *yeh*³ *kuan*¹-*shang*⁴ *ch'uang*¹-

1. Do you want to open the window or the door ?
   I want to open the window.
2. Who opened that door ?   That lady opened it.
3. Please open that window. (Please you take hold of that window open.)
   All right, when I have finished writing I will open it.
4. Has that door been opened ?
   That door has not been opened yet.
5. May I ask you, is this door shut ?
   This door is not shut.
6. Who has closed the door ?
   The teacher has closed the door.
7. Please open the door and close the window.
   I have opened the door and closed the window.

LESSON 21

IV

(問答) wen⁴-ta²
question and answer

Q. Nin² ken¹ shui² hsüeh² chung¹-kuo² hua⁴ na¹?
A. Wo³ ken¹ Kuan¹ hsien¹-sheng¹ hsüeh² na¹.
Q. Kuan¹ hsien¹-sheng¹ chin¹-t'ien¹ lai²-la¹ ma¹?
A. Chin¹-t'ien¹ mei² lai².
Q. T'a¹ to¹-tsan² lai²?
A. T'a¹ shuo¹ t'a¹ ming²-t'ien¹ lai².
Q. Nin² chin¹-t'ien¹ yao⁴ tso⁴ shen²-ma¹ ch'ü⁴?
A. Wo³ yao⁴ mai³ tien-'rh³ tung¹-hsi¹ ch'ü⁴.
Q. Nin² yao⁴ mai³ shen²-ma¹ tung¹-hsi¹?
A. Wo³ yao⁴ mai³ chi³ p'ing²-tzu¹ chiu³, chi³ p'ing²-tzu¹ niu²-nai³ ken¹ chi³ chin¹ nai³-yu².
Q. Nin² yao⁴ mai³ tung¹-hsi¹ ch'ü⁴, ch'ing³ nin² pa³ ch'uang¹-hu⁴, men², tou¹ kuan¹-shang⁴.
A. Shih⁴ shih⁴. Wo³ tou¹ kuan¹-shang⁴-la¹.

Q. With whom are you learning Chinese?
A. I am learning with Mr. Kuan.
Q. Has Mr. Kuan come today?
A. (He) has not come today.
Q. When will he come?
A. He says he will come tomorrow.
Q. What do you want to go out for today?
A. I want to go and buy a few things.
Q. What (things) do you want to buy?

A. I want to buy some bottles of wine, some bottles of milk and several pounds of butter.

Q. (If) you want to go out to buy things, please shut all the windows and doors.

A. Yes. I will shut (them) all.

V

(問答) wen⁴-ta²
question and answer

Q. *Nin² tsai⁴* **na-'rh³ chu⁴ na¹** *?*
A. *Wo³ tsai⁴* **chung¹-kuo² ta⁴-chieh¹ chu⁴ na¹.**
Q. *Nin² ken¹* **shui² i²-k'uai-'rh⁴ lai²-***ti¹ ?*
A. *Wo³ ken¹ wo³* **fu⁴-mu² i²-k'uai-'rh⁴** *lai²-ti¹.*
Q. *Ni³-men² tso⁴* **shen²-ma¹** *lai²-la¹ ?*
A. *Wo³-men² yao⁴ mai³* **chi³ chien⁴ i¹-shang¹.**
Q. *Ni³-men² yao⁴ mai³* **shen²-ma¹ yen²-se⁴-***ti¹ **i¹-shang¹** *?*
A. *Yao⁴ mai³ i²* **chien⁴ hung²-*ti¹*, *liang³* chien⁴ lan²-*ti¹.**
Q. *Tsai⁴* **na⁴-***li³* **yu³** *mai⁴-hsieh²-ti¹ mei² yu³ ?*
A. *Tsai⁴* **na⁴-***li³* **yu³** *mai⁴-hsieh²-ti¹.*
Q. *Nin² ch'uan¹-ti¹ che⁴* **shuang¹ hsieh² shih⁴** *tsai⁴* **na-'rh³**
A. *Yeh³ shih⁴ tsai⁴* **na⁴-***li³ mai³-ti¹.*   [*mai³-ti¹ ?*
Q. *Na⁴ t'iao² chieh¹* **shang⁴ yeh³** *yu³* **shu¹-p'u⁴** *ma¹ ?*
A. *Yu³* **shu¹-p'u⁴.**
Q. *T'a¹-men² mai⁴* **chung¹-kuo² shu¹, wai⁴-kuo² shu¹** *?*
A. *T'a¹-men² chung¹-kuo² shu¹, wai⁴-kuo² shu¹,* **tou¹ mai⁴.**
Q. *Na⁴ ke⁴* **shu¹-p'u⁴ shih⁴ chung¹-kuo² shu¹-p'u⁴** *ma¹ ?*
A. *Pu² shih⁴, shih⁴* **wai⁴-kuo² shu¹-p'u⁴.**

LESSON 21

Q. *Nin² * **yeh³** *tsai⁴ t'a¹-men²* **na⁴-li³ mai³** *shu¹ ma¹ ?*
A. **Tui⁴**-*la¹, wo³-men²-ti¹* **k'e⁴-pen³ tou¹ shih⁴** *tsai⁴* **na⁴-li³**
⎣*mai³-ti¹.*
Q. *T'a¹-men²* **hui⁴ shuo¹** *chung¹-kuo² hua⁴ pu² hui⁴ ?*
A. *T'a¹-men²* **yu³ hui⁴**-*ti¹,* **yu³ pu² hui⁴ shuo¹**-*ti¹.*

Q. Where do you live ?
A. I live in *Chung-kuo* street.
Q. Whom did you come with ?
A. I came with my parents.
Q. What did you (pl.) come for ?
A. We want to buy some clothes.
Q. What colour clothes do you want to buy ?
A. (We) want to buy one red one and two blue ones.
Q. Is there a shoe-seller here ?
A. There is a shoe-seller here.
Q. Where did you buy this pair of shoes (that) you are wearing ?
A. (They) were also bought there.
Q. Is there also a book-shop in that street ?
A. There is a book-shop.
Q. Do they sell Chinese books and foreign books ?
A. They sell both Chinese books and foreign books.
Q. Is that book-shop a Chinese book-shop ?
A. No, it is a foreign book-shop.
Q. Do you also buy books at their (place) ?
A. Right, our text-books are all bought there.
Q. Can they speak Chinese ?
A. Some of them can and some of them can't speak.

VI

看 k'an⁴
to look, to look at, to see

1. *Ch'ing³ ni³-men² k'an⁴, tsai⁴ che⁴ chang¹ hua-'rh⁴ shang⁴, hua⁴-ti¹ shih⁴ shen²-ma¹ tung¹-hsi¹?*
Tsai⁴ na⁴ chang¹ hua-'rh⁴ shang⁴, hua⁴-ti¹ shih⁴ p'ing²-tzu⁴ ken¹ chiu³-pei¹, shen²-ma¹-ti¹
2. *Nin² k'an⁴, che⁴ chi³ ke⁴ tzu⁴ hsieh³-ti¹ hao³ pu⁴ hao³?*
Che⁴ chi³ ke⁴ tzu⁴ hsieh³-ti¹ pu⁴ ta⁴ hao³.
3. *Ch'ing³ nin⁴ k'an⁴, che⁴ shih⁴ wo³-ti¹ k'e⁴-pen³ pu² shih⁴, na⁴ shih⁴ nin²-ti¹ k'e⁴-pen³.* ⌊*shih⁴?*
4. *Nin² tsai⁴ na⁴-li³ k'an⁴ shen²-ma¹ na¹?*
Wo³ tsai⁴ na-'rh⁴ k'an⁴ hua-'rh⁴ na¹.
5. *Ni³ k'an⁴, shih⁴ che⁴ chang¹ hua-'rh⁴ hua⁴-ti¹ hao³, shih⁴ na⁴ chang¹ hua-'rh⁴ hua⁴-ti¹ hao³?*
Hai² shih⁴ che⁴ chang¹ hua-'rh⁴ hua⁴-ti¹ hao³.

1. Please look, what things are drawn in that picture?
In that picture are drawn a bottle, a wine-glass, etc.
2. Look! Are these characters well written?
These characters are not written very well.
3. Please look; this is my text-book isn't it?
Yes, that is your text-book.
4. What are you looking at (over) there?
I am looking at a picture.
5. Look! Is this picture better drawn than that picture?
This picture is better drawn.

LESSON 21

VII

報 pao⁴ newspaper(s)　(〇份報) = fen⁴ pao⁴ — newspaper(s)

信 hsin⁴ letter(s)　(〇封信) = feng¹ hsin⁴ — letter(s)

看 k'an⁴ to read { (書) shu¹ book(s)　(信) hsin⁴ letter(s)
(報) pao⁴ newspaper(s) }

1. Che⁴ shih⁴ nin² mai³-ti¹ pao⁴ ma¹?
   Shih⁴, che⁴ shih⁴ wo³ mai³-ti¹ pao⁴.
2. Che⁴ shih⁴ chung¹-kuo² pao⁴ shih⁴ wai⁴-kuo² pao⁴ ni¹?
   Che⁴ shih⁴ wai⁴-kuo² pao⁴.
3. Che⁴ i² fen⁴ pao⁴ to¹-shao³ ch'ien²?
   Che⁴ i² fen⁴ pao⁴ i⁴ mao²-ch'ien².
4. Nin² chin¹-t'ien¹ yao⁴ k'an⁴ chung¹-kuo² pao⁴ ma¹?
   Shih⁴, wo³ chin¹-t'ien¹ yao⁴ k'an⁴ chung¹-kuo² pao⁴.
5. Nin² k'an⁴ shen²-ma¹ shu¹ na¹?
   Wo³ k'an⁴ wai⁴-kuo² shu¹ na¹.
6. Wo³ nien⁴ shu¹, t'a¹ k'an⁴ shu¹.
7. Che⁴ i¹ feng¹ hsin⁴ shih⁴ shui² hsieh³-ti¹?
   Shih⁴ wo³ mu³-ch'in¹ hsieh³-ti¹.
8. Ni³ yao⁴ kei³ shui² hsieh³ hsin⁴?
   Wo³ yao⁴ kei³ wo³ chang⁴-fu¹ hsieh³ hsin⁴.
9. Nin² k'an⁴-ti¹ shih⁴ shui²-ti¹ hsin⁴?
   Wo³ k'an⁴-ti¹ shih⁴ Kuan¹ hsien¹-sheng¹-ti¹ hsin⁴.
10. Nin² tsai⁴ na-'rh⁴ k'an⁴ shen²-ma¹ na¹?
    Wo³ k'an⁴ hsin⁴ na¹.

11. *Che⁴ fen⁴ pao⁴* **shih⁴ nin² ʻkʻan⁴**-*ti¹ ma¹?*
    Shih⁴ *wo³ kʻan⁴-ti¹.*

1. Is this the newspaper you bought?
   Yes, this is the newspaper I bought.
2. Is this a Chinese newspaper or a foreign newspaper?
   This is a foreign newspaper.
3. How much is this paper? This paper is ten-cents.
4. Shall you read the Chinese newspaper today?
   Yes, I shall read the Chinese newspaper today.
5. What book are you reading?
   I am reading a foreign book.
6. I study (books), he reads books.
7. Who wrote this letter? My mother wrote it.
8. To whom will you write a letter?
   I will write a letter to my husband.
9. Whose letter did you read? I read Mr. Kuan's letter.
10. What are you reading there? I am reading a letter.
11. Have you read this newspaper? I have read it.

VIII

聽 **tʻing¹**
to listen, to listen to

1. *Chʻing³ ni³-men² tʻing¹, wo³ yao⁴ kei³ ni³-men² chiang³ kung¹-kʻe⁴.*
2. *Hsien¹-sheng¹ chiang³ kung¹-kʻe⁴,* **shen²-ma¹** *jen² tʻing¹?*
   Hsien¹-sheng¹ chiang³ kung¹-kʻe⁴ **hsüeh²-sheng¹-men²** *tʻing¹.*

LESSON 21

3. *Nin² t'ing¹, shui² tsai⁴ na⁴-li³ shuo¹-hua⁴ na¹?*
   Ch'ien² *t'ai⁴-t'ai⁴* ken¹ Huang² *t'ai⁴-t'ai⁴ tsai⁴ na-'rh⁴ shuo¹-hua⁴ na¹.*
4. *T'a¹ t'ing¹ shen²-ma¹ na¹?*
   T'a¹ t'ing¹ wo³-men² liang³ ke⁴ jen² shuo¹-ti¹ shih⁴ shen²-ma¹ hua⁴.

1. Please listen; I will explain the lesson to you.
2. Who listens (when) the teacher explains the lesson?
   The students listen (when) the teacher explains the lesson.
3. Listen! Who is speaking (over) there?
   Mrs. Ch'ien and Mrs. Huang are speaking (over) there.
4. What is he listening to?
   He is listening to what we two (men) are saying.

IX

看一看 k'an⁴-i¹-k'an⁴
to look

聽一聽 t'ing¹-i¹-t'ing¹
to listen

1. *Ch'ing³ nin² k'an⁴-i¹-k'an⁴, wo³ hsieh³-ti¹ che⁴ feng¹ hsin⁴ tui⁴ pu² tui⁴? Hsieh³-ti¹ tui⁴-la¹.*
2. *Nin² mai³-ti¹ chiu³-pei¹ mei² kei³ nin² fu⁴-ch'in¹ k'an⁴-i¹-k'an⁴ ma¹? Kei³ wo³ fu⁴-ch'in¹ k'an⁴-la¹.*
3. *Ch'ing³ nin² k'an⁴-i¹-k'an⁴, t'a¹ tsai⁴ chia¹ li³ mei² yu³? T'a¹ tsai⁴ chia¹ na¹.*
4. *Chang¹ hsieh¹-sheng¹ lai²-la¹ mei² yu³? Wo³ k'an⁴-i¹-k'an⁴ ch'ü⁴.*

5. *Hsien¹-sheng¹, ch'ing³ nin² t'ing¹-i¹-t'ing¹, wo³ nien⁴-ti¹ hsin⁴ tui⁴ pu² tui⁴? Hao³, wo³ t'ing¹-i¹-ting¹.*
6. *Ch'ing³ nin² t'ing¹-i¹-t'ing¹, t'a¹-men² shuo¹-ti¹ chung¹-kuo² hua⁴ hao³ pu⁴ hao³?*
   T'a¹-men² shuo¹-ti¹ hen² hao³ la¹.

1. Please look; have I written this letter correctly?
   It is written correctly.
2. Haven't you shown your father the wine-glass (that) you bought?
   (You bought wine-glass not give your father look?)
   I have shown it to my father.
3. Please see (if) he is at home or not? He is at home.
4. Has Mr. Chang come? I will go and see.
5. Teacher! Please listen to me while I read out this letter and tell me if it is correct?
   (Please listen me read aloud letter correct not correct?)
   All right, I am listening.
6. Please listen; do they speak Chinese well?
   They speak Chinese very well.

LESSON 21

NOTES

88. 開 k'ai¹ — to open. In colloquial usage this character is often repeated: 開開 k'ai¹-k'ai¹.

你把那個門開開！ } Open that door!
ni³ pa³ na⁴ ke⁴ men² k'ai¹-k'ai¹!

那個門開開了麼？ } Has that door been opened?
na⁴ ke⁴ men² k'ai¹-k'ai¹-la¹ ma¹?

89. 關 kuan¹ — to close, to shut. In colloquial usage this character is often followed by 上 shang: 關上 kuan¹-shang⁴.

把這個窗戶關上！ } Close this window!
pa³ che⁴ ke⁴ ch'uang¹-hu⁴ kuan¹-shang⁴!

90. 看 k'an⁴ may be translated as: to look, to look at, to see or to read, according to its context.

看書 } to read a book,
k'an⁴ shu¹ } to glance through a book

念書 } to read a book aloud,
nien⁴ shu¹ } to study

看信 } to read a letter
k'an⁴ hsin⁴

念信 } to read a letter out aloud
nien⁴ hsin⁴

看畫兒 } to look at a picture
k'an⁴ hua-'rh⁴

91. Repetition of Verbs with 一 i¹. There are many examples of this form in the colloquial language. It implies that the action is one of duration — that it lasts for a few moments.

看 一 看 { to take a look at, to look at for a few moments
k'an¹-i¹-k'an¹

聽 一 聽 { to listen for a moment
t'ing¹-i¹-t'ing¹

LESSON 22

I

上 〇 去 shang⁴ — ch'ü⁴
to go to —

1. *Nin² shang⁴ shen²-ma¹ ti⁴-fang¹ ch'ü⁴?*
   Wo³ shang⁴ t'a¹ chia¹ li³ ch'ü⁴.
2. *Na⁴ wei⁴ hsüeh²-sheng¹ shang⁴ hsüeh²-t'ang² ch'ü⁴-la¹ ma¹? T'a¹ shang⁴ hsüeh²-t'ang² ch'ü⁴-la¹.*
3. *Nin² ming²-t'ien¹ shang⁴ shui² chia¹ ch'ü⁴?*
   Wo³ yao⁴ shang⁴ Chang¹ hsien¹-sheng¹ chia¹ li³ ch'ü⁴.
4. *Nin² shang⁴ Chang¹ hsien¹-sheng¹ chia¹ li³ ch'ü⁴ tso⁴ shen²-ma¹ ch'ü⁴?*
   Wo³ yao⁴ ch'ing³ t'a¹ kei³ wo³-men² chiang³ kung¹-k'e⁴.
5. *Tso²-t'ien¹ shang⁴ nin² chia¹ li³ ch'ü⁴-ti¹ na⁴ ke⁴ jen² shih⁴ shui²? Na⁴ shih⁴ wo³-men²-ti¹ hsien¹-sheng¹.*

1. Where are you going to? (You to what place go?)
   I am going to his home.
2. Has that pupil gone to school?
   He has gone to school.
3. Whose house are you going to tomorrow?
   I will go to Mr. Chang's house.
4. What are you going to Mr. Chang's house for?
   I want to ask him to explain the lessons for us.
5. Who was that man who came to your house yesterday?
   That was our teacher.

II

上那裡(兒)? shang⁴ na² li³ (-'rh³)?
where to ? where ? whither ?

上街 shang⁴ chieh¹
up the street

1. *Ch'ing³ wen⁴* **nin²** *na¹,* **nin²** **chin¹**-*t'ien¹* **yao⁴ shang⁴ na-'rh³** *ch'ü⁴?* *Wo³ yao⁴ mai³* **cho¹**-*tzu¹ ch'ü⁴.*
   Shang⁴ **na²**-*li³ mai³ ch'ü⁴?*
   Shang⁴ **na⁴** *ke⁴* **cho¹**-*i³*-*p'u⁴ mai³ ch'ü⁴.*
2. *Nin² nien⁴* **wan²**-*la¹* **shu¹,** *hai² yao⁴ shang⁴* **na²**-*li³ ch'ü⁴?*
   Wo³ **na-'rh³** *yeh³ pu² ch'ü⁴-la¹.*
3. *Pai² hsien¹-sheng¹ shang⁴* **na²-li³** *la¹?*
   Wo³ **hai⁴** *pu² chih¹-tao⁴ shang⁴* **na-'rh³** *la¹ na¹.*
4. *Wo³ shang⁴ chieh¹ ch'ü⁴,* **nin²** *shang⁴* **na-'rh³** *ch'ü⁴?*
   Wo³ yeh³ shang⁴ chieh¹ ch'ü⁴.
5. *Ni³* **chih¹-tao⁴** *t'a¹ shang⁴* **na-'rh³** *ch'ü⁴-la¹ ma¹?*
   Wo³ **chih¹**-*tao⁴ t'a¹ shang⁴* **na-'rh³** *ch'ü⁴-la¹.*

1. May I ask you, where will you go today ?
   I will go and buy a table. Where will you go to buy it ?
   I will go to that furniture shop to buy it.
2. When you have finished studying where will you go ?
   I will not go anywhere. (I where even will not go.)
3. Where has Mr. Pai (gone) to ?
   I still don't know where (he) has (gone) to.
4. I am going up the street, where are you going ?
   I am also going up the street.

LESSON 22

5. Do you know where he has gone to?
   I do know where he has gone.

III

從 ○ 來   ts'ung² — lai²
          to come from —

1. *Nin² ts'ung² chia¹ li³ lai² ma¹?*
   Shih⁴, wo³ ts'ung² chia¹ li³ lai².
2. *T'a¹ ts'ung² shen²-ma¹ ti⁴-fang¹ lai²?*
   T'a¹ yeh³ ts'ung² chia¹ li³ lai².
3. *Nin² ts'ung² shu¹-p'u⁴ mai³-la¹ shen²-ma¹ lai²-la¹?*
   Wo³ mai³-la¹ liang³ pen³ shu¹ lai².
4. *Che⁴ chi³ p'ing²-tzu¹ chiu³ shih⁴ ts'ung² chia¹ li³ na²-lai²-ti¹ ma¹?*
   Pu² shih⁴, shih⁴ ts'ung² p'u⁴-tzu¹ na²-lai²-ti¹.
5. *Na⁴ wei⁴ hsien¹-sheng¹ shih⁴ ts'ung² wai⁴-kuo² ch'ing³ lai²-ti¹ ma¹?*
   Tui⁴-la¹, shih⁴ ts'ung² wai⁴-kuo² ch'ing³ lai²-ti¹.

1. Are you coming from (your) home?
   Yes, I am coming from (my) home.
2. Where is he coming from? (He from what place comes?)
   He is also coming from (his) home.
3. What did you buy from the book-shop?
   I bought two books.
4. Were these (numerous) bottles of wine brought from
   No, they were brought from a shop.   [home?

5. Was that teacher invited to come from abroad ?
   Right, (he) was invited to come from abroad.

IV

從那裡(兒)？ ts'ung² na²-li³ (-'rh³)?
where from ?, whence ?

1. *Nin² ts'ung² na-'rh³ lai²?*
   Wo³ ts'ung² mai³-mai⁴ chieh¹ lai².
2. *Che⁴ ke⁴ mien⁴-pao¹ shih⁴ ts'ung² na²-li³ mai³ lai²-ti¹?*
   Shih⁴ ts'ung² wo³-men² na⁴ t'iao² chieh¹ shang⁴, na⁴ ke⁴ mien⁴-pao¹-fang² li³, mai³ lai²-ti¹.
3. *Shang⁴ ni³-men² hsüeh²-t'ang², yao⁴ ts'ung² na-'rh³ ch'ü⁴? Yao⁴ ts'ung² chung¹-kuo² ta⁴-chieh¹ ch'ü⁴.*
4. *T'a¹-men² mai⁴-ti¹ tung¹-hsi¹ tou¹ shih⁴ ts'ung² na²-li³ mai³ lai²-ti²? Tou¹ shih⁴ ts'ung² wai⁴-kuo² mai³ lai²-ti¹.*
5. *Nin² ming² t'ien¹ ts'ung² na²-li³ shang⁴ hsüeh²-t'ang² ch'ü⁴?*
   Wo³ ming²-t'ien¹ ts'ung² Pao¹ hsien¹-sheng¹ na-'rh⁴, shang⁴ hsüeh²-t'ang² ch'ü⁴.

1. Where have you come from ? (Where are you coming from ?)
   I am coming from *Mai-mai* Street.
2. Where was this bread bought ?
   It was bought from the baker's on our street.
3. From what place must I go to get to your school ?
   (To your school want from where go ?)
   (You) must go from *Chung-kuo* street.

4. Where do they buy all the things that they sell?
   (They sold things all are from where bought came?)
   They are all bought from abroad.
5. Where will you go to school from tomorrow?
   Tomorrow I will go to school from Mr. Pao's.

V

上那裡(兒) shang⁴ na⁴-li³ (-'rh⁴)
there, to there, thither

1. *Nin² tso²-t'ien¹ shang⁴* **na-'rh³** *ch'ü⁴-la¹?*
   Wo³ shang⁴ Ch'ien² **hsien¹-sheng¹ na-'rh⁴** *ch'ü⁴-la¹.*
2. *Shang⁴ na-'rh⁴ tso⁴ shen²-ma¹ ch'ü⁴-la¹?*
   Wo³ **ken¹ t'a¹** *yu³* **hua⁴ shuo¹.**
3. *Shang⁴ nin² na⁴-li³ ch'ü⁴-ti¹* **na⁴ wei⁴.** *kuei⁴ hsing⁴?*
   T'a¹ hsing⁴ **Lan².**
4. *Nin² shang⁴* **t'a¹ na-'rh⁴** *ch'ü⁴-la¹ ma¹?*
   Hai² mei² ch'ü⁴ na¹.
5. *Nin²* **hai²** *shang⁴ na⁴-li³* **mai³ hsieh²** *ch'ü⁴* **ma¹?**
   Wo³ **pu²** *ch'ü⁴-la¹,* **na-'rh⁴-ti¹ hsieh²** *t'ai⁴ kuei⁴.*

1. Where did you go to yesterday?
   I went to Mr. Ch'ien's.
2. What did you go there for?
   I had something to say to him.
3. What is the name of that person (who) came (to see) you there?   His name is Lan.

4. Have you gone (to see) him there?
   I have not gone yet.
5. Will you go there again to buy shoes?
   I won't go, the shoes there are too expensive.

VI

上這裡(兒) shang⁴ che⁴-li³ (-'rh⁴)
here, to here, hither

1. *T'a¹ shang⁴ che-'rh⁴ tso⁴ shen²-ma¹ lai²-la¹?*
   T'a¹ yao⁴ ken¹ nin² shuo¹ chi³ chü⁴ hua⁴.
2. *Nin² chin¹-t'ien¹ shang⁴ che⁴-li³ lai², nin² ming²-t'ien¹ hai² lai² ma¹? Wo³ ming²-t'ien¹ hai² lai².*
3. *Ming²-t'ien¹ shih⁴ nin² shang⁴ t'a¹ na-'rh⁴ ch'ü⁴, shih⁴ t'a¹ shang⁴ nin² che-'rh⁴ lai²?*
   Hai² shih⁴ t'a¹ shang⁴ wo³ che-'rh⁴ lai².
4. *Shang⁴ che-'rh⁴ lai²-ti¹ tou¹ shih⁴ tso⁴ shen²-ma¹-ti¹?*
   Tou¹ shih⁴ hsüeh²-sheng¹.
5. *Nin² tso²-t'ien¹ mei² shang⁴ che-'rh⁴ lai², nin² shang⁴ na²-li³ ch'ü⁴ la¹? Wo³ mai³ tung¹-hsi¹ ch'ü⁴-la¹.*

1. What has he come here for?
   He wants to talk (over) a few (things) with you.
2. You have come here today, will you come again tomor-
   I will come again tomorrow.   [row?
3. Will you go to him tomorrow, or will he come to you here?
   He will come to me here.

LESSON 22

4. What do all the people who have come here do?
   (They) are all pupils.
5. Yesterday you did not come here, where did you go to?
   I went (out) to buy things.

VII

從那裡(兒) ts'ung² na⁴-li³ (-'rh⁴)
from there, thence

1. T'a¹ ts'ung² na²-li³ na²-lai²-ti¹ nlu²-nai³?
   T'a¹ ts'ung² na-'rh⁴ na²-lai²-ti¹.
2. Nin² ts'ung² na-'rh⁴ shang⁴ na-'rh³ ch'ü⁴?
   Wo³ ts'ung² na⁴-li³ shang⁴ hsüeh²-t'ang² ch'ü⁴.
3. Ts'ung² na⁴ ke⁴ shu¹-p'u⁴ na-'rh⁴ mai³ lai²-ti¹ shu¹ tou¹ shih⁴ wai⁴-kuo² shu¹ ma¹?
   Pu² shih⁴, yeh³ yu³ chung¹-kuo² shu¹.
4. Che⁴ ting³ mao⁴-tzu¹ shih⁴ ts'ung² na-'rh³ mai³ lai²-ti¹?
   Pu² shih⁴ mai³-ti¹, shih⁴ ts'ung² Ch'ien² t'ai⁴-t'ai⁴ na⁴-li³ na²-lai²-ti¹.
5. Ch'ing³ wen⁴ hsien¹-sheng¹, che⁴ pen³ shu¹ ts'ung² na-'rh³ nien⁴? Ts'ung² na-'rh⁴ nien⁴.

1. Where did he bring the milk from?
   He brought it from (over) there.
2. Where are you going from there?
   I am going to school from there.
3. Are all those books bought from that book-shop foreign
   No, (they) also have Chinese books.   [books?

4. Where was this hat bought from ?
It was not bought, it was brought from Mrs. Ch'ien's.
5. May I ask (you) teacher, where should I start reading from in this book ? (This book from where read ?) Read from there.

NOTES

92. 上 **shang⁴** has more than one translation. In this lesson it indicates direction to or towards.

上　學　堂　去 ｜ Towards school go,
shang⁴ *hsüeh²-t'ang²* **ch'ü⁴** ｜ (To go to school)

上　先　生　家　裡　去
shang⁴ *hsien¹-sheng¹* **chia¹** *li³* **ch'ü⁴**
Towards teacher house in go, (To go to the teacher's)

93. Adverbs of Place. The following adverbs are formed with 上 **shang⁴** — to, towards, and 從 **ts'ung²** — from :

(a)　上　這　兒　(裡) ｜ Towards here,
　　　shang⁴ *che-'rh⁴* *(li³)* ｜ (Hither) (Here)

　　　上　那　兒　(裡) ｜ Towards there,
　　　shang⁴ *na-'rh⁴* *(li³)* ｜ (Thither) (There)

　　　上　那　兒　(裡)? ｜ Towards where ?
　　　shang⁴ *na-'rh³* *(li³)* ? ｜ (Whither ?) (Where to ?)

(b)　從　這　兒　(裡) ｜
　　　ts'ung² *che-'rh⁴* *(li³)* ｜ From here, Hence

　　　從　那　兒　(裡) ｜
　　　ts'ung² *na-'rh⁴* *(li³)* ｜ From there, Thence

　　　從　那　兒　(裡)? ｜ From where ? Whence ?
　　　ts'ung² *na-'rh³* *(li³)* ? ｜ Where from ?

94. 上街 **shang⁴ chieh¹** is translated in this lesson as : up the street. It is a vague expression which implies : to go out, to go for a walk.

LESSON 23

I

從這裡(兒) tsung² che⁴-li³ (-'rh⁴) from here, hence

1. Nin² ts'ung² che-'rh⁴ shang⁴ na-'rh³ ch'ü⁴?
   Wo³ ts'ung² che⁴-li³ shang⁴ chieh¹ mai³ i¹-shang¹ ch'ü⁴.
   Nin² yao⁴ mai³ shen²-ma¹ yen²-se⁴-ti¹ i¹-shang¹?
   Wo³ yao⁴ mai³ i² chien⁴ hei¹-ti¹, i² chien⁴ lan²-ti¹.
2. T'a¹ tso²-t'ien¹ ts'ung² che⁴-li³ shang⁴ na²-li³ ch'ü⁴-la¹?
   Wo³ hai² pu⁴ chih¹-tao⁴ t'a¹ shang⁴ na-'rh³ ch'ü⁴-la¹ na¹.
3. Che⁴ pen³ shu¹ shih⁴ ts'ung² che-'rh⁴ chiang³-ti¹ ma¹?
   Pu² shih⁴, shih⁴ ts'ung² na-'rh⁴ chiang³-ti¹.
4. Nin² ts'ung² che-'rh⁴ shih⁴ shang⁴ hsüeh²-t'ang² ma¹?
   Shih⁴, wo³ ts'ung² che-'rh⁴ shang⁴ hsüeh²-t'ang².
5. Na⁴ chi³ wan³ k'a¹-fei⁴ shih⁴ ts'ung² che-'rh⁴ kei³ t'a¹-men² na²-ch'ü⁴-ti¹ ma¹?
   Tui⁴-la¹, shih⁴ ts'ung² che-'rh⁴ na²-ch'ü⁴-ti¹.

1. Where are you going from here?
   I am going up the street from here to buy clothes.
   What colour clothes will you buy?
   I will buy one black one and one blue one.
2. Where did he go to from here yesterday?
   I don't know yet where he went to.
3. Is this book explained from here (on)?
   No, it is explained from there (on).

4. Will you go to school from here?
   Yes, I will go to school from here.
5. Were those cups of coffee brought to them from here?
   Right, (they) were brought from here.

II

學校 hsüeh²-hsiao⁴
school(s)

大學校 ta⁴-hsüeh²-hsiao⁴
High School(s), University

中學校 chung¹-hsüeh²-hsiao⁴
Middle School(s)

小學校 hsiao³-hsüeh²-hsiao⁴
Primary School(s)

1. Nin²-ti¹ chang⁴-fu¹ shih⁴ ta⁴-hsüeh²-hsiao⁴-ti¹ hsien¹-sheng¹ ma¹?
   Shih⁴, t'a¹ shih⁴ ta⁴-hsüeh²-hsiao⁴-ti¹ hsien¹-sheng¹.
2. Nin²-ti¹ ku¹-niang² tsai⁴ shen²-ma¹ hsüeh²-hsiao⁴ nien⁴ shu¹ na¹? T'a¹ tsai⁴ ta⁴-hsüeh²-hsiao⁴ nien⁴ shu¹.
3. Tsai⁴ che-'rh⁴ yu³ hsiao³-hsüeh²-hsiao⁴ mei² yu³?
   Tsai⁴ che⁴-li³ yu³ hen³ to¹-ti¹ hsiao³-hsüeh²-hsiao⁴ na¹.
4. Tsai⁴ hsiao³-hsüeh²-hsiao⁴ nien⁴ wan²-la¹ shu¹, chiu⁴ yao⁴ shang⁴ shen²-ma¹ hsüeh²-hsiao⁴ nien⁴ shu¹ ch'ü⁴?
   Yao⁴ shang⁴ chung¹-hsüeh²-hsiao⁴ nien⁴ shu¹ ch'ü⁴.
5. Na⁴ so³ hung² fang²-tzu¹ shih⁴ chung¹-hsüeh²-hsiao⁴ shih⁴ hsiao³-hsüeh²-hsiao⁴?
   Shih⁴ chung¹-hsüeh²-hsiao⁴.

6. *Na⁴ chi³ wei⁴ hsüeh²-sheng¹ shih⁴* **shen²-ma¹** *hsüeh²-hsiao⁴-ti¹* **hsüeh²-sheng¹** *?*
   T'a¹-men² shih⁴ **ta⁴-hsüeh²-hsiao⁴-ti¹** *hsüeh²-sheng¹.*

1. Is your husband a University teacher ?
   Yes, he is a University teacher.
2. At what school is your daughter studying ?
   She is studying at a University.
3. Is there a Primary School here ?
   There are a great many Primary Schools here.
4. When (one) has finished studying at a Primary School, what school will (one) go to to study.
   (One) will go to a Middle School to study.
5. Is that red house a Middle School or a Primary School ?
   It is a Middle School.
6. What school are those (several) students from ?
   They are University students.

III

事情 shih⁴-*ch'ing*²
business, affair(s), work

(○件事情) — *chien⁴ shih⁴-ch'ing²*
— business, — affair(s)

事 shih⁴
business, affair(s), work

1. *Nin² chin¹-t'ien¹ yu³* shih⁴-*ch'ing² mei² yu³ ?*
   Wo³ chin¹-t'ien¹ yu³ shih⁴-*ch'ing².*

LESSON 23

2. *Nin² ch'in¹-t'ien¹ yu³ shen²-ma¹ shih⁴?*
   Wo³ yao⁴ mai³ tung¹-hsi¹ ch'ü⁴.
3. *Ch'ing³ wen⁴, Ch'ien² hsien¹-sheng¹-ti¹ shih⁴-ch'ing² hao³ pu⁴ hao³? T'a¹-ti¹ shih⁴-ch'ing² pu² ta⁴ hao³.*
4. *T'a¹ tso²-t'ien¹ mei² yu³ shih⁴-ch'ing², chin¹-t'ien¹ yeh³ mei² yu³ shih⁴-ch'ing² ma¹?*
   T'a¹ chin¹-t'ien¹ yeh³ mei² shih⁴-ch'ing².
5. *Chang¹ hsien¹-sheng¹ tso⁴ shen²-ma¹ shih⁴-ch'ing² na¹?*
   Wo³ hai² pu⁴ chih¹-tao⁴ t'a¹ tso⁴ shen²-ma¹ shih⁴-ch'ing² [na¹.
6. *Wo³ yu³ i² chien⁴ shih⁴-ch'ing² yao⁴ ken¹ nin² shuo¹.*
   Ch'ing³ shuo¹.
7. *Che⁴ chien⁴ shih⁴-ch'ing² shih⁴ wo³-ti¹, na⁴ chien⁴ shih⁴-ch'ing² shih⁴ t'a¹-ta¹.*
8. *Hsien¹-sheng¹ yu³ hsien¹-sheng¹-ti¹ shih⁴-ch'ing², hsüeh²-sheng¹ yu³ hsüeh²-sheng¹-ti¹ shih⁴-ch'ing².*

1. Have you any work today? Today I have some work.
2. What business have you got today?
   I want to go (out) and buy some things.
3. May I ask (you), how are Mr. Ch'ien's affairs?
   (Mr. Ch'ien's business good not good?)
   His affairs are not doing very well.
   (His affairs not big good.)
4. Yesterday he had no business, has he also no business Today he also has no business.   [today?
5. What sort of work does Mr. Chang do?
   I still don't know what sort of work he does.

6. I have a piece of business (that I) want to talk to you (about). Please tell me. (Please say.)
7. This affair is mine, that affair is his.
8. The teacher has the teacher's business, the pupil has the pupil's business.

IV

火車站 huo³-ch'e¹-chan⁴
railway station(s)

車票 ch'e¹-p'iao⁴
railway ticket(s), (bus ticket, tram ticket, etc.)

1. *Nin² shang⁴ na-'rh³ ch'ü⁴-la¹?*
   Wo³ shang⁴ huo³-ch'e¹-chan⁴ ch'ü⁴-la¹.
2. *Nin² shang⁴ huo³-ch'e¹-chan⁴ tso⁴ shen²-ma¹ ch'ü⁴-la¹?*
   Wo³ mai³ ch'e¹-p'iao⁴ ch'ü⁴-la¹.
3. *Nin² kei³ shui² mai³ ch'e¹-p'iao⁴ ch'ü⁴-la¹?*
   Wo³ kei³ Pai² hsien¹-sheng¹ mai³ ch'e¹-p'iao⁴ ch'ü⁴-la¹.
4. *Chin¹-t'ien¹ huo³-ch'e¹-chan⁴ jen² to¹ pu⁴ to¹?*
   Chin¹-t'ien¹ jen² pu⁴ shao³.
5. *Che⁴ chang¹ ch'e¹-p'iao⁴ shih⁴ lü⁴-ti¹, na⁴ chang¹ shih⁴ shen²-ma¹ yen²-se⁴-ti¹? Na⁴ chang¹ shih⁴ huang²-ti¹.*

1. Where have you been to?
   I have been to the railway station.
2. What did you go to the railway station for?
   I went to buy a railway ticket.
3. Whom did you go and buy a ticket for?
   I went to buy a ticket for Mr. Pai.

LESSON 23

4. Were there many people at the railway station today?
   There were many poeple today. (Today people not few.)
5. This railway ticket is green, what colour is that one?
   That one is yellow.

V

郵政局 yu²-cheng⁴-chū²
post-office(s), The Chinese Post Office

郵票 yu²-p'iao⁴
postage stamp(s)

(一分票) I⁴ fen¹ p'iao⁴
one cent postage stan..

(三分票) san¹ fen¹ p'iao⁴
three cent postage stamp

(半分票) pan⁴ fen¹ p'iao⁴
half-cent postage stamp

來信 lai² hsin⁴
to receive a letter

去信 ch'ü⁴ hsin⁴
to send a letter

回信 hui²-hsin⁴
reply (answer) to a letter

票 p'iao⁴
ticket(s), bank-note(s), warrant(s)

1. Ch'ing³ wen⁴ nin² na¹, che⁴ t'iao² chieh¹ shang⁴ yu³ yu²-cheng⁴-ch'ū² mei² yu³?
   Che⁴ t'iao² chieh¹ shang⁴ yu³ yu²-cheng⁴-chü².
2. Nin² yao⁴ shang⁴ yu²-cheng⁴-chü² ma¹?
   Tui⁴-la¹, wo³ yao⁴ shang⁴ yu²-cheng⁴-chü².

3. *Nin² shang⁴ yu²-cheng⁴-chü² tso⁴ shen²-ma¹ ch'ü⁴?*
   Wo³ yao⁴ mai³ yu²-p'iao⁴ ch'ü⁴.
4. *Nin² mai³ yu²-p'iao⁴ tso⁴ shen²-ma¹?*
   Wo³ yao⁴ kei³ wo³ mu³-ch'in¹ hsieh³ hsin⁴.
5. *Nin² mu³ ch'in¹ kei³ nin² lai² hsin⁴ la¹ ma¹?*
   Kei³ wo³ lai² hsin⁴ la¹.
6. *Shih⁴ to¹-tsan² lai²-ti¹ hsin⁴?*
   Shih⁴ tso²-t'ien¹ lai²-ti¹ hsin⁴.
7. *Nin² yao⁴ kei³ shui² ch'ü⁴ hsin⁴?*
   Wo³ yao⁴ kei³ Lan² hsien¹-sheng¹ ch'ü⁴ hsin⁴.
8. *Che⁴ liang³ feng¹ hsin⁴ tou¹ shih⁴ kei³ Kuan¹ hsien¹-sheng¹ ch'ü⁴-ti¹ hsin⁴ m i¹?*
   Pu² shih⁴, i⁴ feng¹ shih⁴ kei³ wo³ mu³-ch'in¹ ch'ü⁴-ti¹, i⁴ feng¹ shih⁴ kei³ Kuan¹ hsien¹-sheng¹ ch'ü⁴-ti¹.
9. *Nin² kei³ t'a¹-men² ch'ü⁴ hsin⁴, t'a¹-men² lai² hui²-hsin⁴ ma¹? T'a¹-men² lai² hui²-hsin⁴.*
10. *Che⁴ shih⁴ i⁴ fen¹ p'iao⁴, na⁴ shih⁴ chi³ fen¹ p'iao⁴?*
    Na⁴ shih⁴ pan⁴ fen¹ p'iao⁴.
11. *Yu³ pan⁴ fen¹ p'iao⁴, i⁴ fen⁴ p'iao⁴, hai² yu³ chi³ fen¹-ti¹?*
    Hai² yu³ ssu⁴ fen¹-ti¹, wu³ fen¹-ti¹, shen²-ma¹-ti¹.
12. *Che⁴ chang¹ p'iao⁴ shih⁴ chi³ fen¹-ti¹?*
    Che⁴ chang¹ p'iao⁴ shih⁴ ssu⁴ fen¹-ti¹.
13. *Nin² yao⁴ mai³ chi³ fen¹ p'iao⁴?*
    Wo³ yao⁴ mai³ liang³ chang¹ wu³ fen¹-ti¹, ssu⁴ chang¹ i⁴ fen¹-ti¹.
14. *Nin² yu³ san¹ fen¹-ti¹ yu²-p'iao⁴ ma¹?*
    Wo³ mei² yu³ san¹ fen¹-ti¹, wo³ yu³ i⁴ fen¹-ti¹.

LESSON 23

15. **Che⁴** *chang¹* **p'lao⁴ shih⁴ shen²**-*ma¹* *p'iao⁴?*
    Che⁴ chang¹ shih⁴ ch'e¹-p'iao⁴.

1. May I ask you, is there a post-office in this street?
   There is a post-office in this street.
2. Do you want (to go) to the post-office?
   Right, I want (to go) to the post-office.
3. What do you want to go to the post-office for?
   I want to go and buy a postage stamp.
4. What do you want to buy a postage stamp for?
   I want to write a letter to my mother.
5. Have you received a letter from your mother?
   (Your mother give you received letter?)
   I have received a letter. (Give me received letter.)
6. When did you receive the letter?
   I received the letter yesterday.
7. Whom do you want to send a letter to?
   I want to send a letter to Mr. Lan.
8. Are both these two letters to be sent to Mr. Kuan?
   No, one is to be sent to my mother and one is to be sent to Mr. Kuan.
9. You send letters to them, do they send answers?
   They do send answers.
10. This is a one cent stamp, how many cents is that stamp?
    That is a half-cent stamp.
11. There are half-cent stamps and one cent stamps; what other cent stamps are there?
    There are also four cent stamps, five cent stamps and so on.

12. How many cents is this stamp?
    This stamp is a four cent one.
13. How many cents stamps do you want to buy?
    I want to buy two five cent ones and four one cent ones.
14. Have you any three cent postage stamps?
    I haven't any three cent ones, (but) I have one cent ones.
15. What sort of ticket is this?
    This is a railway ticket.

VI

電報局 tien⁴-pao⁴-chü² telegraph office(s)

電報 tien⁴-pao⁴ telegram(s), telegraphic despatch(es)

(○ 份 電 報) — fen⁴ tien⁴-pao⁴ — telegram(s)

打電報 ta³ tien⁴-pao⁴ to despatch (send) a telegram

來電報 lai² tien⁴-pao⁴ to receive a telegram

去電報 ch'ü⁴ tien⁴-pao⁴ to send a telegram

上海 shang⁴-hai³ Shanghai

1. *Nin² tsai⁴ na-'rh³ tso⁴ shih⁴ na¹?*
   Wo³ tsai⁴ tien⁴-pao⁴-chü² tso⁴ shih⁴ na¹.
2. **Che⁴** *fen⁴ tien⁴-pao⁴ shih⁴ shui² lai²-ti¹?*
   Shih⁴ **Mao²** *hsien¹-sheng¹ lai²-ti¹.*

LESSON 23

3. *Nin² shang⁴ tien⁴-pao⁴-chü² tso⁴ shen²-ma¹ ch'ü⁴?*
   Wo³ ta³ tien⁴-pao⁴ ch'ü⁴.
4. *Ta³ tien⁴-pao⁴, I² ke⁴ tzu⁴ to¹-shao³ ch'ien²?*
   I² ke⁴ tzu⁴ I⁴ mao² to¹ ch'ien².
5. *Nin² shih⁴ kei³ Mao² hsien¹-sheng¹ ta³ tien⁴-pao⁴ a¹, shih⁴ kei³ t'a¹ hsieh³ hsin⁴ ni¹?*
   Wo³ hai² shih⁴ kei³ t'a¹ ta³ tien⁴-pao⁴.
6. *Che⁴ fen⁴ tien⁴-pao⁴ shih⁴ ts'ung² na²-li³ lai²-ti¹?*
   Shih⁴ ts'ung² shang⁴-hai³ lai²-ti¹.
7. *Nin² kei³ t'a¹ ch'ü⁴ tien⁴-pao⁴ tso⁴ shen²-ma¹?*
   Wo³ kei³ t'a¹ ch'ü⁴ tien⁴-pao⁴ chiao⁴ t'a¹ shang⁴ che-'rh⁴ lai².

1. Where do you work? (You at where do business?)
   I work at the telegraph office.
2. Who received this telegram? Mr. Mao received it.
3. What are you going to the telegraph office for?
   I am going to send a telegram.
4. How much is one word (when) sending a telegram?
   One word is more than ten cents.
5. Are you (going) to send a telegram to Mr. Mao or (are you going) to write him letter?
   I am (going) to send him a telegram.
6. Where did this telegram come from?
   It came from Shanghai.
7. What are you sending him a telegram for?
   I am sending him a telegram to tell him to come here.

NOTES

95. 學校 hsüeh²-hsiao⁴ — school. 學堂 hsüeh²-t'ang² also means a school. The former is the more usual form in Peiping colloquial.

96. 票 p'iao⁴ means ticket, bank-note or warrant. The following combinations are found in this lesson:

車 ch'e¹	wheeled vehicle	票 p'iao⁴	ticket	車票 ch'e¹-p'iao⁴	railway ticket
郵 yu²	post, mail	票 p'iao⁴	ticket	郵票 yu²-p'iao⁴	postage stamp

97. Postage Stamp Denominations are expressed as follows:

半 pan⁴	half	分 fen¹	cent	票 p'iao⁴	ticket

半分票 pan⁴-fen¹-p'iao⁴ { half-cent stamp

三 san¹	three	分 fen¹	cent	票 p'iao⁴	ticket

三分票 san¹-fen¹-p'iao⁴ { three cent stamp

98. 信 hsin⁴ — letter, 電報 tien⁴-pao⁴ — telegram. The following combinations are formed:-

來 lai²	come, motion towards	信 hsin⁴	letter	來信 lai² hsin⁴	to receive a letter

LESSON 23

來 *lai²* — come, motion towards
電報 *tien⁴-pao⁴* — telegram

來電報 *lai² tien⁴-pao⁴* — to receive a telegram

去 *ch'ü⁴* — go, motion away from
信 *hsin⁴* — letter

去信 *ch'ü⁴ hsin⁴* — to send a letter

去 *ch'ü⁴* — go, motion away from
電報 *tien⁴-pao⁴* — telegram

去電報 *ch'ü⁴ tien⁴-pao⁴* — to send a telegram

打 *ta³* — to strike
電報 *tien⁴-pao⁴* — telegram

打電報 *ta³ tien⁴-pao⁴* — to send a telegram

回 *hui²* — to return
信 *hsin⁴* — letter

回信 *hui²-hsin⁴* — a reply to a letter

回 *hui²* — to return
電報 *tien⁴-pao⁴* — telegram

回電報 *hui² tien⁴-pao⁴* — a reply to a telegram

LESSON 24

I

飯舘子 fan⁴-kuan³-tzu¹
restaurant(s)

1. *Nin² chin¹-t'ien¹ tsai⁴ na-'rh³ ch'ih¹-ti¹ fan⁴?*
   Wo³ tsai⁴ fan⁴-kuan³-tzu¹ ch'ih¹-ti¹ fan⁴.
2. **Shih⁴** *tsai⁴* **chung¹**-*kuo² fan⁴-kuan³-tzu¹ ch'ih¹-ti¹,* **shih⁴** *tsai⁴* **wai⁴**-*kuo²·fan⁴-kuan³-tzu¹ ch'ih¹-ti¹?*
   Shih⁴ tsai⁴ chung¹-kuo² fan⁴-kuan³-tzu¹ ch'ih¹-ti¹.
3. *Na⁴ t'iao² chieh¹ shang⁴ yeh³ yu³ wai⁴-kuo² fan⁴-kuan³-tzu¹ ma¹? Yeh³ yu³ wai⁴-kuo² fan⁴-kuan³-tzu¹.*
4. **Tso²**-*t'ien¹ ni³-men² tsai⁴ na⁴ ke⁴ fan⁴-kuan³-tzu¹ ch'ih¹ fan⁴, ch'ih¹-la¹ to¹-shao³ ch'ien²?*
   Ch'ih¹-la¹ wu³ k'uai⁴ to¹ ch'ien².
5. *Ni³-men² ch'ih¹ fan⁴-ti¹* **na⁴** *ke⁴ fan⁴-kuan³-tzu¹ ta⁴* **hsiao³**? *Na⁴ ke⁴ fan⁴-kuan³-tzu¹ pu⁴ hsiao³.*

1. Where did you eat today?
   I ate at a restaurant.
2. Did you eat at a Chinese restaurant or at a foreign res-
   I ate at a Chinese restaurant.   [taurant?
3. Is there also a foreign restaurant on that street?
   There is also a foreign restaurant.
4. How much was the food that you ate yesterday at that restaurant? (ate how much money?)

It cost more than five dollars. (ate five dollars more).
5. Is that restaurant where you eat a large one?
That is a large restaurant.

II

旅舘 lü² ⁽³⁾-*kuan*³
inn(s), hotel(s)

1. *Nin² tsai⁴* **na-rh³ chu⁴ na¹?**
   Wo³ tsai⁴ lü²-**kuan³ chu⁴ na¹.**
2. *Tsai⁴* **na³ ke⁴** *lü²-kuan³* **chu⁴ na¹?**
   Tsai⁴ **na⁴ ke⁴ wai⁴-kuo²** *lü²-kuan³* **chu⁴ na¹.**
3. *Nin² tsai⁴* **na⁴ ke⁴** *lü²-kuan³* **chu⁴ chi³ chien¹ wu¹-tzu¹?**
   Chu⁴ liang³ chien¹ wu¹-tzu¹.
4. *To¹-shao³ ch'ien² i⁴ chien¹?*
   Ssu⁴-shih² k'uai⁴-ch'ien² i⁴ chien¹.
5. *Na⁴ ke⁴ lü²-kuan³-ti¹* **wu¹-tzu¹ ta⁴ pu² ta⁴?**
   Wu¹-tzu¹ pu² ta⁴.
6. *Nin² tsai⁴ lü²-kuan³* **chu⁴,** *yeh³ tsai⁴ lü²-kuan³* **ch'ih¹ fan⁴ ma¹?** *Yeh³ tsai⁴ na-'rh⁴ ch'ih¹ fan⁴.*

1. Where are you living? I am living at an inn.
2. What inn are you living at? At that foreign inn.
3. How many rooms do you occupy (live in) at that inn?
   I occupy two rooms.
4. How much is it for one (room)?
   Forty dollars for one (room).

5. Are the rooms in that inn big ? The rooms are not big.
6. You live in the inn and do you also eat in the inn ?
    I also eat there.

III

電影院 tien⁴-*ying*³-yuan⁴
cinema(s)

片子 p'ien⁴-*tzu*¹
film(s)

演電影兒 yen³ *tien*⁴-*ying*³-*erh*²
to show motion pictures (movies)

看電影兒 k'an⁴ *tien*⁴-*ying*³-*erh*²
to look at (to see) motion pictures (movies)

1. Na⁴ *shih*⁴ shen²-*ma*¹ ti⁴-*fang*¹ ?
   Na⁴ *shih*⁴ tien⁴-ying³-yuan⁴.
2. Tien⁴-ying³-yuan⁴ *shih*⁴ tso⁴ shen²-*ma*¹-*ti*¹ ti⁴-*fang*¹ ?
   Tien⁴-ying³-yuan⁴ *shih*⁴ yen³ *tien*⁴-*ying*³-*erh*²-*ti*¹ *ti*⁴-*fang*¹.
3. Tso²-*t'ien*¹ shang⁴ na-'rh³ ch'ü⁴-*la*¹ ?
   Wo³ k'an⁴ tien⁴-ying³-erh² ch'ü⁴-*la*¹.
4. Tso²-*t'ien*¹-*ti*¹ p'ien⁴-*tzu*¹ hao³ pu⁴ hao³ ?
   Tso²-*t'ien*¹-*ti*¹ *p'ien*⁴-*tzu*¹ hen² hao³ *la*¹.
5. Nin² k'an⁴-*ti*¹ *shih*⁴ chung¹-*kuo*² p'ien⁴-*tzu*¹ ma¹ ?
   Shih⁴ *chung*¹-*kuo*² *p'ien*⁴-*tzu*¹.
6. Nin² k'an⁴ wai⁴-*kuo*² p'ien⁴-*tzu*² pu² k'an⁴ ?
   Wo³ yeh³ k'an⁴ *wai*⁴-*kuo*² *p'ien*⁴-*tzu*¹.

1. What is that place ? That is a cinema.

LESSON 24

2. What sort of a place is a cinema?
   A cinema is a place (where they) show motion pictures.
3. Where did you go to yesterday? I went to see a movie.
4. Was yesterday's film a good one?
   Yesterday's film was very good.
5. Did you see a Chinese film? It was a Chinese film.
6. Do you (go) and see foreign films?
   I also see foreign films.

IV

戲 hsi⁴ play(s)

戲園子 hsi⁴-yuan²-tzu¹ theatre(s)

看戲 k'an⁴ hsi⁴ to see a play

聽戲 t'ing¹ hsi⁴ to see (hear) a play

唱 ch'ang⁴ to sing, (to act)

1. *Ch'ing*³ **wen⁴ nin² na¹, na⁴ shih⁴ hsi⁴-yuan²-*tzu*¹ pu² shih⁴?** Na⁴ shih⁴ hsi⁴-yuan²-*tzu*¹.
2. Chin¹-*t'ien*¹ yu³ hsi⁴ mei² yu³? Chin¹-*t'ien*¹ yu³ hsi⁴.
3. Nin² shih⁴ yao⁴ k'an⁴ *t'ien*⁴-ying³-erh² shih⁴ yao⁴ t'ing¹ hsi⁴? Wo³ yao⁴ t'ing¹ hsi⁴.
4. *Tso*²-*t'ien*¹ na⁴ ke⁴ hsi⁴-yuan²-*tzu*¹ k'an⁴ hsi⁴-*ti*¹ to¹ pu⁴ to¹? K'an⁴ hsi⁴-*ti*¹ pu⁴ shao³.
5. K'an⁴ tien⁴-ying³-erh² yao⁴ mai³ p'iao⁴, *t'ing*¹ hsi⁴ yeh³ yao⁴ mai³ p'iao⁴ ma¹? K'an⁴ hsi⁴ yeh³ yao⁴ mai³ p'iao⁴.

6. **Chin¹-t'ien¹ t'a¹-men² ch'ang⁴-ti¹, shih⁴ chung¹-kuo² hsi⁴ shih⁴ wai⁴-kuo² hsi¹ ?**
Chin¹-t'ien¹ t'a¹-men² ch'ang⁴-ti¹ shih⁴ chung¹-kuo² hsi⁴.
7. *Nin² hui⁴ ch'ang⁴ chung¹-kuo² hsi⁴ ma¹ ? Wo³ pu² hui⁴.*

1. Please tell me, that is a theatre isn't it ?
   That is a theatre.
2. Is there a play today ?   There is a play today.
3. Do you want to see a movie or do you want to see a play ?
   I want to see a play.
4. Were there many people seeing the play at that theatre yesterday ?
   There were many (not a few) people seeing the play.
5. One must (is required) to buy a ticket to see a movie, must one also buy a ticket to see a play ?
   One must also buy a ticket to see a play.
6. Are they acting (singing) a Chinese or a foreign play [today ?
   They are acting a Chinese play today.
7. Can you sing Chinese plays ?   I can't.

V

商人 **shang¹-jen²**
merchant(s), trader(s)

作買賣 **tso⁴ mai³-mai⁴**
to buy and sell, to trade

作買賣的 **tso⁴ mai³-mai⁴-ti¹**
merchant(s), trader(s), one who buys and sells

1. *Na⁴ wei⁴ shih⁴ tso⁴ shen²-ma¹-ti¹ ?*
   Na⁴ wei⁴ shih⁴ shang¹-jen².

LESSON 24

2. Shen²-ma¹ shih⁴ shang¹-jen²?
   Shang¹-jen² shih⁴ tso⁴ mai³-mai⁴-ti¹.
3. Tso⁴ mai³-mai⁴-ti¹ tsai⁴ na-'rh³ tso⁴ mai³-mai⁴?
   Tso⁴ mai³-mai⁴-ti¹ tsai⁴ p'u⁴-tzu¹ li³ tso⁴ mai³-mai⁴.
4. Na⁴ ke⁴ jen² shih⁴ tso⁴ shen²-ma¹ mai³-mai⁴-ti¹?
   T'a¹ shih⁴ mai⁴ cho¹-I³-ti¹.
5. Che⁴ ke⁴ ti⁴-fang¹ yeh³ yu³ wai⁴-kuo² shang¹-jen² ma¹?
   Che⁴ ke⁴ ti⁴-fang¹ wai⁴-kuo² shang¹-jen² pu⁴ shao³ na¹.

1. What does that man do? That man is a merchant.
2. What is a merchant?
   A merchant is one who buys and sells.
3. Where do merchants trade?
   Merchants buy and sell in shops.
4. What sort of trade does that man do?
   He is a furniture merchant. (He deals in furniture.)
5. Are there also any foreign merchants in this place?
   There are many (not a few) foreign merchants in this place.

VI

書記 shu¹-chi⁴
secretary, clerk(s)

1. Ni³-men² hsüeh²-hsiao⁴ yu³ chi³ ke⁴ shu¹-chi⁴?
   Yu³ liang³ ke⁴ shu¹-chi⁴.
2. Shu¹-chi⁴ shih⁴ tso⁴ shen²-ma¹-ti¹?
   Shu¹-chi⁴ shih⁴ hsieh³-tzu⁴-ti¹.

3. Na⁴ liang³ ke⁴ shu¹-chi⁴ hui⁴ hsieh³ na³ kuo² tzu⁴?
I² ke⁴ hui⁴ hsieh³ chung¹-kuo² tzu⁴, I² ke⁴ hui⁴ hsieh³ wai⁴-kuo² tzu⁴.

4. Chang¹ hsien¹-sheng¹ chiao⁴ na⁴ ke⁴ shu¹-chi⁴ hsieh³ shen²-ma¹ na¹? T'a¹ chiao⁴ t'a¹ hsieh³ hsin⁴ na¹.

5. Na⁴ ke⁴ hsieh³-tzu⁴-ti¹ shih⁴ shu¹-chi⁴ pu² shih⁴?
T'a¹ pu² shih⁴ shu¹-chi⁴, t'a¹ shih⁴ hsüeh²-sheng¹.

1. How many clerks are there in your school?
   There are two clerks.
2. What does a clerk do?
   A clerk is (one who) writes.
3. What language (letters) can those two clerks write?
   One can write Chinese characters and the other can write foreign letters.
4. What is Mr. Chang telling that clerk to write?
   He is telling him to write a letter.
5. That writer is a clerk isn't he?
   He isn't a clerk, he is a student.

VII

裁縫 t'sai²-feng² tailor(s)

1. Tso²-t'ien¹ lai²-ti¹ na⁴ ke⁴ jen² shih⁴ tso⁴ shen²-ma¹-ti¹? T'a¹ shih⁴ tso⁴ i¹-shang¹-ti¹.
2. Tso⁴ i¹-shang¹-ti¹ chiao⁴ shen²-ma¹?
   Tso⁴ i¹-shang¹-ti¹ chiao⁴ t'sai²-feng².
3. Na⁴ ke⁴ t'sai²-feng² hsing⁴ shen²-ma¹?
   T'a¹ hsing⁴ Mao².

LESSON 24

4. *Ts'ai²-feng² tso²-t'ien¹* tso⁴ shen²-*ma¹* lal²-*la¹* ?
   Wo³ yao⁴ *chiao⁴ t'a¹ kei³ wo³* tso⁴ *i⁴ chien⁴ i¹-shang¹*.
5. Na⁴ ke⁴ *t'sai²-feng² hui⁴ tso⁴ chung¹-kuo² i¹*-shang¹, yeh³ hui⁴ *tso⁴ wai⁴-kuo² i¹*-shang¹ *ma¹* ?
   T'a¹ hui⁴ *tso⁴ wai⁴-kuo² i¹-shang¹*, yeh³ *hui⁴ tso⁴ chung¹-kuo² i¹-shang¹*.

1. What does that man (who) came yesterday do ?
   He is (a man who) makes clothes.
2. What is a man who makes clothes called ?
   A man who makes clothes is called a tailor.
3. What is the name of that tailor ? His name is Mao.
4. What did the tailor come for yesterday ?
   I want to order him to make an article of clothing for me.
5. Can that tailor make Chinese clothes and also foreign clothes ?
   He can make foreign clothes and he can also make Chinese clothes.

VIII

回來 **huì²-lai²**
to return, to come back

回去 **huì²-ch'ü⁴**
to return, to go back

回國 **huì²-kuo²**
to return to one's native country

(回家來) **huì² chia¹** *lai²*
to return home, to come back home

(回家去) **huì² chia¹** *ch'ü⁴*
to return home, to go back home

北平 **pei³-p'ing²**
Peiping, (Peking)

南京 **nan²-*ching*¹**
Nanking

1. **Pai²** *hsien¹-sheng¹* **huì²-*lai²*-*la*¹** *mei² yu³* ?
   Hai² *mei² huì²-lai² na*¹.
2. **Nin²** **yao⁴** **huì²-ch'ü⁴** **ma**¹ ? **Shih⁴,** *wo³* **yao⁴** **huì²-ch'ü⁴**.
3. **Nin²** *ts'ung² che-'rh⁴* **chiu⁴** **huì²-ch'ü⁴** **ma¹** ?
   Shih⁴, *wo³ ts'ung² che-'rh⁴* **chiu⁴** **huì²-ch'ü⁴**.
4. **Ni³-*men² liang³ ke⁴ jen²* i²-k'uai-'rh⁴** **huì² chia¹** *ch'ü⁴ ma¹* ? **Wo³** **huì² chia¹** *ch'ü⁴*, **t'a¹ pu⁴** **huì² chia¹** *ch'ü⁴*.
5. **T'a¹ shih⁴ ts'ung² na-'rh³** **huì²-*lai²-ti*¹** ?
   T'a¹ shih⁴ ts'ung² Shang⁴-hai³ **huì²-*lai²-ti*¹**.
6. **Nin² ts'ung² yü²-cheng⁴-chü²** **hai² yao⁴ shang⁴ na-'rh³ ch'ü⁴ ma¹** ? **Pu² shang⁴ na²-li³ ch'ü⁴-la¹,** *wo³ ts'ung² che⁴-li³* **chiu⁴ yao⁴** **huì² chia¹** *ch'ü⁴-la¹*.

LESSON 24

7. *Nin² shih⁴ ts'ung² hsi⁴-yuan²-tzu¹* **hui²**-*lai²-ti¹ ma¹*?
   Shih⁴, **shih⁴** *ts'ung² hsi⁴-yuan²-tzu¹ hui²-lai²-ti¹*.
8. *Nin²-ti¹ chang⁴-fu¹ shang⁴ na-'rh³ ch'ü⁴-la¹*?
   T'a¹ **hui²**-*kuo²-la¹*.
9. *Nin²-ti¹ t'ai⁴-t'ai⁴ shang⁴ Pei³-p'ing² ch'ü⁴-la¹*, *to¹-tsan²* **hui²**-*lai²*? *Ming²-t'ien¹* **hui²**-*lai²*.
10. *T'a¹ to¹-tsan² ts'ung² Nan²-ching¹* **hui²**-*lai²*?
    T'a¹ chin¹-t'ien¹ chiu⁴ hui²-lai².   ⌊*lai²-la¹*?
11. *T'a¹-men² hui²-kuo² ch'ü⁴-la¹*, **hai²** **hui²**-*lai²* **pu⁴** *hui²-*
    Wo³ **pu⁴** *chih¹-tao⁴ hai² hui²-lai² pu⁴ hui²-lai²-la¹*.
12. *Ni³* **hai²** **hui²** *hsüeh²-hsiao⁴ ch'ü⁴ ma¹*?
    Shih⁴, *wo³* **hai²** **hui²** *hsüeh²-hsiao⁴ ch'ü⁴*.
13. *Nin² shang⁴ huo³-ch'e¹-chan⁴ ch'ü⁴*, **hai²** **hui²**-*lai²* **pu⁴** *hui²-lai² ni¹*?
    Pu⁴ *hui²-lai²-la¹*, *wo³ ts'ung² huo³-ch'e¹-chan⁴* **hai²** *yao⁴ shang⁴ tien⁴-ying³-yuan⁴ ch'ü⁴*.
14. *T'a¹ ts'ung² Pei³-p'ing² hui² Nan²-ching¹ ch'ü⁴ ma¹*?
    Shih⁴, *hui² Nan²-ching¹ ch'ü⁴*.
15. *Hui² Nan²-ching¹ tso⁴ shen²-ma¹ ch'ü⁴-la¹*?
    K'an⁴ t'a¹-ti¹ fu⁴-mu³ ch'ü⁴-la¹.
16. *T'a¹ shih⁴ hui² Pei³-p'ing² ch'ü⁴-la¹ ma¹*?
    Shih⁴, *t'a¹ hui² Pei³-p'ing² ch'ü⁴-la¹*.
17. *Shu¹-chi⁴* **hui²**-*lai¹-la¹ mei² yu³*?
    Hai² **mei²** *hui²-lai²*.
18. *Na⁴ ke⁴ shang¹-jen² shih⁴ tso²-t'ien¹ hui²-kuo² lai²-.a¹*.

1. Has Mr. Pai returned? He has not returned yet.
2. Do you want to go back? Yes, I want to go back.

3. Will you return from here?
   Yes, I shall return from here.
4. Are you two men going home together?
   I am going home, he is not going home.
5. Where has he returned from?
   He has come back from Shanghai.
6. Where will you go from the post-office?
   I won't go anywhere, I will just go back home from [here.
7. Have you returned from the theatre?
   Yes, I have returned from the theatre.
8. Where has your husband gone to?
   He has returned to his own country.
9. Your wife has gone to Peiping, when will she return?
   She will return tomorrow.
10. When will he come back from Nanking?
    He will return today.
11. They have returned to their native country, will they come back again?
    I don't know whether they will come back or not.
12. Are you going back to school again?
    Yes, I am going back to school.
13. You are going to the railway station, are you coming back or not?
    I won't come back, I will go to the cinema from the railway station.
14. Is he returning to Nanking from Peiping?
    He is returning to Nanking.
15. What did he return to Nanking for?
    He went to see his parents.

LESSON 24

16. Has he returned to Peiping?
    Yes, he has retuned to Peiping.
17. Has the clerk come back? He has not come back yet.
18. That merchant returned from his native country yesterday.

NOTES

99. 他 是 作 甚 麼 的?   He is a do what
    t'a¹ shih⁴ tso⁴ shen²-ma¹-ti¹?   (man)?
    (What does he do?)

    The answer to this enquiry may be:—

    他 是 寫 字 的   He is a writer
    t'a¹ shih⁴ hsieh³-tzu⁴-ti¹   (He is a clerk)
    [書 記 sh'u¹-chi⁴]

    他 是 作 飯 的   He is a make food (man)
    t'a¹ shih⁴ tso⁴-fan⁴-ti¹   (He is a cook)
    [廚 子 ch'u²-tzu¹]

    他 是 作 買 賣 的   He is a do trade
    t'a¹ shih⁴ tso⁴ mai³-mai⁴-ti¹   (man)
    [商 人 shang¹-jen²]   (He is a merchant)

    他 是 作 衣 裳 的   He is a make clothes
    t'a¹ shih⁴ tso⁴ i¹-shang¹-ti¹   (man)
    [裁 縫 ts'ai²-feng²]   (He is a tailor)

100. 回 來 hui²-lai², 回 去 hui²-ch'ü⁴.

    回   to return   來   come,
    hui²   lai²   motion towards

回 來　to return here,
huí²-lai²　to come back

回　　　　　　　去　　go,
huí²　to return　**ch'ü⁴**　motion away from

回 去　to return there,
huí²-ch'ü⁴　to go back

The object is usually inserted between 回 *huí²* and 來 *lai²* or 去 *ch'ü⁴*:

回　家　來
huí² chia¹ lai²　to come back home

回　家　去
huí² chia¹ ch'ü⁴　to go back home

回　學　校　來
huí² *hsüeh²-hsiao⁴ lai²*　to come back to school

回　學　校　去
huí² *hsüeh²-hsiao⁴ ch'ü⁴*　to go back to school

LESSON 25

I

作飯的 tso⁴-fan⁴-ti¹
one who prepares (cooks) food, cook

廚子 ch'u²-tzu¹
cook(s)

1. *Nin² chia¹ li³ yu³ tso⁴-fan⁴-ti¹ mei² yu³?*
   Yu³ i² ke⁴ tso⁴-fan⁴-ti¹.
2. *Tso⁴-fan⁴-ti¹ chiao⁴ shen²-ma¹?*
   Tso⁴-fan⁴-ti¹ chiao⁴ ch'u²-tzu¹.
3. *Nin²-ti¹ tso⁴-fan⁴-ti¹ hui⁴ tso⁴ chung¹-kuo² fan⁴, hui⁴ tso⁴ wai⁴-kuo² fan⁴ ma¹?*
   Chung¹-kuo² fan⁴, wai⁴-kuo² fan⁴, tou¹ hui⁴ tso⁴.
4. *Na⁴ ke⁴ ch'u²-tzu¹ tso⁴-ti¹ fan⁴ hao³ ch'ih¹ pu⁴ hao³ ch'ih¹? T'a¹ tso⁴-ti¹ fan⁴ hen² hao³ ch'ih¹.*
5. *Nin² yao⁴ kao⁴-su⁴ ch'u²-tzu¹ shen²-ma¹ hua⁴?*
   Wo³ yao⁴ kao⁴-su⁴ t'a¹ chin¹-t'ien¹ to¹ tso⁴ i² ke⁴ jen²-ti¹ fan⁴.

1. Is there someone who cooks the food in your home?
   There is someone who cooks the food.
2. What is a man who cooks food called?
   A man who cooks food is called a cook.
3. Can your cook make Chinese food or foreign food?
   He can cook both Chinese and foreign food.

4. Is the food that cook makes good (to eat)?
   He makes very good food.
5. What do you want to tell the cook? [today.
   I want to tell him to make food for one more person

II

木匠 mu⁴-chiang⁴
carpenter(s)

1. *Ch'ing³ wen⁴ nin²,* **shen²**-*ma¹ jen² hui⁴ tso⁴* **cho¹-i³?**
   Mu⁴-*chiang⁴ hui⁴ tso⁴* **cho¹-i³**.
2. *Mu⁴-chiang⁴* **hai²** *hui⁴ tso⁴* **shen²**-*ma¹?*
   Hai² hui⁴ tso⁴ **ch'uang¹**-*hu⁴,* **men²,** *shen²-ma¹-ti¹*.
3. *Na⁴ ke⁴* **cho¹**-*i³-p'u⁴ li³ yu³* **chi³** *ke⁴* **mu⁴**-*chiang⁴?*
   Yu³ pu⁴ shao³ mu⁴-chiang⁴ na¹.
4. *Nin² shuo¹ shih⁴ che⁴ ke⁴ mu⁴-chiang⁴ tso⁴-ti¹ cho¹-i³
   hao³ a¹,* **hai²** *shih⁴ na⁴ ke⁴ mu⁴-chiang⁴ tso⁴-ti¹ hao³
   ni¹?* **Hai²** *shih⁴ che⁴ mu⁴-chiang⁴ tso⁴-ti¹ hao³.*
5. *Che⁴ chang¹ cho¹-tzu¹ ken¹ na⁴ chi³ pa² i³-tzu¹ tou¹
   shih⁴ shui² kei³ nin² tso⁴-ti¹?*
   Tou¹ shih⁴ na⁴ ke⁴ mu⁴-chiang⁴ kei³ wo³ tso⁴-ti¹.

1. Please tell me, what kind of man can make furniture?
   A carpenter can make furniture.
2. What else can a carpenter make?
   He can also make windows, doors and so on.
3. How make carpenters are there in that furniture shop?
   There are many carpenters.

LESSON 25

4. Whom do you consider makes furniture better, this carpenter or that carpenter?
   This carpenter makes it better.
5. Who made this table and those chairs for you?
   That carpenter made them all for me.

III

作鞋的 tso⁴-hsieh²-ti¹
one who makes shoes, shoemaker

鞋匠 hsieh²-chiang⁴
shoemaker(s)

1. *T'a¹ shih⁴ tso⁴ shen²-ma¹-ti¹?*
   T'a¹ shih⁴ tso⁴-hsieh²-ti¹.
2. *Tso⁴-hsieh²-ti¹ shih⁴ hsieh²-chiang⁴ pu² shih⁴?*
   Tso⁴-hsieh²-ti¹ shih⁴ hsieh²-chiang⁴.
3. *Na⁴ ke⁴ hsieh²-chiang⁴ tsai⁴ na³ ke⁴ hsieh²-p'u⁴ li³ tso⁴ hsieh²?*
   T'a¹ tsai⁴ na⁴ ke⁴ wai⁴-kuo² hsieh²-p'u⁴ li³ tso⁴ hsieh².
4. *Na⁴ chi³ ke⁴ hsieh²-chiang⁴ hui⁴ tso⁴ chung¹-kuo² hsieh² pu² hui⁴?*
   T'a¹-men² pu² hui⁴ tso⁴ chung¹-kuo² hsieh², t'a¹-men² hui⁴ tso⁴ wai⁴-kuo² hsieh².
5. *Che⁴ liang³ shuang¹ hsieh² shih⁴ na³ ke⁴ hsieh²-chiang⁴ tso⁴-ti¹? Shih⁴ na⁴ ke⁴ wai⁴-kuo² hsieh²-chiang⁴ tso⁴-ti¹.*

1. What does he do? He makes shoes.
2. A man who makes shoes is a shoemaker isn't he?
   A man who makes shoes is a shoemaker.

3. In which shoe-shop does that shoemaker make shoes?
   He makes shoes in that foreign shoe-shop.
4. Can those shoemakers make Chinese shoes?
   They can't make Chinese shoes, (but) they can make foreign shoes.
5. Which shoemaker made these two pairs of shoes?
   That foreign shoemaker made (them).

IV

買東西的 mai³-tung¹-hsi¹-ti¹ one who buys things, buyer
賣東西的 mai⁴-tung¹-hsi¹-ti¹ one who sells things, seller

1. Wo³-men² shang⁴ p'u⁴-tzu¹ mai³ tung¹-hsi¹, wo³-men² shih⁴ tso⁴ shen²-ma¹-ti¹?
   Wo³-men² shih⁴ mai³-tung¹-hsi¹-ti¹.
2. Tso⁴ mai³-mai⁴-ti¹ chiao⁴ shang¹-jen², hai² chiao⁴ shen²-ma¹? Hai² chiao⁴ mai⁴-tung¹-hsi¹-ti.
3. Na⁴ t'iao² chieh¹ shang⁴ mai⁴-tung¹-hsi¹-ti¹ to¹ pu² to¹? Mai⁴-tung¹-hsi¹-ti pu⁴ hen³ to¹.
4. Che⁴ ke⁴ jen² shih⁴ mai⁴ shen²-ma¹-ti¹?
   Wo³ yeh³ pu⁴ chih¹-tao⁴ shih⁴ mai⁴ shen²-ma¹-ti¹.
5. Na⁴ ke⁴ mai³-tung¹-hsi¹-ti¹ ken¹ shui² shuo¹ hua⁴ na¹?
   T'a¹ ken¹ mai⁴-tung¹-hsi¹-ti¹ shuo¹ hua⁴ na¹.

1. (If) we go to the shops to buy things, what do we do?
   We are people who buy things.

LESSON 25

2. One who trades is called a merchant, what else is he called?
   He is also called a seller.
3. Are there many people selling things on that street?
   There are not many people selling things.
4. What does this man sell?
   I don't know what he sells.
5. With whom is that buyer speaking?
   He is speaking to the seller.

V

病 **ping⁴**
sickness, disease, to be ill

得病 **te² ping⁴**
to become ill, to get sick

大夫 **tai⁴-fu¹**
doctor, physician

治 **chih⁴**
to treat (medically) to heal, to cure,

醫院 **i¹-yuan⁴**
hospital

1. Ch'ien² hsien¹-sheng¹ chin¹-t'ien¹ lai²-la¹ mei² yu³?
   T'a¹ mei² lai², t'a¹ ping⁴-la¹.
2. T'a¹ te² shen²-ma¹ ping⁴ la¹?
   Wo³ hai² pu⁴ chih¹-tao⁴ na¹.
3. Chang¹ hsien¹-sheng¹-ti¹ ping⁴ hao³-la¹ mei² yu³?
   Hai² mei² hao³ na¹.
4. T'a¹ ch'ing³ tai⁴-fu¹ la¹ ma¹? Ch'ing³-la¹.

5. **Huang**² *tai*⁴*-fu*¹ **shang**⁴ **na-'rh**³ **ch'ü**⁴*-la*¹ ?
   *T'a*¹ *kei*³ *jen*² **chih**⁴ **ping**⁴ *ch'ü*⁴*-la*¹.
6. *Chih*⁴ *ping*⁴ *ti*¹ *ti*⁴*-fang*¹ **chiao**⁴ **shen**²*-ma*¹ ?
   *Chih*⁴ *ping*⁴ *ti*¹ *ti*⁴*-fang*¹ **chiao**⁴ **i**¹*-*yūan⁴.
7. *Na*⁴ *ke*⁴ *i*¹*-yüan*⁴ *li*³ *yu*³ **to**¹*-*shao³ *wei*⁴ **tai**⁴*-fu*¹ ?
   *Yu*³ **shih**² **chi**³ *wei*⁴ *tai*⁴*-fu*¹.   [*ma*¹ ?
8. *Na*⁴ *ke*⁴ *i*¹*-yüan*⁴ *li*³ *ti*¹ *tai*⁴*-fu*¹ **tou**¹ **shih**⁴ **hao**³ *tai*⁴*-fu*¹
   *Na*⁴ *ke*⁴ *i*¹*-yüan*⁴ *li*³ **mei**² *yu*³ **pu**⁴ *hao*³*-ti*¹ *tai*⁴*-fu*¹.
9. *Kei*³ **nin**² *chih*⁴ *ping*⁴*-ti*¹ *na*⁴ *wei*⁴ *tai*⁴*-fu*¹, **yeh**³ **shih**⁴ *na*⁴ *ke*⁴ *i*¹*-yüan*⁴*-ti*¹ *tai*⁴*-fu*¹ *ma*¹ ?
   Tui⁴*-la*¹, *t'a*¹ **yeh**³ **shih**⁴ *na*⁴ *ke*⁴ *i*¹*-yüan*⁴*-ti*¹ *tai*⁴*-fu*¹.
10. *Che*⁴ *t'iao*² *chieh*¹ *shang*⁴ **chiu**⁴ *yu*³ **i**² *ke*⁴ **i**¹*-*yūan⁴ *ma*¹?
    *Pu*² *shih*⁴, **hai**² *yu*³ *i*² *ke*⁴ **wai**⁴*-kuo*² *i*¹*-yüan*⁴ *na*¹.

1. Has Mr. Ch'ien come today?
   He has not come, he is ill.
2. What sort of sickness has he got? I don't know yet.
3. Is Mr. Chang's illness all right (now)?
   He is still not all right.
4. Has he asked a doctor to come?
   (He has) asked (for one).
5. Where has Dr. Huang gone?
   He has gone to treat a patient (man).
6. What is a place where they treat diseases called?
   A place where they treat diseases is called a hospital.
7. How many doctors are there in that hospital?
   There are ten odd doctors.
8. Are the doctors in that hospital all good doctors?
   There are no bad boctors in that hospital.

9. Is the physician who cured you (also) a physician of that hospital?

Right, he is (also) a physician of that hospital.

10. Is there only one hospital on this street?

No, there is a foreign hospital besides.

VI

辦公 pan⁴ kung¹
to transact business, to work (in an office)

職員 chih²-yüan²
official(s)

當 tang¹
to act as, to be employed as

行 hsing²
it will do!

不行 pu⁴ hsing²
it won't do!

1. Pao¹ *hsien¹-sheng¹* tsai⁴ tien⁴-pao⁴-chü² pan⁴ kung¹ ma¹? *T'a¹* tsai⁴ tien⁴-pao⁴-chü² pan⁴ kung¹.

2. *T'a¹-men²* na-'rh⁴ yu³ to¹-shao³ wei⁴ chih²-yüan²? *Yu³* san¹-shih² to¹ wei⁴.

3. *Hsüeh²-hsiao⁴ li³* yu³ *hsien¹-sheng¹*, yeh³ *yu³* chih²-yüan² ma¹? *Hsüeh²-hsiao⁴ li³* yeh³ yu³ chih²-yüan².

4. *Hsüeh²-hsiao⁴ li³* ti¹ chih²-yüan² yeh³ chiang³ kung¹-k'e⁴ ma¹? *T'a¹-men²* pu⁴ chiang³ kung¹-k'e⁴.

5. *Nin²-ti¹* fu⁴-*ch'in¹* tsai⁴ na⁴ ke⁴ hsüeh²-hsiao⁴ li³ shih⁴ hsien¹-*sheng¹* shih⁴ chih²-yüan²? *T'a¹* shih⁴ chih²-yüan².

6. *Ch'ing³ wen⁴ nin², yu²-cheng⁴-chü²* **ming²-t'ien¹ pan⁴ kung¹ pu² pan⁴ kung¹?** *Ming²-t'ien¹* **pan⁴ kung¹.**
7. *Chih²-yüan² shuo¹ pan⁴ kung¹,* **shang¹-jen² yeh³ shuo¹ pan⁴ kung¹ ma¹?** *Shang¹-jen² yao⁴ shuo¹ tso⁴ mai³-*
8. **Lao² hsien¹-sheng¹ shih⁴ shang¹-jen² ma¹?**   [*mai⁴.*
   T'a¹ pu² shih⁴ shang¹-jen², t'a¹ shih⁴ tien⁴-pao⁴-chü²-ti¹ **chih²-yüan².**
9. *T'a¹ tsai⁴ yu²-cheng⁴-chü²* **tang¹ shu¹-chi⁴ ma¹?**
   Tui⁴-la¹, tang¹ shu¹-chi⁴.
10. *Tang¹ shu¹-chi⁴ ti¹ pu² hui⁴ hsieh³ tzu⁴, hsing² ma¹?*
    Na⁴ pu⁴ hsing².
11. *K'an⁴ tien⁴-ying³-erh² pu⁴ mai³ p'iao⁴,* **hsing² pu⁴ hsing²?** *Pu⁴ mai³ p'iao⁴ pu⁴ hsing².*
12. *T'a¹ te²-ti¹ na⁴ ke⁴ ping⁴ pu² shang⁴ i¹-yüan⁴ chih⁴ ch'ü⁴,* **hsing² pu⁴ hsing²?**
    Pu² shang⁴ i¹-yüan⁴ ch'ü⁴ pu⁴ hsing².

1. Does Mr. Pao work in the telegraph office?
   He does work in the telegraph office.
2. How many officials have they there?
   They have thirty odd.
3. There are teachers in the school, are there also offi-
   There are also officials in the school.   [cials?
4. Do the school officials also give (explain) lessons?
   They don't give lessons.
5. Is your father a teacher or an official in that school?
   He is an official.
6. Please tell me, will the post-office be open tomorrow?

LESSON 25

(Post-office tomorrow transact business not transact business?)

It will be open tomorrow.

7. One says that an official transacts business, does one also say that a merchant transacts business?

One should say that a merchant trades.

8. Is Mr. Lan a merchant?

He isn't a merchant, he is a post-office official.

9. Is he employed as a clerk in the post-office?

Right, he is employed as a clerk.

10. Will it do if one who is employed as a clerk, can't write?

That won't do.

11. Will it do if one doesn't buy a ticket to see a movie?

It won't do not to buy a ticket.

12. Will it do if he doesn't go to hospital to be treated for for that illness he has got?

It won't do if he doesn't go to hospital.

NOTES

101. 得病 **te² ping⁴**

得 / **te²** — to get, to have, to become
病 / **ping⁴** — illness, disease

得病 / **te² ping⁴** — to become sick, to get ill

102. Combinations with 好 **hao³**. This character has been translated as: good, well, all right. It retains its essential meaning in the following cases:

他的病好了
t'a¹-ti¹ ping⁴ hao³-la¹ His sickness all right, (He has recovered)

大夫把他的病治好了
tai⁴-fu⁴ pa³ t'a¹-ti¹ ping⁴ chih⁴ hao³-la¹
The doctor took hold of his sickness cured all right
(The doctor cured his disease)

103. 就 **chiu⁴** is translated in this lesson — para. V, as 'only', which is one of the many translations of this difficult though frequently used character. (see § 62.)

就有一本書
chiu⁴ *yu³ i⁴ pen³ shu¹* Just have one book,
(Have only one book) (There is only one book)

就有一個醫院
chiu⁴ *yu³ i² ke⁴ i¹-yüan⁴* Just have one hospital,
(There is only one hospital)

EXERCISES FOR REVISION

I.	The Family (i)
II.	Shopping (i)
III.	Clothes
IV.	The Restaurant (i)
V.	The House
VI.	At School (i)
VII.	At School (ii)
VIII.	The Family (ii)
IX.	Shopping (ii)
X.	The Post Office
XI.	The Telegraph Office
XII.	The Cinema
XIII.	The Hospital
XIV.	The Restaurant (ii)
XV.	The Hotel
XVI.	Tradesmen

REVISION I

THE FAMILY (i)

家 chia¹   問答 wen⁴-ta²

Q. Nin² kuei⁴ hsing⁴?
A. Chien⁴ hsing⁴ Chang¹.
Q. Nin² tsai⁴ na-'rh³ tso⁴ shih⁴?
A. Wo³ tsai⁴ huo³-ch'e¹-chan⁴ tso⁴ shih⁴.
Q. Nin² chia¹ li³ yu³ chi³ kou-'rh³ jen²?
A. Wo³ chia¹ li³ yu³ ch'i¹ kou-'rh³ jen².
Q. Nin² tou¹ yu³ shen²-ma¹ jen²?
A. Wo³ yu³ fu⁴-ch'in¹, mu³-ch'in¹, wo³ yu³ t'ai⁴-t'ai⁴, hai² yu³ i² ke⁴ erh²-tzu¹, liang³ ke⁴ ku¹-niang².
Q. Nin² fu⁴-ch'in¹ shih⁴ tso⁴ shen²-ma¹-ti¹?
A. T'a¹ shih⁴ shang¹-jen².
Q. Nin²-ti¹ hai²-tzu¹-men² tsai⁴ chia¹ li³ nien⁴ shu¹ ma¹?
A. Pu² shih⁴. Wo³-ti¹ ta⁴ ku¹-niang² tsai⁴ ta⁴-hsüeh²-hsiao⁴ nien⁴ shu¹, wo³-ti¹ erh²-tzu¹ ken¹ wo³-li¹ hsiao³ ku¹-niang² tsai⁴ hsiao³-hsüeh²-hsiao⁴ nien⁴ shu¹.
Q. Nin²-ti¹ mu³-ch'in¹ ken¹ nin²-ti¹ t'ai⁴-t'ai⁴ tsai⁴ chia¹ li³ tso⁴ shen²-ma¹?
A. T'a¹-men² tsai⁴ chia¹ li³ kei³ wo³-men² tso⁴ fan⁴.

Q. What is your name?
A. My name is Chang.

Q. Where do you work?
A. I work at the railway station.
Q. How many people are there in your house?
A. There are seven.
Q. Who are they all?
A. There is my father and mother, my wife and also my son and two daughters.
Q. What does your father do?
A. He is a merchant.
Q. Do your children study at home?
A. No. My elder daughter studies at the university while my son and small daughter study at a Primary School.
Q. What do your mother and wife do at home?
A. They cooked the food for us.

REVISION II

SHOPPING (i)

賣東西 ma⁴ tung¹-hsi¹   問答 wen⁴-ta²

Q. Ni³-men² che-'rh⁴ mai⁴ shen²-ma¹ tung¹-hsi¹?

A. Wo³-men² che-'rh⁴ mai⁴ ch'a²-yeh⁴, k'a¹-fei⁴, chiu³, nai³-yu², niu²-nai³, shen²-ma¹-ti¹.

Q. Che⁴ ke⁴ ch'a²-yeh⁴ to¹-shao³ ch'ien² i¹ chin⁴?

A. Che⁴ ke⁴ ch'a²-yeh⁴ san¹ k'uai⁴ pan⁴ ch'ien² i¹ chin⁴.

Q. K'a¹-fei⁴ yeh³ shih⁴ san¹ k'uai⁴ pan⁴ ch'ien² i¹ chin⁴ ma¹?

A. Pu² shih⁴, k'a¹-fei⁴ shih⁴ liang³ k'uai⁴ san¹ i¹ chin⁴.

Q. Nai³-yu² to¹-shao³ ch'ien² i¹ chin⁴, niu²-nai³ to¹-shao³ ch'ien² i⁴ p'ing²-tzu¹?

A. Nai³-yu² liu⁴ mao²-ch'ien² i¹ chin⁴, niu²-nai³ i⁴ mao² erh⁴ i⁴ p'ing²-tzu¹.

Q. Ni³-men² che-'rh⁴ hai² mai⁴ shen²-ma¹ tung¹-hsi¹?

A. Wo³-men² che-'rh⁴ hai² mai⁴ ch'a²-wan³, fan⁴-wan³, po¹-li²-pei¹, chiu³-pei¹, shen²-ma¹-ti¹.

Q. Ni³-men² yeh³ mai⁴ mien⁴-pao¹ ma¹?

A. Wo³-men² yu³ pai² mien⁴-pao¹, mei² yu³ hei¹ mien⁴-pao¹.

Q. What do you sell here?
A. We sell tea, coffee, wine, butter, milk and so forth.
Q. How much is this tea a pound?
A. It is three and a half dollars a pound.

Q. Is coffee also three and a half dollars a pound?
A. No. Coffee is two dollars thirty a pound.
Q. How much is butter a pound and how much is milk per bottle?
A. Butter is sixty cents a pound and milk is twelve cents a bottle.
Q. What else do you sell here?
A. We also sell tea-cups, rice-bowls, tumblers, wine-glasses, and so on.
Q. Do you sell bread too?
A. We have white bread but no black bread.

REVISION III

CLOTHES

人 jen² 穿的 ch'uan¹-ti¹ 戴的 tai⁴-ti¹ 問答 wen⁴-ta²

Q. Nin² tso²-t'ien¹ shang⁴ na-'rh³ ch'ü⁴-la¹?

A. Wo³ mai³ i¹-shang¹ ch'ü⁴-la¹.

Q. Tou¹ kei³ shui² mai³ a¹?

A. Wo³-men² chia¹ li³ ti¹ jen², wǎ³ kei³ t'a¹-men² i² ke⁴ jen² mai³ i¹ chien⁴.

Q. Mai³-ti¹ tou¹ shih⁴ shen²-ma¹ i¹-shang¹ a¹?

A. Kei³ wo³ fu⁴-ch'in¹ mai³ la¹ i¹ chien⁴ ch'ang²-ti¹, kei³ wo³ mu³-ch'in¹ mai³-la¹ i¹ chien⁴ tuan³-ti¹, kei³ wo³-ti¹ erh²-tzu¹, ku¹-niang²-men² tou¹ mai³-ti¹ shih⁴ hsüeh²-sheng¹-ti¹ i¹-shang¹, hai² kei³ wo³ t'ai⁴-t'ai⁴ mai³-la¹ i¹-chien⁴ pu⁴ hen³ ch'ang²-ti¹.

Q. Na⁴-hsieh¹ chien⁴ i¹-shang¹ tou¹ shih⁴ shen²-ma¹ yen²-se⁴-ti¹?

A. Wo³ fu⁴-mu³-ti¹ tou¹ shih⁴ lan² yen²-se⁴-ti¹, ku¹-niang²-ti¹ shih⁴ lü⁴ yen²-se⁴-ti¹, wo³ erh²-tzu¹-ti¹ shih⁴ hung² yen²-se⁴-ti¹, wo³ t'ai⁴-t'ai⁴-ti¹ shih⁴ huang²-ti¹.

Q. Nin² mai³-ti¹ na⁴ chien⁴ i¹-shang¹ kuei⁴ chien⁴ na¹?

A. Yu³ chiu³ k'uai⁴ wu³ mao²-ch'ien²-ti¹, yu³ shih²-i¹ k'uai⁴ pan⁴-ti¹, na⁴ hsiao³ hai²-tzu¹-ti¹ i¹-shang¹ tou¹ shih⁴ liu⁴ k'uai⁴ wu³ i¹ chien⁴, nin² shuo¹ kuei⁴ pu² kuei⁴ a¹?

REVISION III

Q. *Wo³ shuo¹* **tou¹ hen³** *chien⁴,* **i⁴-*tien*-'rh³** *pu² kuei⁴. Nin²* **ch'uan¹**-*ti¹* **che⁴ chien⁴** *i¹-shang¹* **yeh³ shih⁴ hsin¹ mai³**-*ti¹* **ma¹**?

A. **Pu² shih⁴, che⁴ shih⁴ chiu⁴**-*ti¹, wo³ tso²-t'ien¹* **chiu⁴ mai³**-*la¹* **i⁴** *ting³* **mao⁴**-*tzu¹,* **i⁴** *shuang¹* **hsieh², mei²** *mai³ i¹-shang¹.*

Q. *Na⁴ ting³ mao⁴-tzu¹ to¹-shao³ ch'ien² na¹?*

A. **Liang³** *k'uai⁴* **wu³.**

Q. *Na⁴ shuang¹* **hsieh² shih⁴ chi³** *k'uai⁴-ch'ien²* **mai³**-*ti¹?*

A. **Hsieh² shih⁴ ch'i²** *k'uai⁴* **pa¹** *mao²* **wu³ mai³**-*ti¹.*

Q. *Nin² shuo¹* **shih⁴ tsai⁴** *i¹-shang¹-p'u⁴ li³ mai³ i¹-shang¹* **hao³** *a¹,* **hai² shih⁴ chiao⁴** *ts'ai²-feng² tsai⁴ chia¹ li³* **tso⁴ hao³** *ni¹?*

A. *Wo³ shuo¹ na⁴ yu³* **ch'ien²**-*ti¹* **hai² shih⁴ chiao⁴** *ts'ai²-feng² tsai⁴ chia¹ li³ tso⁴ hao³, na⁴* **mei² ch'ien²**-*ti¹ mai³ i¹ chien⁴ ch'uan¹* **yeh³ hsing²** *la¹.*

Q. Where did you go yesterday?
A. I went out to buy some clothes.
Q. Whom did you buy them for?
A. I bought one garment for each member of our family.
Q. What clothes did you buy?
A. I bought a long one for my father, a short one for my mother, school clothes for my son and daughters and also and not very long one for my wife.
Q. What colours are they all?
A. My parent's (clothes) are both blue, my daughters' are green, my son's are red and my wife's yellow.
Q. Were these clothes expensive?

A. Some were nine dollars fifty and some were eleven dollars fifty each; the childrens' clothes were all six fifty a piece, do you think that was expensive ?
Q. I should say they were all cheap and not a bit expensive. Are the clothes you are wearing also new ?
A. No, these are old ones, I only bought a hat and a pair of shoes yesterday, I didn't buy any clothes.
Q. How much was that hat ?
A. Two dollars fifty.
Q. How much was that pair of shoes ?
A. They were seven dollars eighty-five cents.
Q. Do you think it is better to buy clothes in a shop or to have a tailor make them at home ?
A. I should say that for people who have money it is better to have a tailor make them at home, but for people who haven't much money it is better to buy ready-made clothes.

REVISION IV

THE RESTAURANT (i)

人 jen² 吃的 ch'ih¹-ti¹ 喝的 he¹-ti¹ 問答 wen⁴-ta²

A. *Nin² hao³ a¹!*

Q. *Hao³ hao³. Nin² yeh³ hao³ a¹!*

A. *Hsieh⁴-hsieh⁴, wo³ yeh³ hao³.*

Q. *Nin² ts'ung² na-'rh³ lai²?*

A. *Ts'ung² fan⁴-kuan³-tzu¹ lai².*

Q. *Shang⁴ fan⁴-kuan³-tzu¹ tso⁴ shen²-ma¹ ch'ü⁴-la¹?*

A. *Ch'ih¹ fan⁴ ch'ü⁴-la¹.*

Q. *Shih⁴ nin² i² ke⁴ jen² ch'ih¹-ti¹ a¹, hai² shih⁴ ken¹ jen² i²-k'uai-'rh⁴ ch'ih¹-ti¹ ni¹?*

A. *Shih⁴ ken¹ jen² i²-k'uai-'rh⁴ ch'ih¹-ti¹.*

Q. *Ken¹ shui² i²-k'uai-'rh⁴ ch'ih¹-ti¹?*

A. *Yu³ tien⁴-pao⁴-chü²-ti¹ i¹ wei⁴ chih²-yüan², yu²-cheng⁴-chü²-ti¹ i¹ wei⁴ shu¹-chi⁴, ken¹ Pei³-p'ing² i¹-yüan⁴-ti¹ Huang² tai⁴-fu¹, hai² yu³ i¹ wei⁴ shang¹-jen², wo³-men² liu⁴ ke⁴ jen² i²-k'uai-'rh⁴ ch'ih¹-ti¹.*

Q. *Ch'ih¹-ti¹ shih⁴ chung¹-kuo² fan⁴ shih⁴ wai⁴-kuo² fan⁴?*

A. *Chih¹-ti¹ shih⁴ chung¹-kuo² fan⁴.*

Q. *Ch'ih¹-ti¹ tou¹ shih⁴ shen²-ma¹ ni¹?*

A. *Ch'ih¹-ti¹ shih⁴ niu², yang², chu¹ jou⁴ ken¹ yü², shen²-ma¹-ti¹.*

Q. *Ni³-men² he¹ chiu³ la¹ ma¹?*
A. *He¹ chiu³ la¹.*
Q. *He¹-ti¹ chiu³ to¹ pu⁴ to¹ a¹?*
A. *Wo³-men² he¹-ti¹ pu⁴ to¹, chiu⁴ he¹-la¹ liang³ p'ing²-tzu¹, na⁴ chi³ wei⁴ yu³ he¹ ch'i¹ pa¹ pei¹-ti¹, yu³ he¹ wu³ liu⁴ pei¹-ti¹, wo³ chiu⁴ he¹-la¹ liang³ pei¹.*
Q. *Ni³-men² liu⁴ wei⁴ ch'ih¹-la¹ to¹-shao³ ch'ien²?*
A. *Ch'ih¹-la¹ liu⁴ k'uai⁴ erh⁴ mao²-ch'ien².*
Q. *Shih⁴ shui² kei³-ti¹ ch'ien² na¹?*
A. *Shih⁴ Huang² tai⁴-fu¹ ch'ing³-ti¹.*
Q. *Ni³-men² ch'ih¹ wan²-la¹ fan⁴, tso⁴ shen²-ma¹ ch'ü⁴-la¹?*
A. *Ch'ih¹ wan²-la¹ fan⁴ he¹-la¹ i⁴-tien-'rh³ ch'a², chiu⁴ shang⁴ tien⁴-ying³-yüan⁴ k'an⁴ tien⁴-ying³-erh² ch'ü⁴-la¹, k'an⁴ wan²-la¹ tien⁴-ying³-erh² chiu⁴ tou¹ hui² chia¹ la¹.*

A. How are you?
Q. I am very well, and how are you?
A. Thank you, I am also well.
Q. Where have you been?
A. I have been to a restaurant.
Q. What did you go to a restaurant for?
A. I went to get something to eat.
Q. Did you eat by yourself or with other people?
A. I ate with some other people.
Q. Who were you with?
A. There were two telegraph-office officials, a clerk from the post-office, Dr. Huang from the Peiping hospital and also a business man. The six of us ate together.

Q. Did you have Chinese food or foreign food?
A. We had Chinese food.
Q. What did you have to eat?
A. We had beef, mutton, pork, fish and so forth.
Q. Did you have any wine?
A. We did.
Q. Did you drink much wine?
A. We didn't drink much — only two bottles. Some of them drank seven or eight glasses (cups) and some five or six glasses, but I only drank two glasses.
Q. How much money did the six of you spend?
A. We spent six dollars twenty cents..
Q. Who paid?
A. It was Dr. Huang who invited us.
Q. Where did you go after you had finished eating?
A. When we had finished eating we drank a little tea and then went to a cinema to see a movie. After we had seen the movie we all went home.

REVISION V

THE HOUSE

人 jen² 住的 chu⁴-ti¹

問答 wen⁴-ta²

Q. Nin² tsai⁴ che⁴ so³ fang²-tzu¹ chu⁴ ma¹?

A. Shih⁴, wo³ tsai⁴ che⁴ so³ fang²-tzu¹ chu⁴.

Q. Nin² chu⁴ chi³ chien¹ wu¹-tzu¹?

A. Wo³ chu⁴ i⁴ chien¹ wu¹-tzu¹.

Q. Nin² chu⁴-ti¹ wu¹-tzu¹ yu³ chi³ ke⁴ men². chi³ ke⁴ ch'uang¹-hu¹?

A. Wo³ chu⁴-ti¹ wu¹-tzu¹ yu³ i² ke⁴ men², liang³ ke⁴ ch'uang¹-hu¹.

Q. Ni³ chu⁴-ti¹ wu¹-tzu¹, men², ch'uang¹-hu¹, ti⁴-pan³, ting³-p'eng² ken¹ ch'iang², tou¹ shih⁴ shen²-ma¹ yen²-se⁴-ti¹?

A. Men², ch'uang¹-hu¹, ting³-p'eng² tou¹ shih⁴ pai² yen²-se⁴-ti¹, ssu⁴ mien⁴ ch'iang² shih⁴ lan² yen²-se⁴-ti¹, ti⁴-pan³ shih⁴ huang²-ti¹.

Q. Tsai⁴ ch'iang² shang⁴ kua⁴ shen²-ma¹ tung¹-hsi¹?

A. Tsai⁴ ch'iang² shang⁴ kua⁴ liang³ chang¹ hua-'rh⁴.

Q. Tsai⁴ hua-'rh shang⁴ hua⁴-ti¹ shih⁴ shen²-ma¹ tung¹-hsi¹?

A. I⁴ chang¹ hua⁴-ti¹ shih⁴ i⁴ chih¹ yang², i¹ k'ou² chu¹, liang³ t'ou² niu², na⁴ i⁴ chang¹ hua⁴-ti¹ shih⁴ i¹ so³ fang²-tzu¹.

REVISION V

Q. *Tsai⁴ nin²-ti¹ chu⁴-ti¹ wu¹-tzu¹ li³* **tou¹** *yu³* **shen²-*ma¹* tung¹-hsi¹ ?*

A. *Tsai⁴ wo³-ti¹ wu¹-tzu¹ li³ yu³ i⁴ chang¹* **shu¹**-*cho¹-tzu¹, i⁴ chang¹* **fan**⁴-*cho¹-tzu¹, ssu⁴ pa² l³-tzu¹, shen²-ma¹-ti¹.*

Q. Do you live in this house ?
A. Yes, I live in this house.
Q. How many rooms do you live in ?
A. I live in one room.
Q. How many doors and windows has the room you live in ?
A. The room I live in has one door and two windows.
Q. What colour are the door, windows, floor, ceiling and walls of the room you live in ?
A. The door, windows and ceiling are white, the four walls are blue and the floor is yellow.
Q. What hangs on the walls ?
A. There are two pictures hanging on the walls.
Q. What is painted in the pictures ?
A. In one of the pictures is a sheep, a pig and two cows, in the other there is a house.
Q. What sort of things are there in your room ?
A. In my room I have a desk, a dining-table, four chairs and so on.

REVISION VI

AT SCHOOL (i)

我們的學堂 wo³-men²-ti¹ hsüeh²-t'ang²
問答 wen⁴-ta²

Q. Nin² tsai⁴ **shen²-ma¹** hsüeh²-t'ang² **nien⁴ shu¹**?

A. Wo³ tsai⁴ chung¹-hsüeh²-t'ang² nien⁴ shu¹.

Q. Ni³-men² hsüeh²-t'ang² yu³ **chi³** wei⁴ hsien¹-sheng¹, to¹-shao³ wei⁴ hsüeh²-sheng¹?

A. Wo³-men² hsüeh²-t'ang² li³ yu³ **shih²** chi³ wei⁴ hsien¹-sheng¹, **san¹-pai³** to¹ wei⁴ hsüeh²-sheng¹.

Q. Chung¹-kuo² hsüeh²-sheng¹ wai⁴-kuo² hsüeh²-sheng¹ tou¹ yu³ ma¹?

A. Yu³ chung¹-kuo² hsüeh²-sheng¹, **mei²** yu³ wai⁴-kuo² hsüeh²-sheng¹.

Q. Chung¹ wai⁴ kuo²-ti¹ shu¹ tou¹ nien⁴ ma¹?

A. **Tou¹** nien⁴.

Q. Ni³-men² hsüeh²-t'ang² li³ yu³ to¹-shao³ ke⁴ chiang³-t'ang²?

A. Wo³-men² hsüeh²-t'ang² li³ yu³ **shih²-san¹** ke⁴ chiang³-t'ang².

Q. Chiang³-t'ang² shih⁴ tso⁴ shen²-ma¹-ti¹ ti⁴-fang¹?

A. Chiang³-t'ang² shih⁴ **chiang³** kung¹-k'e⁴-ti¹ ti⁴-fang¹.

Q. Tsai⁴ chiang³-t'ang² shang⁴ tou¹ yu³ shen²-ma¹ tung¹-hsi¹?

A. *Tsai⁴ chiang³-t'ang² shang⁴ yu³* **shu¹**-*cho¹-tzu¹, yu³ i³-tzu¹, tsai⁴* **ch'iang²** *shang⁴ yu³* **hei¹**-*pan³,* **hua-'rh⁴,** *shen²-ma¹-ti¹.*

Q. *Hsien¹-sheng¹ na²* **shen²**-*ma¹* **pi³** *tsai⁴* **hei¹**-*pan³ shang⁴ hsieh³ tzu⁴ ?*

A. *Hsien¹-sheng¹ na²* **fen²**-*pi³ tsai⁴ hei¹-pan³ shang⁴ hsieh³ tzu⁴.*

Q. *Hsüeh²-sheng¹ na²* **shen²-ma¹ pi³** *hsieh³ tzu⁴, tsai⁴* **shen²-ma¹ shang⁴** *hsieh³ tzu⁴ ?*

A. *Hsüeh²-sheng¹ na²* **kang¹**-*pi³ tsai⁴* **pen³**-*tzu¹ shang⁴ hsieh³ tzu⁴.*   [*ma¹ ?*

Q, *Hsüeh²-sheng¹-men² nien⁴-ti¹ tou¹ shih⁴* **hsin¹** *k'e⁴-pen³*

A. **Pu²** *shih⁴, yu³-ti¹ hsüeh²-sheng¹ nien⁴-ti¹ shih⁴* **hsin¹** *k'e⁴-pen³, yu³-ti¹ hsüeh²-sheng¹* **hai²** *shih⁴ chiu⁴ k'e⁴-pen³.*

Q. *Ni³-men² tsai⁴ chiang³-t'ang² shang⁴* **tso⁴** *shen²-ma¹ ?*

A. *Wo³-men² tsai⁴ chiang³-t'ang² shang⁴* **t'ing¹ hsien¹**-*sheng¹ chiang³ kung¹-k'e⁴. Hsien¹-sheng¹* **wen⁴** *wo³-men², wo³-men² chiu⁴* **hui²**-*ta².*

Q. *Ni³-men²-ti¹ kung¹-k'e⁴ yu³ pu⁴ ming²-pai²-ti¹ ti⁴-fang¹* **yao⁴ wen⁴ shui² ?**

A. *Wo³-men²* **ch'ing³** *hsien¹-sheng¹ kei³ wo³-men² chiang³.*

Q. *Kung¹-k'e⁴ wan²-la¹ ni³-men²* **chiu⁴ hui² chia¹** *ma¹?*

A. **Shih⁴,** *kung¹-k'e⁴ wan²-la¹ wo³-men²* **chiu⁴ hui² chia¹** *ch'ü⁴.*

Q. Which school do you study.at?
A. We are studying at the Middle School.
Q. How many teachers and pupils are there in your school?
A. In our school there are about ten teachers and more than three hundred pupils.

Q. Are there Chinese and foreign pupils?
A. There are Chinese pupils but no foreign ones.
Q. Do you read Chinese and foreign books?
A. We read both.
Q. How many classrooms are there in your school?
A. There are thirteen classrooms in our school.
Q. What do they do in the classrooms?
A. They give lessons in the classrooms.
Q. What sort of things are there in the classrooms?
A. In the classrooms there are desks and chairs, and on the walls there are blackboards, pictures, etc.
Q. What does the teacher use to write on the blackboard
[with?
A. The teacher uses a chalk to write on the blackboard
[with.
Q. What do the pupils use to write with and what do they write on?
A. The pupils write with pens in note-books.
Q. Do the pupils only study new text-books?
A. No, some pupils study new text-books and some of them study old ones.
Q. What do you do in the classroom?
A. We listen to the teacher explaining the lesson in the classroom. When the teacher asks us anything we reply.
Q. If you have something that you don't understand in your lesson, whom do you ask?
A. We ask the teacher to explain it to us.
Q. Do you go home when the lessons are finished?
A. Yes, when the lessons are finished we just go home.

REVISION VII

AT SCHOOL (ii)

學堂 hsüeh²-t'ang²　學校 hsüeh²-hsiao⁴

Hsüeh²-t'ang²/hsiao⁴ shih⁴ nien⁴-shu¹-ti¹ ti⁴-fang¹. Yu³ hsiao³-hsüeh²-t'ang²/hsiao⁴, chung¹-hsüeh²-t'ang²/hsiao⁴, hai² yu³ ta⁴-hsüeh²-t'ang²/hsiao⁴. Hsien¹-sheng¹ tsai⁴ hsüeh²-t'ang²/hsiao⁴ li³ chiang³ kung²-k'e⁴, hsüeh²-sheng¹ tsai⁴ hsüeh²-t'ang²/hsiao⁴ li³ nien⁴ shu¹. Hsien¹-sheng¹ chiang³ kung¹-k'e⁴-ti¹ ti⁴-fang¹ chiao⁴ chiang³-t'ang² yeh³ chiao⁴ k'e⁴-t'ang². Chiang³-t'ang² li³ yu³ hei¹-pan³ ken¹ hua-'rh⁴, shen²-ma¹-ti¹. Tsai⁴ che⁴ ke⁴ ti⁴-fang¹ hsiao³-hsüeh²-t'ang²/hsiao⁴ hen³ · to¹, chung¹-hsüeh²-t'ang²/hsiao⁴, ta⁴-hsüeh²-t'ang²/hsiao⁴ yeh³ pu⁴ shao³.

A school is a place where one studies. There are Primary Schools, Middle Schools and High Schools. In a school the teacher gives lessons and the pupils study. The place where the teacher gives lessons is called a classroom. In the classroom there are blackboards, pictures, etc. In this place there are many Primary Schools and also many Middle Schools and High Schools.

學堂(校) hsüeh²-t'ang² (hsiao⁴)
問話 wen⁴-hua⁴

1. Hsüeh²-t'ang²/hsiao⁴ shih⁴ tso⁴ shen²-ma¹-ti¹ ti⁴-fang¹?
3. Tsai⁴ hsüeh²-t'ang²/hsiao⁴ nien⁴-shu¹-ti¹ shih⁴ shen²-ma¹ jen²? shen²-ma¹ jen²?
2. Tsai⁴ hsüeh²-t'ang²/hsiao⁴ li³ chiang³ kung¹-k'e⁴-ti¹ shih⁴
4. Hsien¹-sheng¹ chiang³ kung¹-k'e⁴-ti¹ wu¹-tzu¹ chiao⁴ shen²-ma¹?
5. Hsien¹-sheng¹ na² shen²-ma¹ pi³ tsai⁴ hei¹-pan³ shang⁴ hsieh³ tzu⁴?
6. Tsai⁴ ch'iang² shang⁴ kua⁴-li¹ na⁴ chang¹ hua-'rh⁴ shih⁴ hsien¹-sheng¹ hua⁴-ti¹, shih⁴ hsüeh²-sheng¹ hua⁴-ti¹?
7. Na⁴ ke⁴ wai⁴-kuo² hsüeh²-t'ang² shih⁴ ta⁴-hsüeh²-t'ang² shih⁴ chung¹-hsüeh²-t'ang²?
8. Che⁴ ke⁴ ti⁴-fang¹ tou¹ yu³ shen²-ma¹ hsüeh²-t'ang²?

1. What does one do in a school?
2. Who gives lessons in school?
3. Who studies in school?
4. What is the room where the teacher gives lessons called?
5. What does the teacher use to write on the blackboard [with?
6. Was the picture hanging on the wall drawn by the teacher or a student?
7. Is that foreign school a High School or a Middle School?
8. What sort of schools are there in this place?

REVISION VIII

THE FAMILY (ii)

 chia¹

Na⁴ so³ fang²-tzu¹ yu³ liang³ chia¹ chu⁴, i⁴ chia¹ hsing⁴ Ch'ien² shih⁴ tso⁴ mai³-mai⁴-ti¹ (shang¹-jen²), i⁴ chia¹ hsing⁴ Chang¹ shih⁴ tai⁴-fu¹. Ch'ien² chia¹ chia¹ li³ yu³ ssu⁴ k'ou-'rh³ jen², Chang¹ chia¹ chia¹ li³ yu³ san¹ k'ou-'rh³ jen². Na⁴ ke⁴ hsing⁴ Ch'ien²-ti¹ yu³ i² ke⁴ shu¹-p'u⁴, tung¹-hsi¹ hen² hao³, mai¹-ti¹ yeh³ hen³ chien⁴, mai³-mai⁴ hen² hao³. Na⁴ ke⁴ hsing⁴ Chang¹-ti¹ shih⁴ tsai⁴ Nan²-ching¹ i¹-yüan⁴ li³ tang¹ tai⁴-fu¹.

Two families live in that house; one is the Ch'ien family who are business people (merchants), the other is the Chang family who is a doctor. In the Ch'ien family house there are four people, and in the Chang family house there are three people. Ch'ien has a book-shop where the goods are excellent and very cheap — his business is doing well. Chang is a physician at the Nanking hospital.

家 chia¹   問話 wen⁴-hua⁴

1. *Nin² chia¹ li³ yu³* chi³ *k'ou-'rh³ jen²?*
2. *Nin² chia¹ li³* tou¹ *yu³* shen²-ma¹ *jen²?*
3. *Nin²* ken¹ *nin²-ti¹* fu⁴-mu³ tsai⁴ *i²-k'uai-'rh⁴* chu⁴ ma¹?
4. *Nin²-ti¹* chang⁴-*fu¹* tsai⁴ na-'rh³ tso⁴ shih⁴?
5. *Nin²-ti¹ t'ai⁴-t'ai⁴* tsai⁴ chia¹ *li³* na¹ ma¹?
6. *Nin²-ti¹* fu⁴-*ch'in¹* shih⁴ shang¹-*jen²* ma¹?
7. *Nin²-ti¹* mu³-*ch'in¹* tsai⁴ chia¹ *li³* tso⁴ shen²-ma¹?
8. *Nin²* yu³ chi³ ke⁴ hai²-*tzu¹?*
9. *Nin²-ti¹* erh²-*tzu¹* shih⁴ tsai⁴ chia¹ *li³* nien⁴ shu¹ ma¹?
10. *Nin²-ti¹* ku¹-*niang²* tsai⁴ shen²-ma¹ hsüeh²-*t'ang² hsiao⁴* nien⁴ *shu¹?*
11. *Che⁴ t'iao² chieh¹ shang⁴* yu³ hsing⁴ Pai²-*ti¹* ma¹?
12. *Chang¹ chia¹* shih⁴ che-'rh⁴ chu⁴ ma¹?
13. *Nin²-ti¹* fu⁴-mu³ tsai⁴ chia¹ na¹ ma¹?
14. *T'a¹* ken¹ *t'a¹-ti¹ t'ai⁴-t'ai⁴* chu⁴ chi³ chien¹ wu¹-*tzu¹?*

1. How many are there in your family?
2. Who are the members of your family?
3. Do you live with your parents?
4. Where does your husband work?
5. Is your wife at home?
6. Is your father a business man?
7. What does your mother do at home?
8. How many children have you?
9. Does your son study at home?

REVISION VIII

10. Which school does your daughter go to ?
11. Is there anyone called Pai in this street ?
12. Does the Chang family live here ?
13. Are your parents at home ?
14. How many rooms do he and his wife live in ?

REVISION IX

SHOPPING (ii)

舖子 p'u⁴-tzu¹

Na⁴ t'iao² chieh¹ shang⁴ yu³ hen³ to¹ p'u⁴-tzu¹: shen²-ma¹ shu¹-p'u⁴, cho¹-i³-p'u⁴, mien⁴-pao¹-fang², hsieh²-p'u⁴, pi³-p'u⁴, tou¹ yu. T'a¹-men² mai⁴-ti¹ tung¹-hsi¹ yu³ kuei⁴-ti¹, yu³ chien⁴-ti¹. Tsai⁴ na-'rh⁴ yeh³ yu³ wai⁴-kuo² p'u⁴-tzu¹, tso⁴ mai³-mai⁴-ti¹ yeh³ tou¹ shih⁴ wai⁴-kuo² jen². T'a¹-men²-ti¹ tung¹-hsi¹ tou¹ shih⁴ ts'ung² wai⁴-kuo² mai³ lai²-ti¹.

On that street there are a great many shops : book shops, furniture shops, bakers, shoemakers and stationers. Some of the things they sell are expensive and some are cheap. There are also some foreign shops and the shop-keepers are all foreigners. Their goods are all bought from abroad.

舖子 p'u⁴-tzu¹   問話 wen⁴-hua⁴

1. *P'u⁴-tzu¹ shih⁴ mai⁴ tung¹-hsi¹-ti¹ ti⁴-fang¹ ma¹?*
2. *Tsai⁴ che⁴ t'iao² chieh¹ shang⁴ tou¹ yu³ shen²-ma¹ p'u⁴-tzu¹?*
3. *Cho¹-i³-p'u⁴ mai⁴ shen²-ma¹ tung¹-hsi¹?*
4. *Shu¹-p'u⁴ li³ yeh³ mai⁴ pen³-tzu¹ ma¹?*
5. *Na⁴ ke⁴ hsieh²-p'u⁴ mai⁴-ti¹ hsieh² kuei⁴ chien⁴?*

6. *Ch'ing³ wen⁴ nin²,* **na⁴ ke⁴** *p'u⁴-tzu¹ shih⁴* **mien⁴-***pao¹-fang²* **shih⁴ jou⁴-***p'u⁴?*
7. *Na⁴ ke⁴ wai⁴-kuo² p'u⁴-tzu¹* **mai⁴-***ti¹* **tou¹** *shih⁴* **wai⁴-***kuo² **tung¹-***hsi¹* **ma¹?**
8. *P'u⁴-tzu¹ li³* **tso⁴** *mai³-mai⁴-ti¹ shih⁴* **shen²-***ma¹ jen²?*
9. *Tsai⁴ pi³-p'u⁴ li³* **shen²-***ma¹ pi³* **tou¹ mai⁴ ma¹?**
10. *Tsai⁴ na⁴ ke⁴ p'u⁴-tzu³ li³* **yeh³** *mai⁴* **mao⁴-***tzu¹ ma¹?*

1. Is a shop a place where things are sold?
2. What sort of shops are there on this street?
3. What do they sell at a furniture shop?
4. Does a book-store also sell note-books?
5. Are the shoes sold at that shoemaker's expensive?
6. Will you please tell me, is that a baker's or a butcher's?
7. Do they only sell foreign goods at that foreign shop?
8. What sort of people are the shop-keepers?
9. Do they sell all kinds of pens at the stationer's?
10. Does that shop also sell hats?

REVISION X

THE POST OFFICE

郵政局 yu²-cheng⁴-chü²

Wo³ tso²-t'ien¹ hsieh³-la¹ **liang³ feng¹ hsin⁴,** **i⁴ feng¹** *shih⁴ kei³ wo³* **mu³-ch'in¹** *ch'ü⁴-ti¹,* **i⁴ feng¹ shih⁴ kei³ Mao²** *hsien¹-sheng¹ ch'ü⁴-ti¹. Che⁴ liang³ feng¹ hsin⁴* **yao⁴ mai³ chi³ fen¹** *yu²-p'iao⁴,* **shen²-ma¹** *ti⁴-fang¹* **mai⁴** *yu²-p'iao⁴, wo³* **tou¹** *pu⁴ chih¹-tao¹. Wo³* **chiu⁴ wen⁴ Chang¹** *hsien¹-shen¹ ch'ü⁴-la¹. Chang¹ hsien¹-sheng¹* **kao⁴-su⁴** *wo³, che⁴ liang³ feng¹ hsin⁴ yao⁴ mai³* **liu⁴ fen¹** *p'iao⁴, mai⁴ yu²-p'iao⁴-ti¹ ti⁴-fang¹* **chiao⁴** *yu²-cheng⁴-chü².*

Yesterday I wrote two letters, one to my mother and one to Mr. Mao. I did not know what postage stamps to buy for these two letters nor where stamps were sold. I therefore went to ask Mr. Chang. Mr. Chang told me that I must buy six cents stamps for these two letters and that the place where stamps were sold was called a post office.

郵政局 yu²-cheng⁴-chü² 問話 wen⁴-hua⁴

1. *Ch'ing³ wen⁴ nin², na-'rh³ yu³ yu²-cheng⁴-chü²?*
2. *Na⁴ ke⁴ yu²-cheng⁴-chü² li³ yu³ to¹-shao³ wei⁴ chih²-yüan²?*

3. *Yu²-cheng⁴-chü² li³ yu³* hui⁴ *shuo¹* wai⁴-*kuo²* hua⁴-*ti¹* chih²-*yüan² ma¹ ?*
4. *Nin²-ti* hsien¹-*sheng¹ kei³ nin² lai² *hsin⁴ la¹ ma¹ ?*
5. *T'a¹* shang⁴ *yu²-cheng⁴-chü²* mai³ shen²-*ma¹ ch'ü⁴-la¹ ?*
6. *Na⁴ chang¹ yu²-p'iao⁴ shih⁴ chi³ fen¹-ti¹ ?*
7. *Tso²-t'ien¹ nin² kei³* shui² *ch'ü⁴* hsin⁴ *?*
8. *Che⁴ feng¹* hsin⁴ shih⁴ chin¹-*t'ien¹ lai²-ti¹ ma¹ ?*

1. Please tell me, where is the post office ?.
2. How many officials are there in that post office ?
3. Are there any officials who can speak foreign languages in the post office ?
4. Has your teacher sent you a letter ?
5. What has he gone to buy at the post office ?
6. How many cents is that stamp ?
7. Whom did you send a letter to yesterday ?
8. Did this letter come today ?

REVISION XI

THE TELEGRAPH OFFICE

電報局 tien⁴-pao⁴-chü²

Wo³ fu⁴-ch'in¹ kei³ wo³ lai²-la¹ i⁴ fen⁴ tien⁴-pao⁴. Wo³ chin¹-t'ien¹ yeh³ kei³ t'a¹ ch'ü⁴-la¹ i⁴ fen⁴ tien⁴-pao⁴. T'a¹ kei³ wo³ lai²-ti¹ tien⁴-pao⁴ yu³ shih² chi³ ke⁴ tzu⁴, wo³ kei³ t'a¹ ch'ü⁴-ti¹ tien⁴-pao⁴ yu³ erh⁴-shih² to¹ ke⁴ tzu⁴. Ta³ tien⁴-pao⁴-ti¹ ti⁴-fang¹ chiao⁴ tien⁴-pao⁴-chü². Tsai⁴ wo³ chu⁴-ti¹ na⁴ ke⁴ ti⁴-fang¹, yu³ i² ke⁴ hen³ ta⁴-ti¹ tien⁴-pao⁴-chü². Na⁴ ke⁴ tien⁴-pao⁴ chü² li³ chih²-yüan² hen³ to¹, shang⁴ na-'rh⁴ ta³ tien⁴-pao⁴-ti¹ yeh³ pu⁴ shao³.

My father sent me a telegram. Today I also sent him a telegram. The telegram that he sent me had ten odd words, but the telegram that I sent him had about twenty words. The place where they send telegrams is called a telegraph office. Where I live there is a very large telegraph office. In that telegraph office there are a great many officials and also very many people sending off telegrams.

電報局 tien⁴-pao⁴-chü² **問話** wen⁴-hua⁴

1. *Che⁴ fen⁴ tien⁴-pao⁴ shih⁴ shui² lai²-ti¹ ?*
2. *Nin² kei³ t'a¹ ch'ü⁴ tien⁴-pao⁴ la¹ ma¹ ?*

3. Ch'ien² t'ai⁴-t'ai⁴ kei³ t'a¹ chang⁴-fu¹ ch'ü⁴-ti¹ tien⁴-pao⁴ yu³ to¹-shao³ ke⁴ tzu⁴ ?
4. Ta³ tien⁴-pao⁴, i² ke⁴ tzu⁴ to¹-shao³ ch'ien² ?
5. Ta³ tien⁴-pao⁴ yao⁴ shang⁴ shen²-ma¹ ti⁴-fang¹ ch'ü⁴ ?

1. Who sent this telegram ?
2. Have you sent him a telegram ?
3. How many words were there in the telegram that Mrs. Ch'ien sent to her husband ?
4. How much is it a word when sending a telegram ?
5. Where must one go to send a telegram ?

REVISION XIJ

THE CINEMA

電影院 tien⁴-*ying*³-yŭan⁴

戲園子 hsi⁴-*yüan*²-*tzu*¹

*Jen*² *tso*⁴ *wan*²-*la*¹ *shih*⁴-*ch'ing*², **hen**² **hao**³ *shih*⁴ **k'an**⁴ **tien**⁴-*ying*³-*erh*² *ch'ü*⁴. *Pu*⁴ *k'an*⁴ *tien*⁴-*ying*³-*erh*², **t'ing**¹ **hsi**⁴ *ch'ü*⁴ *yeh*³ *hen*² *hao*³. **Yen**³ *tien*⁴-*ying*³-*erh*²-*ti*¹ *ti*⁴-*fang*¹ **chiao**⁴ **tien**⁴-*ying*³-**yüan**⁴. **Ch'ang**⁴-*hsi*⁴-*ti*¹ *ti*⁴-*fang*¹ **chiao**⁴ **hsi**⁴-*yüan*²-*tzu*¹. **Chang**¹ *hsien*¹-*sheng*¹ *shuo*¹ *chin*¹-*t'ien*¹ **na**⁴ **ke**⁴ *hsi*⁴-*yüan*²-*tzu*¹ **hsi**⁴ **hen**² **hao**³, *na*⁴ *ke*⁴ *tien*⁴-*ying*³-*erh*²-*ti*¹ **p'ien**⁴-*tzu*¹ *pu*² *ta*⁴ *hao*³.

When people have finished their work it is very pleasant to go and see a moving-picture. If one doesn't go and see a moving-picture, it is also very pleasant to go to a play. The place where they show moving-pictures is called a cinema. The place where they give plays is called a theatre. Mr. Chang says that the play on at that theatre today is very good, but the film at that cinema is not very good.

REVISION XII

電影院 tien⁴-ying³-yüan⁴

戲園子 hsi⁴-yüan²-tzu¹

問話 wen⁴-hua⁴

1. Nin² shang⁴ tien⁴-ying³-yüan⁴ tso⁴ shen²-ma¹ ch'ü⁴-la¹?
2. K'an⁴ tien⁴-ying³-erh² yeh³ yao⁴ mai³ p'iao⁴ ma¹?
3. Tien⁴-ying³-yüan⁴ yen³-ti¹ p'ien⁴-tzu¹ tou¹ shih⁴ wai⁴-kuo² p'ien⁴-tzu¹ ma¹?
4. Chin¹-t'ien¹ na⁴ ke⁴ tien⁴-ying³-yüan⁴-ti¹ p'ien⁴-tzu¹ hao³ pu⁴ hao³?
5. Che⁴ ke⁴ ti⁴-fang¹ yu³ hsi⁴-yüan²-tzu¹ mei² yu³?
6. Nin² shuo¹ shih⁴ k'an⁴ tien⁴-ying³-erh² hao³ shih⁴ t'ing¹ hsi⁴ hao³?
7. Wo³-men² shuo¹ t'ing¹ hsi⁴ ch'ü⁴ hsing², wo³-men² shuo¹ k'an⁴ hsi⁴ ch'ü⁴ hsing² pu⁴ hsing²?
8. Tso²-t'ien¹ ni³-men² chi³ wei⁴ k'an⁴ hsi⁴ ch'ü⁴-la¹ ma¹?

1. What did you go to the cinema for?
2. Must one buy a ticket to see a movie?
3. Are the films that are shown in the cinemas all foreign [films?
4. Is the film on at that cinema today a good one?
5. Is there a theatre in this place?
6. Which do you think is better, to see a movie or to go to a play?
7. We say *t'ing hsi ch'ü*, but can we say *k'an hsi ch'ü*?
8. Did you all go to a play yesterday?

REVISION XIII

THE HOSPITAL

醫院 I¹-yüan⁴

Tsai⁴ wo³-men² che-'rh⁴ yu³ i² ke⁴ hen³ ta⁴-ti¹ I¹-yüan⁴. Na⁴ ke⁴ i¹-yüan⁴ li³ tai⁴-fu¹ hen³ to¹. Tsai⁴ na⁴ ke⁴ ti⁴-fang¹ chu⁴-ti¹ jen² yu³-la¹ ping⁴, tou¹ shih⁴ shang⁴ na-'rh⁴ chih⁴ ch'ü⁴. Na⁴ ke⁴ i¹-yüan⁴-ti¹ tai⁴-fu¹ tou¹ shih⁴ hen² hao³ ti¹ tai⁴-fu¹. Wo³ fu⁴-ch'in¹-ti¹ ping⁴ ken¹ Huang² hsien¹-sheng¹-ti¹ ping⁴, tou¹ shih⁴ tsai⁴ na⁴ ke⁴ i¹-yüan⁴ chih⁴ hao³ la¹ ti¹.

We have a very large hospital here. There are a great many doctors in that hospital. The people living in that place all go there to be treated when they get ill. The doctors in that hospital are all excellent. Both my father's illness and Mr. Huang's were cured at that hospital.

醫院 I¹-yüan⁴   問話 wen⁴-hua⁴

1. Che-'rh⁴ yu³ I¹-yüan⁴ ma¹?
2. Na⁴ ke⁴ i¹-yüan⁴ li³ yu³ to¹-shao³ wei⁴ tai⁴-fu¹?
3. Na⁴ ke⁴ i¹-yüan⁴ shih⁴ wai⁴-kuo² i¹-yüan⁴ pu² shih⁴?
4. Huang² tai⁴-fu¹ shih⁴ na³ ke⁴ i¹-yüan⁴-ti¹ tai⁴-fu¹?

5. *Tsai*⁴ *Shang*⁴-*hai*³ *i*¹-*yüan*⁴ *li*³ **chih**⁴ *ping*⁴ **kuei**⁴ *pu*² *kuei*⁴ ?
6. *Nin*²-*ti*¹ *ping*⁴ *shih*⁴ **na**³ *ke*⁴ *i*¹-*yüan*⁴ *li*³ **chih**⁴ **hao**³ *la*¹ *ti*¹ ?

1. Is there a hospital here ?
2. How many physicians are there in that hospital ?
3. Is that a foreign hospital ?
4. What hospital is Dr. Huang from ?
5. Is it expensive to be treated at the Shanghai Hospital ?
6. At which hospital was your illness cured ?

REVISION XIV

THE RESTAURANT (ii)

飯舘子 fan⁴-kuan³-*tzu*¹

*Tso²-t'ien*¹ **Kuan**¹ **hsien**¹**-sheng**¹ **ch'ing**³ *wo*³*-men*² **chi**³ *ke*⁴ *jen*² *tsai*⁴ **fan**⁴**-kuan**³**-***tzu*¹ *li*³ **ch'ih**¹ **fan**⁴. *Wo*³*-men*² **ch'ih**¹**-***ti*¹ *yu*³ **niu**²**-jou**⁴, **yang**²**-jou**⁴, **chu**¹**-jou**⁴, **yü**², **shen**²**-ma**¹**-***ti*¹. *Wo*³*-men*² **hai**² **he**¹**-***la*¹ **hen**³ **to**¹**-***ti*¹ **chiu**³. *Wo*³*-men*³ **ch'ih**¹ **wan**²**-***la*¹ **fan**⁴, **Kuan**¹ **hsien**¹**-sheng**¹ **chiu**⁴ **wen**⁴ *wo*³*-men*², **shui**² **he**¹ **ch'a**² **shui**² **he**¹ **k'a**¹**-fei**⁴. *Wo*³*-men*² **kao**⁴**-su**⁴ *t'a*¹, *wo*³*-men*² **tou**¹ *pu*⁴ **he**¹ **k'a**¹**-fei**⁴. *T'a*¹ **chih**¹**-tao**⁴ *wo*³*-men*² **tou**¹ *pu*⁴ **he**¹ **k'a**¹**-fei**⁴, **chiu**⁴ **kei**³ *wo*³*-men*² **i**² *ke*⁴ *jen*² **tao**⁴**-***la*¹ *i*⁴ **wan**³ **ch'a**². *Wo*³*-men*² **he**¹ **wan**²**-***la*¹ **ch'a**², **chiu**⁴ **tou**¹ **hui**² **chia**¹ **ch'ü**⁴**-***la*¹.

Yesterday Mr. Kuan invited us to have a meal at a restaurant. We ate some beef, mutton, pork, fish and so on. We also drank a lot of wine. When we had finished eating, Mr. Kuan asked us if we drank tea or coffee. We told him that none of us drank coffee. When he learned that none of us drank coffee, he poured out a cup of tea for each of us. After we had finished our tea we all went home.

飯舘子 fan⁴-kuan³-*tzu*¹ 問話 wen⁴-*hua*⁴

1. *Na*⁴ *ke*⁴ fan⁴-*kuan*³-*tzu*¹ *shih*⁴ chung¹-*kuo*² fan⁴-*kuan*³-*tzu*¹, *shih*⁴ wai⁴-*kuo*² fan⁴-*kuan*³-*tzu*¹?
2. *Tsai*⁴ fan⁴-*kuan*³-*tzu*¹ ch'ih¹ *fan*⁴ kuei⁴ chien⁴?
3. *Tso*²-*t'ien*¹ *t'a*¹-*men*² ssu⁴ *wei*⁴ *tsai*⁴ fan⁴-*kuan*³-*tzu*¹ ch'ih¹ *fan*⁴, ch'ih¹-*la*¹ to¹-*shao*³ *ch'ien*²?
4. *Ni*³-*men*² *tsai*⁴ fan⁴-*kuan*³-*tzu*¹ *li*³ ch'ih¹-*ti*¹ tou¹ shih⁴ shen²-*ma*¹?
5. *Nin*² *ch'ing*³ *na*⁴ *erh*⁴ *wei*⁴ *ch'ih*¹ *fan*⁴, shih⁴ *tsai*⁴ fan⁴-*kuan*³-*tzu*¹ *ch'ih*¹, shih⁴ *tsai*⁴ chia¹ *li*³ *ch'ih*¹?

1. Is that a Chinese or a foreign restaurant?
2. Is it expensive to eat at a restaurant?
3. How much did the four of them spend at the restaurant yesterday?
4. What did you have to eat at the restaurant?
5. Shall you invite those two to eat at a restaurant or at [home?

REVISION XV

THE HOTEL

旅舘 lü²⁽³⁾-kuan³

Lü²-kuan³ shih⁴ **chu⁴ jen²** *ti¹ ti⁴-fang¹. Lü²-kuan³ yu³* **ta⁴,** *yu³* **hsiao³,** *yu³* **kuei⁴,** *yu³* **chien⁴.** *Tsai⁴ huo³-ch'e¹-chan⁴ na-'rh⁴ yu³ i² ke⁴* **hen³ ta⁴-ti¹** *lü²-kuan³. Na⁴ ke⁴ lü²-kuan³* **ming²-tzu¹ chiao⁴ Pei³-p'ing²** *lü²-kuan³. Pei³-p'ing² lü²-kuan³ li³ chu⁴-ti¹ jen²* **na³ kuo² jen² tou¹** *yu³. Pei³-p'ing³ lü²-kuan³-ti¹ wu¹-tzu¹ yeh³* **hen³ ta⁴,** *ch'uang¹-hu⁴ yeh³ hen³ to¹. T'a¹-men² shuo¹* **shih⁴ shang⁴ che-'rh⁴** *lai²-ti¹ jen²,* **tou¹ shih⁴ chu⁴ Pei³-p'ing²** *lü²-kuan³.*

An hotel is a place where people stay. There are large and small hotels, there are expensive and cheap hotels. At the railway station there is a very large hotel. That hotel is called the Peiping Hotel. There are people of every nationality staying at the Peiping Hotel. The rooms at the Peiping Hotel are very large and there are also numbers of windows. They say that all the people who come here stay at the Peiping Hotel.

旅舘 lü² ⁽³⁾-kuan³ 問話 wen⁴-hua⁴

1. *Na⁴ ke⁴ lü²-kuan³* **ta⁴** *hsiao³?*
2. *Tsai⁴ lü²-kuan³ chu⁴* **kuei⁴** *pu² kuei⁴?*
3. *Nin² tsai⁴ lü²-kuan³ chu⁴* **chi³** *chien¹ wu¹-tzu¹?*
4. *Tsai⁴ lü²-kuan³ chu⁴* **i⁴** *chien¹ wu¹-tzu¹* **to¹**-*shao³ ch'ien²?*
5. *Nin² shang⁴ Shang⁴-hai³* **shih⁴** *tsai⁴ lü²-kuan³ chu⁴,* **hai²** *shih⁴* **tsai¹ Chang¹** *hsien¹-sheng¹* **chia¹** *li³ chu⁴ ni¹?*
6. *Nin² tsai⁴ lü²-kuan³ chu⁴, yeh³ tsai⁴ lü²-kuan³ li³* **ch'ih¹** **fan⁴** *ma¹?*

1. Is that a big hotel?
2. Is it expensive to stay in an hotel?
3. How many rooms do you occupy in the hotel?
4. How much is it for one room in the hotel?
5. Shall you stay at an hotel or at Mr. Chang's house, when you are in Shanghai?
6. You are staying in the hotel, but do you also have meals in the hotel?

REVISION XVI

TRADESMEN

厨子 ch'u²-tzu¹   木匠 mu⁴-chiang⁴

裁縫 t'sai²-feng²   鞋匠 hsieh²-chiang⁴

1. 厨子 ch'u²-tzu¹

Q. *Ch'u²-tzu¹ shih⁴ tso⁴ shen²-ma¹-ti¹?*
A. *Ch'u²-tzu¹ shih⁴ tso⁴-fan⁴-ti¹.*
Q. *Nin² chia¹ li³ yu³ ch'u²-tzu¹ mei² yu³?*
A. *Yu³ ch'u²-tzu¹.*
Q. *Nin²-ti¹ ch'u²-tzu¹ hui⁴ tso⁴ wai⁴-kuo² fan⁴ ma¹?*
A. *T'a¹ hui⁴ tso⁴ wai⁴-kuo² fan⁴.*

Q. What does a cook do?
A. A cook prepares the food.
Q. Is there a cook in your house?
A. There is a cook.
Q. Can your cook make foreign food?
A. He can make foreign food.

2. **木匠** mu⁴-chiang⁴

Q. *Mu⁴-chiang⁴ hui⁴ tso⁴* cho¹-*tzu*¹, *l³-tzu*¹, hai² *hui⁴ tso⁴* shen²-*ma*¹?

A. *T'a*¹-*men*² *hai*² *hui*⁴ *tso*⁴ ch'uang¹-*hu*⁴, *men*², *shen*²-*ma*¹-*ti*¹.

Q. *Na⁴ ke⁴ mu⁴-chiang⁴ tso⁴-ti¹ na⁴ chang¹,* shih⁴ shu¹-*cho¹-tzu¹* shih⁴ fan⁴-*cho¹-tzu¹*?

A. *T'a¹ tso⁴-ti¹ shih⁴* fan⁴-*cho¹-tzu¹*.

Q. *Na⁴ chang¹ fan⁴-cho¹-tzu¹ shih⁴* kei³ *nin² tso⁴-ti¹ ma¹*?

A. *Pu² shih⁴, shih⁴* kei³ *na⁴ wei⁴ hsien¹-sheng¹ tso⁴-ti¹*.

Q. Carpenters can make tables and chairs, what else can they make?
A. They can also make windows, doors, etc.
Q. Did that carpenter make a desk or a dining-table?
A. He made a dining-table.
Q. Was that dining-table made for you?
A. No, it was made for that gentleman.

3. **裁縫** t'sai²-*feng*²

Q. *Nin² chiao⁴ ts'ai²-feng² tso⁴ shen²-ma¹*?
A. *Wo³ chiao⁴ t'a¹* kei³ *wo³ tso⁴ i¹-shang¹*.
Q. *T'a¹* hui⁴ *tso⁴* wai⁴-*kuo² i¹-shang¹ ma¹*?
A. *Wai⁴-kuo² i¹-shang¹ t'a¹ yeh³ hui⁴ tso⁴*.
Q. *Nin²-ti¹ i¹-shang¹ tou¹ shih⁴ t'a¹* kei³ *nin² tso⁴ ma¹*?
A. Tui⁴-*la¹, tou¹ shih⁴ t'a¹ kei³ wo³ tso⁴*.

Q. What did you tell the tailor to do ?
A. I told him to make me some clothes.
Q. Can he make foreign clothes ?
A. He can make foreign clothes.
Q. Does he make all your clothes for you ?
A. Yes, he makes them all for me.

4. 鞋匠 hsieh²-chiang⁴

Q. *Nin² ch'uan¹-ti¹ che⁴ shuang¹ hsieh² shih⁴ hsin¹-ti¹ shih⁴ chiu⁴-ti¹ ?*
A. *Wo³ ch'uan¹-ti¹ shih⁴ hsin¹ hsieh².*
Q. *Tsai⁴ na³ ke⁴ hsieh²-p'u⁴ mai³-ti¹ ?*
A. *Tsai⁴ chung¹-kuo² ta⁴-chieh¹ na⁴ ke⁴ hsieh²-p'u⁴ mai³-*
Q. *To¹-shao³ ch'ien² i⁴ shuang¹ ?* [*ti¹.*
A. *San¹ k'uai⁴ pa¹ i⁴ shuang¹.*

Q. Is the pair of shoes that you are wearing new or old ?
A. I am wearing new shoes.
Q. From which shoemaker were they bought ?
A. They were bought from that shoemaker on *Chung-kuo*
[street.
Q. How much was the pair ?
A. Three dollars eighty the pair.

INDEX TO NOTES

	Paragraph		Paragraph
a^1 啊	45	fu^4-mu^3 父母	80
adverbs of place	93	future time	39
affirmative sentence	1	greeting, forms of	50
approximate numbers	32	hai^2 — na^1 還〇哪	43
articles	8	hai^2 $shih^4$ 還是	44
at	45	hao^3 好, combinations	
cardinal numbers	24, 31	with	102
che^4 這	17, 34	$hsieh^4$-$hsieh^4$ 謝謝	51
che^4 $shih^4$ 這是	11	$hsien^1$-$sheng^1$ 先生	46
chi^3 幾	27	$hsin^4$ 信	98
chi^3 $shih^4$ 幾是	28	$hsüeh^2$-$hsiao^4$ 學校	95
$chia^1$ 家	69	$hsüeh^2$-$t'ang^2$ 學堂	95
$chiao^4$ 叫	60	hui^2-$ch'ü^4$ 回去	100
$chien^4$-$hsing^4$ 賤姓	66	hui^2-lai^2 回來	100
$chiu^4$ 就	62, 103	hui^2-ta^2 回答	54
$chung^1$-kuo^2 中國	84	i^2-$k'uai$-$'rh^4$ 一塊兒	79
$ch'uan^1$ 穿	82	i^4-$tien$-$'rh^3$ 一點兒	59
$ch'ü^4$ 去	49	in, inside	68, 73
classifiers	10, 23	interrogative pronoun	15
comparative degree	20	interrogative sentence	3, 9, 18
comparison	26	$k'ai^1$ 開	88
compound nouns	21	$k'an^4$ 看	90
compound verds	36	ken^1 跟	56
erh^2 兒	59, 78	kei^3 給	65
forms of greeting	50	$kuan^1$ 關	89
foreign nations	86	$kuei^4$-$hsing^4$ 貴姓	66

INDEX TO NOTES

	Paragraph		Paragraph
*lai*² 來	49	personal pronouns	5
*li*³ 裡	78	*pi*³ 筆	71
*mei*² 沒	6	*p'iao*⁴ 票	96
*men*² 們	29	possessive case	16
*ming*²-*pai*² 明白	57	possessive pronouns	14
money	63	postage stamp denominations	97
*na*¹ 哪	42		
*na*² 拿	75	present time	40
*na*²-*ch'ü*⁴ 拿去	76	*pu*⁴⁽²⁾ 不	12
*na*²-*lai*² 拿來	76	*p'u*⁴-*tzu*¹ 鋪子	70
*na*²-*pi*³ 拿筆	72	repetition of verbs with	
*na*³? 那?	77	— *i*¹	91
*na*⁴ 那	17, 34	sentence, affirmative	1
*na*⁴ *shih*⁴ 那是	11	sentence, interrogative	3, 9, 18
national adjectives	87	sentence, negative	2
nations, foreign	86	*shang*⁴ 上	92, 93
negatives	13	*shang*⁴ *chieh*¹ 上街	94
negative sentence	2	*shen*²-*ma*¹ — *tou*¹ 甚麼○都	48
*ni*¹ 呢	45	*shen*²-*ma*¹ — *yeh*³ *mei*² (*pu*⁴)	
*ni*³ 你, *nin*² 您	25	甚麼○也沒(不)	47
*ni*³ *shuo*¹ 你說	58	*shih*² *chi*³ 十幾	28
*nien*⁴ 念	90	*shuo*¹-*hua*⁴ 說話	55
nouns, compound	21	street names	81
numbers, approximate	32	superlative degree	67
numbers, cardinal	24, 31	*tai*⁴ 戴	82
numerators (classifiers)	10, 23	*tao*⁴ 倒	83
on	73	*t'a*¹ *shuo*¹ 他說	58
*pa*³ 把	74, 75, 76	*te*² *ping*⁴ 得病	101
past time	41	*ti*¹ 的	19, 30

INDEX TO NOTES

	Paragraph		Paragraph
tien⁴-pao⁴ 電報	98	verbs, compound	36
to¹-shao³ 多少	27	verbs, repeated with — *i¹*	91
tou¹ 都	33	*wan²* 完	61
tso⁴ 作, 做	37	*wai⁴-kou²* 外國	85
tso⁴ shen²-ma¹? 作甚麼?	99	weights	22
ts'ung² 從	93	*wo³ shuo¹* 我說	58
tzu³⁽¹⁾ 子	59	word order	38
verb	4, 35	*yao⁴* 要	64

ROMANIZATION INDEX

		LESSON	PARA
a^1 ? 啊	interrogative particle	10	VII
$ch'a^2$ 茶	tea	5	VII
$ch'a^2$-wan^3 茶碗	tea-cup	5	VIII
$ch'a^2$-yeh^4 茶葉	tea (in leaf)	6	VI
$chang^1$ 張	classifier for paper, tables, bank-notes, and documents	2	III
$chang^4$-fu^1 丈夫	husband	14	VII
$ch'ang^2$ 長	long	5	V
$ch'ang^4$ 唱	to sing, (to act)	24	IV
che^4 這	this, these	3	I
che-'rh^4 這兒	here	18	IX
che^4-chi^3 這幾	here are several (some)	5	II
che^4-$hsieh^1$ 這些	these	8	II
che^4-li^3 這裡	here	18	IX
$ch'e^1$-$p'iao^4$ 車票	railway ticket, (bus ticket, tram ticket, etc.)	23	iv
chi^3 ? 幾	how many? how much?	2	VI
chi^3 $shih^2$ 幾十	several tens, (dozens)	7	III
chi^3 pai^3 幾百	how many hundred? several hundred	8	I
chi^3 $ch'ien^1$ 幾千	how many thousand? several thousand	8	I
$ch'i^{1\,(2)}$ 七	seven	3	VII
$ch'i^2$-tzu^1 旗子	flag	20	IX
$chia^1$ 家	family, home	15	VI
$chiang^3$ 講	to explain, to expound	14	III
$chiang^3$-$t'ang^2$ 講堂	classroom, lecture-hall	18	X

ROMANIZATION INDEX

		LESSON	PARA
*ch'iang*² 牆	wall	16	III
*chiao*⁴ 叫	to call, call by name, to summon, to order.	13	(I-II)
*chieh*¹ 街	street	19	IV
*chien*¹ 間	classifier for rooms *(wu*¹*-tzu*¹*)*	15	I
*chien*⁴ 件	classifier for clothing *(i*¹*-shang*¹*)* and business *(shih*⁴*-ch'ing*²*)*	23	III
*chien*⁴ 賤	cheap	14	I
*chien*⁴ *hsing*⁴ 賤姓	humble name, my humble name is...	14	II
*ch'ien*¹ 千	thousand	7	VIII
*ch'ien*¹ *to*¹ 千多	over a thousand, a thousand odd	8	I
*ch'ien*¹*-pi*³ 鉛筆	pencil	1	VI
*ch'ien*² 錢	money	13	III
*chih*¹ 枝	classifier for pens, flowers, and other long things	2	V
*chih*¹*-tao*⁴ 知道	to know	5	VI
*chih*¹ 隻	classifier for sheep *(yang*²*)*	6	III
*chih*²*-yüan*² 職員	official	25	VI
*chih*³ 紙	paper	1	I
*chih*⁴ 治	to heal, to cure, to treat (medically)	25	IV
*ch'ih*¹ 吃	to eat	9	VIII
*ch'ih*¹*-mo*⁴*-chih*³ 吃墨紙	blotting paper	17	VI
*chin*¹ 斤	catty (1 ⅓ lbs.)	6	IV
*chin*¹*-t'ien*¹ 今天	today	10	I
*ch'ing*³ 請	please, to invite, request, ask (polite form)	11	(VII-VIII)

		LESSON	PARA
*ch'ing*³ *tso*⁴ 請坐	please sit down	11	VII
*chiu*³ 九	nine	3	VII
*chiu*³ 酒	wine	19	VIII
*chiu*³-*pei*¹ 酒盃	wine-glass	19	IX
*chiu*⁴ 就	then, when, thereupon, just, immediately	13	II
*chiu*⁴ 舊	old (of time, persons, places, things)	20	III
*cho*¹-*tzu*¹ 棹子	table	3	VI
*chu*¹ 猪	pig	6	III
*chu*¹-*jou*⁴ 猪肉	pork	6	IV
*chu*⁴ 住	to live, to live in, to dwell, to inhabit	15	V
*ch'u*²-*tzu*¹ 廚子	cook	25	I
*ch'uan*¹ 穿	to put on, to wear (of clothes)	19	V
*ch'uang*¹-*hu*⁴ 窗戶	window	15	III
*chung*¹-*hsüeh*²-*t'ang*² 中學堂	Middle School	17	V
*chung*¹-*hsüeh*²-*hsiao*⁴ 中學校	Middle School	23	II
*chung*¹-*kuo*² 中國	China, Chinese	20	V
*chung*¹-*kuo*² *jen*² 中國人	Chinese (person), The Chinese people	20	VI
*chung*¹-*kuo*² *hua*⁴ 中國話	Chinese language, Chinese	20	VII
*chung*¹-*kuo*² *tzu*⁴ 中國字	Chinese character	20	VIII
*chü*⁴ 句	sentence, phrase	12	III

		LESSON	PARA
*ch'ü*⁴ 去	to go, to go away, to go out, motion away from	11	VI
*ch'ü*⁴ *hsin*⁴ 去信	to send a letter	23	V
*ch'ü*⁴ *tien*⁴*-pao*⁴ 去電報	to send a telegram	23	VI
*erh*² 兒	colloquial ending (note § 59)	12	-
*erh*²*-tzu*¹ 兒子	son, boy	6	II
*erh*⁴ 二	two	6	VII
*erh*⁴*-shih*² *chi*³ 二十幾	over twenty, twenty odd	7	III
*fan*⁴ 飯	food, cooked rice	5	VII
*fan*⁴*-cho*¹*-tzu*¹ 飯桌子	dining-table, dinner-table	6	I
*fan*⁴*-kuan*³*-tzu*¹ 飯館子	restaurant	24	I
*fan*⁴*-wan*³ 飯碗	rice-bowl	5	VIII
*fang*²*-tzu*¹ 房子	house	15	IV
*fen*¹*-ch'ien*² 分錢	cent	13	III
*fen*¹*-p'iao*⁴ 分票	cent postage stamp	23	V
*fen*² ⁽³⁾*-pi*³ 粉筆	chalk, crayon	16	IV
*fen*⁴ 份	classifier for newspaper *(pao*⁴*)*	21	VII
	and telegram *(tien*⁴*-pao*⁴*)*	23	VI
*feng*¹ 封	classifier for letter *(hsin*⁴*)*	21	VII
*fu*⁴*-ch'in*¹ 父親	father	6	II
*fu*⁴*-mu*³ 父母	parents	19	II
*hai*² 還	still more, besides, still, yet, also	10	III
*hai*² *shih*⁴ 還是	or	10	VII
*hai*² *shih*⁴ 還是	(denotes comparison)	10	VIII
*hai*²*-tzu*¹ 孩子	child, children	19	III
*hao*³ 好	good, well, all right	10	VI
*hao*³ *ch'ih*¹ 好吃	good to eat, tasty	10	VIII
*hao*³*-hsieh*¹*-ke*¹ 好些個	a good many, a great many	12	VIII

		LESSON	PARA
he^1 喝	to drink	9	VII
hei^1 黑	black	16	I
hei^1-pan^3 黑板	blackboard	16	IV
$hen^{3(2)}$ 很	very	14	I
hsi^4 戲	play	24	IV
hsi^4-$yüan^2$-tzu^1 戲園子	theatre	24	IV
$hsiao^3$ 小	small, mean, little	5	IV
$hsiao^3$-$hsüeh^2$-$hsiao^4$ 小學校	Primary School	23	II
$hsiao^3$-$hsüeh^2$-$t'ang^2$ 小學堂	Primary School	17	V
$hsieh^2$ 鞋	shoe, slipper	19	VII
$hsieh^2$-$chiang^4$ 鞋匠	shoemaker	25	III
$hsieh^3$ 寫	to write	9	IV
$hsieh^4$-$hsieh^4$ 謝謝	thanks, thank you	11	VII
$hsien^1$-$sheng^1$ 先生	teacher, Mr.	4	IV
$hsien^1$-$sheng^1$-ti^1 先生的	teacher's	5	I
$hsin^1$ 新	new, recent, recently	20	III
$hsin^4$ 信	letter	21	VII
$hsing^2$ 行	it will do!	25	VI
$hsing^4$ 姓	surname	13	I
$hsüeh^2$ 學	to learn, to study	21	I
$hsüeh^2$-$hsiao^4$ 學校	school	23	II
$hsüeh^2$-$sheng^1$ 學生	student, pupil	4	IV
$hsüeh^2$-$sheng^1$-ti^1 學生的	student's, pupil's	5	I
$hsüeh^2$-$t'ang^2$ 學堂	school	15	VII
hua^4 畫	to draw, to paint	16	V

		LESSON	PARA
*hua-'rh*⁴ 畫兒	drawing, painting	16	V
*huang*² 黃	yellow	16	I
*hui*² 回	a time	12	VII
*hui*²*-chia*¹ 回家	to return home	24	VIII
*hui*²*-ch'ü*⁴ 回去	to return, to go back	24	VIII
*hui*²*-hsin*⁴ 回信	reply (answer) to a letter	23	V
*hui*²*-kuo*² 回國	to return to one's native country	24	VIII
*hui*²*-lai*² 回來	to return, to come back	24	VIII
*hui*²*-ta*² 回答	to reply, to answer	12	II
*hui*⁴ 會	to be able, can	9	VI
*hung*² 紅	red	16	I
*huo*³*-ch'e*¹*-chan*⁴ 火車站	railway station	23	IV
*i*² (2,4) 一	one	2	I
*i*²*-kuai-'rh*⁴ 一塊兒	together	19	I
*i*⁴*-tien-'rh*³ 一點兒	a little	12	VIII
*i*¹*-shang*¹ 衣裳	clothes, clothing	19	V
*i*¹*-yüan*⁴ 醫院	hospital	25	IV
*i*³*-tzu*¹ 椅子	chair	3	VI
*i*⁴*-ssu*¹ 意思	meaning, intention, idea	14	IV
*jen*² 人	man, men, person, people	4	III
*jou*⁴ 肉	meat	6	IV
*k'a*¹*-fei*⁴ 咖啡	coffee	6	VI
*k'ai*¹ 開	to open	21	III
*k'an*⁴ 看	to look, to look at, to see	21	IV
*k'an*⁴ *hsi*⁴ 看戲	to see a play	24	IV
*k'an*⁴*-i*¹*-k'an*⁴ 看一看	to look, to take a look at	21	IX
*k'an*⁴ *pao*⁴ 看報	to read a newspaper	21	VII
*k'an*⁴ *shu*¹ 看書	to read a book	21	VII

		LESSON	PARA
k'an⁴ tien⁴-ying³-erh² 看電影兒	to see (look at) motion pictures	24	III
kang¹-pi³ 鋼筆	pen, steel pen	1	VI
kao⁴-su⁴ 告訴	to tell	14	V
ke⁴ 個	general classifier	2	II
k'e⁴-pen³ 課本	text-book	20	IV
k'e⁴-t'ang² 課堂	classroom	18	X
kei³ 給	to give, for, on behalf of, to	13	V-VI
ken¹ 跟	with, and	12	III-IV
k'ou³ 口	classifier for pig (chu¹)	6	III
ku¹-niang² 姑娘	daughter, girl, Miss	6	II
kua⁴ 掛	to hang up, to suspend	17	I
k'uai⁴ 塊	classifier, bit, piece, lump	6	V
k'uai⁴-ch'ien² 塊錢	dollar	13	III
kuan¹ 關	to close, to shut	21	III
kuei⁴ 貴	dear, expensive	14	I
kuei⁴-hsing⁴ 貴姓	honourable name, what is your honourable name?	14	II
kung¹-k'e⁴ 功課	lesson	14	III
kuo² 國	country	20	V
la¹ 了	particle denoting the past tense	10	I
lai² 來	to come, motion towards	11	VI
lai² hsin⁴ 來信	to receive a letter	23	V
lai² tien⁴-pao⁴ 來電報	to receive a telegram	23	VI
lan² 藍	blue	16	I
li³ 裡	in, inside	15	II
liang³ 兩	two	2	I

ROMANIZATION INDEX

		LESSON	PARA
*liang*³ 兩	Chinese ounce, tael	20	I
*ling*² 零	zero, nought	7	VII
*liu*⁴ 六	six	3	VII
*lü*²⁽³⁾-*kuan*³ 旅館	hotel, inn	24	II
*lü*⁴ 綠	green	16	I
*ma*¹ 麼	interrogative particle	1	VII
*mai*³ 買	to buy	13	VII
*mai*³-*tung*¹-*hsi*¹-*ti*¹ 買東西的	one who buys things, buyer	25	III
*mai*⁴ 賣	to sell	13	VII
*mai*⁴-*tung*¹-*hsi*¹-*ti*¹ 賣東西的	one who sells things, seller	25	III
*mao*²-*pi*³ 毛筆	writing-brush, brush-pen	4	I
*mao*²-*ch'ien*² 毛錢	ten-cents	13	III
*mao*⁴-*tzu*¹ 帽子	hat	19	VI
*mei*² 沒	no, not (notes § 13)	3	–
*mei*² *yu*³ 沒有	have not, has not, have not got, has not got	1	IV
*men*² 們	plural particle (of persons)	7	V
*men*² 門	door, gate	15	III
*mien*⁴ 面	classifier for walls *(ch'iang²)* and flags *(ch'i²-tzu¹)*	16	III
*mien*⁴-*pao*¹ 麵包	bread	6	VI
*ming*²-*pai*¹ 明白	to understand	12	IV
*ming*²-*t'ien*¹ 明天	tomorrow	10	I
*ming*²-*tzu*¹ 名子	name, personal name	13	I
*mo*⁴-*shui*-'*rh*³ 墨水兒	ink	16	IV
*mu*³-*ch'in*¹ 母親	mother	6	II
*mu*⁴-*chiang*⁴ 木匠	carpenter	25	II

ROMANIZATION INDEX

		LESSON	PARA
*na*¹ 哪	final particle	10	IV
*na*² 拿	to take, to grasp, to take hold of	16	VI
*na*²-*ch'ü*⁴ 拿去	to take away, to take	17	III
*na*²-*lai*² 拿來	to bring here, to bring	17	III
*na*² *pi*³ 拿筆	to hold a pen, to use a pen (to write with)	16	VI
*na*³? 那?	which?	18	VIII
na-'*rh*³? 那兒?	where?	18	IX
*na*²⁽³⁾-*li*³? 那裡?	where?	18	IX
*na*⁴ 那	that, those	3	I
na-'*rh*⁴ 那兒	there	18	IX
*na*⁴ *chi*³ 那幾	there are several, some	5	II
*na*⁴-*hsieh*¹ 那些	those	8	II
*na*⁴-*li*³ 那裡	there	18	IX
*nai*³-*yu*² 奶油	butter	19	X
*nan*²-*ching*¹ 南京	Nanking	24	VIII
*ni*¹ 呢	interrogative final particle	10	VII
*ni*³ 你	you (usual form)	1	II
*ni*³-*men*² 你們	you (plural)	7	V
*ni*³-*men*²-*ti*¹ 你們的	your (pl), yours (pl)	7	VI
*ni*³ *shuo*¹ 你說	you say, your opinion is	12	VI
*ni*³-*ti*¹ 你的	your, yours (usual form)	4	VI
*nien*⁴ 念	to read, to study	9	V
*nin*² 您	you (polite form)	1	II
*nin*² *hao*³ *a*¹? 您好啊	how are you? are you well?	11	VII
*nin*² *shuo*¹ 您說	you say, your opinion is	12	VI
*nin*²-*ti*¹ 您的	your, yours (polite form)	4	VI
*niu*² 牛	cow, ox	6	III

ROMANIZATION INDEX

		LESSON	PARA
niu²-nai³ 牛奶	milk	19	X
niu²-jou⁴ 牛肉	beef	6	IV
pa¹⁽²⁾ 八	eight	3	VII
pa³⁽²⁾ 把	classifier for chairs, knives	3	VII
pa³ 把	to take hold of	17	II
pai² 白	white	16	I
pai³ 百	hundred	7	VII
pai³ to¹ 百多	over a hundred, a hundred odd	8	I
pan⁴ 半	half, ½	20	I
pan⁴ fen¹ p'iao⁴ 半分票	half cent postage stamp	23	V
pan⁴ kung¹ 辦公	to transact business	25	VI
pao⁴ 報	newspaper	21	VII
pei³-p'ing² 北平	Peiping, Peking	24	VIII
pen³ 本	classifier for books (shu¹)	2	IV
pen³-tzu¹ 本子	note-book	1	I
pi³ 筆	pen, instrument for writing	16	VI
p'iao⁴ 票	ticket, warrant, banknote	23	V
p'ien⁴-tzu¹ 片子	film	24	III
ping⁴ 病	sickness, illness, to be ill	25	IV
p'ing²-tzu¹ 瓶子	bottle	19	VIII
po¹-li²-pei¹ 玻璃盃	glass, tumbler	5	VIII
pu⁴⁽²⁾ 不	no, not (notes § 13)	3	I
pu⁴ hao³ 不好	bad, not well, badly	10	VI
pu⁴ hsing² 不行	it won't do!	25	VI
pu² shih⁴ 不是	no, it isn't, is not so	3	II
pu² ta⁴ hao³ 不大好	not very good, not very well	14	I
pu² tui⁴ 不對	incorrect, wrong	12	V
p'u⁴-tzu¹ 鋪子	shop, store	15	VIII

		LESSON	PARA
san¹ 三	three	2	I
shang¹-jen² 商人	merchant, trader	24	V
shang⁴ 上	on	17	I
shang⁴ che-'rh⁴ 上這兒	here, to here, hither	22	VI
shang⁴ che⁴-li³ 上這裡	here, to here, hither	22	VI
shang⁴ chieh¹ 上街	up the street	22	II
shang⁴ — ch'ü⁴ 上〇去	to go to —	22	I
shang⁴-hai³ 上海	Shanghai	23	VI
shang⁴ na-'rh³? 上那兒?	where to? where? whither?	22	II
shang⁴ na²-li³? 上那裡?	where to? where? whither?	22	II
shang⁴ na-'rh⁴ 上那兒	there, to there, thither	22	V
shang⁴ na⁴-li³ 上那裡	there, to there, thither	22	V
shao³ 少	few	7	I
shen²-ma¹? 甚麼?	what? what sort of?	4	II
shen²-ma¹-ti¹ 甚麼的	etc., and so on	8	I
shen²-ma¹ — tou¹ 甚麼〇都	everything, all kinds of, any kind of	11	I
shen²-ma¹ — yeh³ mei² 甚麼〇也沒	not — any, — nothing	11	I
shen²-ma¹ — yeh³ pu⁴ 甚麼〇也不	not — any, — nothing	11	I
shih² 十	ten	3	VII
shih² chi³ 十幾	over ten, ten odd	7	III
shih⁴ 是	is, are, yes	3	I-II
shih⁴ 事	business, affair, work	23	III
shih⁴-ch'ing² 事情	business, affair, work	23	III
shu¹ 書	book	1	I
shu¹-chi⁴ 書記	secretary	24	VI
shu¹-cho¹-tzu¹ 書桌子	writing table	6	I

ROMANIZATION INDEX

		LESSON	PARA
shuang¹ 雙	a pair	19	VII
shui²? 誰?	who? which?	4	V
shui²-ti¹? 誰的?	whose?	4	VII
shui² tou¹ 誰都	everyone, everybody	11	I
shui² yeh³ mei² 誰也沒	no one, nobody	11	I
shui² yeh³ pu⁴ 誰也不	no one, nobody	11	I
shui³ 水	water	5	VII
shuo¹-hua⁴ 說話	(to speak words), to speak, to say	12	III
so³ 所	classifier for buildidgs (*fang²-tzu¹*)	15	IV
ssu⁴ 四	four	2	I
ta³ tien⁴-pao⁴ 打電報	to despatch (send) a telegram	23	VI
ta⁴ 大	large, great, big, tall	5	IV
ta⁴-hsüeh²-hsiao⁴ 大學校	High School, University	23	II
ta⁴-hsüeh²-t'ang² 大學堂	High School, University	17	V
t'a¹ 他, 她, 牠	he, him, she, her, it	1	II
t'a¹-men² 他們	they, them	7	V
t'a¹-men²-ti¹ 他們的	their, theirs	7	VI
t'a¹ shuo¹ 他說	he says, his opinion is	12	VI
t'a¹-ti¹ 他的	his, her, hers, its	4	VI
tai⁴ 戴	to wear (on the head)	19	VI
tai⁴-fu¹ 大夫	doctor, physican	25	IV
t'ai⁴ 太	too, very	14	VI
t'ai⁴-t'ai⁴ 太太	wife, lady, Mrs., Madam	14	VII
tang¹ 當	to act as, to be employed as	25	VI
tao⁴ 倒	to pour, to pour out	20	II
te² ping⁴ 得病	to become ill, to get sick	25	IV
ti¹ 的	possessive particle	4	VI

		LESSON	PARA
*ti*¹ 的	particle denoting the past participle	10	II
*ti*⁴-*fang*¹ 地方	place	15	VII
*ti*⁴-*pan*³ 地板	floor, wooden floor	16	II
*t'iao*² 條	classifier for streets, dogs, fish, and long slender things	6 19	V IV
*tien*⁴-*pao*⁴ 電報	telegram, telegraphic despatch	23	VI
*tien*⁴-*pao*⁴-*chü*² 電報局	telegraph office	23	VI
*tien*⁴-*ying*³-*erh*² 電影兒	motion pictures, movies	24	III
*tien*⁴-*ying*³-*yüan*⁴ 電影院	cinema	24	III
*ting*³ 頂	classifier for hats (*mao*⁴-*tzu*¹)	19	VI
*ting*³-*p'eng*² 頂棚	ceiling	16	II
*t'ing*¹ 聽	to listen, to listen to	21	VIII
*t'ing*¹ *hsi*⁴ 聽戲	to hear a play, to see a play	24	IV
*t'ing*¹-*i*¹-*t'ing*¹ 聽一聽	to listen	21	IX
*to*¹ 多	many, much, more	7	I
*to*¹-*shao*³? 多少?	how many? how much?	7	II
*to*¹-*tsan*²? 多喒?	when?	21	II
*tou*¹ 都	all, both	8	I
*t'ou*² 頭	classifier for cow, ox (*niu*²)	6	III
*tsai*⁴ 再	again, a second time, more	12	VII
*tsai*⁴-*chien*⁴ 再見	we shall meet again, goodbye, au revoir	11	VII
*tsai*⁴ 在	in, at	15	II
*tsai*⁴ *che*-'*rh*⁴ 在這兒	here	18	IX
*tsai*⁴ *che*⁴-*li*³ 在這裡	here	18	IX
*tsai*⁴—*li*³ 在○裡	in, at	15	II
*tsai*⁴ *na*-'*rh*³? 在那兒?	where?	18	IX
*tsai*⁴ *na*²-*li*³? 在那裡?	where?	18	IX

ROMANIZATION INDEX

		LESSON	PARA
tsai⁴ na-'rh⁴ 在那兒	there	18	IX
tsai³ na⁴-li³ 在那裡	there	18	IX
tsai⁴—shang⁴ 在〇上	on	17	I
ts'ai²-feng² 裁縫	tailor	24	VII
tso²-t'ien¹ 昨天	yesterday	10	I
tso⁴ 作	to make, to do, (notes § 37)	9	I
tso⁴ 做	to make, to do, (notes § 37)	9	I
tso⁴ fan⁴ 作飯	to prepare food, to cook	9	III
tso⁴-fan⁴-ti¹ 作飯的	one who prepares food, cook	25	I
tso⁴-hsieh²-ti¹ 作鞋的	one who makes shoes, shoemaker	25	III
tso⁴-mai³-mai⁴ 作買賣	to buy and sell, to trade	24	V
tso⁴-mai³-mai⁴-ti¹ 作買賣的	merchant, one who buys and sells	24	V
tso⁴ shu¹ 作書	to compose (write) a book	9	II
ts'ung² che-'rh⁴ 從這兒	here, from here, hence	22	VI
ts'ung² che⁴-li³ 從這裡	here, from here, hence	22	VI
ts'ung²—lai² 從〇來	to come from	22	III
ts'ung² na-'rh³? 從那兒?	where from? whence?	22	IV
ts'ung² na²-li³? 從那裡?	where from? whence?	22	IV
ts'ung² na-'rh⁴ 從那兒	from there, thence	22	VII
ts'ung² na⁴-li³ 從那裡	from there, thence	22	VII
tuan³ 短	short	5	V
tui⁴ 對	correct, right	12	V
tung¹-hsi¹ 東西	thing	4	III
tzu³ ⁽¹⁾ 子	colloquial ending (notes § 59)	12	-
tzu⁴ 字	character, letter	7	IV
wai⁴-kuo² 外國	foreign country, abroad	20	V

ROMANIZATION INDEX

		LESSON	PARA
wai⁴-kuo² hua⁴ 外國話	foreign language	20	VII
wai⁴-kuo² jen² 外國人	foreigner	20	VI
wai⁴-kuo² tzu⁴ 外國字	foreign word, foreign letter	20	VIII
wan² 完	to complete, to finish	13	II
wan³ 碗	bowl, cup	5	VIII
wei⁴ 位	classifier for persons (polite form)	4	IV
wen⁴ 問	to ask	12	I
wo³ 我	I, me	1	II
wo³-men² 我們	we, us	7	V
wo³-men²-ti¹ 我們的	our, ours	7	VI
wo³ shuo¹ 我說	I say, my opinion is	12	VI
wo³-ti¹ 我的	my, mine	4	VI
wu¹-tzu¹ 屋子	room	15	I
wu³ 五	five	2	I
yang² 羊	sheep	6	III
yang²-jou⁴ 羊肉	mutton	6	IV
yao⁴ 要	to want, will, shall	9	IX
yao⁴ 要	to want, to require	13	IV
yeh³ 也	also, even	3	V
yen²-se⁴ 顏色	colour	16	I
yen³ tien⁴-ying³-erh² 演電影兒	to show motion pictures (movies)	24	III
yu²-cheng⁴-chü² 郵政局	post office, the Chinese Post Office	23	V
yu²-p'iao⁴ 郵票	postage stamp	23	V
yu³ 有	have, has, have got, has got	1	III
yü² 魚	fish	6	IV

ENGLISH INDEX

		LESSON	PARA
able, to be 會	hui⁴	9	VI
abroad 外國	wai⁴-kuo²	20	V
act as, to 當	tang¹	25	VI
affair 事情	shih⁴-ch'ing²	23	III
again 再	tsai⁴	12	VII
all 都	tou¹	8	I
all kinds of 甚麽○都	shen²-ma¹ — tou¹	11	I
all right 好	hao³	10	VI
also 也, 還	yeh³, hai²	3 v, 10	III
and 跟	ken¹	12	IV
and so on 甚麽的	shen²-ma¹-ti¹	8	I
any kind of 甚麽○都	shen²-ma¹ — tou¹	11	I
answer, to 回答	hui²-ta²	12	II
answer, to a letter 回信	hui²-hsin⁴	23	V
are 是	shih⁴	3	I
are you well? 您好啊？	nin² hao³ a¹?	11	VII
ask, to 問	wen⁴	12	I
ask, to (polite) 請	ch'ing³	11	VIII
at 在	tsai⁴	15	II
au revoir 再見	tsai⁴-chien⁴	11	VII
bad 不好	pu⁴ hao³	10	VI
badly 不好	pu⁴ hao³	10	VI
bank-note 票	p'iao⁴	23	V
beef 牛肉	niu²-jou⁴	6	IV
besides 還	hai²	10	III
big 大	ta⁴	5	IV

ENGLISH INDEX

		LESSON	PARA
bit 塊	k'uai⁴	6	V
black 黑	hei¹	16	I
blackboard 黑板	hei¹-pan³	16	IV
blotting-paper 吃墨紙	ch'ih¹-mo⁴-chih³	17	VI
blue 藍	lan²	16	I
book 書	shu¹	1	I
both 都	tou¹	8	¶
bottle 瓶子	p'ing²-tzu¹	19	VIII
bowl 碗	wan³	5	VIII
boy 兒子	erh²-tzu¹	6	II
bread 麵包	mien⁴-pao¹	6	VI
bring, to 拿來	na²-lai²	17	III
brush-pen 毛筆	mao²-pi³	4	I
business 事情	shih⁴-ch'ing²	23	III
business, to transact 辦公	pan⁴ kung¹	25	VI
butter 奶油	nai³-yu²	19	X
buy, to 買	mai³	13	VII
call, to 叫	chiao⁴	13	I
can (able) 會	hui⁴	9	VI
carpenter 木匠	mu⁴-chiang⁴	25	II
catty 斤	chin¹	6	IV
ceiling 頂棚	ting³-p'eng²	16	II
cent 分	fen¹	13	III
cent stamp 分票	fen¹-p'iao⁴	25	V
chair 椅子	i³-tzu¹	3	VI
chalk 粉筆	fen²⁽³⁾-pi³	16	IV
character 字	tzu⁴	7	IV
cheap 賤	chien⁴	14	I
child 孩子	hai²-tzu¹	19	III

ENGLISH INDEX

		LESSON	PARA
China 中國	*chung¹-kuo²*	20	V
Chinese 中國	*chung¹-kuo²*	20	V
cinema 電影院	*tien⁴-ying³-yüan⁴*	24	III
classroom 講堂, 課堂	*chiang³-t'ang² k'e⁴-[t'ang²*	18	X
clerk 書記	*shu¹-chi⁴*	24	VI
close, to 關	*kuan¹*	21	III
clothes 衣裳	*i¹-shang¹*	19	V
coffee 咖啡	*k'a¹-fei⁴*	6	VI
colour 顏色	*yen²-se⁴*	16	I
come, to 來	*lai²*	11	VI
come back, to 回來	*hui²-lai²*	.24	VIII
complete, to 完	*wan²*	13	II
compose, to (a book) 作書	*tso⁴ shu¹*	9	II
cook 廚子	*ch'u²-tzu¹*	25	I
cook, to 做(作)飯	*tso⁴ fan⁴*	9	III
cooked rice 飯	*fan⁴*	5	VII
correct 對	*tui⁴*	12	V
cow 牛	*niu²*	6	III
crayon 粉筆	*fen²⁽³⁾-pi³*	16	IV
cup 碗	*wan³*	5	VII
cure, to 治	*chih⁴*	25	IV
CLASSIFIERS			
for books 本	*pen³*	2	IV
» buildings 所	*so³*	15	IV
» chairs 把	*pa³⁽²⁾*	3	VII
» clothes 件	*chien⁴*	19	V
» cows 頭	*t'ou²*	6	III
» fish, streets 條	*t'iao²*	6	V

ENGLISH INDEX

			LESSON	PARA
» flags 面	mien⁴		20	IX
general 個	ke⁴		2	II
for hats 頂	ting³		19	VI
» letters 封	feng¹		21	VII
» newspapers 份	fen⁴		21	VII
» paper 張	chang¹		2	II
» pens 枝	chih¹		2	V
» persons 位	wei⁴		4	IV
» pigs 口	k'ou³		6	III
» rooms 間	chien¹		15	I
» sheep 隻	chih¹		6	III
» walls 面	mien⁴		16	III
daughter 姑娘	ku¹-niang²		6	II
dear 貴	kuei⁴		14	I
despatch, to 打	ta³		23	VI
dining-table 飯桌子	fan⁴-cho¹-tzu¹		6	I
dinner-table 飯桌子	fan⁴-cho¹-tzu¹		6	I
disease 病	ping⁴		25	IV
do, to 作	tso⁴		9	I
doctor 大夫	tai⁴-fu¹		25	IV
dollar 塊錢	k'uai⁴-ch'ien²		13	III
door 門	men²		15	III
dozens 幾十	chi³ shih²		7	III
draw, to 畫	hua⁴		16	V
drawing 畫兒	hua-'rh⁴		16	V
drink, to 喝	he¹		9	VII
dwell, to 住	chu⁴		15	V
eat, to 吃	ch'ih¹		9	VIII
eight 八	pa¹⁽²⁾		3	VII

ENGLISH INDEX 341

		LESSON	PARA
employed as, to be 當	*tang*¹	25	VI
etc. 甚麼的	*shen²-ma¹-ti¹*	8	I
even 也	*yeh³*	3	V
everybody 誰都	*shui² tou¹*	11	I
everyone 誰都	*shui² tou¹*	11	I
everything 甚麼○都	*shen²-ma¹ — tou¹*	11	I
expensive 貴	*kuei⁴*	14	I
explain, to 講	*chiang³*	14	III
expound, to 講	*chiang³*	14	III
family 家	*chia¹*	15	VI
father 父親	*fu⁴-ch'in¹*	6	II
few 少	*shao³*	7	I
film 片子	*p'ien⁴-tzu¹*	24	III
finish, to 完	*wan²*	13	II
fish 魚	*yü²*	6	IV
five 五	*wu³*	2	I
flag 旗子	*ch'i²-tzu¹*	20	IX
floor 地板	*ti⁴-pan³*	16	II
food 飯	*fan⁴*	5	VII
for 給	*kei³*	13	V
foreign 外國	*wai⁴-kuo²*	20	V
foreign country 外國	*wai⁴-kuo²*	20	V
foreigner 外國人	*wai⁴-kuo² jen²*	20	VI
four 四	*ssu⁴*	2	I
gate 門	*men²*	15	III
general classifier 個	*ke⁴*	2	II
girl 姑娘	*ku¹-niang²*	6	II
give, to 給	*kei³*	13	VI
glass 玻璃盃	*po¹-li²-pei¹*	5	VIII

		LESSON	PARA
go, to 去	ch'ü^4	11	VI
go away, to 去	ch'ü^4	11	VI
go out, to 去	ch'ü^4	11	VI
good 好	hao^3	10	VI
good to eat 好吃	hao^3 ch'ih^1	10	VIII
good-bye 再見	tsai^4-chien^4	11	VII
good many 好些個	hao^3-hsieh^1-ke^4	12	VIII
grasp, to 拿	na^2	16	VI
great 大	ta^4	5	IV
great many 好些個	hao^3-hsieh^1-ke^4	12	VIII
green 綠	lü^4	16	I
half 半	pan^4	20	I
hang up, to 掛	kua^4	17	I
hat 帽子	mao^4-tzu^1	19	VI
have 有	yu^3	1	III
have got 有	yu^3	1	III
have not 沒有	mei^2 yu^3	1	IV
have not got 沒有	mei^2 yu^3	1	IV
he 他	t'a^1	1	II
heal, to 治	chih^4	25	IV
hear, to (a play) 聽戲	t'ing^1 hsi^4	24	IV
hence 從這兒(裡)	t'sung^2-che-'rh^4 (li^3)	22	VI
her 他, (她), 他的	t'a^1	1	II
here 這兒, 這裡	che-'rh^4, che^4-li^3	3	I
High School 大學堂(校)	ta^4-hsüeh^2-t'ang^2 (hsiao^4)	17	V
him 他	t'a^1	1	II
hither 上這兒(裡)	shang^4 che-'rh^4 (li^3)	22	VI
his 他的	t'a^1-ti^1	4	VI

ENGLISH INDEX

		LESSON	PARA
hold a pen, to 拿筆	$na^2\ pi^3$	16	VI
home 家	$chia^1$	15	VI
honourable name 貴姓	$kuei^4\text{-}hsing^4$	14	II
hospital 醫院	$i^1\text{-}yuan^4$	25	IV
hotel 旅館	$lü^{2(3)}\text{-}kuan^3$	24	II
house 房子	$fang^2\text{-}tzu^1$	15	IV
how are you? 您好啊?	$nin^2\ hao^3\ a^1?$	11	VII
how many? 幾? 多少?	$chi^3?\ to^1\text{-}shao^3?$	2 VI, 7 II	
how much? 幾? 多少?	$chi^3?\ to^1\ shao^3?$	2 VI, 7 II	
humble name 賤姓	$chien^4\text{-}hsing^4$	14	II
hundred 百	pai^3	7	VII
husband 丈夫	$chang^4\text{-}fu^1$	14	VII
I 我	wo^3	1	II
idea 意思	$i^4\text{-}ssu^1$	14	IV
ill, to be 病	$ping^4$	25	IV
ill, to become 得病	$te^2\ ping^4$	25	IV
immediately 就	$chiu^4$	13	II
in 在○裡, 裡	$tsai^4 - li^3,\ li^3$	15	II
incorrect 不對	$pu^2\text{-}tui^4$	12	V
inhabit, to 住	chu^4	15	V
ink 墨水兒	$mo^4\text{-}shui\text{-}'rh^3$	16	IV
inn 旅館	$lü^{2(3)}\text{-}kuan^3$	24	II
inside 裡	li^3	15	II
intention 意思	$i^4\text{-}ssu^1$	14	IV
interrogative particle 麼, 啊	$ma^1?\ a^1?$	1 VII, 10 VII	
interrogative final particle 呢	$ni^1?$	10	VII
invite, to 請	$ch'ing^3$	11	VIII
is 是	$shih^4$	3	I
it 他 (牠)	$t'a^1$	1	II

ENGLISH INDEX

		LESSON	PARA
it will do 行	*hsing*²	25	VI
it won't do 不行	*pu*⁴ *hsing*²	25	VI
its 他(牠)的	*t'a*¹-*ti*¹	4	VI
just 就	*chiu*⁴	13	II
know, to 知道	*chih*¹-*tao*⁴	5	VI
lady 太太	*t'ai*⁴-*t'ai*⁴	14	VII
large 大	*ta*⁴	5	IV
learn, to 學	*hsüeh*²	21	I
lecture-hall 講堂, 課堂	*chiang*³-*t'ang*², *k'e*⁴-*t'ang*²	18	X
lesson 功課	*kung*¹-*k'e*⁴	14	III
letter (alphabet) 字	*tzu*⁴	7	IV
letter 信	*hsin*⁴	21	VII
listen, to 聽	*t'ing*¹	21	VIII
little 小	*hsiao*³	5	IV
little, a 一點兒	*i*⁴-*tien*-'*rh*³	12	VIII
to live in 住	*chu*⁴	15	V
long 長	*ch'ang*²	5	V
look, to 看	*k'an*⁴	21	VI
lump 塊	*k'uai*⁴	6	V
madam 太太	*t'ai*⁴-*t'ai*⁴	14	VII
make 作	*tso*⁴	9	I
man 人	*jen*²	4	III
many 多	*to*¹	7	I
me 我	*wo*³	1	II
mean 賤	*chien*⁴	14	I
meaning 意思	*i*⁴-*ssu*¹	14	IV
meat 肉	*jou*⁴	6	IV
merchant 商人	*shang*¹-*jen*²	24	V

ENGLISH INDEX 345

LESSON PARA

middle school 中學堂(校)	chung¹-hsüeh²-t'ang² (hsiao⁴) 17	V
milk 牛奶	niu²-nai³ 19	X
mine 我的	wo³-ti¹ 4	VI
Miss 姑娘	ku¹-niang² 6	II
money 錢	ch'ien² 13	III
mother 母親	mu³-ch'in¹ 6	II
motion pictures 電影兒	tien⁴-ying³-erh² 24	III
more 多	to¹ 7	I
more (again) 再	tsai⁴ 12	VII
movies 電影兒	tien⁴-ying³-erh² 24	III
Mr. 先生	hsien¹-sheng¹ 4	IV
Mrs. 太太	t'ai⁴-t'ai⁴ 14	VII
much 多	to¹ 7	I
mutton 羊肉	yang²-jou⁴ 6	IV
my 我的	wo³-ti¹ 4	VI
name, to call by 叫	chiao⁴ 13	I
name, honourable 貴姓	kuei⁴-hsing⁴ 14	II
name, humble 賤姓	chien⁴-hsing⁴ 14	II
name, personal 名子	ming²-tzu¹ 13	I
name, surname 姓	hsing⁴ 13	I
Nanking 南京	nan²-ching¹ 24	VIII
new 新	hsin¹ 20	III
newspaper 報	pao⁴ 21	VII
nine 九	chiu³ 3	VII
no 不, 沒	pu⁴, ⁽²⁾ mei² 3 I, 1	IV
nobody 誰也沒(不)	shui² yeh³ mei² (pu⁴) 11	I
no one 誰也沒(不)	shui² yeh³ mei² (pu⁴) 11	I
not 不, 沒	pu⁴ ⁽²⁾, mei² 3 I, 1	IV

		LESSON	PARA
not well 不好	pu⁴ hao³	10	VI
note-book 本子	pen³-tzu¹	1	I
nothing 甚麽○也沒	shen²-ma¹—yeh³ mei²	11	I
nought 零	ling²	7	VII
numerator see classifier			
— odd ○幾	— chi³	7	III
official 職員	chih²-yuan²	25	VI
old 舊	chiu⁴	20	III
on 在○上	tsai⁴ — shang⁴	17	I
on behalf of 給	kei³	13	VI
one 一	i¹ (2)(4)	2	I
open, to 開	k'ai¹	21	III
or 還是	hai² shih⁴	10	VII
order, to 叫	chiao⁴	13	II
ounce 兩	liang³	20	I
our 我們的	wo³-men²-ti¹	7	VI
ours 我們的	wo³-men²-ti¹	7	VI
over — ○幾	— chi³	7	III
ox 牛	niu²	6	III
paint, to 畫	hua⁴	16	V
pair, a 雙	shuang¹	19	VII
paper 紙	chih³	1	I
parents 父母	fu⁴-mu³	19	II
PARTICLES			
— denoting past participle 的	ti¹	10	II
— denoting past tense 了	la¹	10	I
— final 哪	na¹	10	IV
— interrogative 麽	ma¹ ?	1	VII
— interrogative 啊	a¹ ?	10	VII

ENGLISH INDEX

		LESSON	PARA
— interrogative final 呢	*ni*¹ ?	10	VII
— plural of persons 們	*men*²	7	v
— possessive 的	*ti*¹	4	VI
Peiping, Peking 北平	*pei*³-*p'ing*²	24	VIII
pen 筆	*pi*³	16	VI
pen, steel 鋼筆	*kang*¹-*pi*³	1	VI
pencil 鉛筆	*ch'ien*¹-*pi*³	1	VI
people 人	*jen*²	4	III
person 人	*jen*²	4	III
personal name 名子	*ming*²-*tzu*¹	13	I
phrase 句	*chü*⁴	12	III
physician 大夫	*tai*⁴-*fu*¹	25	IV
picture 畫兒	*hua-'rh*⁴	16	v
piece 個	*ke*⁴	2	II
pig 猪	*chu*¹	6	III
place 地方	*ti*⁴-*fang*¹	15	VII
play 戲	*hsi*⁴	24	IV
please 請	*ch'ing*³	11	VII
please sit down 請坐	*ch'ing*³ *tso*⁴	11	VII
pork 猪肉	*chu*¹-*jou*⁴	6	IV
post-office 郵政局	*yu*²-*cheng*⁴-*chü*²	23	v
postage stamp 郵票	*yu*²-*p'iao*⁴	23	v
pour out, to 倒	*tao*⁴	20	II
prepare food, to 作飯	*tso*⁴ *fan*⁴	9	III
Primary School 小學堂(校)	*hsiao*³-*hsüeh*²-*t'ang*² (*hsiao*⁴)	17	v
pupil 學生	*hsüeh*²-*cheng*¹	4	IV
put on, to (clothes) 穿	*ch'uan*¹	19	v
put on, to (on the head) 戴	*tai*⁴	19	VI

ENGLISH INDEX

		LESSON	PARA
railway station 火車站	huo³-ch'e¹-chan⁴	23	IV
railway ticket 車票	ch'e¹-p'iao⁴	23	IV
read, to 念	nien⁴	9	V
receive a letter, to 來信	lai² hsin⁴	23	V
recent, recently 新	hsin¹	20	III
red 紅	hung²	16	I
reply, to 回答	hui²-ta²	12	II
reply, (to a letter) 回信	hui²-hsin⁴	23	V
request, to 請	ch'ing³	11	VIII
require, to 要	yao⁴	13	IV
restaurant 飯館子	fan⁴-kuan³-tzu¹	24	I
return, to 回去, 回來	hui²-ch'ü⁴, hui²-lai²	24	VIII
return home, to 回家	hui² chia¹	24	VIII
return to one's native country, to 回國	hui² kuo²	24	VIII
rice, cooked 飯	fan⁴	5	VII
rice-bowl 飯碗	fan⁴-wan³	5	VIII
right 對	tui⁴	12	V
room 屋子	wu¹-tzu¹	15	I
say, to 說話	shuo¹ hua⁴	12	III
school 學校, 學堂	hsüeh²-hsiao⁴,	23	II
	hsüeh²-t'ang²	15	VII
second time, a 再	tsai⁴	12	VII
secretary 書記	shu¹-chi⁴	24	VI
see a play, to 看戲	k'an⁴ hsi⁴	24	IV
sell, to 賣	mai⁴	13	VII
seller 賣東西的	mai⁴-tung¹-hsi¹-ti¹	25	III
send a letter, to 去信	ch'ü⁴ hsin⁴	23	V
sentence 句	chü⁴	12	III

ENGLISH INDEX

		LESSON	PARA
seven 七	*ch'i*¹ ⁽²⁾	3	VII
several 幾	*chi*³	7	III
Shanghai 上海	*shang*⁴*-hai*³	23	VI
shall 要	*yao*⁴	9	IX
she 他 (她)	*t'a*¹	1	II
sheep 羊	*yang*²	6	III
shoe 鞋	*hsieh*²	19	VII
shoemaker 鞋匠	*hsieh*²*-chiang*⁴	25	III
shop 鋪子	*p'u*⁴*-tzu*¹	15	VIII
short 短	*tuan*³	5	V
show motion-pictures, to 演電影兒	*yen*³ *tien*⁴*-ying*³*-erh*²	24	III
shut, to 關	*kuan*¹	21	III
sick, to get 得病	*te*² *ping*⁴	25	IV
sickness 病	*ping*⁴	25	IV
sing (a play), to 唱 (戲)	*ch'ang*⁴ *(hsi)*⁴	24	IV
six 六	*liu*⁴	3	VII
slipper 鞋	*hsieh*²	19	VII
small 小	*hsiao*³	5	IV
some 幾	*chi*³	7	III
son 兒子	*erh*²*-tzu*¹	6	II
speak, to 說話	*shuo*¹*-hua*⁴	12	III
stamp, postage 郵票	*yu*²*-p'iao*⁴	23	V
still 還	*hai*²	10	III
still more 還	*hai*²	10	III
store 鋪子	*p'u*⁴*-tzu*¹	15	VIII
street 街	*chieh*¹	19	IV
student 學生	*hsüeh*²*-sheng*¹	4	IV
student's 學生的	*hsüeh*²*-sheng*¹*-ti*¹	5	I

ENGLISH INDEX

		LESSON	PARA
study, to 學, 念書	hsüeh², nien⁴ shu⁴	21	I, 9 V
summon, to 叫	chiao⁴	13	I, II
surname 姓	hsing⁴	13	I
suspend, to 掛	kua⁴	17	I
table 桌子	cho¹-tzu¹	3	VI
tael 兩	liang³	2	I
tailor 裁縫	ts'ai²-feng²	24	VII
tall 大	ta⁴	5	IV
take, to 拿去	na²-ch'ü⁴	17	III
take hold of, to 拿	na²	16	VI
tasty 好吃	hao³ chih¹	10	VIII
tea 茶	ch'a²	5	VII
tea (in leaf) 茶葉	ch'a²-yeh⁴	6	VI
tea-cup 茶碗	ch'a²-wan³	5	VIII
teacher 先生	hsien¹-sheng¹	4	IV
teacher's 先生的	hsien¹-sheng¹-ti¹	5	I
telegram 電報	tien⁴-pao⁴	23	VI
telegraph office 電報局	tien⁴-pao⁴-chü²	23	VI
tell, to 告訴	kao⁴-su⁴	14	V
ten 十	shih²	3	VII
ten-cents 毛錢	mao²-ch'ien²	13	III
text-book 課本	k'e⁴-pen³	20	IV
thanks, thank you 謝謝	hsieh⁴-hsieh⁴	11	VII
that 那	na⁴	3	I
theatre 戲園子	hsi⁴-yüan²-tzu¹	24	IV
their 他們的	t'a¹-men²-ti¹	7	VI
theirs 他們的	t'a¹-men²-ti¹	7	VI
them 他們	t'a¹-men²	7	V
then 就	chiu⁴	13	II

ENGLISH INDEX

		LESSON	PARA
thence 從那兒(裡)	*t'sung² na-'rh⁴ (li³)*	22	VII
there 在那兒(裡)	*tsai⁴ na-'rh⁴ (li³)*	18	IX
thereupon 就	*chiu⁴*	13	II
these 這些	*che⁴-hsieh¹*	8	II
they 他們	*t'a¹-men²*	7	V
thing 東西	*tung¹-hsi¹*	4	III
this 這	*che⁴*	3	I
thither 上那兒(裡)	*shang⁴ na-'rh⁴ (li³)*	22	V
those 那些	*na⁴-hsieh¹*	8	II
thousand 千	*ch'ien¹*	7	VIII
three 三	*san¹*	2	I
ticket 票	*p'iao⁴*	23	V
time, a 回	*hui²*	12	VII
today 今天	*chin¹-t'ien¹*	10	I
together 一塊兒	*i²-kuai-'rh⁴*	19	I
to-morrow 明天	*ming²-t'ien¹*	10	I
too 太	*t'ai⁴*	14	VI
trade, to 作買賣	*tso⁴ mai³-mai⁴*	24	V
trader 商人	*sheng¹-jen²*	24	V
transact business, to 辦公	*pan³ kung¹*	25	VI
treat (medically), to 治	*chih⁴*	25	IV
tumbler 玻璃盃	*po¹-li²-pei¹*	5	VIII
two 二	*erh⁴*	6	VII
two 兩	*liang³*	2	I
understand, to 明白	*ming²-pai²*	12	IV
university 大學堂(校)	*ta⁴-hsüeh²-t'ang²*	17	V
	(hsiao⁴)	23	II
up the street 上街	*shang⁴ chieh¹*	22	II
us 我們	*wo³-men²*	7	V

ENGLISH INDEX

		LESSON	PARA
very 很	*hen³*	14	I
wall 牆	*ch'iang²*	16	III
want, to 要	*yao⁴*	9	IX
warrant 票	*p'iao⁴*	23	V
water 水	*shui³*	5	VII
we 我們	*wo³-men²*	7	V
wear, to 穿	*ch'uan¹*	19	V
wear (on the head), to 戴	*tai⁴*	19	VI
what? 甚麼?	*shen²-ma¹?*	4	II
what sort of? 甚麼?	*shen²-ma¹?*	4	II
when? 就, 多咱?	*chiu⁴, to¹-tsan²?*	13 II,	21 II
whence? 從那兒(裡)?	*ts'ung² na-'rh³ (li³)?*	22	IV
where? 那兒?, 那裡?	*na-'rh³?, na²-li³?*	18	IX
which? 那?	*na³?*	18	VIII
whither? 上那兒(裡)?	*shang⁴ na-'rh³ (li³)*	22	II
white 白	*pai²*	16	I
who? 誰?	*shui²?*	4	V
whose? 誰的?	*shui²-ti¹?*	4	VII
wife 太太	*t'ai⁴-t'ai⁴*	14	VII
will 要	*yao⁴*	9	IX
will do! 行	*hsing²*	25	VI
window 窗戶	*ch'uang¹-hu⁴*	15	III
wine 酒	*chiu³*	19	VIII
wine-glass 酒盃	*chiu³-pei¹*	19	IX
with 跟	*ken¹*	12	III
with, (together) 一塊兒	*i²-k'uai-'rh⁴*	19	I
won't do! 不行	*pu⁴ hsing²*	25	VI
wooden floor 地板	*ti⁴-pan³*	16	II
work 事情	*shih⁴-ch'ing²*	23	III

ENGLISH INDEX

		LESSON	PARA
work (in an office), to 辦公	*pan⁴ kung¹*	25	VI
write, to 寫	*hsieh³*	9	IV
writing-brush 毛筆	*mao²-pi³*	4	I
writing-table 書桌子	*shu¹-cho¹-tzu¹*	6	I
wrong 不對	*pu² tui⁴*	12	V
yellow 黃	*huang²*	16	I
yes 是	*shih⁴*	3	II
yesterday 昨天	*tso²-t'ien¹*	10	I
yet 還	*hai²*	10	III
you (plural) 你們	*ni³-men²*	7	V
you (polite) 您	*nin²*	1	II
you (usual) 你	*ni³*	1	II
your (plural) 你們的	*ni³-men²-ti¹*	7	VI
your (polite) 您的	*nin²-ti¹*	4	VI
your (usual) 你的	*ni³-ti¹*	4	VI
yours (plural) 你們的	*ni³-men²-ti¹*	7	VI
yours (polite) 您的	*nin²-ti¹*	4	VI
yours (usual) 你的	*ni³-ti¹*	4	VI
zero 零	*ling²*	7	VII

練習四聲表 TONE

第幾課 LESSON NUMBER	練習四聲次序	第一次	第二次	第三次	第四次	第五次
1	1 2 3 4	書 shu^1	紙 $chih^3$	本 pen^3	子 $tzu^{3,(1)}$	我 wo^3
2	1 4 2 3	您 nin^2	你 ni^3	他 $t'a^1$	有 yu^3	沒 mei^2
3	1 3 2 4	鉛 $ch'ien^1$	筆 pi^3	鋼 $kang^1$	麼 ma^2	一 $i^{1,2,4}$
4	1 4 3 2	二 erh^4	兩 $liang^3$	三 san^1	四 ssu^4	五 wu^3
5	1 2 4 3	個 ke^4	張 $chang^1$	幾 chi^3	這 che^4	那 na^4
6	1 3 4 2	不 $pu^{4,2}$	是 $shih^4$	也 yeh^3	桌 cho^1	六 liu^4
7	2 3 4 1	七 $ch'i^{1,2}$	八 $pa^{1,2}$	九 $chiu^3$	毛 mao^2	甚 $shen^2$
8	2 1 3 4	人 jen^2	東 $tung^1$	西 hsi^1	先 $hsien^1$	生 $sheng^1$
9	2 4 1 3	學 $hsüeh^2$	位 wei^4	誰 $shui^2$	的 ti^1	大 ta^4
10	2 4 3 1	小 $hsiao^3$	短 $tuan^3$	道 tao^4	茶 $ch'a^2$	飯 fan^4
11	2 1 3 4	碗 wan^3	父 fu^4	親 $ch'in^1$	母 mu^3	姑 ku^1
12	2 3 1 4	娘 $niang^2$	羊 $yang^2$	牛 niu^2	頭 $t'ou^2$	猪 chu^1
13	3 4 2 1	口 $k'ou^3$	肉 jou^4	斤 $chin^1$	塊 $k'uai^4$	魚 $yü^2$

TABLE 練習四聲表

第幾課 LESSON NUMBER	練習四聲次序	第一次	第二次	第三次	第四次	第五次
14	3 4 1 2	條 t'iao²	麵 mien⁴	包 pao¹	咖 k'a¹	啡 fei⁴
15	3 2 1 4	多 to¹	少 shao³	們 men²	百 pai³	零 ling²
16	3 2 4 1	都 tou¹	些 hsieh¹	作 tso⁴	念 nien⁴	會 hui⁴
17	3 1 2 4	喝 he¹	吃 ch'ih¹	要 yao⁴	天 t'ien¹	明 ming²
18	3 1 4 2	了 la¹	還 hai²	好 hao³	啊 a¹	來 lai²
19	4 3 2 1	去 ch'ü⁴	請 ch'ing³	再 tsai⁴	見 chien⁴	問 wen⁴
20	4 2 1 3	說 shuo¹	話 hua⁴	跟 ken¹	句 chü⁴	對 tui⁴
21	4 3 1 2	點 tien³	姓 hsing⁴	叫 chiao⁴	份 fen⁴	給 kei³
22	4 1 3 2	買 mai³	貴 kuei⁴	很 hen³	講 chiang³	功 kung¹
23	4 1 2 3	課 k'e⁴	告 kao⁴	訴 su⁴	太 t'ai⁴	裡 li³
24	4 2 3 1	窗 ch'uang¹	戶 hu⁴	房 fang²	所 so³	家 chia¹
25	1 2 3 4	堂 t'ang²	鋪 p'u⁴	紅 hung²	黃 huang²	綠 lü⁴

華語入門
卷壹

著作者　哈爾濱法政大學校教授　吳索福

繙譯者　廸瑞德

出板者　魏　智

排印者　北京西什庫印刷所

發行者　北京法文圖書館

"早期北京话珍本典籍校释与研究"
丛书总目录

早期北京话珍稀文献集成

（一）日本北京话教科书汇编

《燕京妇语》等八种　　　　　　　四声联珠
华语跬步　　　　　　　　　　　官话指南·改订官话指南
亚细亚言语集　　　　　　　　　京华事略·北京纪闻
北京风土编·北京事情·北京风俗问答
伊苏普喻言·今古奇观·搜奇新编

（二）朝鲜日据时期汉语会话书汇编

改正增补汉语独学　　　　　　　修正独习汉语指南
高等官话华语精选　　　　　　　官话华语教范
速修汉语自通　　　　　　　　　无先生速修中国语自通
速修汉语大成　　　　　　　　　官话标准：短期速修中国语自通
中语大全　　　　　　　　　　　"内鲜满"最速成中国语自通

（三）西人北京话教科书汇编

寻津录　　　　　　　　　　　　北京话语音读本
语言自迩集　　　　　　　　　　语言自迩集（第二版）
官话类编　　　　　　　　　　　言语声片
华语入门　　　　　　　　　　　华英文义津逮
汉语口语初级读本·北京儿歌　　汉英北京官话词汇
北京官话：汉语初阶

（四）清代满汉合璧文献萃编

清文启蒙　　　　　　　　　　清话问答四十条
一百条·清语易言　　　　　　清文指要
续编兼汉清文指要　　　　　　庸言知旨
满汉成语对待　　　　　　　　清文接字·字法举一歌
重刻清文虚字指南编

（五）清代官话正音文献

正音撮要　　　　　　　　　　正音咀华

（六）十全福

（七）清末民初京味儿小说书系

新鲜滋味　　　　　　　　　　过新年
小额　　　　　　　　　　　　北京
春阿氏　　　　　　　　　　　花鞋成老
评讲聊斋　　　　　　　　　　讲演聊斋

（八）清末民初京味儿时评书系

益世余谭——民国初年北京生活百态
益世余墨——民国初年北京生活百态

早期北京话研究书系

早期北京话语法研究
早期北京话语法演变专题研究
早期北京话语气词研究
晚清民国时期南北官话语法差异研究
基于清后期至民国初期北京话文献语料的个案研究
高本汉《北京话语音读本》整理与研究
北京话语音演变研究
文化语言学视域下的北京地名研究
语言自迩集——19世纪中期的北京话（第二版）
清末民初北京话语词汇释